ENGRAVING THE SAVAGE

ENGRAVING THE SAVAGE

The New World and
Techniques of Civilization

Michael Gaudio

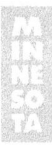

University of Minnesota Press / Minneapolis London

An early version of chapter 1 appeared in *Art and the British Empire,* ed. Timothy Barringer, Geoff Quilley, and Douglas Fordham (Manchester: Manchester University Press, 2006). An early version of chapter 3 was originally published as "The Space of Idolatry: Reformation, Incarnation, and the Ethnographic Image," *RES* 41 (Spring 2002): 73–91; copyright by the President and Fellows of Harvard College; reprinted by permission of the Peabody Museum Press, Harvard University.

Published by the University of Minnesota Press
111 Third Avenue South, Suite 290
Minneapolis, MN 55401-2520
http://www.upress.umn.edu

Library of Congress Cataloging-in-Publication Data

Gaudio, Michael.
    Engraving the savage : the New World and techniques of civilization / Michael Gaudio.
       p. cm.
    Includes bibliographical references and index.
    ISBN-13: 978-0-8166-4846-7 (hc : alk. paper)
    ISBN-10: 0-8166-4846-8 (hc : alk. paper)
    ISBN-13: 978-0-8166-4847-4 (pb : alk. paper)
    ISBN-10: 0-8166-4847-6 (pb : alk. paper)
    1. Indians in art. 2. America—Discovery and exploration—European—Historiography.
3. Difference (Philosophy) in art. 4. Art—Reproduction. 5. Prints—Technique. I. Title.
    N8217.I5G38 2008
    704.9'42—dc22

                               2007031468

Printed in the United States of America on acid-free paper

The University of Minnesota is an equal-opportunity educator and employer.

15 14 13 12 11 10 09 08   10 9 8 7 6 5 4 3 2 1

Contents

Acknowledgments

If *Engraving the Savage* had a moment of inspiration, it must have been in the first lecture of Charles Eldredge's course on early American art at the University of Kansas in the spring of 1995, when he projected onto the screen John White's watercolor drawing of an Algonquian shaman. I thought it a very strange picture, fitting into none of my preconceived notions about the moment of New World "discovery," and this sense of strangeness has sustained my interest in the work of White and de Bry through the completion of this book. The book itself had its beginnings as a dissertation in the Department of Art and Art History at Stanford University, supervised by Alex Nemerov. Alex's reading of my work was always discerning and full of insight; as a writer, teacher, and critic, he has provided me with an unparalleled model for practicing art history, and I am deeply grateful to him for this. Others at Stanford also provided critical guidance and support in the early stages of this book, especially Wanda Corn, Suzanne Lewis, Pamela Lee, Paula Findlen, Patricia Parker, and Roland Greene. During a memorable year in the Department of Art History at the University of Illinois, made possible by Jonathan Fineberg, I had the good fortune to share an office with Rachael DeLue; many conversations with Rachael and with colleagues in the Descartes and the Modernist reading groups helped me rethink my arguments at a crucial stage in the book's development. In the Department of Art History at the University of Minnesota, I am grateful especially to Rick Asher, who as chair of the department showed unfailing support during the preparation of my manuscript, and to Jane Blocker, an incomparable colleague, critic, and friend. My students at Minnesota have been a constant pleasure, and I thank them for letting me share my ideas with them and for providing me, in turn, with the pleasure of their own sparkling intelligence. The University of Minnesota has been a particularly exciting place to pursue early modern studies. My work on *Engraving the Savage* was carried out in tandem with my involvement in the Theorizing Early Modern Studies (TEMS) research collaborative. At a time when the mantra of "interdisciplinarity" is everywhere, my work on TEMS with Juliette Cherbuliez and JB Shank has shown me what it might really mean to practice such a thing. I also thank Bronwen Wilson for her most thoughtful reading of the manuscript, and Richard Morrison, my editor at the University of Minnesota Press, for the support he has shown this project from the beginning.

I could not have completed this book without the support of various institutions and foundations. Fellowship support at Stanford from the Department of Art and Art History and from the Whiting Foundation made the writing of the dissertation possible. The Stanford Humanities Center provided an ideal scholarly community within which I worked out my initial arguments. Fellowships from the Huntington Library and from the Paul Mellon Centre for Studies in British Art provided critical support at the dissertation stage. At the University of Minnesota, the Graduate School has been most supportive: a Faculty Summer Research Fellowship and a McKnight Summer Fellowship allowed me to carry out research for the second chapter, and a single semester leave gave me time to write it. I thank the Department of Art History for research funds that made it possible to pay for photographs and permissions. Staffs of many libraries and collections have been extremely helpful with locating and using materials: the British Library, the James Ford Bell Library at the University of Minnesota, Stanford University Special Collections, the Annenberg Rare Book and Manuscript Library at the University of Pennsylvania, the Rare Book and Manuscript Library at the University of Illinois, the Houghton Library, the Newberry Library, Princeton University Rare Books and Special Collections, the New York Public Library, the Huntington Library, and the prints and drawings collections at the British Museum, the Metropolitan Museum of Art, and the Minneapolis Institute of Arts.

While working on this book I have received helpful feedback from audiences at a variety of conferences and seminars. Portions of chapters were presented at College Art Association conferences in 2001 and 2006; the 2004 Renaissance Society of America meeting; the "Art and the British Empire" conference at the Tate Britain in 2001; the Theorizing Early Modern Studies workshop in 2003; the Newberry Seminar in Early American History and Culture in October 2003; the "Rethinking Descartes" conference at the University of Illinois in 2002; the 2001 Group for Early Modern Cultural Studies conference; and the graduate student conference "Speaking in Signs" held at the McNeil Center for Early American Studies in 1999.

I would like to express my gratitude to my family, and particularly to my parents, for their support and encouragement over the years. That it took so long to complete this book may have something to do with the fact that my children Anna and Adam came along while it was in the works: I can think of no better reason for a delay. I dedicate this book to Kerry, who has sustained its writing over the past ten years with her criticism, patience, and love.

Introduction: White Pebbles in the Dark Forest

> From Léry or Thévet to De Bry, things seen and seeable mark off the writing,
> engendered by distance. White pebbles in the dark forest of the text.
>
> —Michel de Certeau, "Writing vs. Time:
> History and Anthropology in the Works of Lafitau"

This book is about what Michel de Certeau eloquently terms "white pebbles in the dark forest." These pebbles can be found scattered throughout numerous early modern volumes (those of Léry, Thévet, de Bry, and many others) that describe the customs and habits of the "savages" of America, volumes in which our eyes jump from pages dense and congested with type to settle on the luminous presence of the image. Paging through Jean de Léry's *Histoire d'un voyage faict en la terre du Brésil* (1578; *History of a Voyage to the Land of Brazil*), for example, one halts at the full-page ethnographic "portrait" of a Tupinamba family (Figure 1).[1] In his text, Léry has just provided a thorough description of the "accoutrements and ornaments with which our Tupinamba customarily outfit themselves in their country." Léry then addresses the reader directly: "picture to yourself a savage according to this description," and he directs us to the woodcut on the opposing page.[2] There we are confronted by a naked Tupinamba man who stands with a bow in his left hand and arrows in his right as "one of his women," standing behind him and carrying a child in a sling, drapes her arm over his shoulder; the group stands amid exotic artifacts of the New World, including a hammock and pineapple. Having looked at this image, having observed with our own eyes what Léry and his contemporaries called the "savage,"[3] we can then return to the written text with a new grounding in the visible reality of distant Brazil.

Léry's appeal to the visible is hardly unusual; indeed, it is a structural element of early modern ethnographic discourse and of eyewitness travel accounts in general. As Francis Bacon, the philosophical spokesman for this new attention to observed phenomena, writes in his *Instauratio magna* (1620): "all depends on keeping the eye steadily fixed upon the facts of nature and so receiving their images simply as they are. For God forbid that we should give out a dream of our own imagination for a pattern

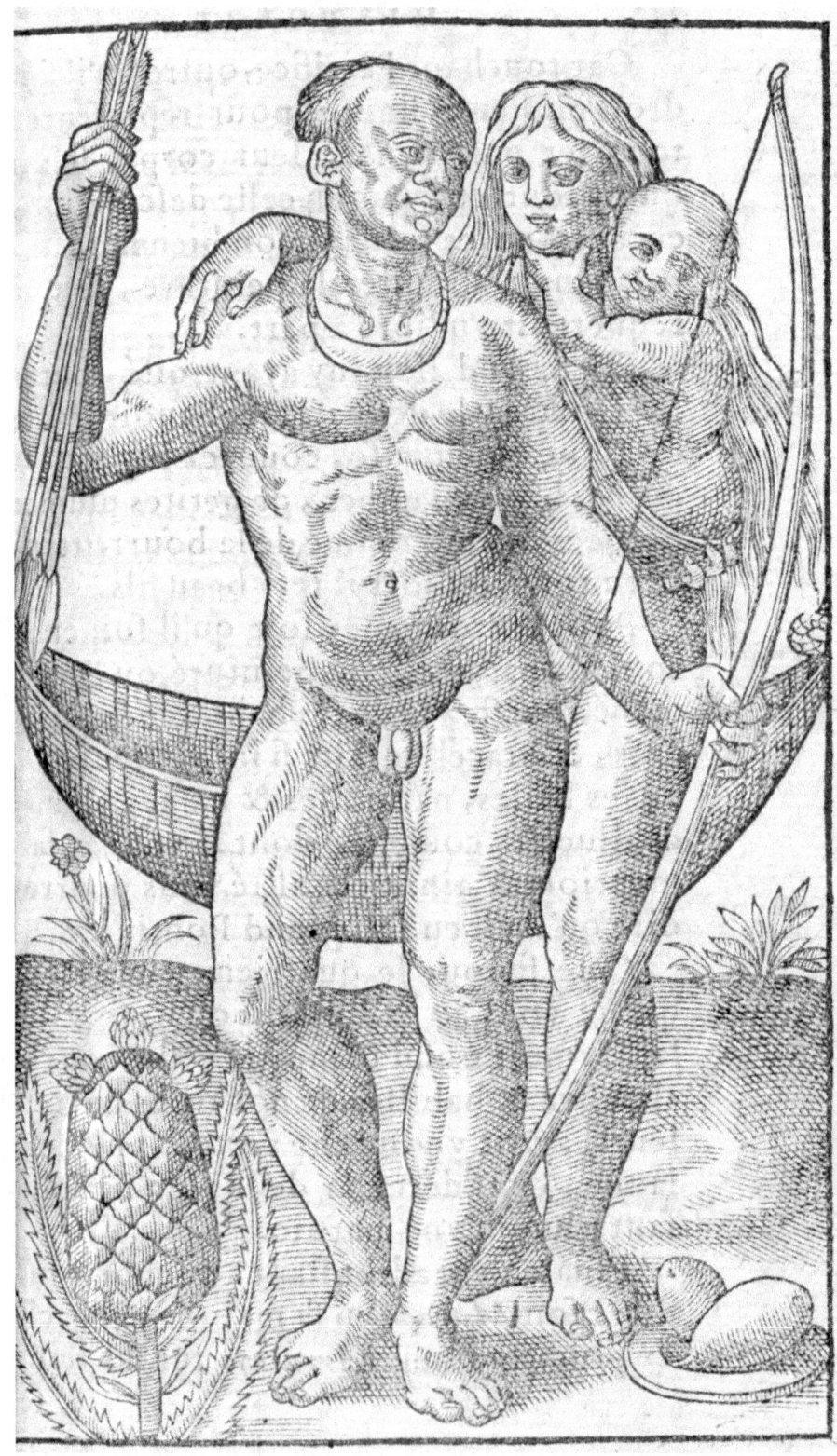

Figure 1. Tupinamba family, from Jean de Léry, *Histoire d'un voyage faict en la terre du Brésil* (La Rochelle, 1578). From the Collections of the University Libraries, University of Minnesota, Minneapolis.

of the world."[4] In recent years, art historians have demonstrated how new modes of picturing in the sixteenth and seventeenth centuries answered Bacon's demand for visual fact. Words and phrases like *contrafacta* (counterfeit) and *ad vivum* (from the life) belonged to a new visual language describing a reportorial mode of image-making that recorded things and events as they were witnessed by the eye, not as they were composed by the artist.[5] It was not a shared style or subject matter that defined these new classes of images, but a shared epistemological status as uninterpreted nature. By means of such images, and through actual physical objects collected for the cabinet of curiosities, the Americas were brought back to Europe in raw, visible fragments.

A common rhetorical convention in the literature of travel is that words cannot adequately describe the strangeness of the new continent. One must see it to believe it. And even vision, while it remained the true experiential measure, could barely take in that strangeness. In the preface to his *History*, Léry fears that if the people of France are reluctant to believe the horrific events he had described four years previously in his published account of the siege of Sancerre—events that had occurred within France's own borders—then "how will they believe what can only be seen two thousand leagues from where they live: things never known (much less written about) by the Ancients; things so marvelous that experience itself can scarcely engrave *[engrauer]* them upon the understanding even of those who have seen them?"[6] For Léry, even though experience—by which he means a visual experience—can scarcely account for the strangeness of the New World, in the absence of textual authority it is nevertheless to visual experience that we must turn. He therefore includes in his book eight woodcuts that present the visible facts from which the author produces his text. While Léry's woodcuts are unquestionably shaped by what we might call, borrowing Bacon's phrase, "dreams of our own imagination"—that is to say, by stylistic influences, iconographic conventions, ideological assumptions—their structural value within a larger descriptive enterprise is nevertheless the preservation of a visible reality that stands prior to the imposition of any cultural schema or preconception.[7] In other words, before we reflect on the meaning of the male figure's classical contrapposto in Léry's woodcut; before we begin comparing this Brazilian couple to contemporary depictions of Adam and Eve; before we consider the projection of European norms of gender difference onto Tupinamba society; before we add meaning in any of these ways, the image has *already* performed its task of serving—simply by virtue of its visibility—as the occasion for Léry's writing. As de Certeau notes about the plates in Joseph-François Lafitau's great work of comparative ethnology, *Mœurs des sauvages ameriquains, comparées aux mœurs des premiers temps* (1724), their "essential value is in their belonging to the order of the visible. They permit a *reseeing*. Or they allow the *belief* that one can *see* the beginnings once again."[8] The "white pebble" of the ethnographic image does not, therefore, merely illustrate the text; as the signifier of a savage otherness that has yet to be written, it is the thing against which the text *generates itself*. This strange and untenable yet hugely productive claim that the visual image can capture the otherness of America and preserve it within the pages of the text will be one of the chief concerns of this book.

In the passage quoted above, Léry raises another important point about the role of the visual image in communicating truths about the New World. By using the word *engrave* to describe the work of vision on the viewer's understanding, he suggests how printmaking was implicated at a fundamental level in the transmission of knowledge about the native inhabitants of the Americas. It will be a central claim of this book that the technique of engraving was, through the nineteenth century, a formative element in the production of ethnographic knowledge. Despite Bacon's rhetoric, Europeans did not passively receive images of the New World "simply as they are"; de Certeau's white pebbles were engraved and imprinted upon European minds through the tools and techniques of printmakers. In the following chapters, I want to retain the sense of materiality implicit in that phrase *white pebbles,* which suggests an irreducible physical presence: walking though the dark forest as our eyes struggle to find the horizon, the brightness of the white pebbles draws our gaze to the ground, forcing us to stop and reexamine the very substance on which we tread. It is easy to lose this "pebbleness" of the image for the dark forest of the text, to explain away the physical substance of the engraving as the neutral agent of a symbolic meaning, a cultural belief, an ideology. Against this tendency to see beyond materials to their meaning, a tendency evidenced in the scores of books and articles that attempt to decipher the European "iconography" of the encounter, this book will attend to the peculiar materiality of the engraver's art. While the image of the savage may have a powerful distancing effect in its placement of the viewer in the elsewhere of a new world, an attention to materials has the effect of bringing us back to the earth, back to the workshop where the engraver, at work with his tools, crafts alterity out of lines cut with a burin into a copper plate.

My focus will be an extraordinary group of engravings that has had an exceptionally long and influential life in the ethnographic literature on the Americas. They originate in a set of watercolor drawings by the sixteenth-century English painter John White (see Figures 27, 39, 50). Under the patronage of Sir Walter Raleigh, White accompanied a 1585 exploratory expedition to Virginia as its artist, returning in 1587 to serve as governor of the short-lived Roanoke colony. His collection of drawings from that initial expedition, now housed in the British Museum, includes a descriptive title page that identifies the contents as "the pictures of sondry things collected and counterfeited according to the truth in the voyage made by Sᵣ: Walter Raleigh knight, for the discouery of La Virginea."⁹ White's surviving pictures are indeed "sondry." They include maps of the eastern coast of North America, bird's-eye views of forts and encampments in the West Indies, coastal profiles, natural history studies, ethnographic studies of Carolina Algonquians along with views of their towns and various customs and practices, and further ethnographic studies of both New and Old World subjects, including several highly imaginative renderings of ancient Picts and Britons. The immediate audience for this collection was, as White's title page suggests, the patronage circle surrounding "Sᵣ: Walter Raleigh knight."

Thanks to the efforts of Flemish engraver Theodor de Bry, White's pictorial studies of Carolina Algonquians, along with his maps of the Virginia coast and his pictures of the ancient peoples of Britain, reached a broad audience in England and throughout Protestant Europe. A Protestant refugee from Liège, de Bry established an engraving and publishing house in Frankfurt am Main in the late 1580s that was to become one of the most important in Europe, known above all for its lavishly illustrated travel accounts. The first of these accounts appeared in 1590 when de Bry published at his own expense, and in four languages, a short but remarkable book titled *A Briefe and True Report of the New Found Land of Virginia* (referred to hereafter as the *Report*). The book was a collaborative effort between its engraver-publisher and two veterans of the 1585 Virginia expedition: John White and the mathematician and scientist Thomas Harriot, the author of the text.[10] While visiting London in 1588, de Bry had acquired a copy of Harriot's text and had also obtained, from the tireless promoter of English colonial efforts, Richard Hakluyt, a set of John White's ethnographic drawings: "I was verye willinge to offer vnto you," writes de Bry to the readers of the *Report,* "the true Pictures of those people wich by the hel[p]e of Maister Richard Hakluyt of Oxford Minister of Gods Word, who first Incouraged me to publish the Worke, I [acquired] out of the verye original of Maister Ihon White."[11] This volume became the first in de Bry's extraordinarily popular *America* (1590–1634), a thirteen-volume project, fiercely anti-Spanish and anti-Catholic in its sympathies, that was continued by de Bry's family after his death in 1598.[12] Through the many editions of the *Report* and many later texts that borrow directly or indirectly from de Bry's engravings, this collection served into the nineteenth century as a visual prototype for the North American Indian. When John Adams wrote to Thomas Jefferson in 1812 for suggestions on where to learn about the traditions of the American Indians, Jefferson directed him to de Bry's *America,* the first three volumes of which he proudly held in his own library.[13] That a scholar like Jefferson would have recommended de Bry to a learned friend (even if Jefferson remained somewhat suspicious of de Bry's mingling of "facts and fable") suggests the important role this group of images has played in a long project—a project at once scholarly and popular—of producing knowledge about the indigenous peoples of North America.

While the *Report* has long been considered an important ethnographic source on Southeastern Indians, in recent years it has also attracted a good deal of attention from literary and cultural historians informed by a postcolonial recognition that ethnography can no longer maintain the illusion of a neutral, perspectival distance from its object.[14] As James Clifford writes, "there seem no distant places left on the planet where the presence of 'modern' products, media, and power cannot be felt. An older topography and experience of travel is exploded. One no longer leaves home confident of finding something radically new, another time or space."[15] We thus return to the early modern moment of New World encounter, not to determine the origins of a triumphant science of culture, but to examine—in the face of our own hybrid reality—the contingencies of that older topography through which the West conjured its savages into existence. The *Report* has proven to be a remarkably suggestive text for such a project. And yet the scholarship on this book, and on early modern Europe's visual response to the Americas more generally, has had little to say about one of the chief media involved in the production of New World texts—the medium of engraving. In an important study of the illustrations for de Bry's *America,* for example, structural anthropologist Bernadette Bucher describes her book as one in which "we shall uncover the formation of an ideology, still unaware of itself, masked by the hieroglyphics of the image."[16] For Bucher, the deep structure and thus the true significance of de Bry's engravings lies beyond visual surfaces, beyond the deceiving "hieroglyphics of the image." The astute viewer will look *through,* not *at,* the engraving. Bucher's dismissal of visual surface is not surprising, and indeed it has been a typical response by scholars when confronted with apparently nonartistic—that is, merely reproductive—engravings such as de Bry's. A proper analysis of such engravings surely cannot be sustained by a "connoisseur's" interest in technique and process; instead, one searches for a deeper content, for the forest of ideology that lies beyond surfaces. In the following chapters, I will make a case for looking *at* the engravings made after John White's watercolor collection, for dwelling at length upon their surface hieroglyphics. How might this attention to the materials and techniques of the engraver reveal the structures as well as the limits and ambiguities in the imagining of primitive origins? What did it mean to *engrave* the savage?[17]

It may not be immediately apparent why engravings of the customs and habits of American Indians should warrant special consideration over other types of subject matter. Common sense would suggest that a study of engraved maps, for instance, or engravings of flora and fauna, would lead to the same conclusions about the role of this reproductive medium in the production of New World knowledge. But there are indeed special reasons to focus on ethnographic subjects over others, since the practice of engraving has sometimes been, as this book will demonstrate, intimately engaged with a Western fantasy of primitive origins. We can tease the basic terms of this engagement out of a series of prints designed around 1580 by the Flemish artist Jan van der Straet. Engraved in Antwerp in the workshop of Philips Galle, this set of twenty engravings, titled *Nova reperta* [New Reports], illustrates the various inventions and discoveries that for van der Straet defined the modern age. Certainly the best-known image in the series is the first plate, titled *America,* an allegory of Europe's encounter with the New World (Figure 2). In this print, Amerigo Vespucci, bearing an astrolabe in his left hand and with his right hand supporting a standard with the stars of the Southern Cross (Vespucci was reportedly the first European to witness them), steps onto the shores of the New World and awakens the female figure of America, whose languorous state is signified by the sloth hanging from the tree behind her. "Americus rediscovers America," reads the text below, "—He called her but once and thenceforth she was always awake."[18] Surrounded by the exotic fauna of the New World, America begins to rise from her hammock and makes a gesture with her right hand that acknowledges Vespucci's arrival and at the same time directs the viewer to the background, where a cannibal feast is underway. It is from this savage, anthropophagous state that Vespucci will presumably deliver his new "discovery."

Van der Straet's *America* has generated much commentary, and it is a testament to the enduring power of the image in the discourse of the encounter that this print has so often served as the point of departure for the postcolonial return to the moment of "discovery."[19] In this recent critical commentary, however, the image hardly serves as a white pebble promising access to untainted origins; on the contrary, the interest of van der Straet's visual allegory derives from the fact that here the American encounter already appears as a dark forest overlaid with multiple levels of significance. For de Certeau, whose suggestive discussion of the print in the preface to *The Writing of History* (1975/1988) is an unavoidable starting point for recent interpretations, Vespucci's encounter with America serves as an allegory for nothing less than a Western system of representation. De Certeau reads Vespucci's arrival as a conquest of writing: "This is *writing that conquers*. It will use the New World as if it were a blank, 'savage' page on which Western desire will be written."[20] Others have developed and nuanced this reading by further considering how gender and cannibalism operate in van der Straet's *America* to produce an imperial subject and its savage other. While I will not enter here into an extended discussion of the recent literature on this image, I would nevertheless like to add one further layer to the allegory, one that instead of immediately

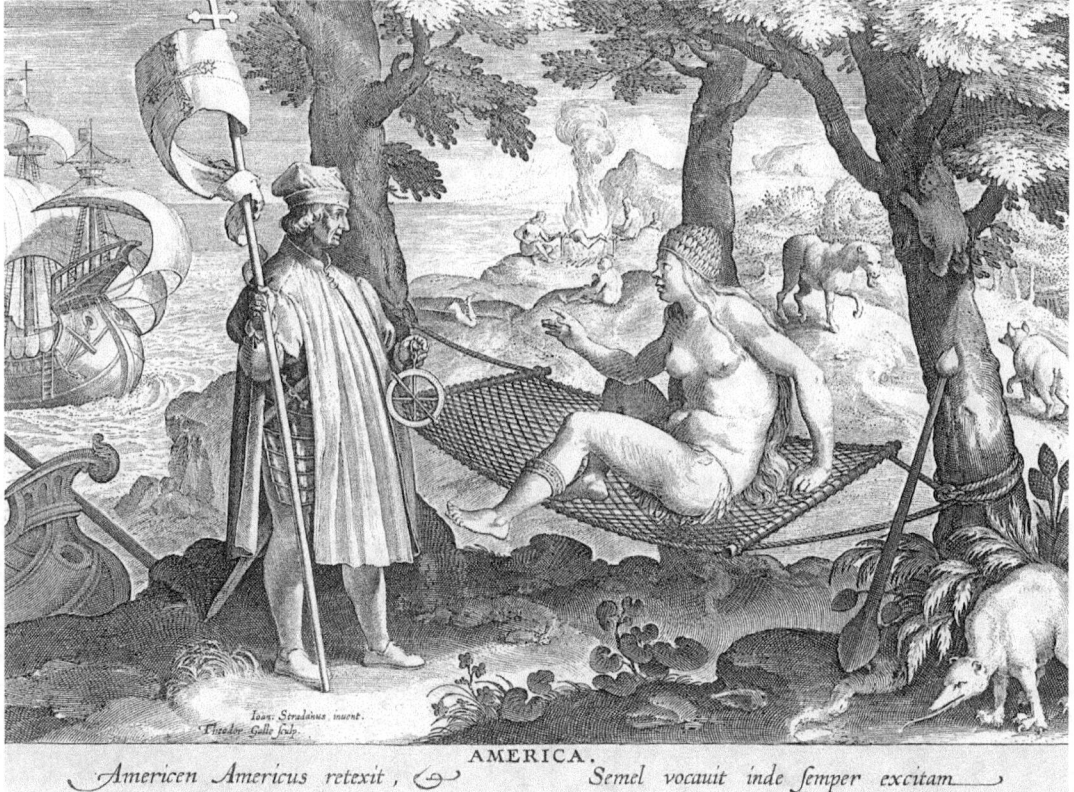

Figure 2. Theodor Galle after Jan van der Straet, *America*, Plate 1 from *Nova reperta*, early 1580s. The Burndy Library, Cambridge, Massachusetts.

thrusting us into theories of representation or the nebulous realm of colonial ideology, places us first in the very real space of the engraver's workshop where this print was made. And it requires no leap of imagination on our part to enter this space, for van der Straet in fact places us there: his series of "new reports," which opens with the discovery of America, concludes with the invention of copper-plate engraving.

The final plate of *Nova Reperta* is entitled *Sculptura in æs* ["Engraving on copper"] (Figure 3). In addition to the discovery of America and other inventions such as the magnetic compass, the printing press, and the iron clock, copper-plate engraving is for van der Straet one of the new reports that sets his age apart from previous ones. The caption reads: "By a new art the sculptor carves figures on beaten sheets and reproduces them on a press." In the scene above, engravers go about their work in a busy atelier, an idealized version of an engraver's workshop like the one in Antwerp where this very print was engraved, or like the de Bry workshop in Frankfurt (de Bry in fact lived in Antwerp from 1577 to 1585, and possibly even worked under Galle at the time *Nova Reperta* was published).[21] Figures young and old are engaged in the various stages of this new art of cutting and printing metal plates. In the foreground an apprentice draws with a quill pen as he copies a design that will eventually be engraved. At the

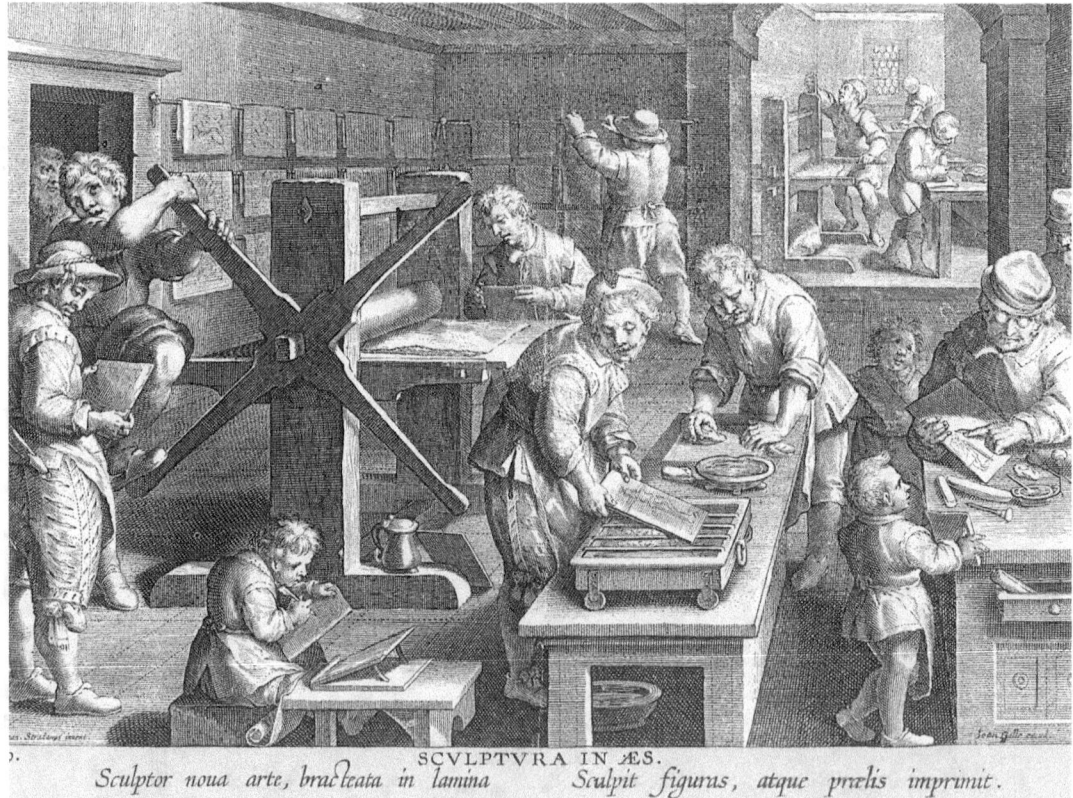

SCVLPTVRA IN ÆS.

Sculptor noua arte, bracteata in lamina   Sculpit figuras, atque prælis imprimit.

Figure 3. Engraving after Jan van der Straet, *Sculptura in æs*, Plate 19 from *Nova Reperta*. The Burndy Library, Cambridge, Massachusetts.

far right we see the actual work of engraving a copper plate: as two apprentices look on, a man wearing spectacles (another of van der Straet's new inventions, illustrated in plate 15) produces the image of an old man with a cane by digging into the plate with his sharp burin. The man's handle on the plate may appear awkward, but in fact it accurately demonstrates the method of creating curved lines, which required the engraver to push the burin with one hand while using the other hand to turn the plate against the burin. On a table at the center of the workshop a man warms a plate bearing the engraved image of a crucified Christ in preparation for inking; behind him, another man wipes a cloth across the surface of the plate to remove excess ink prior to printing. On the far left of the workshop we see the final stages of the engraving process—the printing of the plates as they are sent through the roller press, and the damp prints hung up to dry.

Engravers like Galle and de Bry were proud of their affiliation with this new "art" (a word that needs to be understood in its early modern sense of *technê*), an art that for van der Straet has a special role to play, along with the other novel technologies illustrated in *Nova reperta,* in the advancement of European civilization. Indeed, engraving belongs with the various technological and educational practices that since the Renaissance have shaped human habits and manners through what Norbert Elias has termed "the civilizing process."[22] As a metallic art, engraving held a special status among these civilizing technologies. As the great metallurgist of the Renaissance, Georgius Agricola, noted in his *De re metallica* (1556): "When an art is so poor that it lacks metals, it is not of much importance."[23] The place of metallic arts within a humanist notion of civility is proclaimed in van der Straet's *America,* in which the opposition between metallic and nonmetallic elements plays a key role in the construction of a civil-savage dichotomy. Vespucci, with astrolabe in hand and the shimmering steel of his armor visible beneath his cloak, is directly linked to two of the metallic inventions celebrated in *Nova reperta* (the polishing of armor and the astrolabe are illustrated in plates 17 and 18, respectively). Naked America, in contrast, possesses only the nonmetallic technologies of her hammock and wooden club.

Similarly, in the *Report* de Bry makes very clear his own status as the practitioner of a metallic art, declaring no less than three times that he has taken pains to "cutt in copper" his plates. He also suggests in the preface to his engravings that it is precisely through the use of metals that the inhabitants of Virginia may in the future become as civilized as those of modern Europe. Praising the Virginians for their "Dexteritye of witte, in makinge without any instrument of mettall thinges so neate and so fine," de Bry leaves his reader to imagine what such a promising people might be able to accomplish *with* the use of metals.[24] We can contemplate this developmental narrative in pictorial terms by turning to de Bry's engraving of a *A cheiff Lorde of Roanoac,* who wears a metallic plate around his neck (Figure 4). In the caption below the engraving, provided by Harriot, we learn that it is a "plate of copper" worn "in token of authorityе."[25] But this token of authority is also noticeably empty of any markings—a "blank, 'savage' plate," to paraphrase de Certeau, that invites comparison with the improved plates—polished, engraved, inked, and printed—that we see in *Sculptura in æs.* The temptation to read this Algonquian ornament in relation to de Bry's own art is hard to resist. While the uninscribed plate speaks to a potential for improvement, this savage has yet to develop the art that could transform his copper plate into a very different kind of token, the kind through which de Bry represents his own authority in the engravings of the *Report.*

I do not wish to overstate the case for technology as a measure of civilization during the early phase of European exploration and settlement of the Americas.[26] Regardless of the praise heaped on new inventions in *Nova reperta* or in Francis Bacon's claim that it was the great triad of magnetic compass, printing press, and gunpowder that distinguished civilized Europe from the "wildest and most barbarous districts of New India," early travelers were very much aware of their own vulnerability in the face of the dangerous conditions of transatlantic voyages.[27] In addition, there was hardly universal agreement that Native American societies were hopelessly backward. De Bry's praise of the Virginians' "dexteritye of witte" shows a high regard for Algonquian arts, and in general the White/de Bry images, far from presenting Algonquian society as merely a "blank, 'savage' page," often apply a European visual language of civil

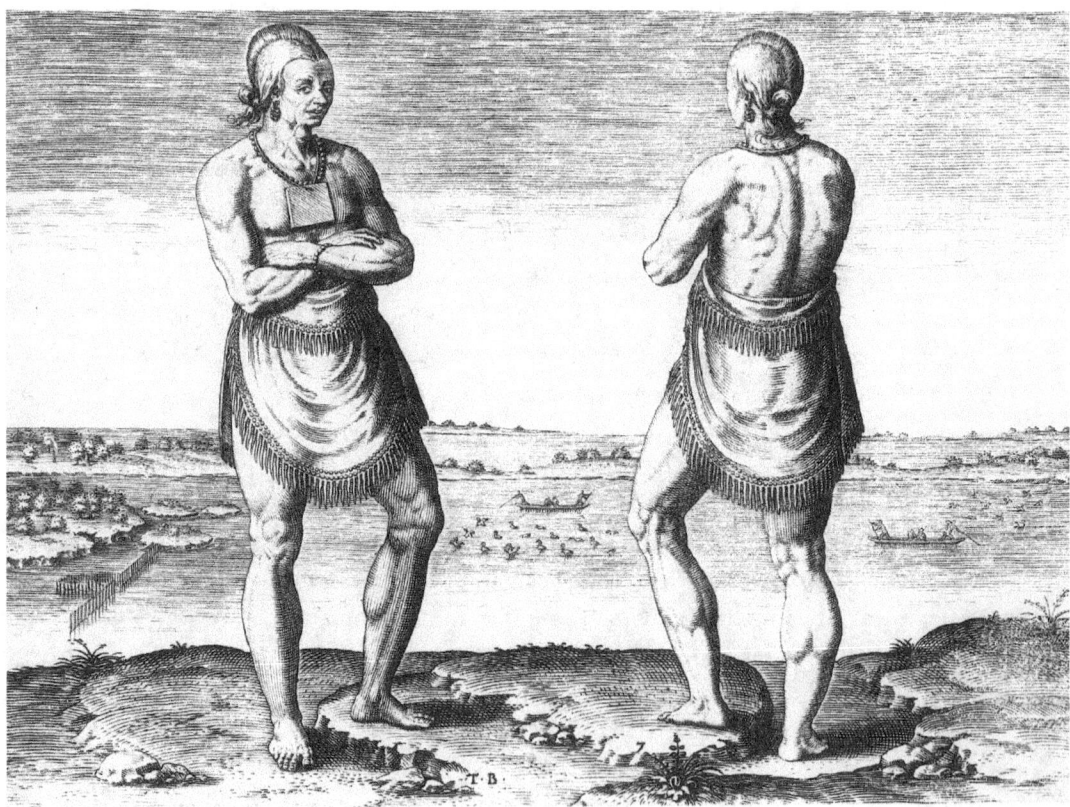

Figure 4. Theodor de Bry after John White, *A cheiff Lorde of Roanoac* (detail), from Harriot, *A Briefe and True Report of the New Found Land of Virginia* (Frankfurt am Main, 1590). Courtesy and with permission of British Library G.6837.

bodily comportment to their subjects. According to the caption, for example, the *Cheiff Lorde of Roanoac* folds his arms over his chest "in signe of wisdom."[28]

Nevertheless, a sense of the technological inferiority of the Americas remains a defining feature even in this early period, and is by no means in conflict with European admiration for the "noble savage." It is worth reflecting a bit further on why technology might have been such a powerful marker of difference, as when Harriot, within the pages of the *Report,* invokes his own scientific instruments in order to call attention to the difference between the English and savages:

> Most thinges they sawe with us, as Mathematicall instruments, sea compasses, the vertue of the loadstone in drawing yron, a perspectiue glasse whereby was shewed manie strange sightes, burning glasses, wildefire woorkes, gunnes, bookes, writing and reading, spring clocks that seeme to goe of themselues, and manie other thinges that wee had, were so straunge unto them, and so farre exceeded their capacities to comprehend the reason and meanes how they should be made and done, that they thought they were rather the works of gods then of men, or at the leastwise they had bin giuen and taught us of the gods.[29]

As Harriot makes clear in this passage, it is more than just the lack of superior technologies that defines the savage; it is the savage's inability "to comprehend the reason and meanes how they should be made and done." Harriot's mention of the perspective glass (telescope) and its "manie strange sightes" is of particular interest here and brings us to the heart of a basic Western myth of what it means to be a savage, which is that a savage is precisely one who *lacks* perspective on the world.[30] What defines the savage as such, in other words, is his inability to undertake a subject position from which he might wield the very instruments described by Harriot. Harriot's litany of European technologies—the sea compass, the perspective glass, writing and reading, clocks, etc. (it is a list to which we could easily add engraving)—is more than a set of sophisticated techniques for measuring and surveying the universe; it is a set of techniques for positioning oneself *within* the universe, for achieving a point of view. We could thus call it a "mechanical perspectivalism" that van der Straet, Bacon, and Harriot celebrate in their paeans to modern technologies. If we want to understand the function of the metallic art of engraving within early ethnographic representation, we must understand that, like the perspective glass, engraving is a perspectival technology. When the viewers of the *Report* gazed at its images of American Indians, they were declaring their difference from the savage by doing precisely that which the savage cannot do—by achieving a perspective on the world.[31]

To possess the art of mechanical reproduction, to experience the world through this art, was thus to be aware of oneself as living in an advanced and ever-advancing state of civilization. This evolutionary paradigm, already clearly at work in *Nova reperta,* has been an enduring feature of the historiography of engraving since the first history of the medium was published during the seventeenth century. As Peter

Parshall has noted, John Evelyn's fascination with the history and techniques of engraving expressed in his *Sculptura, or the History, and Art of Chalcography and Engraving in Copper* (1662) is a product of the intense interest in the mechanical trades present in Evelyn's day within the circles surrounding the newly founded Royal Society.[32] Since the knowledge gained from these trades was to provide the experiential basis for the new science and its grand Baconian project of improving the situation of mankind, the state of the mechanical trades at any given time could serve as a gauge of the state of civilization itself: "So long as they find favour," Bacon writes, the mechanical arts "are always thriving and growing, as if endowed with a certain spirit; at first, primitive, then useful, finally highly developed, and always improving."[33] This Baconian narrative of technological progress is still clearly at work in the most important book of this past century on print history, William M. Ivins's *Prints and Visual Communication* (1953). "Prints are among the most important and powerful tools of modern life and thought," writes Ivins, and without them "we should have very few of our modern sciences, technologies, archaeologies, or ethnologies."[34] Even John Ruskin, who in his *Ariadne Florentina: Six Lectures on Wood and Metal Engraving* (1876) has grave doubts about the "progress" promised by the reproducibility of the print, understands the actual labor of engraving in fundamentally evolutionary terms. For all of these authors, engraving is a civilizing art.

While my book benefits enormously from the work of Evelyn, Ivins, and Ruskin, all of whom make appearances in the following chapters, I do not share their faith in the civilizing nature of the printed image. On the one hand, engraving is indeed a technology that, by allowing a level of standardization in reproduction, served as a critical tool in the formation of the various modern disciplines (art history no less than anthropology) from the mid-sixteenth century until its replacement by photomechanical reproduction around 1900. On the other hand, engraving is notable precisely for the way it has stood stubbornly *between* the viewer and the world, as a technology whose very materiality refuses the space of difference sought in its representations. If in van der Straet's *America* Vespucci stands on the shores of the New World and looks outward toward America in a gaze of colonial desire and conquest, in the enclosed space of *Sculptura in æs* almost all the figures look downward, oblivious of the world around them. This is a workshop full of artisans preoccupied with their materials and labor as they focus on the matter of making reproductions. The engraver at right who is at work cutting his plate can serve as an emblem of the conditions that reign here. Although he wears spectacles that presumably aid him in his work (according to the plate that illustrates this invention, eyeglasses "remove dark veils from the eyes"), the opaque white lenses curiously make him appear blind as he feels his way across the plate with his prosthetic burin, much as the old (blind?) man he has engraved on the plate feels his way forward with his walking stick. Invented to aid human vision, the engraver's spectacles speak to the visual strain that was a consequence of the difficult and minute labor of engraving.[35] They also speak to the problematic place of the workshop throughout engraving's history as the chief reproductive medium in the West. While it was a space that promised to advance the condition of mankind by achieving a clarity of vision unthinkable in the past, it was also a space that reminds us how vision was mediated by imperfect human beings working with tools and copper plates.

Informed by recent interest in the materiality of prints and the printed text, I attempt to negotiate between the representation of the savage and the matter of engraving.[36] The white pebble in the dark forest is not a disembodied light but a palpable thing, an impression made by forcing ink into the absorbent fibers of a sheet of paper, an index of the workshop. Like the opaque white lenses of the engraver's spectacles in *Sculptura in æs,* the white pebble of the ethnographic image represents both the desire for and the impossibility of unmediated access to origins. It must therefore be reckoned with in all its *thingness.* In each of the following chapters I do this by dwelling on the material remainders left over from the workshop, remainders that consistently trouble the stability of the civil-savage opposition that structures ethnographic representation. These remainders, it turns out, take us very near to that which the representation would distance us from. Engraving begins to look, for example, a lot like the tattoos with which the savage marks his body (chapter 1); or like the basely material image that the savage worships as his idol (chapter 3). Or, to return to our example of *A cheiff Lorde of Roanoac,* engraving begins to look a lot like the matter with which the savage signifies his own authority. While we can indeed read the chief lord's copper plate as an emblem of the blankness of America, ripe for the engraver to inscribe his own subjectivity on the New World, we can also read it as a leftover of that very work of inscription, something (uncomfortably) close to those "beaten sheets" of copper being worked on in van der Straet's print. In this book I argue that the leftovers of representation, like the chief lord's copper plate, are precisely the stuff the savage is made of. In other words, we owe the very idea of the "savage" to a strongly felt need in the Christian West to imagine a failure to rise above a base materialism. The savage is thus imagined as one who fails to transcend medium; unable to recognize that the copper plate is not an end in itself, he instead makes the mistake of wearing it around his neck as his "token of authoritye."[37]

The European, in contrast, sees the copper plate as a means to an end. Its value lies in its potential as a tool, as a medium for transforming one thing into another— in the way a tool such as Vespucci's brass astrolabe (made of a copper alloy) transforms the night skies into useful knowledge for the mariner, or in the way a copper coin can be exchanged for useful items in a money economy. As an eminently useful metal, copper was in fact one of the chief "marchantable commodities" of Virginia mentioned in the *Report.* Ralph Lane, the governor of the first Roanoke colony of 1585–86, writes in Hakluyt's *Principall Navigations* (1589) that "Of this metall the Mangoaks [an Iroquoian tribe encountered on an exploratory expedition] haue so great store, by report of all the sauages adioyning, that they beautifie their houses with great plates of the same."[38] Lane's comment, like de Bry's engraving of the chief lord, showcases the Indians' failure to recognize practical utility: the Mangoaks' copper plates, with which they "beautifie their houses," are conspicuously *useless* in their society.[39] By emphasizing an unexploited supply of metal, Lane is of course trying to turn his audience on to what he sees as a great potential for copper mining in Virginia. This apparent bounty could be one of the reasons that publishing a book about Virginia was of such interest to Theodor de Bry. As the head of an engraving workshop, copper was for him a particularly valuable commodity, and not for its monetary value alone.[40] Copper was the key medium of exchange in the representational economy of his workshop, a workshop that during the late sixteenth and early seventeenth centuries became an engine for transforming copper into New World knowledge. In de Bry's workshop, copper was cut from sheets, polished to a lustrous red sheen, engraved, and then printed as representations on paper for dissemination to a wide audience in the form of book illustrations. The figures on the right side of van der Straet's *Sculptura in æs* who seem so devoted to their copper plates—hugging the plate to the body while engraving its surface, warming it over coals, wiping off excess ink—thus represent only the early and middle stages of a larger process of transforming copper into meaning. And yet, to page through de Bry's *Report,* to stop at the engraving of *A cheiff Lorde of Roanoac* and contemplate the meaning of the copper he proudly displays around his neck, is to return ourselves to the kind of loving attention that van der Straet's engravers show their plates. This chief lord's "token of authoritye" is the white pebble that draws our eyes downward to the tables of the workshop; it reminds us that the matter of engraving can never be entirely left behind.

The chief lord's copper plate is, ultimately, a very strange token, because as a remainder it sits comfortably neither here nor there. It belongs *both* to the art of engraving, as its leftover, *and* to the savage, as his defining feature; it fails to map onto the rationalized grid of ethnography, which depends on charting the boundaries between new world and old, savage and civil.[41] A consideration of the remainder can therefore help us rethink what it has meant to imagine the savage in the West. There has, of course, been a good deal of attention to the history of the savage as an intellectual/ideological construct; scholars have located the savage within Western thought by considering its status as belief, idea, symbol, image, attitude, concept, and myth.[42] This has been important and necessary historical work, although it has tended to create the illusion of a successful rationalization, leading us to believe that some kind of final meaning (however ideological) was in fact achieved in the effort to give shape to the other. In contrast, what attention to the materiality of engraving can offer is an understanding of the savage as a product of representation's failure. Engraving the savage never was the illustration of a coherent idea; it was a confrontation with medium, a struggle—never complete—to make meaning out of matter.

Chapter 1, "Savage Marks: The Scriptive Techniques of Early Modern Ethnography," focuses on de Bry's engraving of a tattooed Algonquian warrior. It is an image that raises some very basic questions about the European project of translating Native Americans that accompanied early modern colonial ventures like the Roanoke voyages. How can the body of a New World native be translated into an object of European knowledge? More specifically, how can marks like tattoos be translated into the alphabetical signs with which de Bry indexes them? How can arrows—instruments the tattooed warrior holds in his hand—be translated into emblems of savagery? I attempt to answer such questions by situating de Bry's project of translation within a humanist network of scriptive practices around 1600 that includes alphabetical writing, the quill pen, and the burin. In doing so, I deconstruct any easy distinctions we might draw between savage tattoos and civilized letters, or between the savage arrow and the civilizing quill. Moreover, within this scriptive network in which there can be no clear distinctions between the savage and the civil, I situate the labor of the engraver himself. Although in his self-portrait of 1597 de Bry declares for himself the authority of an engraver working in the tradition of Dürer, an authority that would seem to transcend the (potentially violent) materiality of the engraver's burin, he nevertheless remains an artisan engaged in a labor of inscription not unlike the "savage" work of inscribing tattoos. By dwelling on the relation between engraving and tattooing, I attempt to give some historical specificity to the allegorical reading of America as a blank page awaiting the inscription of Western desire.

Chapter 2, "Making Sense of Smoke: Engraving and Ornament in de Bry's *America*," examines de Bry's predilection for composing ornate, smoky passages in his engravings of Virginia. In a number of his plates, the Algonquians' fires produce an elaborate display of twisting and turning lines that disrupt the illusionistic space of the image by freeing the engraved line from its representational duties. While ornament is typically understood to be an art of surfaces, I argue that ornament in fact plays a central and defining role within the *Report*'s representational project. Drawing on Hubert Damisch's *A Theory of /Cloud/,* which argues that clouds and smoke have performed a key semiotic function in Western art as the nebulous remainders of perspectival representation, I argue that de Bry's smoke performs a similar function in this late sixteenth-century colonial text: smoke makes ethnographic representation possible precisely by signifying its limits. In this regard, the ornamental lines of de Bry's smoke are similar to the grotesque printer's ornaments that appear throughout the *Report*—another marginal element of the text that is easy to overlook. Like these playful grotesques, the ornamental play of line in de Bry's smoke becomes a safe space to display the very irrationality that defines the savage as such. Born in, or rather *as,* the ornamental margins of representation, the savage is less a coherent object of de Bry's descriptive project than its formal condition of possibility.

Chapter 3, "Flatness and Protuberance: Reforming the Image in Protestant Print Culture," considers the reception of one of the most popular engravings based on White's collection, a highly perspectival representation of Algonquian idolatry. I examine how, within this scene, perspectival space appears to contain New World idolatry even as it reveals the impossibility of that containment. Specifically, I focus on the appearance of this image in two eighteenth-century texts: Robert Beverley's *The History and Present State of Virginia* (1705) and the multivolume work of comparative religion, *The Ceremonies and Religious Customs of the Various Nations of the Known World*

(1733–39). Both of these staunchly Protestant texts make image-worship into an object of empirical inquiry, and in doing so they pull this scene of Algonquian idolatry into their service. In its overinscription of perspectival space, however, the engraving suggests that idolatry may be something more than an exclusively New World or even "papist" phenomenon. Precisely because these illustrated texts draw on the viewer's sensual desire to look, the Protestant viewer is always on the verge of becoming an idolater, a "worshiper" of the graven image. What Erwin Panofsky called the "two-edged sword" of perspective—the way in which it distances the world of objects at the same time that it draws those sensuous objects within the domain of the viewer—thus becomes the paradoxical logic of a Protestant anthropology that struggles to distance idolatry from the viewer even as it depends on a repressed desire for the idol.

In the concluding chapter, "The Art of Scratch: Wood Engraving and Picture-Writing in the 1880s," I consider engraved reproductions of White's watercolors created at the end of the nineteenth century, during engraving's last gasp as the primary medium for the mass reproduction of images in the West. Sixteen engravings of White's ethnographic images were made for a series of articles on colonial American history published during the 1880s in *Century Magazine*. Although this was the decade during which the halftone was introduced as a viable form of reproduction, wood engraving was in fact the preferred reproductive method at the time. This chapter examines the ways in which the labor of the wood engraver—the subject of much discussion in *Century* and in other periodicals during this decade—is implicated in the ethnological discourse of the late nineteenth century. Drawing on John Ruskin's writings on engraving, I argue that the engraver's lines demonstrate the process of civilization in action—that is, the process of evolution. To understand wood engraving in these terms is to see how this important reproductive practice of the 1880s, a practice nearly forgotten by art history at the beginning of the twenty-first century, was not simply a vehicle for replicating White's collection but a constitutive element of its meaning. In the wood engraver's lines we witness a peculiarly nineteenth-century investment in White's collection, an evolutionary investment that, in its struggle to evolve beyond the primitive scratches of the American savage, returns us to the contingencies of the reproductive practice that Ruskin called "the art of scratch."

As a final note, it hardly needs saying that the savage I write about in each of these chapters is not to be mistaken for the indigenous societies that the English actually encountered when they arrived in Virginia in 1585. The savage is a (by-)product of Western representation, not a living and breathing agent in history. That I have chosen to focus on a Western construct is not, however, a cynical conclusion on my part about the impossibility of thinking about visual practices across cultures. Although this book is not a study in cross-cultural communication, as have been some of the most stimulating recent works on the cultural history of the Atlantic World, by no means do I wish to close down the possibility of cross-cultural readings of the de Bry engravings and their descendants.[43] Each of my chapters, in fact, suggests how such a reading might proceed. Chapters 1 and 4, in deconstructing the opposition between

European and Native American practices of inscription, suggest that we could think about encounters between Europeans and indigenous societies as negotiations that have taken place through a variety of engraving techniques. Chapters 2 and 3, in turn, open the possibility of thinking about the cross-cultural efficacy of images in terms of what Alfred Gell has called "technologies of enchantment."[44] Though none of my chapters offers a detailed engagement with Native American visual cultures, I do hope that by showing the limits of a Western category for capturing the other I have gestured toward a space, neither savage nor civil, where such an engagement might begin.

1. Savage Marks
The Scriptive Techniques of Early Modern Ethnography

Our world has just discovered another one: and who will answer for its being the last of its brothers, since up till now its existence was unknown to the daemons, to the Sybils, and to ourselves? It is no less big and full and solid than our own; its limbs are as well developed: yet it is so new, such a child, that we are still teaching it its ABC.

—Michel de Montaigne, "Of Coaches"

Designed to encourage investment in Sir Walter Raleigh's Virginia colony, Harriot's *Report* is organized into three parts. It begins with about thirty pages of text by Harriot that evaluate Virginia's mercantile and colonial prospects and then go on to describe the "nature and manners of the people of the countrey." The second part, "the true pictures and fashions of the people" of Virginia, consists of a series of ethnographic images engraved in de Bry's Frankfurt workshop (mostly by de Bry himself), and for the most part based directly on watercolor drawings by John White. The final section of the *Report* includes five engravings of the ancient inhabitants of Britain, again based primarily on White's drawings, and the purpose of which, according to de Bry, is "to show how that the Inhabitants of the great Bretannie have bin in times past as sauvage as those of Virginia" (see Figure 38).[1]

At once a voyage account, an advertisement for investment in a colonial venture, and a work of comparative ethnology (although that science was, of course, nonexistent in 1590), the *Report* belongs to no one discipline or discourse. Mary Campbell has provided a useful term for thinking about the book's function by suggesting that we consider it an exercise in *coloniology*, a word that aptly describes a project wherein what we would now call ethnological data are produced and arranged in the service of explicitly colonial aims.[2] De Bry's contribution to this coloniology, then, was to find compelling visual strategies that could place Virginia—its people, its products, its spaces—in the service of such an endeavor. The question I will take up here is what those strategies were and how they operated at the most concrete level; that is, at the level of the specific representational machineries that organize the *Report*'s data—

1

machineries that include the Roman alphabet, the writer's quill, the engraver's burin. While we may not be able to name a specific discipline to which this text belongs, we can most certainly name the materials and techniques through which it constitutes itself *as* a text and, more generally, through which an early modern ethnography constituted its subjects and objects. According to de Certeau, "Western ethnological science is written on the space that the body of the other provides for it."[3] My reading of the *Report* through the letter, the quill, and the burin is an effort to think seriously and literally through the implications of de Certeau's assertion in a late sixteenth-century context. One of de Bry's plates, an image that offers ample occasion to reflect on techniques of inscription, will serve as my guide.

In the *Report*'s final image of Virginia's natives, titled *The Marckes of sundrye of the Cheif mene of Virginia,* we gaze upon the back of a muscled warrior, an American Doryphorus who has traded his spear for bow and arrows (Figure 5).[4] His right hand, contorted in a difficult mannerist gesture, grasps two arrows horizontally, their tips pointed toward his shoulder. With his left hand, he props up an unstrung bow, its spiraling string echoing the contrapposto of his body. A quiver is slung across his buttocks, and from behind the quiver hangs a tail (as Harriot notes in the caption to an earlier plate, "They hange before them the skinne of some beaste very feinelye dresset in suche sorte, that the tayle hangeth downe behynde"). A mark—of the kind which, following Cook's voyages, would become known in the English-speaking world as a "tattoo"—is etched into the man's left shoulder. Surrounding him on the page are a number of marks that reproduce the patterns of this tattoo and six others from Indians of the region. Each of these patterns corresponds to a letter of the Latin alphabet, *A* through *G,* and these letters in turn correspond to meanings explicated in the text below.

Within the pictorial space of the engraving, de Bry guides his viewer through what we can think of tentatively as four discrete levels of signification. The first is the level of factual description, or what Erwin Panofsky in his classic essay on "Iconography and Iconology" termed the "primary or natural subject matter" of a picture. On this level, the two arrows in the man's hand simply denote weapons that were actually observed among the Indians of Virginia during the sixteenth century, while the tattoo on his left shoulder is nothing more than a bodily ornament the English observed on Indians of the region. The second level of signification is that of iconographical meaning, Panofsky's "secondary or conventional subject matter."[5] The two arrows in particular stand out as objects rich in iconographical significance in the late sixteenth century: by 1590 an arrow or arrows held in the hand had become a standard element in the depiction of the American Indian as well as in allegorical representations of America. This pictorial convention can therefore be understood, when it appears in the appropriate context, as an emblem of the savage. As early as 1505, for example, a New World native is pictured on the woodcut frontispiece of Amerigo Vespucci's *Mundus novus* holding two emblematic arrows in similar fashion (Figure 6). Like Vespucci's savage, de Bry's figure holds up these arrows in a gesture of display,

The Marckes of sundrye of the XXIII.
Cheif mene of Virginia.

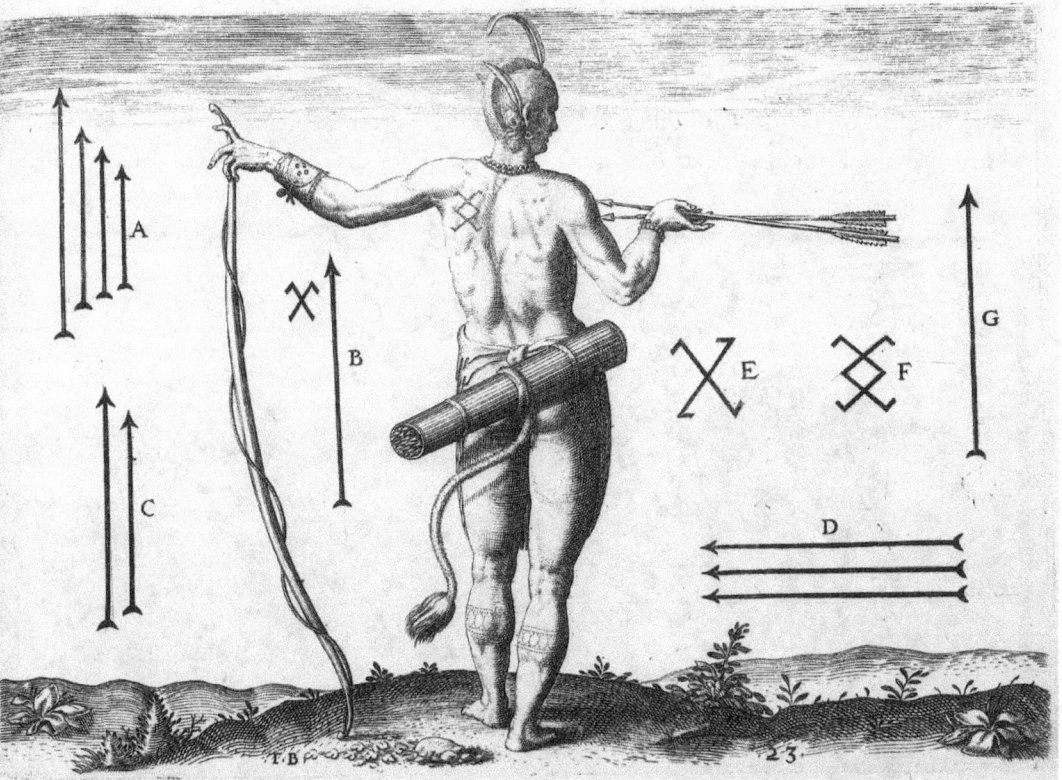

He inhabitāts of all the cūntrie for the most parte haue marks rased on their backs, wherby yt may be knowen what Princes subiects they bee, or of what place they haue their originall. For which cause we haue set downe those marks in this figure, and haue annexed the names of the places, that they might more easelye be discerned. Which industrie hath god indued them withal although they be verye simple, and rude. And to confesse a truthe I cannot remember, that euer I saw a better or quietter people then they.

The marks which I obserued amonge them, are heere put downe in order folowinge.

The marke which is expressed by A. belongeth tho Wingino, the cheefe lorde of Roanoac.

That which hath B. is the marke of Wingino his sisters husbande.

Those which be noted with the letters, of C. and D. belonge vnto diverse chefe lordes in Secotam.

Those which haue the letters E. F. G. are certaine cheefe men of Pomeiooc, and Aquascogoc.

Figure 5. Theodor de Bry, *The Marckes of sundrye of the Cheif mene of Virginia,* from *A Briefe and True Report.* Courtesy and with permission of British Library G.6837.

as if he were presenting them specifically as objects for our observation and reflection, perhaps even encouraging us to think about the relationship between primary and secondary meanings as well as the relationship between these types of pictorial meaning and a third level of signification in the engraving, which is that of the various tattoo designs distributed across the plate. These "primitive" markings, now detached from the skin and thus appearing on the page as fully abstract signs, are visually linked to the real arrows in the figure's hand through the repeated use of a schematic arrow form. As it appears in these tattoos, however, the arrow has now become a fully conventionalized and manipulable element within a Native American system of symbolic communication for marking identity. As Harriot's caption explains, the tattoos make known "what Princes subiects they bee, or of what place they haue their original," and

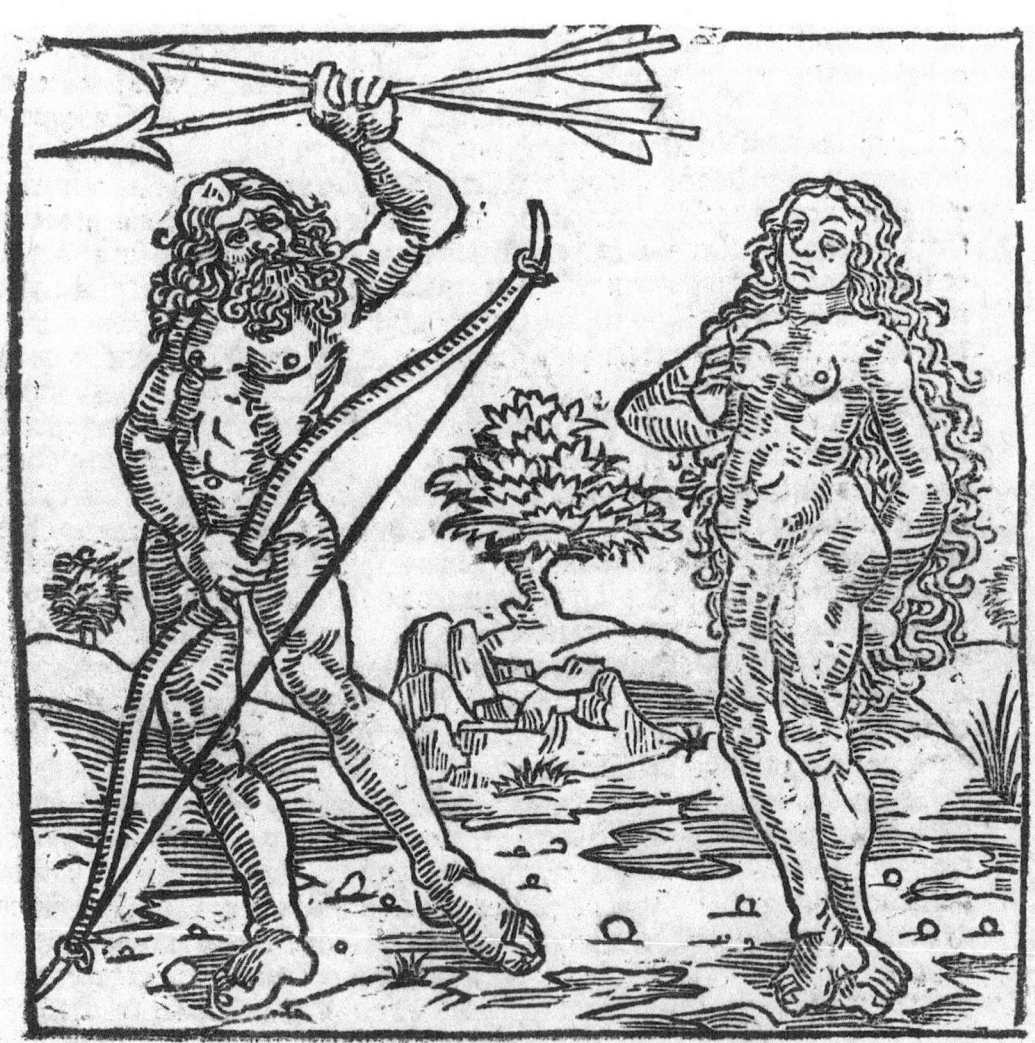

Figure 6. Frontispiece from Amerigo Vespucci, *Mundus novus* (Rostock?, 1505). Courtesy and with permission of British Library C.20.e.18.

he goes on to attach the various marks to specific native groups: "Those which haue the letters E, F, G," for example, "are certain cheefe men of Pomeiooc, and Aquascogoc." The tattoos require this sort of explanation because they are unfamiliar symbols for a sixteenth-century European audience. They stand in contrast, therefore, to a fourth and final level of signification in the engraving, which is that of the familiar, phonetic signs of the Latin alphabet that index each of the tattoos.

The purpose of de Bry's engraving is to decode the savage, to translate the otherness of a New World body, denoted at the primary level of visual meaning, into the familiarity of a European sign system (alphabetical writing). But the way in which de Bry visually juxtaposes what appear to be entirely different orders of signification begs certain questions about this process of producing ethnographic knowledge, about the very stability of oppositions like visual/verbal and savage/civilized on which this translation of knowledge is based. What exactly *are* the differences between savage tattoos and civilized letters, or between illusionistic arrows and arrow-shaped tattoos? What assumptions are made, consciously or unconsciously, when we make the leap from one kind of sign to another? Where, moreover, amidst this proliferation of signs, are we to situate the labor of the productive self indexed at the bottom left of the plate with the letters *TB*—the mark of the engraver whose burin first produced the marks which now present to us this exemplary image of mark-making? All these questions, which are part of a more general question about the conditions of producing ethnographic authority in the late sixteenth century, are raised by de Bry's engraving of *The Marckes of sundrye of the Cheif mene of Virginia.*

We can begin to address these questions by considering two possible interpretations of de Bry's engraving. One approach would be to treat this image as a visual codification of sixteenth-century beliefs about the transcendent authority of writing in the New World encounter. Understood in these terms, de Bry's engraving stages a writing lesson upon the body of an American Indian. For it is precisely alphabetical writing (via the letters indexing the tattoos) that provides us with the key to reading the savage, just as it is the lack of an alphabet that prevents the savage—who stands with his back to us and is thus unaware of our gaze—from turning around and reading us. De Bry's engraving is in this sense entirely consistent with views on alphabetical writing disseminated in the new humanist grammars and instruction manuals of the sixteenth century. In these texts the alphabet became a defining instrument in the production of a distinctly *civil,* and by extension *colonial,* authority. Indeed, the link between the teaching of writing and the production of empire can be traced back to the epochal year of 1492. In addition to marking the completion of the *Reconquista* and the opening of the New World to territorial conquest with Columbus's discovery, the year 1492 also marks the publication of the Castilian grammar of Spanish humanist Elio Antonio de Nebrija. In the prologue to that text, Nebrija announces the role that writing would play in future conquests by claiming that his grammar would prove useful as Queen Isabella places "her yoke upon barbarians who speak outlandish tongues."[6] In short, Europe's civilizing mission in the New World would be a grammatical mission;

as Montaigne put it nearly one hundred years after Nebrija's remark (see epigraph), it would be a matter of teaching a new world "its ABC."

Falling squarely within the tradition of such humanist rhetoric, de Bry's writing lesson teaches his viewers to make alphabetical meaning out of the base matter of the New World. The engraving's reception, the basic elements of which are clearly spelled out for us, becomes an exercise in the constitution of a civil self through the production of its savage other: to progress through its chain of signification is to rehearse one's own advancement from a savage or "natural" state, bound to the material body and to a corporeal, preverbal form of communication (in giving his back to us, the figure echoes the viewer's own physical orientation to the page and thus encourages a *bodily* identification), to a civilized state that locates knowledge in the written word. Interpretation is thus a process of coming into recognition of one's own civility, a civility that is in this case defined as *literacy*. Like the pedagogical manuals of the sixteenth century, de Bry's engraving teaches the use of letters and at the same time provides guidance in the proper discipline of the body: literally, the viewer is taught how to be released from the pictorial register of the tattooed body by entering a textual apparatus that, as the privileged site of knowledge, can now *contain* the matter of the image as the newly discovered object of its proto-ethnographic discourse.

An alternative interpretation, however, might read de Bry's image in the opposite direction. Instead of treating it as a rehearsal of the evolution from a savage form of communication (the basely material tattoo) to civil communication (the letter as transcendent of matter), we could read the image as a collapsing of this binary. And we would not be unjustified, on historical grounds, in taking this approach. In recent years literary historians, taking up Jacques Derrida's call for a "cultural graphology," have demonstrated the impossibility of separating the history of writing from the histories of its various material supports and methods of inscription. Those materials and practices, it is argued, are not simply the accidental forms that abstract thought and poetic expression have taken, but are instead essential constituents of meaning. Indeed, as Juliet Fleming has argued, the tattoo provides a critical but neglected category for understanding the function of writing in a society (sixteenth-century England) in which "writing embraced its status as a material thing."[7] It is significant, argues Fleming, that antiquarians such as William Camden and John Speed who wrote about the bodily markings of the ancient inhabitants of Britain, as well as writers such as Thomas Harriot and Samuel Purchas who offered accounts of American tattooing, turned to a richly descriptive language tied to European writing practices when they remarked on the curious patterns incised into the skin of their cultural and temporal others. To approach de Bry's image from this standpoint is to see how a mark inscribed on a body and a letter inscribed on a copper plate might share a common materiality, again raising the question: What *is* the difference between a tattoo and a letter? While their appearance side by side may imply difference, it could imply resemblance as well. In significant ways, we shall see the letters on the page are *like* the tattoos they index.

Similarly, the arrows in the Indian's hand need not be interpreted exclusively as emblems of difference.[8] To be sure, European artists had at their disposal a well-developed iconography of otherness, and the bow and arrow became an important part of this iconography during the sixteenth century.[9] When a figure is intended to stand for America, or simply to embody the savage condition of the New World, we can usually expect to find a bow and arrow in the hands or at the feet. This iconography is codified in the figure of America that appears in the first illustrated edition of Cesare Ripa's *Iconologia* (1603) (Figure 7), and we can even find a textual source in an illustrated New World travel account of 1578, Jean de Léry's *History of a Voyage to the Land of Brazil*, a book that de Bry knew well (it serves as the basis for part 3 of de Bry's *America*). In reference to an illustration that displays the physical appearance of a Tupinamba man and his family, Léry writes that the savage must have, in order "to keep himself in countenance, his loose bow and his arrows in his hands" *(pour contenance son arc desbandé, & ses flesches aux mains)* (See Figure 1).[10] An iconographical interpretation that grounds itself in such sources would certainly be useful for putting de Bry's Indian "in countenance." But it could tell us only *what* these arrows signify, not *how* they signify: iconographical readings, by treating the image as a vehicle for a meaning external to itself, adhere to the same logic that privileges the meaning of a letter over its physical properties. In both cases, the material body of the signifying mark becomes a secondary or accidental quality subordinated to its emblematic value.[11] To read the arrows iconographically as cultural symbols pointing us outward toward a nexus of historically specific ideas, beliefs, and ideologies concerning the savage (secondary meanings), or even to read them as ethnographic observations pointing us to the real (primary meanings), is to reduce the image to a meaning *other* than itself. If, however, we choose to see those arrows as opaque signifiers, as the irreducibly material traces of a historically specific set of European representational practices, then they can point us back toward the question of how in the sixteenth century it was possible to construct meanings about the New World at all. And I would suggest that this picture asks us to do just that, for the arrows in the Indian's hand do not in fact direct us outside the image; rather, they are pointed reflexively at his body, their tips just meeting his right shoulder as if they were in the process, literally, of describing his contours. The arrows, in other words, appear to figure the labor of inscription itself—a labor which, under the sign of the arrow, assumes a corporeality and even a potential violence. This labor will ultimately lead us to de Bry's own practice as an engraver.

I have sketched the outlines of two contradictory readings of de Bry's picture: one in which a savage body is translated/civilized through alphabetical writing; another in which the very writing and scriptive practices that would translate the savage are shown to be of a piece with the unredeemed matter of the New World. Both readings seem plausible, since both are faithful to the visual "facts" and both rely on legitimate contexts for interpretation: in one case, the ideological context of humanism, colonialism, and an emerging ethnological discourse; in the other, the historical field of mediation—that is, technologies, bodies, and scriptive practices and their deployment

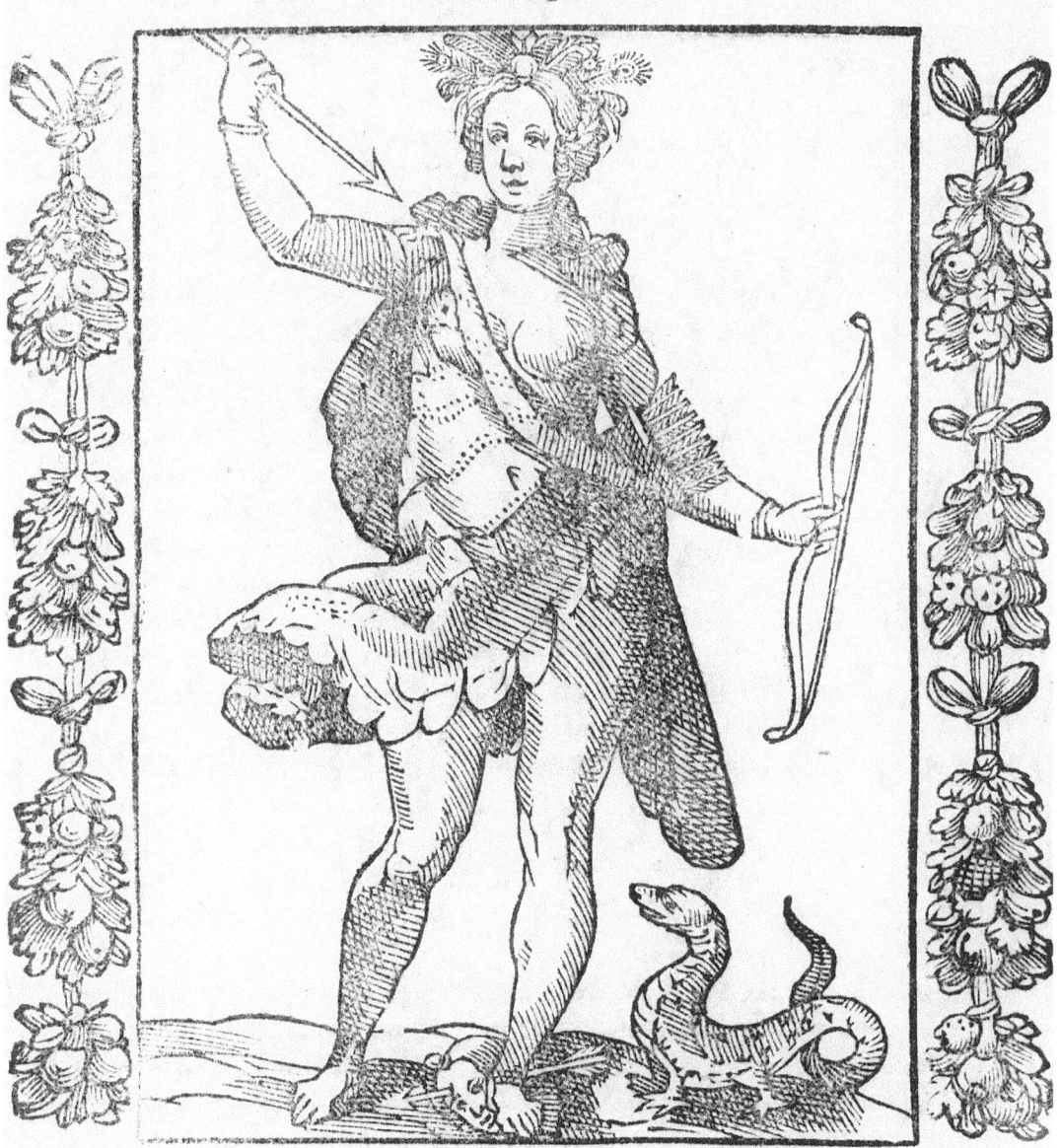

Figure 7. *America,* from Cesare Ripa, *Iconologia* (Rome, 1603). Special Collections, University of Iowa Libraries.

within specific power structures—which it is ideology's task to purify of its untidiness.[12] What distinguishes de Bry's engraving from many other images of the New World is that by explicitly staging the (fraught) translation of an American body, it keeps both the aforementioned readings in play. *The Marckes of sundrye of the Cheif mene of Virginia* is a sixteenth-century example of what W. J. T. Mitchell has called a "meta-picture"—that is, a picture that cannot be reduced to a particular message but, instead, by simultaneously admitting opposing readings, offers a visual meditation on how meaning is produced through images. Metapictures, such as this depiction of a savage who points at himself, are self-referential: they are "pictures that show them-selves in order to know themselves: they stage the 'self-knowledge' of pictures."[13] As a metapicture, then, *The Marckes of sundrye of the Cheif mene of Virginia* reveals the fundamental ambivalence of colonial representation; and only by taking this ambiva-lence seriously will we grasp the radically *incomplete* nature of civility and savagery as they emerge as organizing concepts in the culture of early modern Europe. In the following pages I will attempt to trace the historical parameters of this ambivalence, beginning with the undecidable space between letters and tattoos.

Letter/Tattoo

What is the role of the letter in de Bry's project of coloniology? An answer to this question could begin, by way of comparison, with the engraved frontispiece to Joseph-François Lafitau's *Mœurs des sauvages ameriquains, comparées aux mœurs des premiers temps* (1724; *Customs of the American Indians compared with the Customs of Primitive Times*), an originating text of comparative ethnology in which the Jesuit author traces correspondences between the beliefs of ancient peoples and the recently discovered inhabitants of the New World (Figure 8). Lafitau's frontispiece, the meaning of which he explains in his "Explication des planches et figures," offers a visual allegory of the scientific method that will guide the author in the pages to come, an allegory in which the material letter is precisely that which is overlooked. The engraving displays a pri-vate chamber in which various religious artifacts and texts lie strewn throughout the foreground. Two small "genii" hold up several of the objects for comparison before the female figure of Writing, the ethnographer's muse. Writing looks up from her work to the figure of Time, who directs her gaze to a painting or "mystic vision" in the background that shows Adam and Eve below, and the man and woman of the apoca-lypse above.[14] According to Lafitau, the vision on the wall reveals to Writing "the con-nection between these specimens and the origin of man, the heart of our religion, and all the doctrine of revelation made to our first fathers after their sin."[15]

The fundamental terms of this Jesuit science remain biblical in nature, but as de Certeau has argued in an illuminating reading of this frontispiece, the activity that takes place in the chamber mirrors the procedures of a new science and a new order of writing that emerged during the Enlightenment.[16] The viewer's progress through the room begins with the visible yet disordered collection in the foreground—a collection

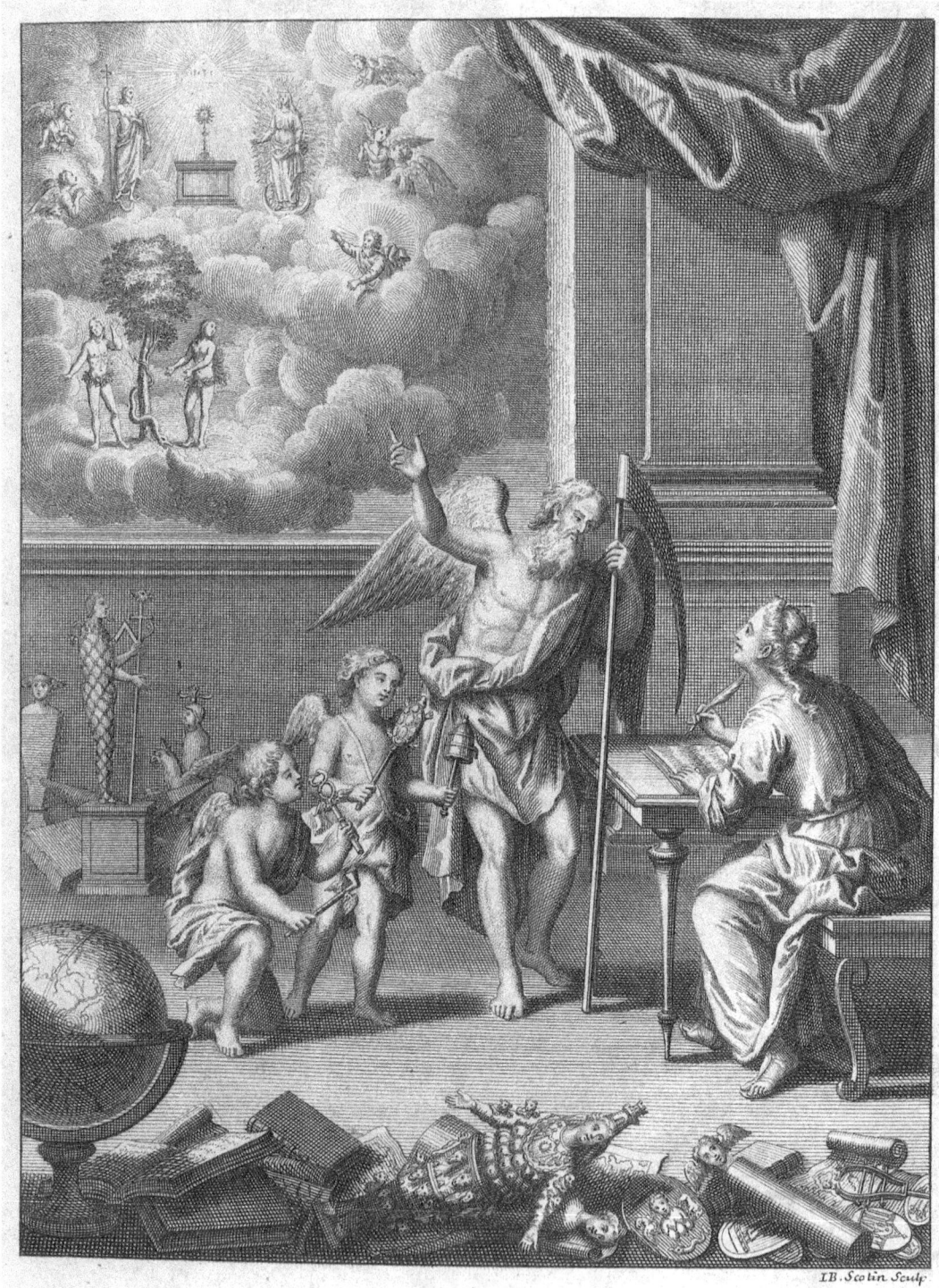

IB.Scotin Sculp.

Figure 8. Frontispiece from Joseph-François Lafitau, *Mœurs des sauvages ameriquains, comparées aux mœurs des premiers temps,* volume 1 (Paris, 1724). From the Collections of the University Libraries, University of Minnesota, Minneapolis.

that provides the evidentiary foundations for Lafitau's comparative project and whose contents will reappear in the forty-one engraved plates interspersed throughout the two-volume quarto—and ends at the vision on the far wall, which is a visual statement of the theoretical principles of Lafitau's ethnology expressed through religious allegory. The actual descriptive work of ethnography belongs to the figure of Writing, whose words transform the fragmentary evidence of the world's religions into a theoretical vision of a universal religious "system."[17] It is worth noting that in this process of translation, the letter *is not seen*: Writing, who looks away from her book and toward a disembodied vision, is unhampered by the materiality of the signs she has scratched out with her quill. In Lafitau's science, the ethnographer's letter is not itself an artifact but a transparent sign on the road from artifact to system.

Lafitau's frontispiece stands not only for the procedures of a new science, but for the structure of a new episteme—Foucault's classical episteme, in which "language has withdrawn from the midst of beings themselves and has entered a period of transparency and neutrality."[18] For Lafitau's muse, the letter occupies an immaterial space of difference, a *non*space in which the materiality of the sign recedes as a positive element in the shaping of knowledge.[19] De Bry's "science," in contrast, responds to a different muse, one who is still firmly rooted in a Renaissance episteme in which the world is conceived as a web of signs woven together through resemblances. The letters that index the Indian's tattoos thus hold a material interest of their own, insofar as they are known through resemblances they may hold to other marks (such as tattoos), and so the eyes of de Bry's viewer must come to rest—or at least I would like to offer the hypothesis that they *should* come to rest—upon the letters themselves.

This is not to say that de Bry's letters have no rational goal; they do, as suggested by the illustrated title page for the *Report,* which makes an instructive point of comparison to Lafitau's frontispiece (Figure 9). Here the goal of de Bry's project is presented, literally, as rational structure: the "unstructured" savage is made to conform to a civilized order embodied in classical architectural forms. The arrangement of the five figures, each of whom represents a figure from Algonquian society and each of whom will later be the subject of a separate engraving, mimics a sixteenth-century European ideal of proper social order: at the top of the pediment sits the Algonquians' idol, Kiwasa; worshiping at his left and right are two religious figures; and below, flanking each column, are a representative Algonquian man and woman. The image displays the heathenism of the savage, who falsely worships an idol rather than God; but at the same time it envisions his assimilation into a proper social hierarchy, an order in which true belief can one day replace idolatry. The rational goal of de Bry's letters, then, is not a scientific knowledge grounded in a set of abstract theoretical principles, as with Lafitau; rather, the goal is to bring the savage within a civilized social order. This order is unequivocally a material one. On the title page, it assumes a solid architectural form: this is by no means the ethereal, cloud-filled vision of Lafitau's frontispiece. Indeed, the function of the architectural supports pictured on de Bry's title page is directly analogous to the function of his letters, for the letters

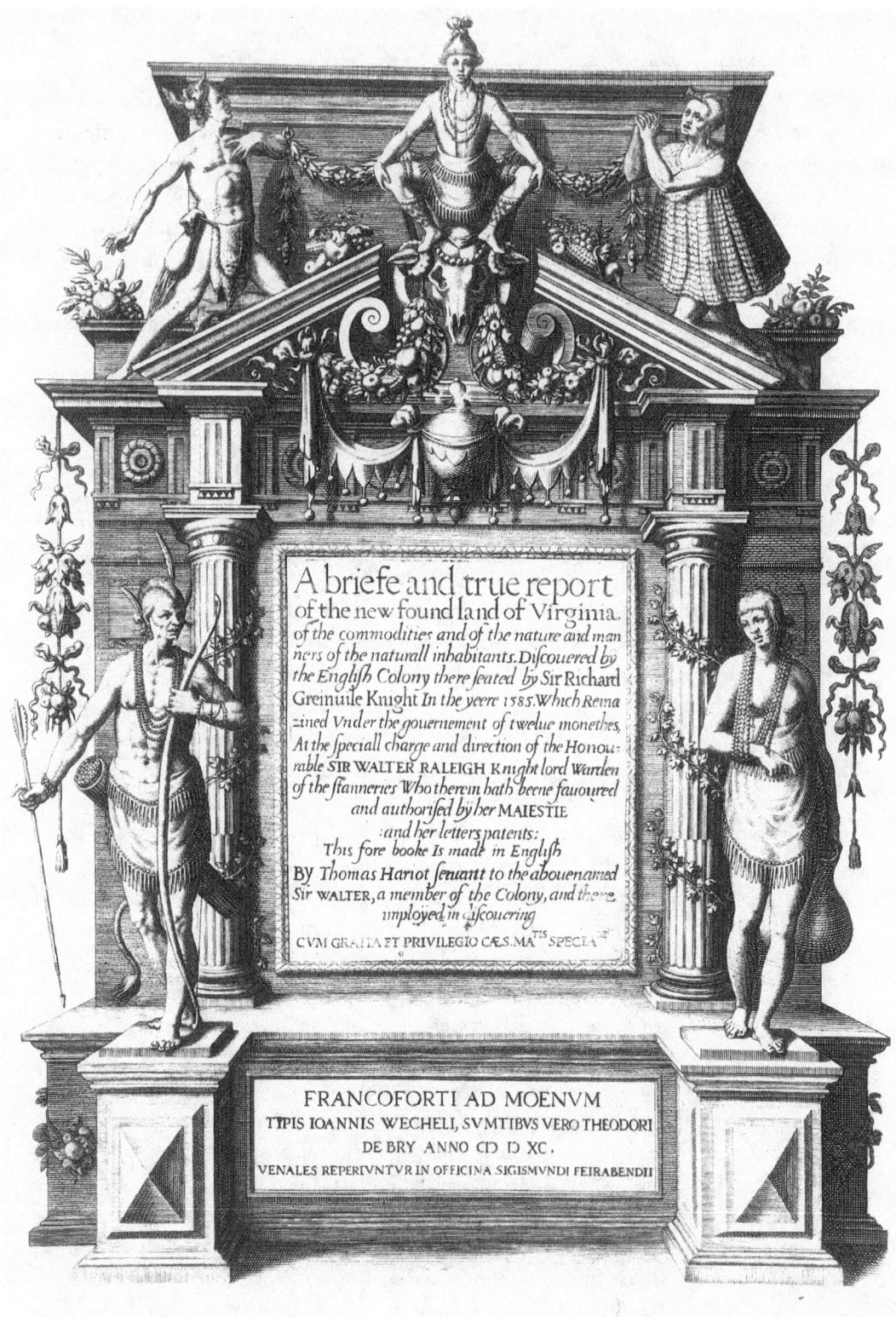

Figure 9. Theodor de Bry, title page from *A Briefe and True Report*. Photograph courtesy of Edward E. Ayer Collection, The Newberry Library, Chicago.

constitute in themselves a foundational material support for the civilized order that is the goal of this Renaissance ethnography.

In an alphabet book published in 1595, de Bry shows quite literally how the letter functions as humanity's chief means of support in a fallen world. The *Nova alphati effictio (Newly Fashioned Alphabet)* consists of twenty-four letters designed by de Bry and engraved by his son, Johann Theodor de Bry. In the initial engraving, the first letter of the alphabet is linked directly to the Fall (Figure 10). Adam and Eve have, so to speak, fallen upon the extended arms of the letter itself, which is intertwined with the branches of the Tree of Knowledge and the snaky limbs of Satan, who assumes the form of a female serpent resting on the top of the *A*. According to the accompanying verses, Adam tasted from the forbidden tree and as a result "the letter now guides the divine soul" *(Litteraque aetheriæ nuncia mentis habet)*. Tasting of the tree, Adam and Eve taste of the letter as well, as they fall into an alphabetical order that is the mark both of their disobedience *and* of the possibility of recovering, through memory, their prelapsarian condition.

De Bry presents his letter *A* as the original supplement: it at once offers to make present mankind's origins (this is, after all, an engraving of Adam and Eve), and at the same time, by virtue of this letter's very existence, it marks mankind's distance from those origins. Letters are the material trappings, the clothing, with which Adam and Eve must now veil the naked self-presence of prelapsarian speech.[20] De Bry's engraving suggests that from this point on—beginning with the Fall—the work of recovering origins (which is the work of the ethnologist, after all) will be mediated by, indeed will have to rest upon, the supportive structure of the alphabet, for nothing in a fallen world is outside the letter. Quite simply, Adam and *A,* the first man and the first letter of the alphabet, go together. "It is of many supposed," writes John Barrett in *An Alvearie or Quadruple Dictionarie* (1580), "that nature hath taught A. to stande in the first place, as wee may easilye perceyve by the first voyce or confuse crying of young infants, which soundeth in the eare most like to A. being also the first letter in the name of our great graundfather Adam."[21] To remove this alphabetical support would be to remove oneself from the Judeo-Christian narrative of fall and redemption, which is a *scriptural* order: as the verses that correspond to de Bry's letter explain, it is only through "knowledge written in sacred books" *(sacris descripta scientia libris)* that we may learn of Adam's "fatal deed." We are now clearly at a distance from Lafitau, where fall and redemption—Adam and Eve and the man and woman of the Apocalypse—are removed from the book and enclosed within the abstract "system" of the ethnologist, a theoretical vision decidedly separate from the world of the ethnographer's letters. Were we to modify Lafitau's frontispiece into an ethnographic allegory more in keeping with de Bry's procedures of knowledge production, the figure of Writing would have to be looking squarely down into a copy of the *Nova alphati* opened to the letter *A*.

De Bry's *A* is not to be taken too literally, however: few Renaissance speculators on the history of letters actually located their origins with Adam and Eve. There were

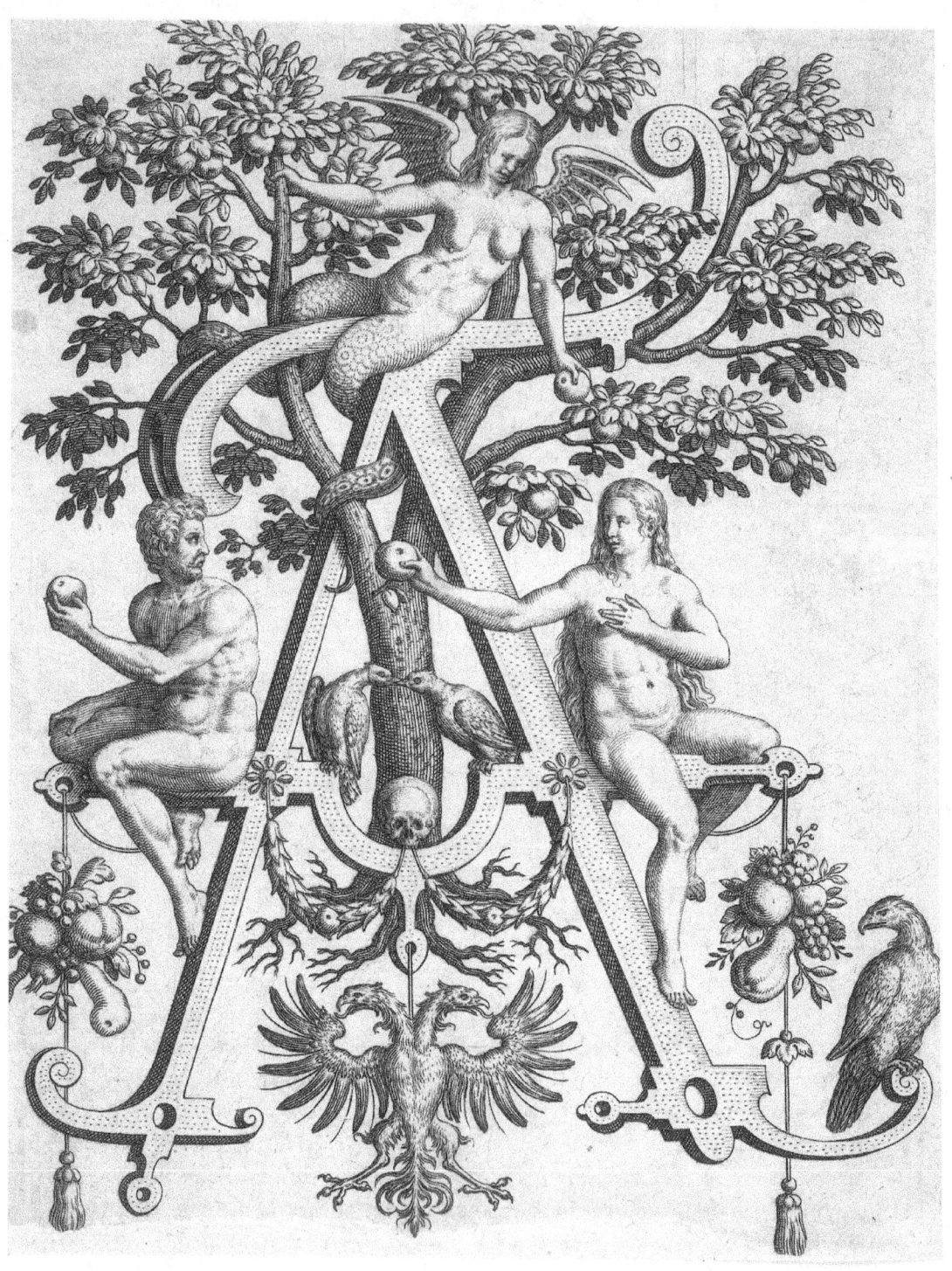

Figure 10. Johann Theodor de Bry after Theodor de Bry, Letter *A*, from Theodor and Johann Theodor de Bry, *Nova alphati effictio* (Frankfurt am Main, 1595). Copyright Trustees of The British Museum.

in fact many different stories at the time, both biblical and secular, as to where and when the writing of letters began.[22] As Jonathan Goldberg has shown, the effort to negotiate between these multiple historical origins and the desire for an originary writing, one that was always there in advance of any human putting a pen to paper or chisel to tablet (de Bry's *A* could be seen as the visualization of this desire), pervades Renaissance literature on writing and letters.[23] Rather, it is the alphabetical *logic* of the *Nova alphati*—the way it absolutely conflates the letter with human origins—and not its status as a serious inquiry into the origins of letters, that makes it a useful guide for understanding the logic behind de Bry's ethnography. Letters may not have originated at the Fall, but it is only through the foundational support of the letter that origins might be recovered. Thomas Harriot notes as much in his text for the *Report* when he remarks that the Indians' lack of letters has led to a confusion over their own origins:

> For mankind they say a woman was made first, which by the woorking of one of the goddes, conceived and brought foorth children: And in such sort they say they had their beginning. But how manie yeeres or ages have passed since, they say they can make no relation, having no letters nor other such meanes as we to keepe recordes of the particularities of times past, but onelie tradition from father to sonne.[24]

The implication is that the Algonquians have their origins all wrong—inverted. Because they lack letters, they have forgotten their true history, a lapse in memory that allows them to place woman before man. But through the letter, through scripture, Harriot is confident "that they may in short time be brought to civilitie, and the imbracing of true religion."[25] Indeed, Harriot did his part in bringing the Indians within an alphabetical order: with the help of two Virginians kidnapped and brought back to London in 1584, he devised a phonetic alphabet for their language so that during the 1585 expedition he could more easily communicate with (i.e., evangelize) the natives. Preparing for his encounter with the confused savages of the New World, hopelessly lost in their orality, the first thing Harriot does, in keeping with the orthographical concerns of the English Renaissance, is to properly ground their speech in the material foundation of the letter.[26] The letters of Harriot's Algonquian alphabet hold the promise of reinscribing the Indians within the scriptural order embodied in the *A* of de Bry's *Nova alphati:* letters will close, or veil, the gap of ignorance between the savage's past and present.

De Bry's visual program for the *Report* is equally set on bringing the natives of the New World within the closure of scripture. However, the problematic element of *time* considerably complicates this task. The difficulty is due to the nature of de Bry's project, which is not only scriptural but ethnological. De Bry's sequence of engravings for the *Report* anticipates the comparative ethnology that will become systematized in Lafitau's *Customs of the American Indians.* The twenty-one plates of New World savages followed by five plates of Old World savages implies a narrative of progress from past to present and from savage to civilized: just as the Britons of Raleigh's day have matured from the savage state of their ancestors, so, too, we are left to assume, will the Virginians mature into civilized British subjects. This narrative, however, raises the possibility that America responds to a different temporality than Europe, and in doing so it throws into question the notion of a sacred history in which all peoples (including pagan) fall within a single, inclusive time. In this regard, de Bry's juxtaposition of "old" world and "new" looks forward to the emergence of a secularized time in the eighteenth century, a time defined by natural history rather than by sacred history. This relativized model of temporality, as Johannes Fabian has argued, fundamentally changed the nature of temporal relations, for now spatial relationships between different parts of the world could be conceived (since time now belonged to the physical world) as temporal relationships.[27] In the illustrations for the *Report,* the spatial distance between Europe and America is collapsed into a temporal distance: Europeans look across the ocean and see themselves as they once were.[28] De Bry thus looks forward to a science of ethnology in which time, as the mediator between the ethnologist and human origins, will take the place of the sacred letter. In Lafitau's eighteenth-century frontispiece, the allegorical figure of Time directs Writing's gaze away from her letters, one form of mediation replacing the other. No longer does the material letter link scripture and New World together in an unbroken chain of signification; now knowledge of the New World is produced in the (non)space of temporal relationships, relationships that will be the ethnologist's task to map.[29]

But de Bry, to repeat a point already made, is not Lafitau. The letter remains at the center of this sixteenth-century ethnography—yet it is an embattled letter, struggling with time for authority. We see this in de Bry's engraving of the Fall, based on a drawing by artist Joos van Winghe, that serves as the frontispiece to the series of Virginia images (Figure 11). In the background, the fallen Adam and Eve live in a state not unlike the Algonquians; clearly we are intended to recognize the similarities between this primitive, partially clad couple—one seeking shelter under a hovel and the other laboring in the soil with the simplest of plows—and the American savages pictured on the pages that follow. Unlike the Adam and Eve of the *Nova alphati,* this couple is inserted into an actual historical chronology: the implied narrative, still scriptural but now ethnological as well, places them and the Indians they resemble at a specific moment in the progress of civilization—namely, in the childhood of man. The engraving thus attempts to reconcile a narrative of human origins held together by *time* with a narrative of human origins held together by the *letter.*

De Bry included the engraving of Adam and Eve because he wanted to leave us with no doubts as to the proper origins of the Indians, and this is precisely because there is so much at stake here—the authority both of the Christian creation story and of the scriptural order on which it rests.[30] This is sensitive subject matter, and it helps us understand why the New World could be such a delicate topic, for there was always the possibility that the American Indian predated Adam and Eve; that the authority of time, taking precedence over the authority of the letter, would produce an Indian who stood outside of and prior to the scriptural order. Of course there were many

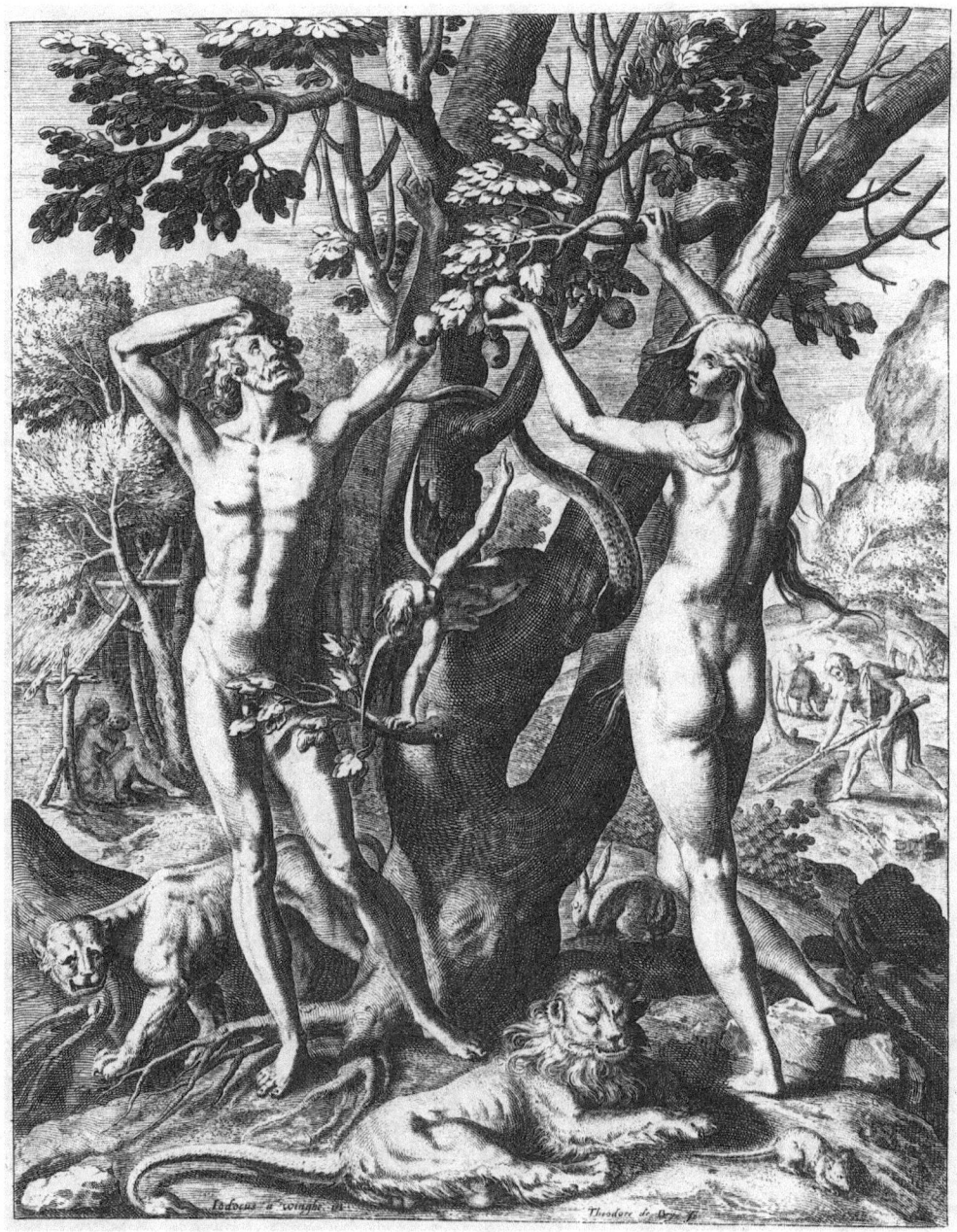

Figure 11. Theodor de Bry after Joos van Winghe, *Adam and Eve,* from *A Briefe and True Report.* Courtesy and with permission of British Library G.6837.

theories that, through various and often intricate arguments, attempted to reconcile the New World with scripture.[31] Among the more common was the belief that the wandering children of Ham, condemned by Noah's curse and alienated from revealed religion, had been responsible for the peopling of America. But such theories did not explain away a basic anxiety that human origins might exceed the letter's capacity to account for them, that there might be no originary writing to secure a place for the Indian within the closure of the Word. It is perhaps for this reason that Arthur Barlowe's discourse on the first (1584) Roanoke voyage, which helped generate interest in sending a larger expedition the following year, included a significant omission in its second edition. As it was first published in Hakluyt's 1589 edition of the *Principall Navigations,* the account claimed that prelapsarian conditions reigned in Virginia: "The earth bringeth foorth all things in aboundance, as in the first creation, without toile or labour"; however, in the second edition (1598–1600) that sentence, with its heterodox implications of a preadamic people, was no longer included.[32] The same anxiety that led to such editorial decisions also fueled charges of atheism against Harriot. Only two years after the publication of de Bry's edition of the *Report,* in which the engraving of Adam and Eve explicitly inscribes the Indians of America within a scriptural order, Thomas Nashe wrote in reference to Harriot, "I heare say there be Mathematitions abroad, that will prooue men before Adam."[33] It goes without saying that an atheist who would "prooue men before Adam" is one who would put his trust in the authority of a profane temporality over the authority of the sacred letter.

We can begin to see the sixteenth-century subtext to the letters that index de Bry's engraving of the tattooed Algonquian, a subtext involving questions of origin that arise when the letter, as the foundation of a long-standing scriptural order, is put into the service of a nascent ethnological science. On the one hand, the logic of the *Nova alphati* is still at work here; the letter still carries the burden of recuperating the savage for scripture. On the other hand, the placement of Latin letters next to Algonquian tattoos puts the letter itself under a kind of ethnological examination, so that its own origins come into question. If we allow ourselves to *see* these letters in the way we are intended to *see* the tattoos, then we have the makings of a comparative science of the letter that, in its organization, is not unlike Lafitau's comparative ethnology: the juxtaposition of two unlike signs sets up a temporal relationship; they become objects of historical inquiry; the tattoo becomes, potentially, a relative of the letter, its primitive ancestor. We are now in a historical or antiquarian mode, the temporal mode adopted by Renaissance authors who conjectured on the historical origins of letters. How does the letter maintain its structural role in de Bry's ethnography under conditions in which that structure is always being undermined by the destructive figure of Time, the scythe-wielding figure of Lafitau's frontispiece? This is the radical question implied in de Bry's juxtaposition of tattoo and letter.

As I have already suggested, it is a question that could be answered ideologically, through a particular definition of writing. As the early literature on the New World makes abundantly clear, there is one critical distinction that separates the tattoo (or any other form of New World mark-making) from the letter, even from the strange letters that make up the phonetic alphabet for the Algonquian language devised by Harriot.[34] While Harriot's Algonquian alphabet may have appeared to those who saw it as exotic as the Algonquians' tattoos (according to John Aubrey's report, Harriot's letters looked "like Devills"[35]), it nevertheless differs in that Harriot's letters, unlike the Algonquian tattoos, are tied to the human voice. According to José de Acosta, author of the *Historia natural y moral de las Indias* (1590; translated into English in 1604 as *The Natural and Moral History of the Indies*), "Letters were invented to signifie properly the words we do pronounce, even as woordes (according to the Philosopher) are the signes and demonstrations of mans thoughtes and conceptions. . . . Signes and markes which are not properly to signifie wordes but things, cannot be called, neyther in trueth are they letters." Acosta, though he placed great value on indigenous non-alphabetic scripts as historical records, goes on to observe that "no Nation of the Indies discovered in our time, hath had the vse of letters and writings, but of the other two sortes, images and figures."[36] Writing is distinguished from other forms of marking because it is the material foundation for speech; tattoos, in contrast, are mere "images and figures." Detached from the voice, they are too close to the status of the image, too close to the look of the "real" arrows in the Indian's hand, to be properly called a form of writing. So on this definitional level we can indeed see the difference between the two kinds of marks represented in this engraving.

The colonial ideology underwriting both the engraving and the *Report* as a whole is founded on this distinction between those who have and those who lack letters. The goal of the Virginia enterprise is eventually to civilize the Indian, to make him like us by replacing tattoos with letters. In the text below, Harriot describes the tattoo as a kind of brand: "the inhabitants of all the cuntrie for the most parte have marks *rased on their backs,* whereby yt may be knowen what Princes subiects they bee" (my italics). The savage, branded as a primitive (i.e., pre-alphabetic) subject, stands with his back turned to us as if he were awaiting a new brand, as if this back were itself a page awaiting a new inscription.[37] Indeed, this Indian, still living in the childhood of man, awaits the alphabetical stamp of Europe, the mark of a new prince who promises to civilize the savage and bring him to completion (by returning him to his origins) in the letter. It is a remarkably efficient logic: through a single act of visual reception, a civil/literate viewer comes into being upon the body of the savage, even as the savage comes into being as the fallen, bodily remainder of an as-yet-unaccomplished literacy.

But this ideological division between the written self and the unwritten savage also masks a basic contradiction within Renaissance conceptions of writing, the contradiction between a "knowledge written in sacred books" that is the source of historical truth, and a historical time that is the source of the letter. We have seen how de Bry grounds knowledge of human origins in the letters of scripture; how his letters are also *products* of history requires further explanation. To better understand de Bry's predicament, we might briefly consider the letter *A* once again. This letter is quite literally embodied in a single-plate illustrated alphabet by de Bry's two sons, Johann Theodor and Johann Israel, from their *Alphabeta et characteres,* first published in 1596 and later published in English in 1628 as *Caracters and Diversitie of Letters Used by Divers Nations in the World* (Figure 12). This antiquarian text, the second alphabet book produced by the de Bry workshop in the 1590s, is comprised mostly of plates reproducing alphabets ancient and modern. The de Brys' fanciful alphabet, in which letters are composed entirely of bodies, is therefore something of an exception in the larger historicizing program of the book, but it does offer a lesson in embodiment that applies to the book as a whole. The alphabet begins with Adam and Eve who, in their original sin, "fall" into each other to become the letter *A*. This corporeal letter, linked to the Fall as surely as the *A* of the *Nova alphati,* once again suggests that in a fallen world it is only by means of the letter that we can embody our scriptural origins. Yet this is also a book full of alphabets in which time makes fallen bodies of letters. The corporeal letter cannot help but play a paradoxical role in a book whose historicizing purpose is to embody the origins of that which embodies *our* origins. It would be easy to explain away this problem by treating the fanciful *A* composed of Adam and Eve as a witty gloss on the simple letter *A* that is given, a priori, just below it; yet this simple *A,* printed in Roman capital, itself turns out to be a gloss on something prior to it. The plate from the *Alphabeta et characteres* illustrating the historicized Roman alphabet proves that this letter exists in time and must therefore be seen as a descendant of, for example, the curious *A*'s of two ancient Egyptian alphabets represented in a separate plate, letters that are themselves descendants of some prior letter (Figure 13). At

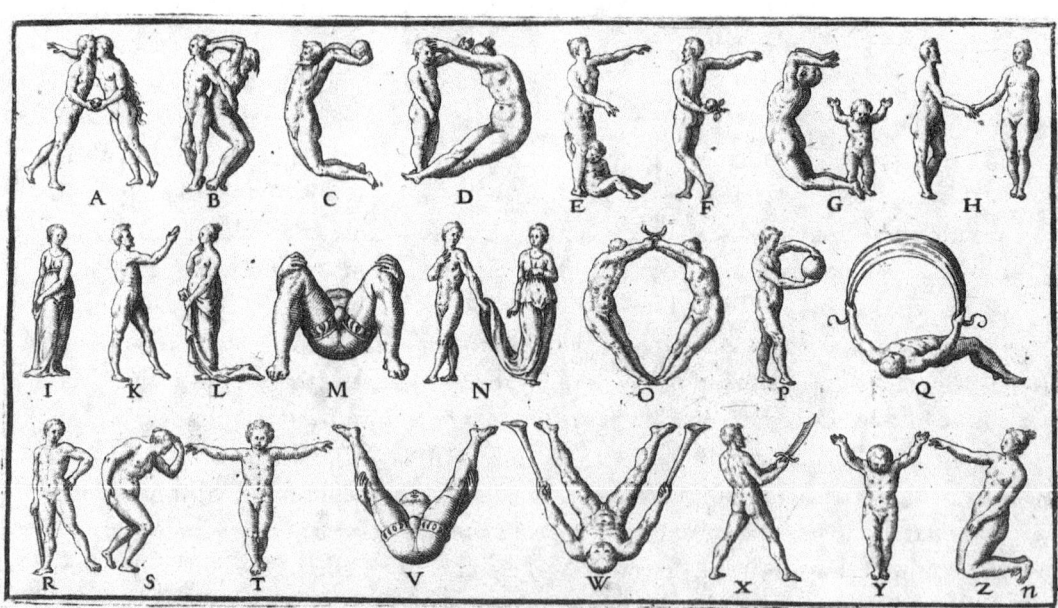

Figure 12. Embodied alphabet, from Johann Theodor and Johann Israel de Bry, *Alphabeta et characteres* (Frankfurt am Main, 1596). Courtesy and with permission of British Library 53.a.19.

some point, if we are to avoid lapsing into this infinite regression in which there will always be one more step to an original writing, a separation must be forced between the sacred truths borne by the letter and the letter as historical artifact.

Perhaps one could argue, with Juliet Fleming, that the form this separation takes in response to the Renaissance tattoo is one of acknowledgment and disavowal.[38] We have seen the ideological work of disavowal, in which the potential sameness of tattoo and letter is renounced through an exclusion of the tattoo from the realm of writing. Such a disavowal is implicit in the introductory remarks to *Caracters and Diversitie of Letters:* "Amongst Men, some are accounted Ciuill, and more both Sociable and Religious, by the Vse of *letters* and Writing, which others wanting are esteemed Brutish, Sauage, Barbarous."[39] But the tattoo, precisely because it stands as a site of disavowal, is the fetish that acknowledges the letter's fallen materiality. In the case of de Bry's engraving, that acknowledgment becomes particularly apparent when we consider alongside the Roman capitals of the *Alphabeta et characteres,* de Bry's Roman capitals that index the Algonquian tattoos. Although de Bry's historicized letters may not properly be "marks rased on their backs," one could certainly see them in terms of inscriptions chiseled into stone, or even as marks "rased" on copper plates. And as physical marks, the letters of the Roman alphabet are no less bound to matter and to a worldly temporality than tattoos. So long as we choose to *see* de Bry's letters (and again I suggest we *should* see them as we see the tattoos), then we must acknowledge

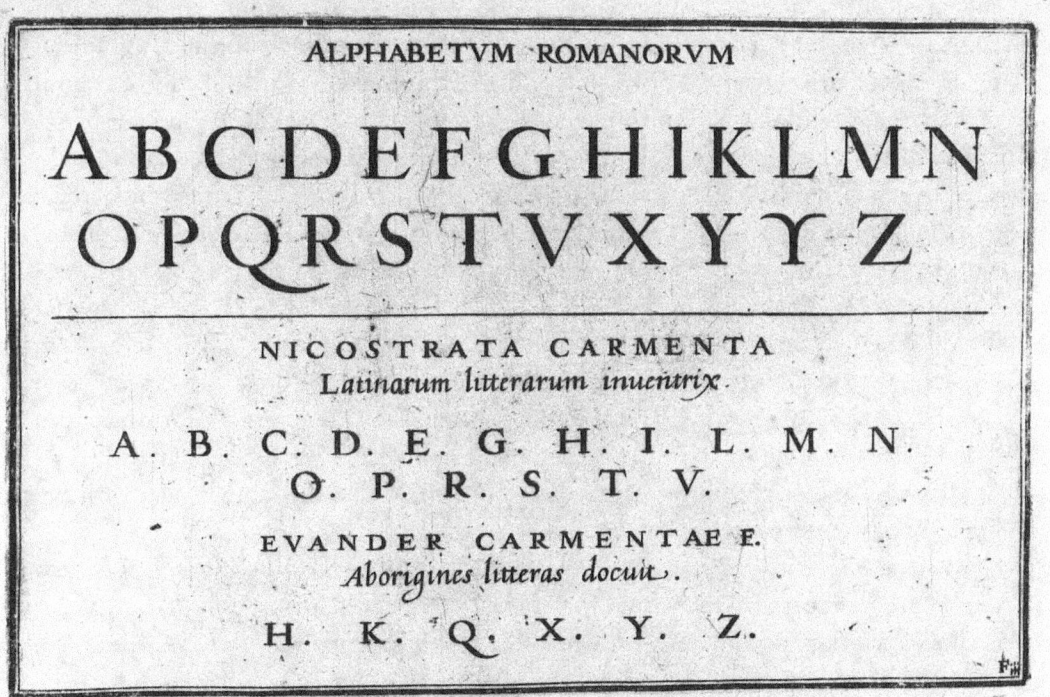

Figure 13. Roman Alphabet, from *Alphabeta et characteres.* Courtesy and with permission of British Library 53.a.19.

a fundamental similarity between letters and tattoos: both are marks that originate *within* time, in a material act of inscription.

Indeed, while tattoos may not be the embodied voice, they are a kind of writing if we think beyond the phonetic and ethnocentric bias that Derrida has called "writing in the narrow sense."[40] The process of making tattoos, which among North American Indians involved the pricking of the flesh with sharp instruments (fish teeth, needles, thorns, sharpened bones) dipped in charcoal or cinnabar, is itself analogous to the two European techniques, at issue in this chapter, for constructing letters: the scratching of a sharpened goose quill dipped in ink onto paper or parchment, and the cutting into a metal plate with a sharp burin. Moreover, in words such as *rase* (which according to the *Oxford English Dictionary [OED]* means to cut or incise, but also to erase) and *pounce* (a word used earlier in the *Report* by Harriot in reference to tattoos, and which also refers to the preparation of paper for writing), the early modern vocabularies of writing and tattooing actually overlap.[41] We must not, of course, neglect the important differences between tattooing practices, of which there are many varieties, and Western alphabetical writing. While the present study is not an investigation of the meaning and function of tattoos within Algonquian society, by no means do I wish to reduce tattooing to a primitive mirror of European writing practices. Tattooing has been shown to be a highly complex form of social reproduction in non-European societies, particularly in Oceania.[42] Among the Indians of North America, the making of sometimes elaborate patterns and figures on the skin was integral to religious and magical practices and functioned as a marker of social standing and bravery in combat.[43] Yet while it is essential to recognize that tattoos in indigenous American societies have their own vital histories, and while these histories are linked to a painful process of application that can be likened to but is certainly not the equivalent of the scratching of ink-stained pens on paper or the carving of copper with a burin, it would nevertheless be a mistake to overlook the shared scriptural status of tattoos and letters. If, as John Hart opens his *Orthographie* (1569), writing is no more than "a reasonable marking or graving, or laying on of some colour differing from the superficies or grounde, to signifie the writers mind to the beholder, which is instructed in that maner," then tattoos—providing we change Hart's "laying on" to "laying in"—seem no less qualified than letters to be called a form of writing.[44] Both tattoo and letter, after all, mark an absent origin. As Harriot's text explains, the tattoo informs us from "what place they [the Algonquians] have their originall."[45] While Harriot clearly does not have biblical origins in mind here, he grants the tattoo the same logic as writing, the logic of the supplement.[46]

I suggested above that an interpretation of de Bry's engraving through the ideological program of the *Report* would read the Indian's back as a figure for a page that awaits inscription, a blank page on which the viewer's mind can write its own subjectivity. But now, taking into consideration the shared materiality of letter and tattoo, we can read this back more ambivalently, as both a translation of the body into a page *and* as the page translated into flesh. The tattoo, the very thing de Bry's letters would not be, returns those letters to their disavowed past, to a history of marking in which the letter is not simply there "in the beginning" but in which it is *made,* "rased" upon a material surface. We are moving now into territory that is in advance of the letter itself. We are still—always—in the material space of writing, but we will now need to think in terms of what Derrida has called "writing before the letter."[47]

Such are the ambivalent alphabetical foundations on which de Bry constructs his ethnography. In the following pages, I will take up the scriptive practices—both writing *and* engraving (before the letter, there is no clear distinction between the two)— whose impossible task is the completion of those foundations. I will first consider the practice of writing, which is invoked in de Bry's engraving by the way the figure holds in his right hand a pair of arrows that suggest, to the eyes of a viewer whose mind is on marking, a pair of quills.

Quill/Arrow

It is no strain on the visual imagination to observe a basic resemblance between the arrow and the quill pen—the tip, shaft, and fletching of the arrow correspond to the nib, shaft, and feather of a quill that has been prepared for writing (compare Figures 5 and 14). It strains the imagination even less to note this resemblance in an engraving that invites the viewer to reflect on the process of inscribing marks upon skin (writing with a quill on parchment, after all, is another version of this process). The arrows, held in the Algonquian warrior's right hand in Figure 5 almost as if he were preparing to write with them, are very much like the civilizing quill; and yet they are definitively not quills, for they are emblems of the savage. The iconography of the arrow is, like the tattoo, the site of an acknowledgment and disavowal: the labor of writing the New World is both acknowledged through the quill's embodiment *as* the arrow, and disavowed through the substitution of the arrow *for* the quill. While keeping the savage connotations of the arrow very much in the forefront of my discussion, I would like to destabilize its iconography by treating it not as something that safely holds the savage, as Léry puts it, "in countenance," but which instead points us toward the practices through which the savage is created. The arrow, one of the great icons of the New World, returns us to the scriptive practices through which the artist constructs the otherness of that world, for it is through this icon that the artist disavows a certain savageness implicit in his own practices of knowledge production by attributing these qualities to the otherness of the arrow-wielding and tattoo-rasing Indian.

An episode from a popular set of Latin dialogues used in the education of schoolboys during the sixteenth century suggests just what it is that will be disavowed by the iconography of the arrow. The tenth dialogue of Juan Luis Vives's *Linguae latinae exercitatio* (1539), titled "Scriptio," takes the schoolboy through a lesson in writing. "But have you come here armed?" asks the teacher. "Not at all, good teacher," replies the student, "we should have been beaten by our teachers if we had dared to merely look at arms, at our age, let alone touch them." The teacher replies, "Ah, ah! I don't speak of the arms of blood-shedding, but of writing-weapons, which are necessary for our purpose. Have you a quill-sheath together with quills in it?"[48] A military metaphor links arrows and quiver to the productive instruments (quill and quill case) of the child just learning to write. For the young "savage" who has not yet learned his proper letters, writing is a training exercise *(exercitatio)* in bodily self-discipline. It is tempting to read de Bry's image as the inverse of Vives's episode: arrows and quiver as the New World version of quill and case; Indian as the New World version of the schoolboy. The engraving then becomes a kind of writing lesson, given under the controlling metaphors of arrow and savage, whose meaning—still to be fully fleshed out—will involve writing on the flesh.

Certainly a great deal separates a Latin dialogue written for the education of children of the aristocracy from an ethnographic report written for potential investors in a New World colony, and one must be careful not to collapse the two together as if those differences in genre were unimportant. It is surely significant, for example, that a textbook can engage in metaphorical play that treats the child simultaneously as the writing subject (a student who wields the writing weapons) and writing's object (the unformed student who is also the object of those weapons) while de Bry's ethnographic work disciplines itself to reject this intertwining of the productive writer (the source of ethnographic authority) and the written body (the Indian). Yet even as they are recast to fit de Bry's colonial project, the scriptive techniques of Vives's humanist pedagogy continue to underwrite the *Report*. Both belong to a humanist project grounded in shared assumptions about the relationship between writing and civility.

Literary and cultural historians now argue that humanism was more than a set of moral principles and high-minded individualism; it was a network of disciplinary practices, most importantly pedagogical exercises and drills for children, the practical purpose of which was, as Anthony Grafton and Lisa Jardine have put it, to train "a social elite to fulfil its predetermined social role."[49] And it was particularly during the sixteenth century, under the reign of what Grafton and Jardine call "northern methodical humanism," that the teaching of proper writing came to the fore to shape young boys into properly civilized subjects. Erasmus, the most influential figure of this pedagogically oriented humanism, inspired a wave of manuals for young students (manuals for teaching reading, writing, grammar, etc.), with Vives's *Linguae latinae exercitatio* being one of the most popular. These books, which played a crucial role in what Norbert Elias has called the "civilizing process," did not teach reading and writing on their own terms; they conjoined the learning of these skills with the acquisition of proper bodily discipline, proper day-to-day behavior for the male children of a social elite: learning to write correctly and the civilizing of young and unruly bodies go hand in hand in these texts.[50] The fact that the de Bry workshop was publishing both alphabet books and colonial texts on New World savages during the 1590s begins to make a little more sense when understood in the context of this general humanist concern with the civilizing mission of writing.[51]

The role of the quill in the "civilizing process" was, as the Vives episode illustrates, a formative one: the quill in the child's hand allowed him to form the letters that are the mark of civilization. Yet at the same time the writing manual had to struggle with the fiction already discussed in the colonial context of the *Report*: that it was the letter, already there in advance of the child, that guided his quill.[52] This is a fiction that the writing manual has some difficulty maintaining, for its terrain is by definition the material scene of writing. Illustrations from sixteenth-century writing manuals are forced to negotiate precisely this tension between the materials of the writer (which produce the letter) and the rational goal of writing (the letter that is already there). This is the tension pictured on the title page of Ugo da Carpi's 1535 writing manual, *Thesauro de scrittori* (Figure 14). From the left side of the page a hand enters holding compasses, the quintessential instrument of rationality, that circumscribe the form of the letter *A,* the first letter of the alphabet and the first letter of *Adam*—a letter that, like the *A* of the *Nova alphati,* is associated with the beginning of history itself. From the right side of the page a hand enters holding a quill that is in the act of producing an *S* (perhaps for *scrivere,* "to write").[53] The *A,* appearing before the *S* as we read from left to right and encompassed within its own imagined rationality, displaces the priority of a quill still in the act of writing. What is the writing manual to do with this quill that, in its pursuit of the civilizing letter, is always occluding its own work, always beginning the letter only to find that the completed letter was already there from the start (just as this *S* appears complete even as it is being written)?

It is but a short distance from the material scene of writing, the precondition and the problem of the writing manual, to puns that play on the violence of the quill, as we saw in the Vives episode. Questions of violence follow the quill because its civilizing work inevitably occurs in the context of power relationships. Even the preparation of the quill is an assertion of power over nature through an act of violence, as the quill is plucked from the bird and then cut and trimmed to produce a writing instrument.[54] This violence is then rehearsed again and again by the writer—in colonial situations, for example, or in the context of the law, as pictured in an engraving by Hendrick Goltzius (Figure 15). Goltzius, the most renowned engraver of his day and a member of the same Protestant, northern-European humanist community to which de Bry belonged, published in 1597 a series of prints showing the *Abuses of the Law.* In his engraving of *The Imperiled Litigation,* the quill is approaching de Bry's arrows even as Goltzius's savage arrows—or perhaps "spears" is more accurate in this case—are being transformed into the rationality of the law. Goltzius makes explicit the violent relationship between the bodies that are disciplined by the law and the writing instruments through which the law is practiced. On each side are figures representing various aspects of legal practice: on the left, True Justice, Loyal Administrator, Skilled Lawyer, and Honest Witness take sides against, on the right, False Witness, Negligent Administrator, Inexperienced Lawyer, and Unjust Judge. Between the two rows, Good Cause runs a gauntlet of giant quills. Victory awaits on the other side, only to be reached *after* the bodily dangers of legal practice have been braved. Below

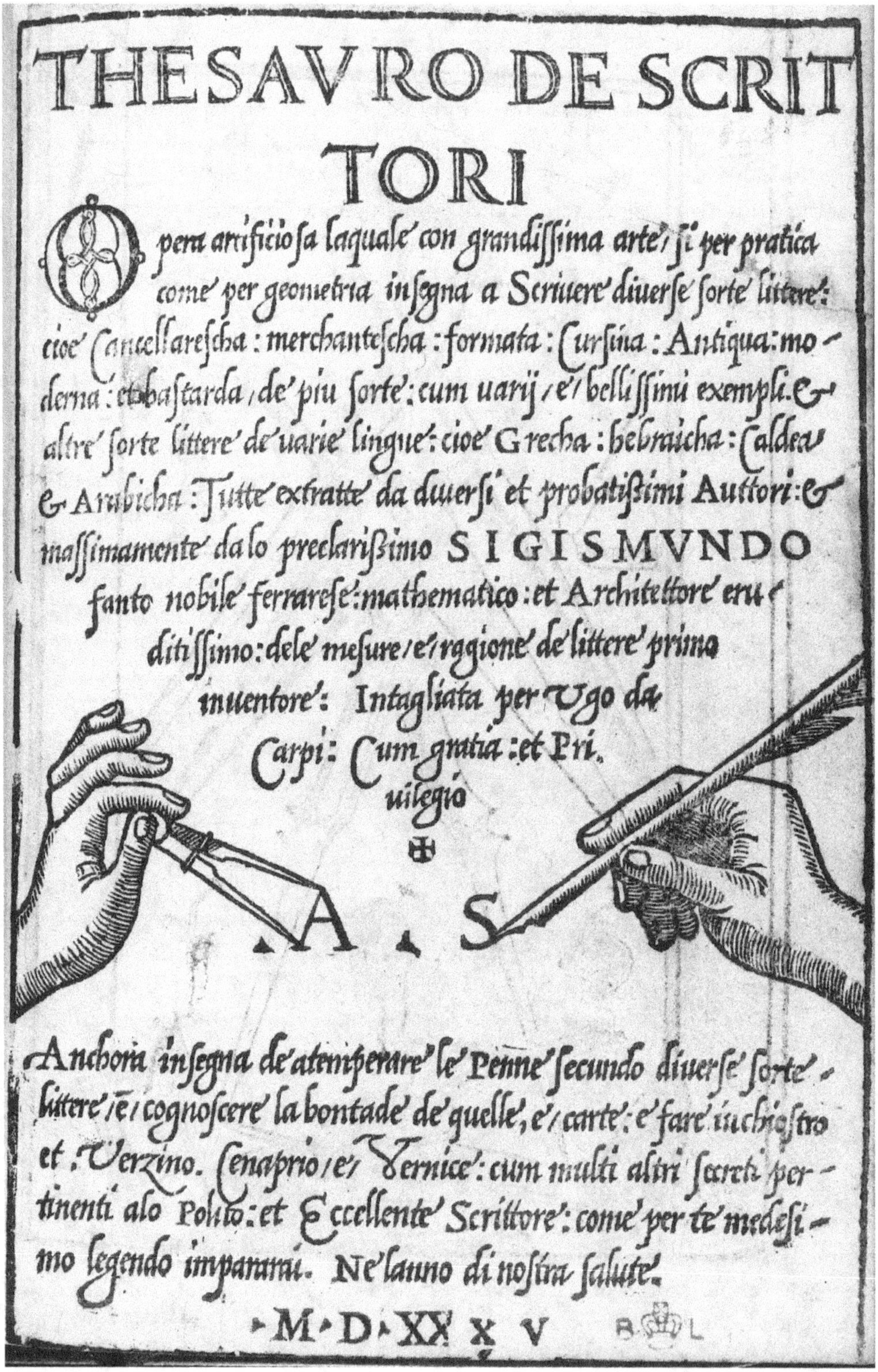

Figure 14. Title page from Ugo da Carpi, *Thesauro de scrittori* (Rome, 1535). Courtesy and with permission of British Library G.648.(2).

the image are several relevant Old Testament quotations, such as Proverbs 25:18: "A man that beareth false witnes against his neighbour is a maule, and a sword, and a sharpe arrow."[55]

The quill-like arrows held by de Bry's tattooed Algonquian, analogous to the arrow-like quills held by Goltzius's legal practitioners, suggest a writing that has not yet transcended its materiality. That ideological leap beyond the material scene of writing, and beyond the violence that may occur there, arrives at the end, like the figure of Victory in the Goltzius engraving. It arrives through the redemptive rationality of the letter of the law, or, in de Bry's case, through the letters that support the work of ethnography. De Bry's tattooed Indian, however, like the figure of Good Cause and like the child just learning to write, stands at the *beginning* of the civilizing process. He is only beginning to learn the techniques of self-inscription and self-origination through writing that will eventually result in his placement within an alphabetical order. He stands for the conditions of what de Certeau has called the modern "scriptural economy," an economy of writing in which "every power, including the power of law, is written first of all on the backs of its subjects." It is an economy of the flesh, one in which

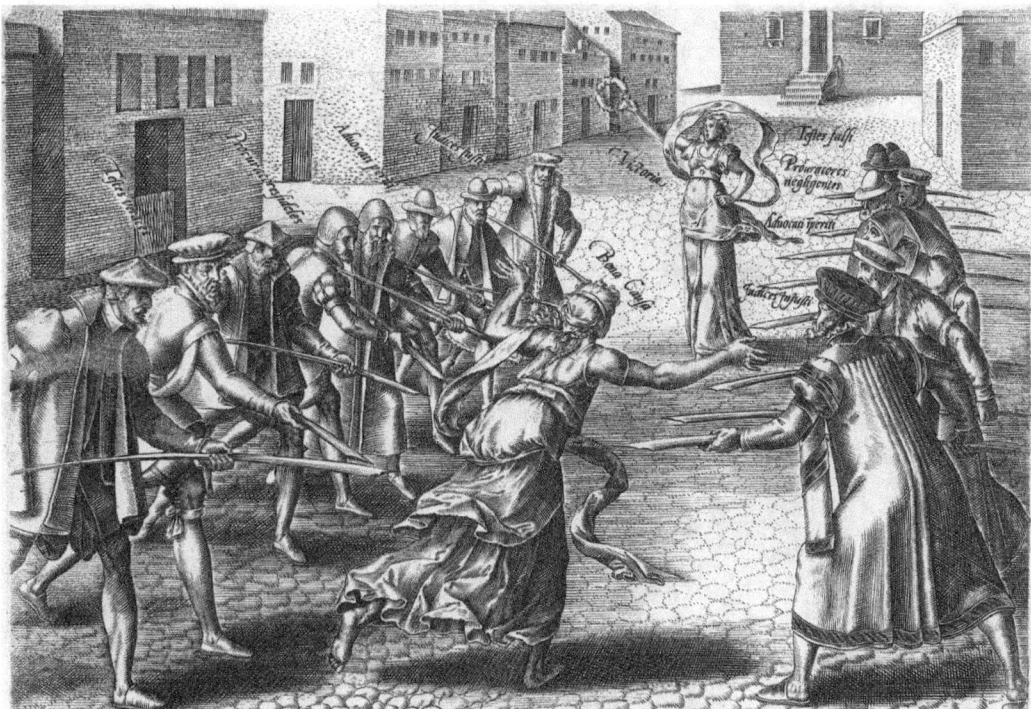

Figure 15. Hendrick Goltzius, *The Imperiled Litigation*, Plate 7 from *The Abuses of the Law*, 1597. The Metropolitan Museum of Art, Harris Brisbane Dick Fund, 1953 [53.601.336(16)]. Photograph from The Metropolitan Museum of Art; all rights reserved.

subjects are produced ambivalently both through suffering, since they are written *upon* ("tattooed," to use de Certeau's terminology), and through pleasure, for it is through inscription on bodies and in books (books, notes de Certeau, "are only metaphors of the body") that selves become recognized and legible within society.[56] The techniques of this scriptural economy are figured explicitly in the points of the Indian's arrow-quills as they meet the line of his shoulder (Figure 16). On the one hand, this reflexive gesture suggests a fantasy of self-constitution in which the childlike savage will one day come into being as a civil subject through his own self-description. On the other hand, these instruments of violence suggest some of the savageness of the scriptural economy. They lead us back to the scriptive practices through which selves and savages are produced; with the tattoo, they direct us to the disavowed, bodily history of the letters that index this page.

This is not to say that writing, understood as a historical practice, must always be linked with violence.[57] If we are to read this Algonquian's arrows as writing instruments, then we must also recognize that he is a rather docile individual; he may carry arrows, but his bow is unstrung (Léry, we have seen, writes that the savage's bow should be *desbandé*), suggesting that he has been disarmed. We should not take the example of Goltzius's engraving too literally: there can be no simple equation between the scriptive practices of ethnography and, for example, the episodes of colonial violence that accompanied English efforts to establish a settlement in Virginia in 1585.[58] I am simply interested in collapsing the division that de Bry's iconography would raise between the two, so that quills and arrows can be recognized as instruments wielded within a shared corporeal sphere. What de Bry looks forward to civilizing in the

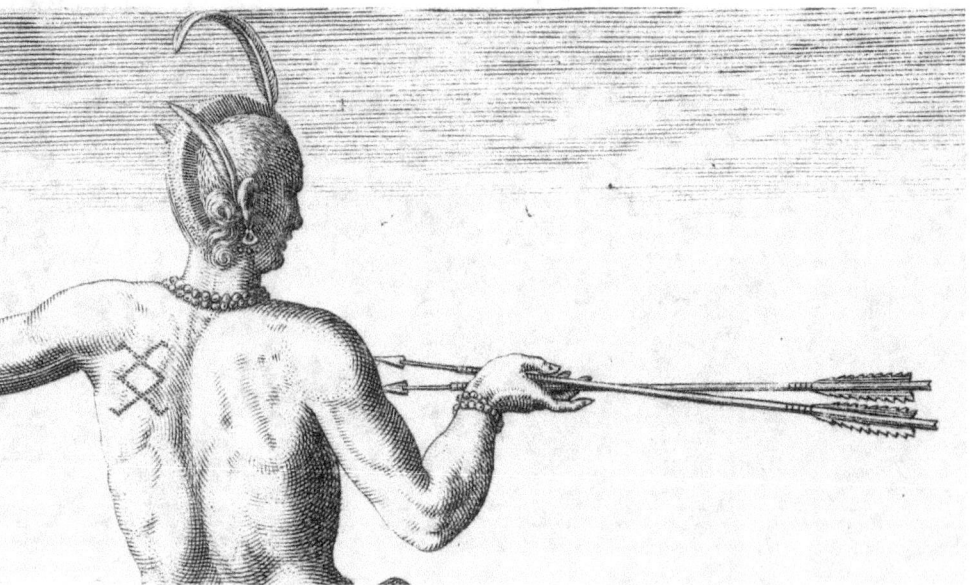

Figure 16. Theodor de Bry, *The Marckes of sundrye of the Cheif mene of Virginia* (detail). Courtesy and with permission of British Library G.6837.

savage, then, is precisely his ethnography's own corporeal history as a pre-alphabetic practice that has not yet left behind its affiliations with arrows and flesh.

Burin/Compasses

"Call them *Point, Stile, Graver, Punction, Polisher,* or what else you please," writes John Evelyn in the opening pages of his *Sculptura: Or the History, and Art of Chalcography and Engraving in Copper* (1662), "we will contend no farther about it; For these *Instruments* (as despicable as they appear) have sometimes proved fatal and dangerous Weapons."[59] Evelyn supports this claim by noting certain episodes in which the historical ancestors of the engraver's burin (or "graver," to use Evelyn's preferred term) have exceeded their intended function and become instruments of violence, as in the cruel death of Cassianus, a third-century Christian schoolteacher who was martyred by pupils wielding styluses. The dangerous tools of the engraver, tools that literally pierce and incise metal surfaces and can do the same to human flesh, provided an effective means for explaining Native American tattooing practices to European audiences. The Recollet friar Gabriel Sagard, for example, in his *Histoire du Canada* (1636), describes the tattoos of the Hurons as marks painfully engraved on the body:

> But that which I find a most strange and conspicuous folly, is that in order to be considered courageous and feared by their enemies they take the bone of a bird or of a fish which they sharpen like a razor, with which they engrave *[grauoient]* themselves and create figures on their bodies by making diverse lines, as we do to swords and armor with a burin *[le burin]*. During this process they exhibit the most admirable courage and patience. They certainly feel the pain, for they are not insensible, but they remain motionless and mute while their companions wipe away the blood that runs from the incisions.[60]

Evelyn and Sagard both remind us that the engraver wields an instrument of potential violence, one that deserves a place alongside the quill in the *Report*'s implements of bodily inscription.

However, it is also important to recognize that the burin is an instrument distinct from the quill in key ways. On a technical level, the activity of using each instrument is quite different: the quill, like any pen, is pulled with relative ease across a sheet, on which it leaves a trace of ink; in contrast, the extremely sharp burin is pushed with significant force into a metal plate as it gouges out a trench in a manner that can be likened—as Ruskin likened it—to the plowing of earth. The quill and burin also occupied distinct, though overlapping, discursive fields during the sixteenth century. The quill, as a concern of the writing manual, is directly involved with the proper construction of the letter, and is thus closely identified with the civilizing process itself; its materiality is one that speaks, as we have seen, to the most basic questions about the nature of the civilized and the savage. The burin, as an instrument that makes its entrance into European intellectual and artistic culture out of its longtime use in an artisanal tradition of metalworking (note that Sagard, in the quotation above, links the burin to the engraving of swords and armor), assumes a place during the sixteenth century in an intellectual discourse of genius versus labor, the liberal arts versus the mechanical arts, and theory versus practice. Where the quill and burin do coincide is in the fact that both belong to a larger sixteenth-century technological network in which knowledge is always in the process of emerging over time from the material practices of representation.

The path I will follow to de Bry's burin takes us through the engraver himself, through his own self-constitution as the artistic authority responsible for the engravings of the *Report*. And what better place to begin than with the letters that index that authority? I refer, of course, to the artist's initials, the simple *TB* that appears at the bottom left of his engraving. On the one hand, these letters lead us to an individual who has earned the right to call this image his own through a certain expenditure of labor. Surely it is fair to assume that—as is typically the case with signatures—de Bry's initials were added at the end when the real work of engraving, the creation of the material artifact itself, was complete. Initials are inscribed afterward as an index of the self, a self that is evidenced in the product of its labor. On the other hand, these letters also establish an authorial identity that *precedes* the artist's labors. Coming at the end, the initials return us to an origin, the subjective origin of the artifact—the productive self.

Like all signatures, the *TB* signifies a unity between the work as objective evidence of the self and the ineffable self as subjective origin of the work; and as with all signatures, this unity is inherently unstable. This is particularly true in the case of a reproductive engraver such as de Bry, who tries to assert the egotistical claims of the author within a cycle of mechanical reproduction that always exceeds authorship's closed circle of self-referentiality.[61] While de Bry was himself a copyist who profited from the artistic labors of John White, he also sought to protect himself against those thieves who would unlawfully copy *his* copies. In his preface to the second section of the *Report,* titled "To the gentle Reader," de Bry writes: "Finallye I hartlye Request thee, that yf any seeke to Contrefaict thes my bookx, (for in this dayes many are so malicious that they seeke to gayne by other men labours) thow wouldest giue noe credit vnto suche conterfaited Drawghte."[62] The fiction of authorship arises precisely at this moment when, in order to make engraving profitable, in order for the engraver to accrue "credit" (both monetary and professional), the self intervenes and puts a halt to the endless dissemination of the artist's labor through copies. And this is precisely the function of the *TB,* which gathers up that labor within the domain of a single productive and inimitable self.

The first engraver of the Renaissance to identify his labor with this noumenal self and to secure this identification through a monogram was Albrecht Dürer. Indeed, we find an antecedent of de Bry's condemnation of counterfeiters in a colophon that Dürer appended to a 1511 edition of his engraved work: "Beware, you envious thieves of the work and invention *(laboris et ingenii)* of others, keep your thoughtless hands from these works of ours."[63] While the copyist has only his "thoughtless hands," the true artist has *ingenium,* an inimitable quality of the self that lies behind Dürer's monogram. Unlike Dürer, however, de Bry makes no special appeal to this power of *ingenium.*[64] Instead, he concludes his brief defense of his authorship with the claim that "dyuers secret marks lye hiddin in my pictures, which wil breede Confusion vnless they bee well obserued."[65] What exactly these "secret marks" are is difficult to say, and they certainly did not stop other printmakers from appropriating de Bry's images for their own work. What this warning does suggest is an engraver's anxiety over the difficulties of maintaining the fiction of authorship in his work;[66] it suggests that the authority behind de Bry's *TB* can only be effective if it is obscured, kept a secret. Indeed, the invocation of secret marks seems a rather transparent attempt to produce authority through a deliberate mystification: de Bry protects his own copies by casting a hex on all other copyists. To be sure, de Bry is making a very practical commercial and legal move, a print publisher's appeal to copyright in an age before the institution of effective copyright laws, but in order to do so he resorts to a mystical, prophetic language that recalls John's words at the end of the book of Revelation: "For I testifie vnto every man that heareth the wordes of the prophesie of this booke, If any man shal adde vnto these things, God shall adde vnto him the plagues, that are written in this booke."[67] Like John, de Bry protects his text by invoking "divine" authority. Only now the authority resides not in God but in the author, whose secret marks—like plagues sent from heaven that "breede Confusion" rather than disease— bring punishment to all counterfeiters.

The self indexed by de Bry's *TB* turns out to be a secret that somehow lies "hiddin" within the engravings of the *Report* as a kind of hermetic knowledge, intelligible only to those who have "well obserued." What lies behind this mystification? What might that secret self look like, if it is to be found at all? Self-portraiture, the genre of visual representation that implicitly stands behind all artists' initials, signatures, and monograms might lead us to some answers. De Bry's 1597 self-portrait (Figure 17), which appears at the beginning of the second volume of Jean Jacques Boissard's *Romane urbis topographia & antiquitatum* (1597), a chorographical and antiquarian study of Rome illustrated by de Bry and his sons, holds its own secrets.[68] In its attempt to imagine a humanist engraver whose images proceed from an intellectual self in full possession of its own labor, de Bry's self-portrait disavows those workshop practices that *precede* the addition of the artist's *TB* to the copper plate. De Bry's initials come at the end of his labor, and then somehow come to signify an authority—the figure pictured in this self-portrait—who has been there all along. This, at least, is the message of the self-portrait's iconography.[69]

The iconographic program, in which the brevity of human life is contrasted with the duration of art, is fairly straightforward. The engraving was made when de Bry was sixty-nine years old, in the year before his death. Two well-established iconographic elements—the shadow cast by the artist's body and the skull upon which his left hand rests—symbolize his mortality. De Bry, who suffered from chronic gout and was presumably well aware of the fragility of human life, underscores this sense of the body's decay and impending death in the text printed on the ledge. First, de Bry offers a prayer: "Lord, teach me to spend the remaining days of my life so that I may live and die in true piety" *(Domine / doce me ita reliquos vitæ mea dies / transigere vt in vera pietate viuam & moriar)*. Beneath this text is de Bry's motto, *Nul Sans Soucy*, a phrase that has the double sense of "not without hard work" and "not without worry." Together, the prayer and the motto suggest an artist who is living out what little time

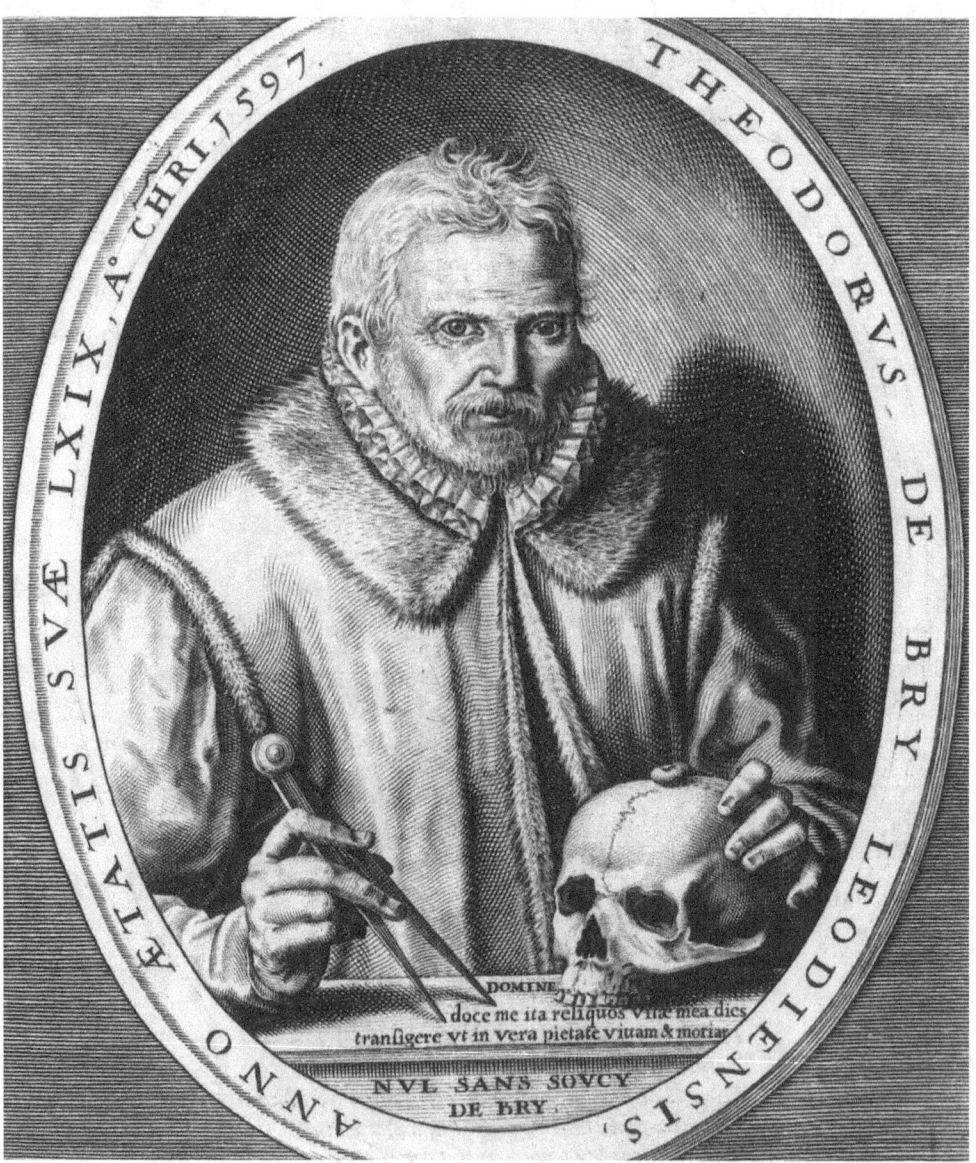

Figure 17. Theodor de Bry, self-portrait, from Jean Jacques Boissard, *Romane urbis topographia & antiquitatum* (Frankfurt am Main, 1597). Courtesy and with permission of British Library 144.f.13.

he has left attending assiduously to his craft, but with the weight of his own mortality on his shoulders.

At the same time, however, this is an artist who is capable of transcending the limitations of the body. As Boissard writes in the celebratory verses that appear immediately below the self-portrait: "while tied up by knots and nodules of untreated gout, [Theodor] has set forth many celebrated monuments before the wide world, and now quite old, he makes for himself an immortal name through many fertile undertakings, and renounces shadows."[70] Boissard's verbal declaration of de Bry's immortality finds its visual equivalent in the compasses the artist holds in his right hand. During the Renaissance, artists like de Bry appropriated the iconography of the compasses from medieval representations of God as *deus artifex,* the divine artificer who on the second day of creation made the firmament by separating the waters. The image of God the father with compasses in hand derives directly, it would seem, from Proverbs 8:27: "When hee prepared the heavens, I was there: when he set a compasse upon the face of the depth." As they appear in de Bry's hand, the compasses stand as emblems for the prosthetic reach of an encompassing intellect, a God-like mind that is capable of imposing order on chaotic matter.[71] Juxtaposed with the skull, the compasses signify the artist's power to transform a mortal and imperfect world into geometric perfection; they elevate the engraver's art above a mere workshop practice (de Bry began his career, like many engravers, as a goldsmith) and declare it to be a product of the rational judgments of his intellect.[72] In short, de Bry's compasses claim for the artist a place among the illustrious intellects of the humanist community whose portraits he engraved for Jean Jacques Boissard's *Icones quinquaginta virorum illustrium (Fifty Portraits of illustrious men),* a book published the same year as his self-portrait.

But de Bry's compasses—like the Algonquian's arrows—also resist such a one-dimensional iconographic reading. In fact, they raise a certain dilemma of self-portraiture: how does the artist represent the immateriality of his intellect? How does he elevate his artistic authority, which is only evidenced in the work of his hands, above the material signs of that labor? Compasses, after all, although they may be used for the construction of perfectly proportioned lines, are also instruments of the *hand.* Theory and practice both have their claims on them, as their emblems from Ripa's 1618 edition of the *Iconologia* suggest (Figures 18, 19). The young woman who represents Theory wears the compasses on her head, for her intellect "is taken up with celestial Things." "The compasses," Ripa's text continues, "are the most proper Instrument of Measuring, which perpetuate the Name of an Author." Practice, in contrast, is an old woman "dress'd in a servile Manner" who, looking down on "abject things," points the compasses toward the earth.[73] It is this baser, practical side of the compasses that an artist with lofty intellectual aspirations like Michelangelo, who also invoked the compasses as a symbol of his authority, could not abide. In his biography of Michelangelo, Vasari relates that at the end of his life, the artist destroyed many of his drawings "to the end that no one might see the labours endured by him and his methods of trying his genius." Vasari then goes on to explain that it was important for Michelangelo

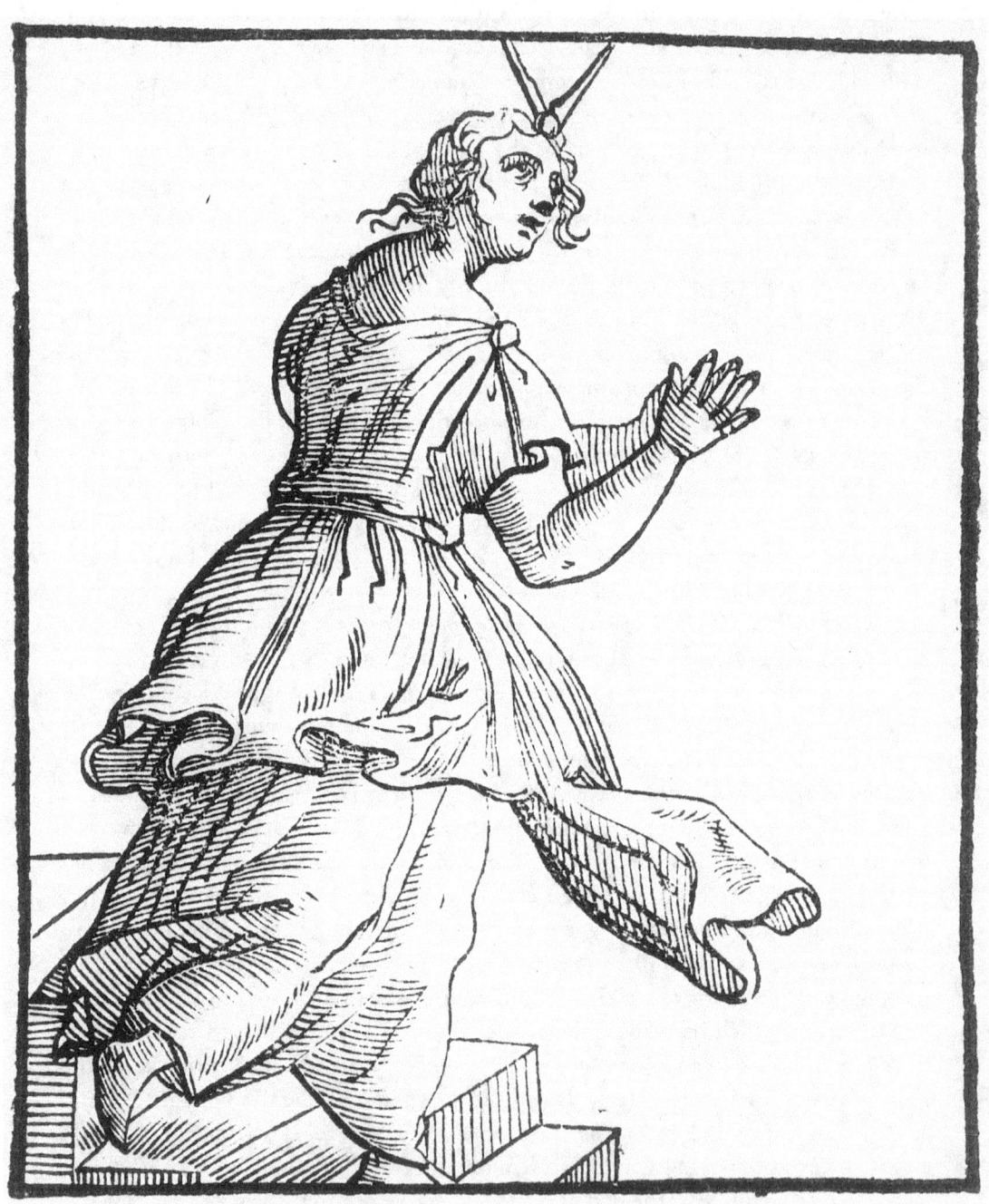

Figure 18. *Theoria,* from Cesare Ripa, *Iconologia* (Padua, 1618). Photograph courtesy of The Newberry Library, Chicago.

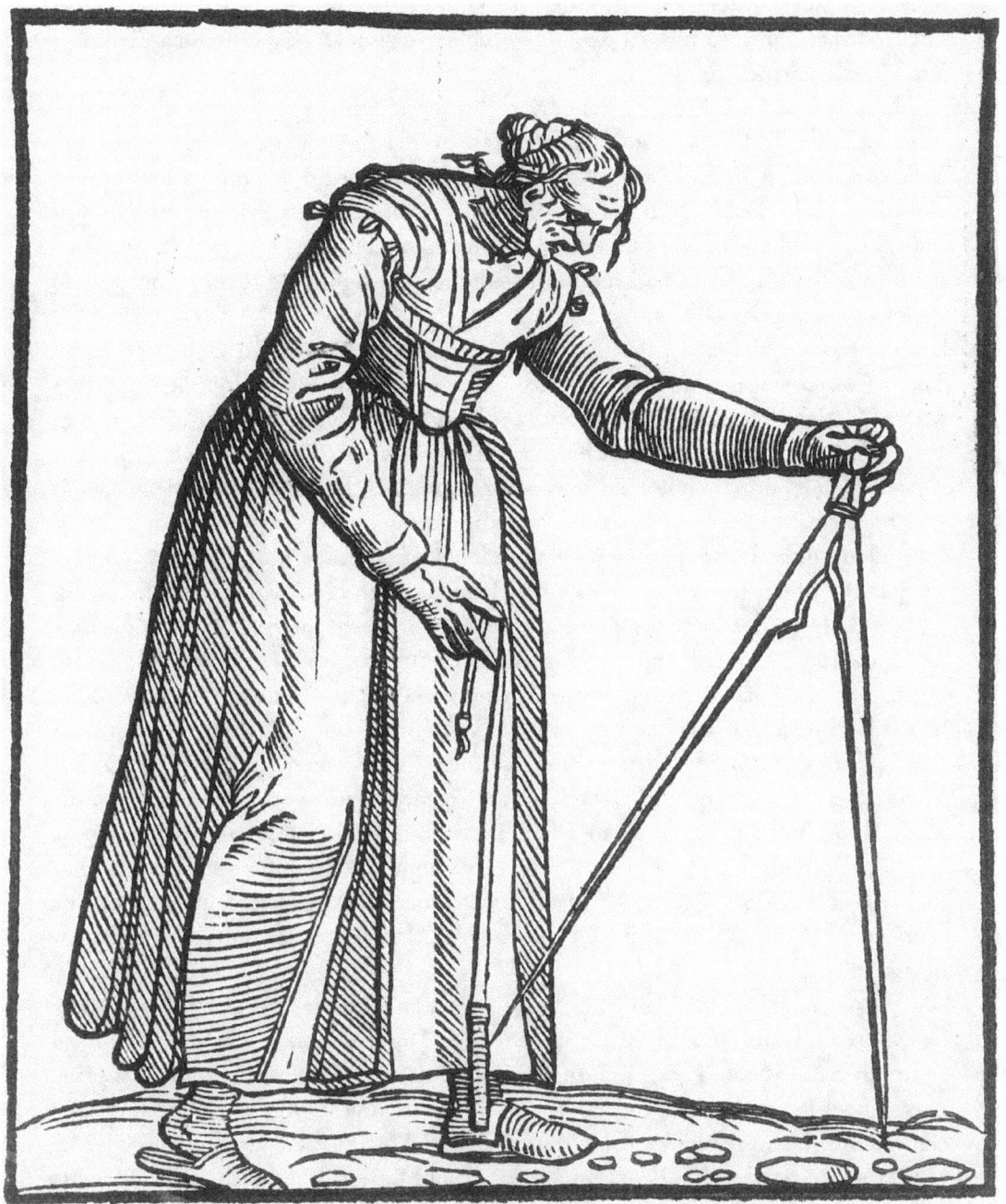

Figure 19. *Prattica*, from *Iconologia*. Photograph courtesy of The Newberry Library, Chicago.

to destroy the evidence of his artistic labors precisely because he identified his art not with his hands but with his intellect: for Michelangelo "it was necessary to have the compasses in the eyes and not in the hand, because the hands work and the eye judges."[74] Compasses held in the hands put the artist too close to the labor of the workshop, and so Michelangelo locates them in the eyes—a good verbal metaphor for intellectual authority, but not a particularly effective visual solution for an artist interested in self-portraiture.

Among Northern European engravers, however, and particularly in the work of Albrecht Dürer and Hendrick Goltzius, this seemingly irreconcilable rift between the work of the hands and the work of the mind is transformed into a productive tension within the image itself. Dürer accomplishes this in his great engraving of 1514, *Melencolia I,* by dividing the double identity of the compasses between two different instruments: the compasses and the burin—the former signifying theory alone, while the problem of practice is displaced onto the latter (Figure 20).[75] The compasses are held, unused, in the lap of the figure of Melancholy, a humanized version of Ripa's Theory who is pensive and earthbound as a result of her impracticality. She is an artist whom "celestial Thoughts" alone cannot lift out of a sublunary inwardness. To her right, however, a putto leans over his plate, deeply immersed in working it with what appears to be a burin. While a putto would seem to offer the antithesis of Melancholy's *gravitas,* his hands are nevertheless the only ones being productive here. With his awkward hold on the burin, he might be considered the equivalent of Dürer's "thoughtless hands," or perhaps a version of Ripa's Practice, with his downcast eyes betraying an interest only in "abject things." However we choose to interpret this curious figure, *Melencolia I* makes it apparent that neither burin nor compasses, neither practice nor theory, is sufficient in itself: the artist who wishes to be productive must combine hands and intellect. This is, at least in part, a recognition born of Dürer's proximity to the craft of metalworking. While Dürer was the most esteemed of the *peintre-graveurs* (the painter-engravers of the first half of the sixteenth-century who elevated the status of engraving from a handicraft to a noble artistic pursuit), he began his training as a goldsmith in his father's workshop.[76] By picturing the relation between practice and theory as a relation between two distinct instruments, Dürer is able to reclaim this artisanal background (the burin) for the intellectual project (the compasses) to which he aspires.

For de Bry, the meaning of the compasses as an emblem of the artist's authority had to be thought—indeed, in the midst of the Dürer renaissance at the end of the sixteenth century, could *only* be thought—in the shadow of Dürer. Through his compasses, held in an elegant right hand with long, tapering, Dürer-like fingers, de Bry claims for himself the intellectual authority signified by the compasses in *Melencolia I.* However, the relationship between compasses and burin has now changed. There is little room in the work of a reproductive engraver such as de Bry to engage, as Dürer had, in a sophisticated dialogue between the two instruments, and this is a result of fundamental changes in the conditions of engraving between 1514 and the 1590s. For

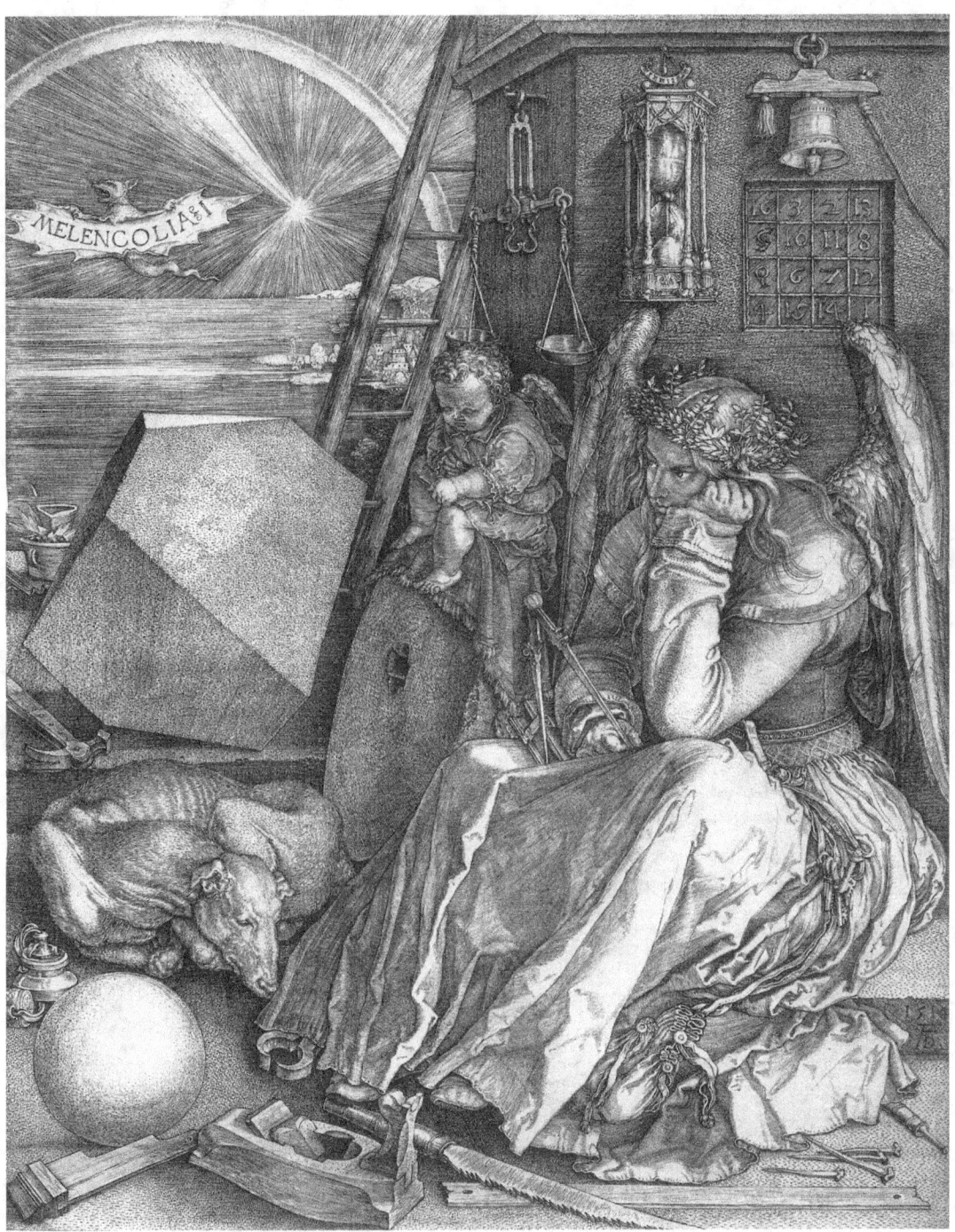

Figure 20. Albrecht Dürer, *Melencolia I*, 1514. The Minneapolis Institute of Arts.

Dürer, the tension between burin and compasses is part of the discourse of genius, in which the artist remakes the expert work of his hands into a sign of his intellect through his own powers of invention, his originality. At the end of the sixteenth century, however, engraving is no longer primarily a medium of invention (with Goltzius as a great exception, as we shall see), but of reproduction. To understand de Bry's compasses, then, we will need to understand his reproductive grammar.

Dürer, as we have seen, denigrates the work of the mere copyist, whose "thoughtless hands" reproduce others' designs without the guidance of *ingenium*. But the day of the *peintre-graveur,* who put extraordinary effort into the invention and execution of each of his engravings, was short-lived. By the second half of the sixteenth century, with the rise of print publishing houses like Hieronymus Cock's in Antwerp, and Antonio Lafreri's in Rome, the focus of the engraver's work gradually shifted from original compositions to the copying of other artists' work. With this commercialization of the print came a different vocabulary for engraving, for the engraver could literally no longer afford the kind of virtuosic burin-work of an artist like Dürer, who took a great deal of time to produce a sense of surfaces and textures in his engravings. We need only compare the technique of Dürer's *Melencolia I* to that of, say, de Bry's *Adam and Eve,* in order to get a sense of this difference (compare Figures 20 and 11). De Bry constructs his figures through a mechanical network of cross-hatching, which is not, like Dürer's technique, intended to reproduce painterly surface-textures, but only to articulate volumes. This reproductive grammar, as William Ivins has described it, is "much like what the geometers call the 'net of rationality,' a geometrical construction that catches all the so-called rational points and lines in space but completely misses the infinitely more numerous and interesting irrational points and lines in space."[77] Because it reduced engraving to the rational essentials, this grammar was a highly teachable one. The first engraving manual, Abraham Bosse's *Traicté des manieres de graver en taille douce* (1645), teaches precisely this method. And it was a profitable grammar as well. De Bry grew wealthy by it, a wealth visible in the elegant fur-lined coat he wears in his self-portrait.[78] Through the application of the net of rationality, de Bry and his sons could with relative ease and uniformity of style copy pictures such as those of John White, and sell them to a public eager to consume images of the New World.

But what did this grammar, so readily imitated, so apparently servile, mean for the authority of the reproductive engraver, particularly when that engraver aspired to a Dürerian model of inimitability? Goltzius in the 1580s and 1590s arrives at one solution to this dilemma: he confronts this reproductive grammar on its own terms, mastering it with such skill that his own virtuosity comes to compete with the artists whose work he copies.[79] As Walter Melion has demonstrated, Goltzius, in his engraved copies of original works by artists such as Bartholomeus Sprangher, displays a Protean skill of appropriating another artist's pictorial invention for his own benefit: the engraver effaces himself by adapting his reproductive grammar to his model, and in the very virtuosity of that self-effacement, he claims his authority. Faced with the anonymity of the standardized techniques of reproductive engraving, Goltzius one-ups them by handling them better than any other engraver of his day.

One of Goltzius's most complete pictorial statements about his own authority as an engraver is his *Venus, Bacchus, and Ceres,* dating from the first years of the seventeenth century.[80] The medium of this work is difficult to classify: executed with a quill, it is one of the artist's so-called "pen-works"; it is also, however, a painting, for it is drawn on a primed canvas over a layer of lead-white ground; finally, it is partly an engraving, for the quill imitates the virtuosic crosshatches of the engraver. Melion has interpreted this work as a complex allegory about love and artisanship. What is of particular interest relative to de Bry's self-portrait is how *Venus, Bacchus, and Ceres* adapts the burin-compasses opposition to Goltzius's reproductive project. In the left background, Goltzius includes a self-portrait that holds what appears at first glance to be a pair of compasses (Figure 21). Upon closer inspection, however, the compasses turn out to be burins simply held so as to look like compasses. As Melion argues, Goltzius is calling attention through this visual pun to the virtue of his burin hand: he decisively returns Michelangelo's compasses (for Melion, Goltzius is in dialogue with Michelangelo rather than Dürer) to the hands, not to reduce the engraver's art to mere manual labor, but to signify his remarkable control over those hands, his unrivalled ability to make his own adeptness with the burin into an expression of his intellectual power as an artist. Through this glorification of artisanship, Goltzius is able to recuperate Dürer's dialogue between burin and compasses for the project of reproductive engraving. He establishes a path of transcendence not unlike that of his *Imperiled Litigation,* in which the artist acknowledges the materiality of the scriptive instrument's work even as he imagines a victorious end for that labor.

De Bry's engravings, however, are hardly virtuosic displays in the manner of Goltzius. This is not to say that de Bry takes no pride in his labors; to the contrary, he brings up this subject at every opportunity. De Bry's motto, after all, declares his work ethic. On the frontispiece of his 1592 emblem book, *Emblemata nobilitati et vulgo scitu digna,* the motto is accompanied by a personal emblem that features the industrious ant. In the pages of the *Report,* de Bry draws attention to his painstaking labor more than once by reminding the reader/viewer that he has taken "ernest paynes in grauinge the pictures."[81] De Bry's collaborators also valued his labor. Boissard, for example, praises it repeatedly in the *Romane urbis topographia.* But the language and emblematic imagery that surrounds de Bry's labor celebrates diligence, not *ingenium.* And in general, de Bry's technique is one that through its rationalization of the engraver's marks makes relatively little effort to draw the viewer's attention to displays of burin-work (with the important exception of de Bry's smoke, as we will see in the next chapter). Nor would it have made much sense for de Bry to compete with the artistic sources of his images, for while Goltzius's technique put him in competition with well-known artists like Sprangher, de Bry would have been in competition with an empty name like "John White."[82] In short, de Bry was engaged in a radically different sort of reproductive project from Goltzius, an ethnographic project that, in its imperative to produce knowledge of a world that was *other* than the artist's, offered relatively little space for reflection on the practices through which it created that world. And yet de Bry would still base his claim to authority on the same Dürerian model invoked by Goltzius.

It is worth recalling at this point that de Bry had no alternative models of "objective" authority to fall back on. It is not a neutral "science" that provides the foundation for ethnographic authority, but the letter—in this case, de Bry's *TB*. And with the reproductive engraver's net of rationality, this assertion of rational authority begins even before the letter. It begins, for example, in the perfectly regular and circular lines on the Algonquian's back, where the savage is *already* rationalized, already encompassed by the engraver's controlling intellect (see Figure 16).[83] And to return to the compasses in de Bry's self-portrait, these, too, like the linear web that aspires to be

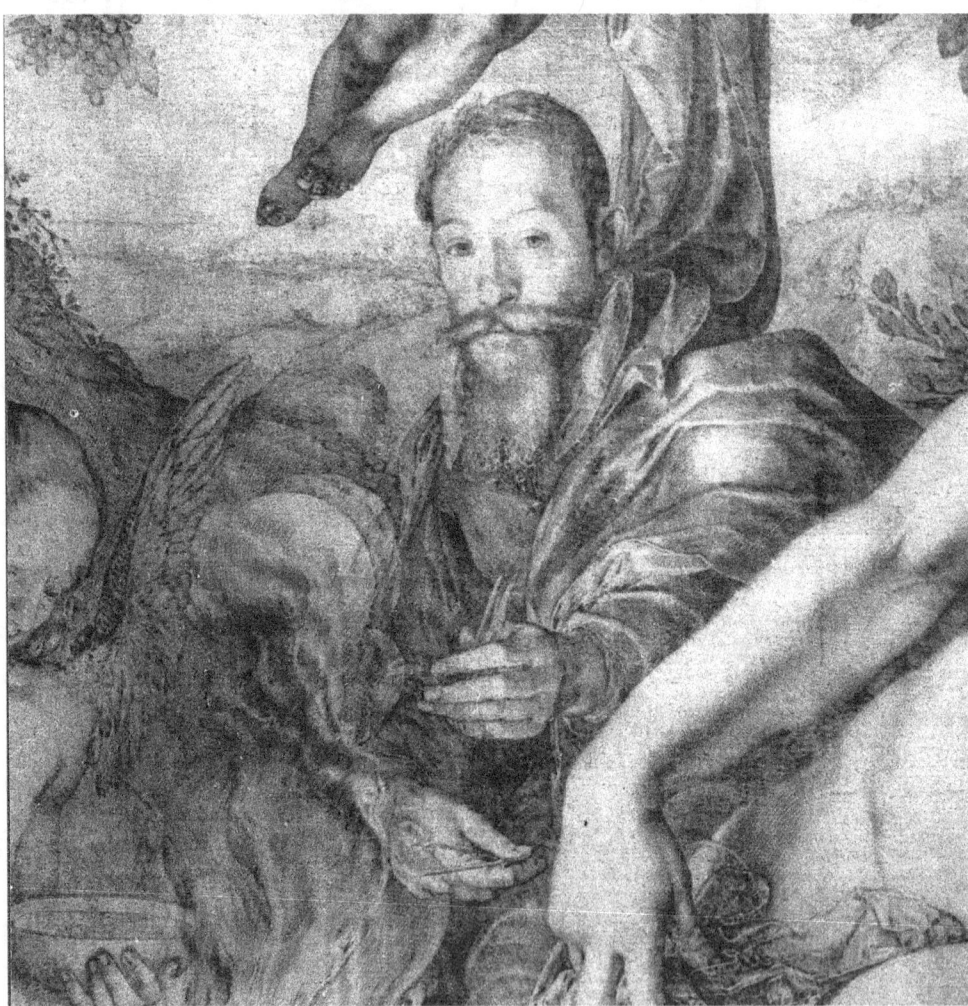

Figure 21. Hendrick Goltzius, *Venus, Bacchus, and Ceres* (detail), pen and ink on canvas, 1606. The State Hermitage Museum, St. Petersburg.

the visual equivalent of reason itself and like the engraver's initials, invoke an authority that comes from elsewhere, from "above." While de Bry's compasses are held in the artist's right hand, his burin hand, they are not—as Goltzius's are—in explicit dialogue with the tool of his trade. Rather, they may be understood once again as the site of an acknowledgment and disavowal: the compasses stand *for* the work of the burin but also stand *in* for that work, as if to exorcize the ghosts of those thoughtless hands that haunt the reproductive engraver.

But Goltzius's pun on burins-as-compasses is present nevertheless, simply because the compasses—as Ripa, Michelangelo, Dürer, and Goltzius all demonstrate—can never fully be divorced from questions of practice, from the artist's necessary relation to abject things. The pun is still there, moreover, because in de Bry's substitution of compasses for burin, the compasses come that much closer to the *work* of the burin. While artists had been including compasses in their self-portraits since the beginning of the sixteenth century—that is, for long enough that Goltzius could play on this custom in 1606 and expect his viewers to get the joke—it is unusual to see the compasses held as de Bry holds them, just so, with the same turned wrist and the same placement of the fingers with which the Algonquian holds his arrows, as if the artist were about to inscribe marks with them. Compare this image, for example, with an early sixteenth-century portrait attributed to Gentile Bellini in the National Gallery, London. A man identified as Giovanni Bellini holds in his right hand a pair of compasses that do not seem to be practical tools at all but are grasped at the base and displayed before the viewer as a token of the liberal rather than the mechanical arts (Figure 22).[84] Next to Bellini's compasses, de Bry's seem all the more closely aligned with the "servile" instruments of Practice.

Reading de Bry's compasses along these lines also demands a reassessment of their relationship to the skull beneath the artist's left hand. Perhaps it is now possible to see this relationship not as one of opposition between divine art and mortal flesh, but as one of resemblance in which the engraver's compasses may not escape the fate of the body after all. The skull, its empty sockets staring at de Bry's compasses, takes on a new significance—it becomes the emblem of practice, of all that is subject to time in the engraver's art. Even the compasses, this skull seems to say, will not outlive the flesh. This message is spelled out for us in the text that appears on the ledge just below the points of the compasses. The tips of the compass legs frame the word *doce,* as the artist calls upon God to "teach" him how to spend the remainder of his life. The proximity of de Bry's instrument to this verbal invocation of God (the upper point, significantly, rests just below the word *Domine*) reinforces the symbolic relation between the compasses and the divine artificer. The lower point, however, falls just above the verb *transigere,* which means to "pass through" or "spend" time, but which also means to pierce or stab with a sharp instrument. De Bry's prayer, in other words, adopts a language of latent violence: compasses in hand, the artist pierces through the remaining days of his life. The word *transigere* thus stands as the verbal acknowledgment that returns de Bry's compasses to a corporeal history, a history of inscribing marks upon

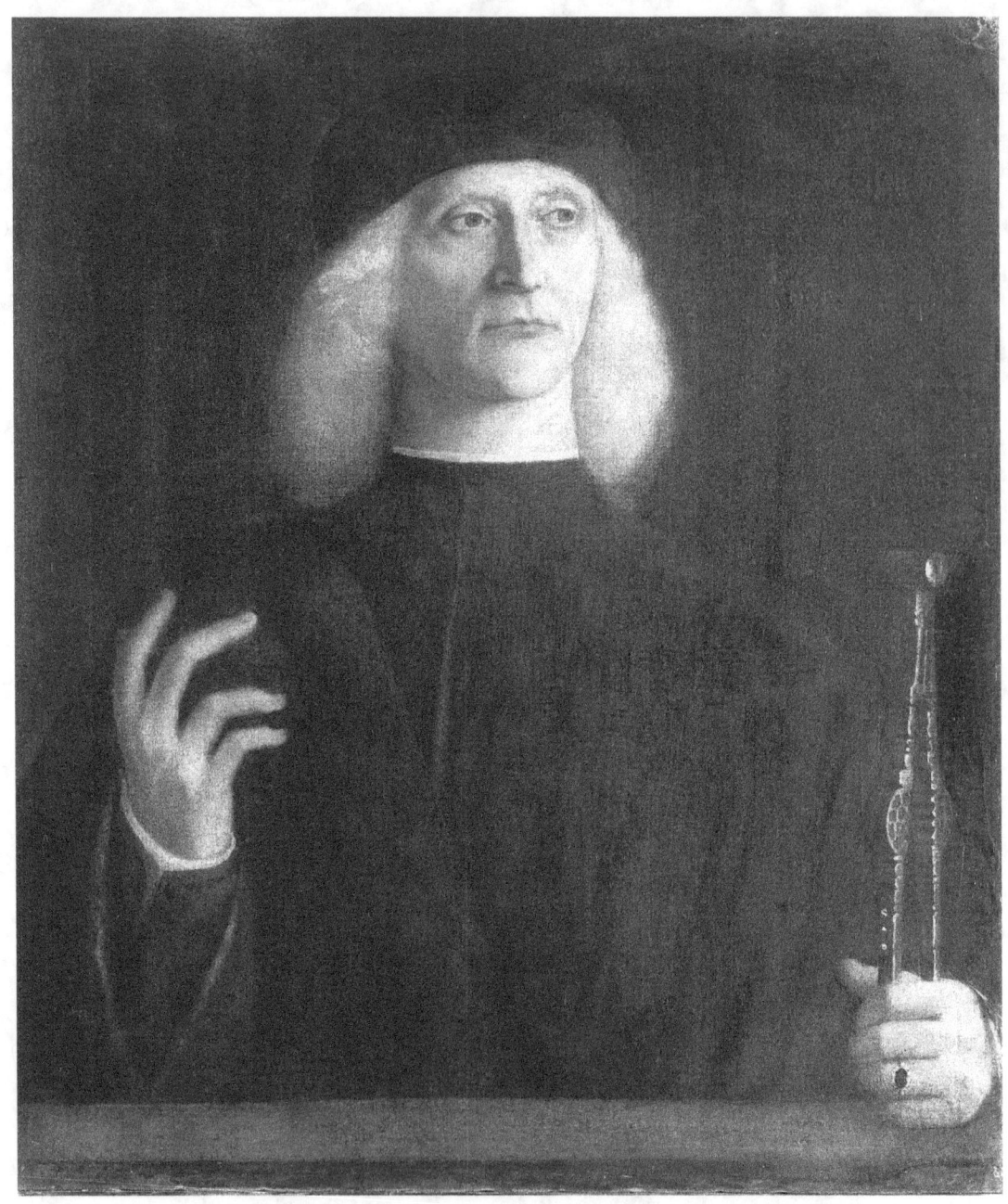

Figure 22. Attributed to Gentile Bellini, *Portrait of man identified as Giovanni Bellini,* oil on canvas, c. 1500. Copyright The National Gallery, London.

the abject matter of the world and a history in which the tools of the engraver have sometimes, to recall Evelyn's remark, "proved fatal and dangerous Weapons."[85]

As instruments that can pierce through time and through bodies, de Bry's burin-compasses also return us to the tattooed savage of the *Report,* for the marks rased on *his* flesh suggest not only, as I have argued, a *writing* before the letter, but also an *engraving* before the letter, a material practice that is always in advance of the consolidation of authority in an artist's initials, in the iconography of authorship, or in the imagined rationality of the engraver's grammar. All that is disavowed in the rational compasses returns in this corporeal savage, with his pre-alphabetical marks and his quill-like arrows. If there is any certain knowledge about "selves" and "others" represented in these two images, one of an engraver and the other of an Algonquian, it is that this knowledge is always a *becoming* rational; it is always a question of tools in the hand producing marks in time, the burin in the process of becoming the compasses, the quill in the process of becoming the arrows. The ghost of the savage thus lingers in de Bry's compasses as the ghost of those pre-rational, pre-alphabetical practices out of which the ethnographer creates the fiction of his own civilized authority. And de Bry's self-portrait returns us finally to a pair of arrows, looking not unlike a pair of quills and even a bit like a pair of compasses, held in the right hand of an unlettered American savage.

2. Making Sense of Smoke
Engraving and Ornament in de Bry's *America*

On any surface of metal, the object of the engraver is, or ought to be, to cover it
with lovely *lines,* forming a lacework, and including a variety of spaces, delicious
to the eye. . . . That [these lines] should mean something, and a good deal of
something, is indeed desirable afterwards; but first we must be ornamental.

—John Ruskin, *Ariadne Florentina:*
Six Lectures on Wood and Metal Engraving

In the previous chapter I looked for traces of the scriptive techniques that produce the savage body; in this chapter, I turn my attention from the instruments of inscription to the engraved line itself. John Ruskin's remarks on the proper ends of engraving provide an appropriate starting point. Lecturing at Oxford in 1872 on the subject of wood and metal engraving, Ruskin declares that the art of the engraver is first and foremost a meaningless activity—it is, quite simply, the decorating or ornamenting of a metal plate with lines. In calling his audience's attention to the materiality of the engraver's mark, over and against its signifying function, Ruskin offers sound guidance for the viewer who is apt to make the leap too quickly from the ornamental lines of the print to a content one might suppose those lines to signify.

Consider de Bry's engraving for the *Report* titled *Their manner of prainge with Rattels abowt te fyer* (Figure 23). Nine Algonquian men and women, five of them shaking rattles, are seated in a circular pattern on the ground, while two additional figures (a man and a woman) stand to the left, apparently engaged in conversation. In the midst of the seated figures burns a large, smoking fire, which provides the focus for the depicted activities. The engraving is rich with potential meaning. There is, first of all, ethnographic content, as the image describes specific customs observed among the coastal Algonquians of Virginia. Harriot explains in the caption on the opposite page:

When they haue escaped any great danger by sea or lande, or be returned from the
warr in token of Ioye they make a great fyer abowt which the men, and woemen sist

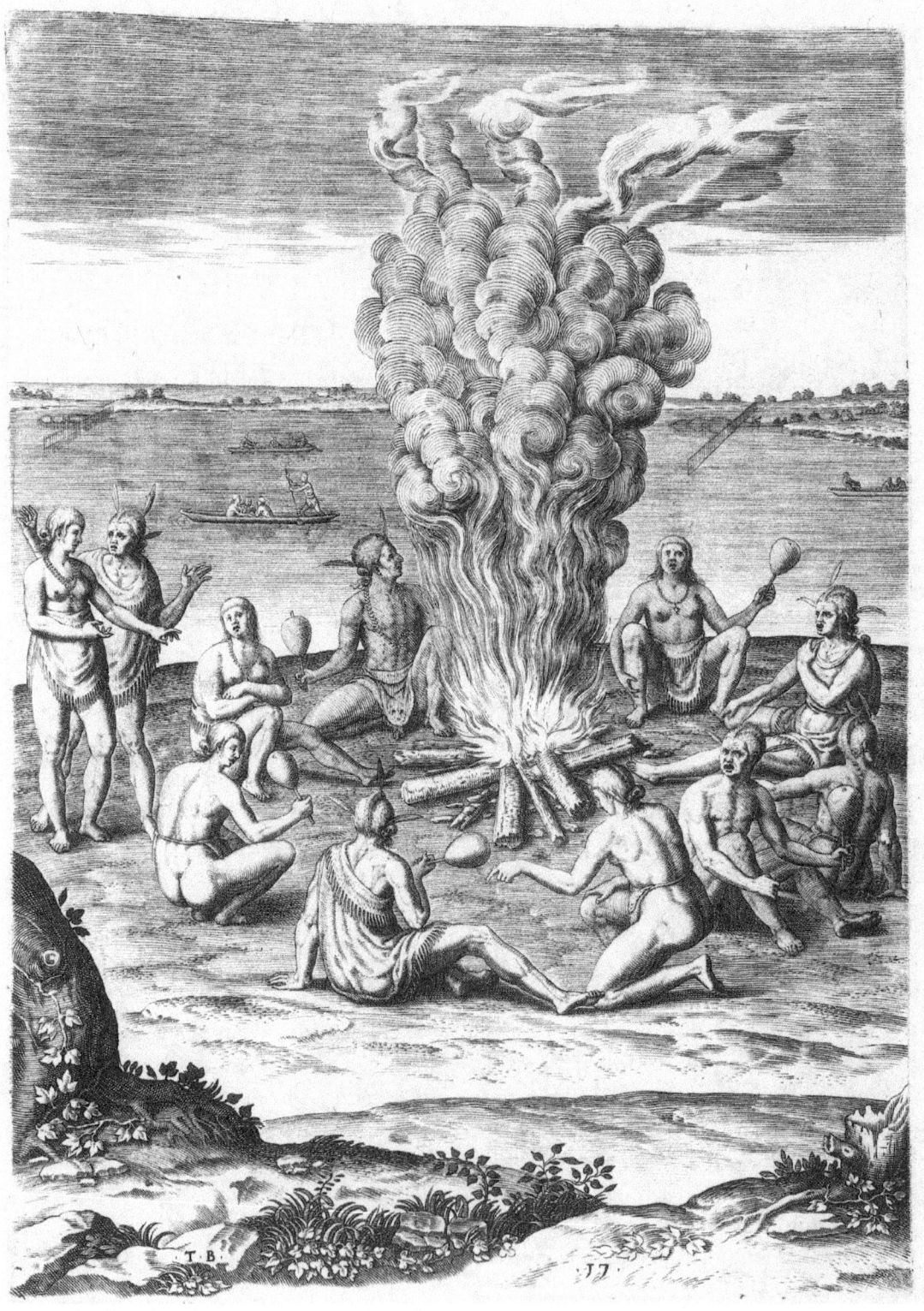

Figure 23. Theodor de Bry after John White, *Their manner of prainge with Rattels abowt te fyer*, from *A Briefe and True Report*. Courtesy and with permission of British Library G.6837.

[sic] together, holdinge a certaine fruite in their hands like vnto a rownde pompion or a gourde, which after they haue taken out the fruits, and the seedes, then fill with smal stons or certayne bigg kernellt to make the more noise, and fasten that vppon a sticke, and singinge after their manner, they make merrie: as myselfe obserued and noted downe at my beinge amonge them. For it is a strange custome, and worth the obseruation.[1]

The caption, of course, includes more information than the engraving itself can offer: from the image alone, we cannot tell why the Virginians have gathered around the fire nor how their rattles were constructed. But because Harriot was there, because he "obserued and noted downe," his words carry the authority of the eyewitness and thus place him in a privileged position for explaining the meaning of the plate. As with the other plates for the *Report,* however, Harriot's caption hardly exhausts the content of the image. Not only does the engraving contain a good deal of descriptive content not addressed by Harriot, it also has potential for connotational meanings that would contextualize it within de Bry's and Harriot's own cultural milieu. These New World savages, for example, as they sing and "make merrie," are engaged (so the title informs us) in a form of prayer, and one can easily imagine de Bry's Protestant audience associating this scene of New World religious ritual with various European contexts: with the "superstitious" rites of pagan antiquity, contemporary witchcraft, and Roman Catholicism, to name three. All these various meanings can and perhaps should be read into this image. Clearly the lines in this engraving *mean* something—indeed, "a good deal of something," to borrow Ruskin's phrase.

And yet before they mean something, they are simply lines. Would it, therefore, be worthwhile, would it tell us anything interesting about the conditions of representing

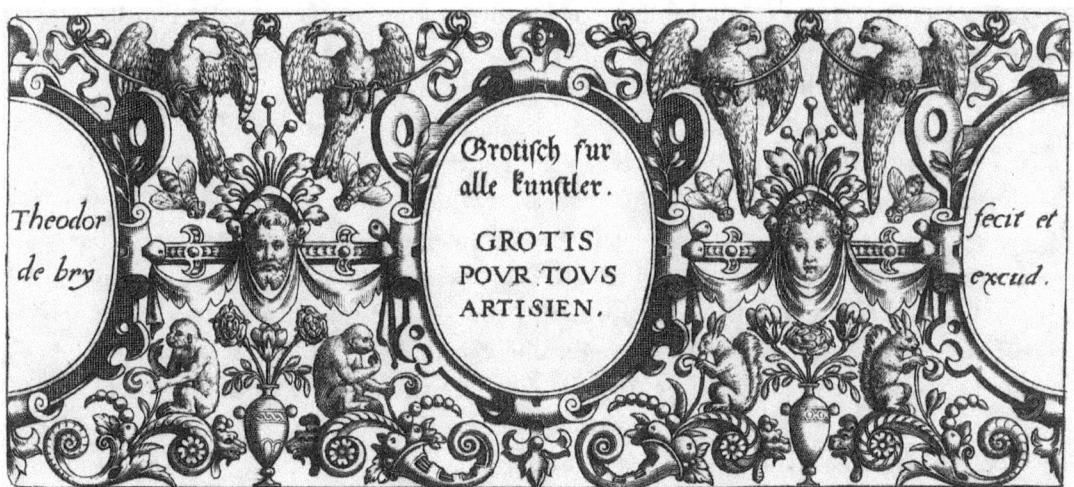

Figure 24. Theodor de Bry, *Grotisch fur alle Kunstler,* title page, late sixteenth century. The Metropolitan Museum of Art, The Elisha Whittelsey Collection, The Elisha Whittelsey Fund, 1951 [51.501.5793(1)]. Photograph from The Metropolitan Museum of Art; all rights reserved.

the New World in the late sixteenth century, to resist the impulse to find content in de Bry's engraving and instead—following Ruskin's cue—to consider this image first as ornament, as simply the decoration of a surface with lines? De Bry, after all, was himself an ornamental engraver and created several series of grotesque designs, such as the four plates of his *Grotisch fur alle Kunstler* (Figure 24). Clearly he was not unaccustomed to engaging in that intense visual concentration on the formal play of line and shape that characterizes ornamental work. And I would suggest that *Their manner of prainge* likewise lends itself to an "ornamental" analysis. Specifically, I would point out the ornamental quality of the roiling, spiraling smoke that occupies the upper portion of the image. The rich linear play of the smoke stands noticeably outside the spatial order that rules throughout the rest of the engraving, where clearly demarcated shapes (flowers, tree stumps, classicized bodies, etc.) occupy a recessional space divided neatly into foreground, middle ground, and background. Ascending from flames that consume a heap of logs positioned securely in the middle ground, the lines of the smoke rise not just toward the sky but also toward the surface of the page. These repeated linear swirls disengage themselves at least partially from representational space, and in doing so they serve as a check upon the historian's impulse immediately to move from inside to outside, from signifier to signified. Here and elsewhere an ornamental quality in de Bry's work plays a disruptive role within his project of New World representation. My concern in this chapter is to arrive at some understanding of this disruption.

The Engraver's Lines

Art historians who wish to take seriously an ornamental impulse within the graphic work of reproductive engravers such as de Bry are met by a certain disciplinary resistance, though it is a resistance that has begun to wane in recent years. Two factors in particular have contributed to this neglect of the reproductive engraver. One is art history's longstanding bias in favor of "originality" in artistic expression, a bias that at least since the publication of Adam von Bartsch's enormously influential catalog *Le Peintre-graveur* (1803–21) has privileged the inventions of painter-engravers such as Dürer over the work of professional engravers who devoted their careers to copying works by other artists. The second factor is the emergence of new photographic technologies in the nineteenth and twentieth centuries. When William Ivins, writing in 1953, described the linear syntax of the early modern reproductive engraver as a "net of rationality," he was indeed looking carefully at the work of professional engravers and offering a new language for critically engaging with their work; but it was also a largely disparaging language that privileged the nearly invisible syntax of twentieth-century photomechanical processes over the engraver's highly visible network of lines. In Ivins's view, the "net of rationality" constituted a "tyranny" that artificially limited the amount of visual information the reproductive engraver could convey.[2] When judged by photomechanical standards, the early modern engraver inevitably failed to measure up. Alternatively, when judged by the standards of originality represented by the *peintre-graveur*, the reproductive engraver once again paled in comparison.

"What we have forgotten," writes Caroline Karpinski, "is the critical, public and artistic confidence that earlier centuries expressed in reproductive prints."[3] Ivins's net of rationality may indeed be a useful concept—as it was in the previous chapter—for coming to terms with a rationalizing impulse within de Bry's graphic work. But it is also a phrase that downplays the extent to which reproductive engravers and their audiences, prior to the advent of photomechanical reproduction, acknowledged the line as a vital and manipulable rather than a "tyrannical" factor in creating meaning within this genre. Art historians have now begun to argue for the importance of attending to the ways in which reproductive engravers—particularly "specialist engravers" such as Hendrick Goltzius and Cornelis Cort, to name two of de Bry's contemporaries—made deliberate and effective use of the tension between the contrived artifice of the engraved line and its power to produce three-dimensional illusion.[4] These artists were not passive recorders of their models, nor did they seek to be; rather, they were skilled interpreters who sought to fix their viewer's attention on lines that wavered provocatively and often spectacularly between representation and ornament.

As I have already argued, we must be careful to distinguish between the virtuosic line of an engraver such as Goltzius, who displayed his *ingenium* by copying the work of prominent artists of his day for the collector, and the lines of de Bry and his assistants, who primarily copied for a more general audience the work of unknown artists. De Bry's lines are serviceable, not spectacular. Deployed within, but rarely against, the representational logic of the net of rationality, they seldom if ever seek the virtuosic effects achieved by the specialist engravers. This does not mean, however, that we should neglect the ornamental value of those lines simply because they do not measure up to Goltzius. De Bry was, after all, a skilled professional engraver, the founder of a printmaking and publishing firm that became known throughout Protestant Europe for the quality of its book illustrations.[5] The *Report* constituted an important step in establishing that reputation, and one sign of its engravers' command of the burin is the smoke that wafts in great, ornamental clouds through several of the book's plates. Smoke, as depicted in engravings such as *Their manner of prainge, The manner of makinge their boates,* and *Their seetheynge of their meate in earthen pottes* (Figures 23, 25, 26), may be the one point in the illustrations for this New World text where the engraver's lines do in fact withdraw, indeed quite dramatically, from their representational obligations and engage in something that approaches a freely ornamental play of line.

The degree to which de Bry's smoke stands out from the other forms in his engravings and commands our visual attention is due in part to the fact that smoke presents the engraver with a special problem of representation: its nebulous immateriality is antithetical to an art whose degree zero is the line. The engraver's solution to the problem of representing smoke is of necessity quite different from that of the watercolorist who provided the models for the engravings of the *Report.* In the prototype

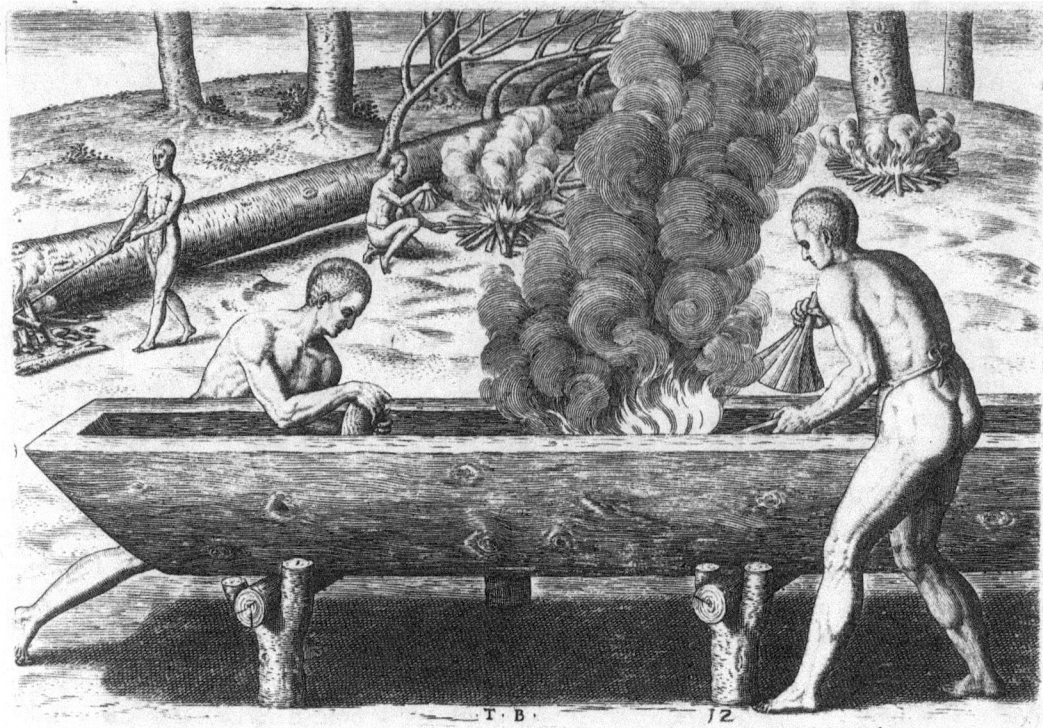

Figure 25. Theodor de Bry, *The manner of makinge their boates,* from *A Briefe and True Report.* Courtesy and with permission of British Library G.6837.

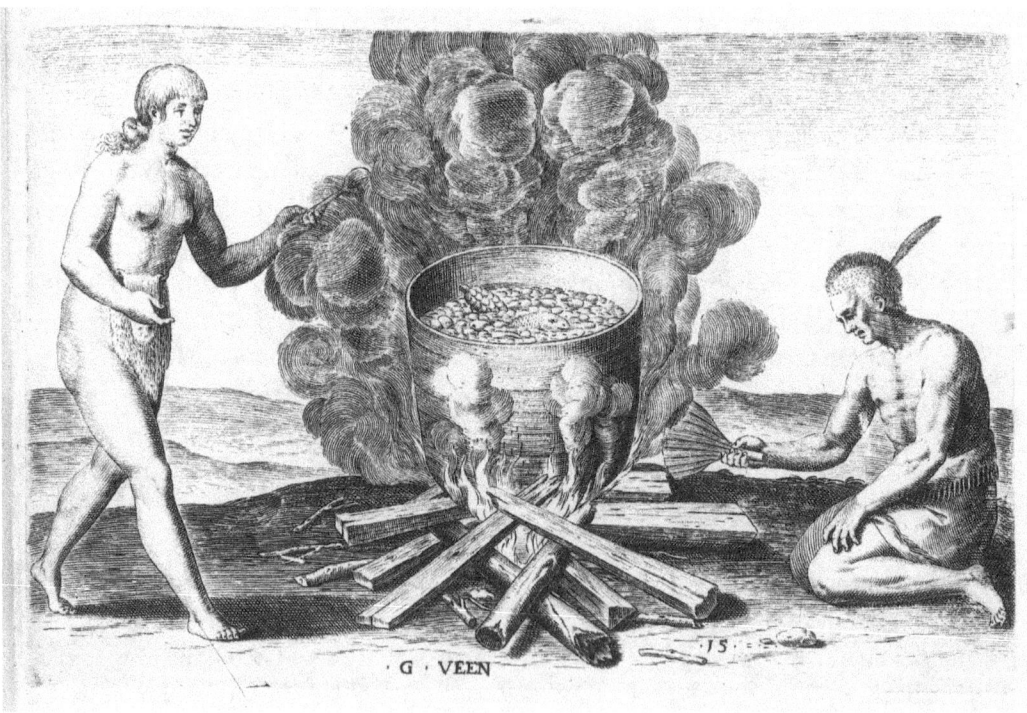

Figure 26. Gijsbert van Veen after John White, *Their seetheynge of their meate in earthen pottes,* from *A Briefe and True Report.* Courtesy and with permission of British Library G.6837.

for *Their manner of prainge,* for example, John White paints his smoke in light, transparent washes through which the ethnographic object—a chanting Indian—is easily discernible (Figure 27). Our visual attention rests not on a display of line or even on painterly virtuosity, but on the "facts"; no medium or projection of ego obstructs our gaze as we see through both the smoke and the artist's technical presence into a new world. White is in fact notable in the history of watercolor painting for the extent to which he added the modern technique of transparent washes to a traditional dense and opaque use of color.[6] But this transparency represents more than a simple technical innovation. It amounts to a strategic use of medium wherein the viewer is invited

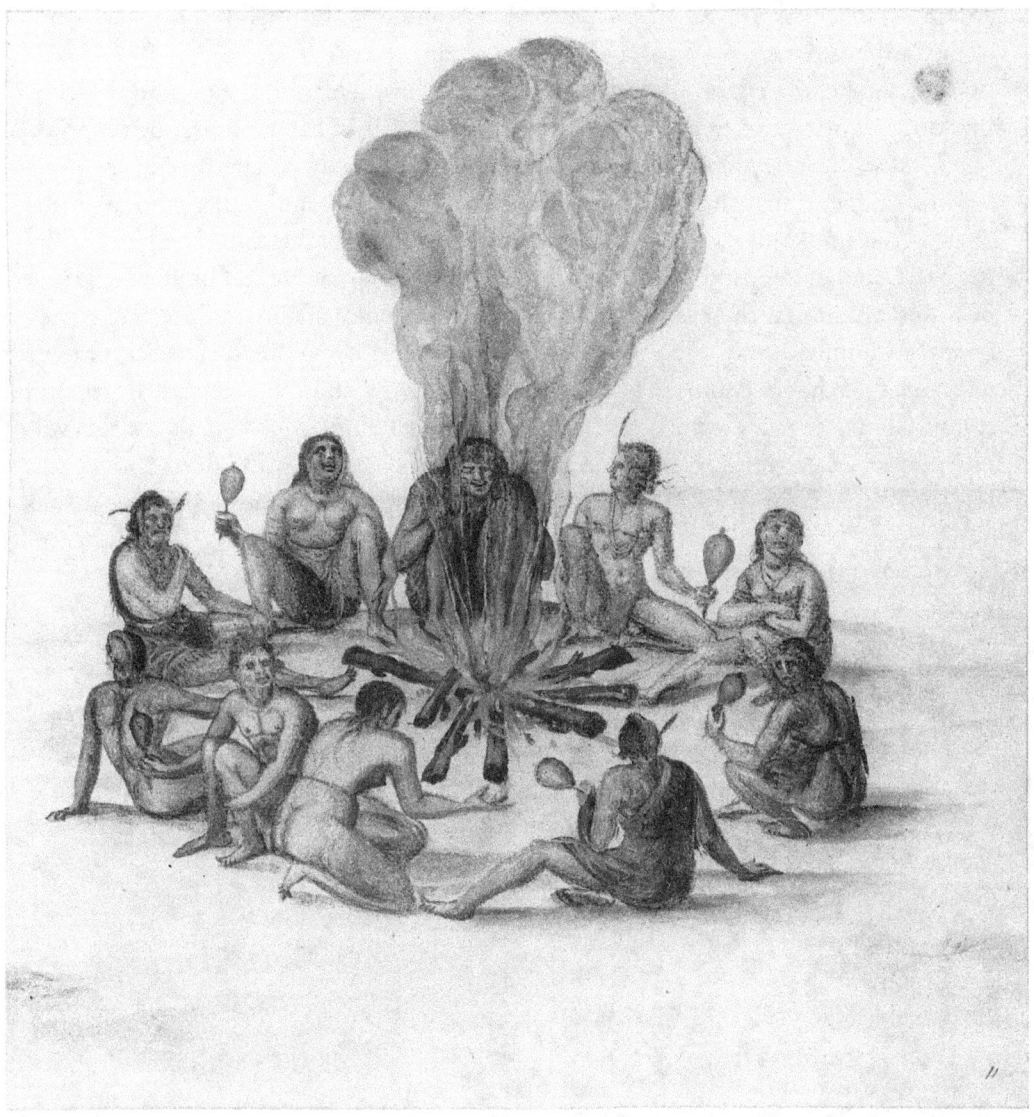

Figure 27. John White, *Algonquians around a fire,* watercolor on paper, c. 1585. Copyright Trustees of The British Museum.

to see through the intrusive hand of the artist by *literally* seeing through the medium itself. Nowhere is this technique more noticeable—or rather, unnoticeable—than in White's manner of depicting smoke.

It is often noted that de Bry's engravings translate White's ethnographically perceptive studies into the classicized forms of European mannerism.[7] But an equally if not more significant translation occurs at the level of the medium itself, where a visual rhetoric of transparency is exchanged for the opacity of the engraved line. This radical shift in visual language is particularly apparent in the artists' respective approaches to the rendering of smoke. There is no seeing through the lines of de Bry's smoke nor through those of Gijsbert van Veen, an engraver in de Bry's workshop whose initials appear on *Their seetheynge of their meate*. The sinuous and sometimes intricate work of the burin in these smoky passages is mesmerizing. In van Veen's and de Bry's depictions of smoke, the engraver's lines are released from their normal function of defining form: compare, for example, the perfectly parallel arcs that circumscribe the felled tree in *The manner of makinge their boates* with the perfectly parallel arcs in the overlapping smoke, which circumscribe nothing specific at all (Figure 28). So released, the lines of the smoke draw our eyes away from the ethnographic subject matter, away from the smoke itself, and into an ornamental display of graphic technique. To be fair, one must admit that there is indeed a compellingly smoky quality to these lines. They appear to mimic certain motions we are accustomed to watching in smoke. Groups of parallel hatchings—some forming serpentine curves, some simple arcs, others full spirals—build one upon the other; areas of cross-hatching suggest shadows and volume and indicate transitions as one smoky pocket bleeds into the next; and all this linear movement seems to defy gravity as it billows upward. However, in none of this

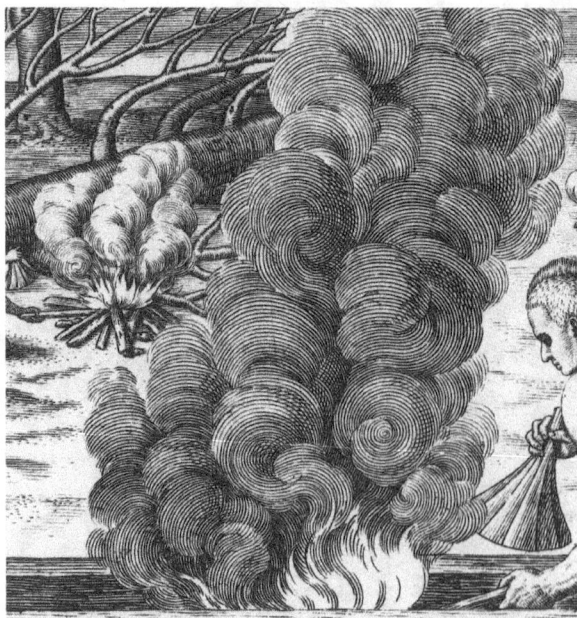

Figure 28. Theodor de Bry, *The manner of makinge their boates* (detail). Courtesy and with permission of British Library G.6837.

smoky play of line do we have the *illusion* of smoke in the way White produces the illusion of smoke's transparency, or in the way an engraver can produce the illusion of more architectural forms such as a tree, a canoe, or even a human body. But if the lines of de Bry's smoke do not give us illusion, they do give us, and to great effect, a display of the linear art involved in the engraver's effort to produce illusion.

One way of coming to terms with these lines (lines that lead us both toward a meaning in the world and toward the art that produces this meaning) is through the semiotic notions first proposed by nineteenth-century American philosopher Charles Sanders Peirce of the iconic sign and the indexical sign. The real interest of de Bry's smoke is in the degree to which it behaves simultaneously as both. For Peirce, the icon is a sign that in some way partakes of the character of its object, even if that object is a purely hypothetical one.[8] De Bry's smoke, as I have described it, functions as an icon insofar is it partakes of a quality, a certain vaporous movement, that any viewer who has ever seen smoke will associate with this ethereal substance. And indeed all other forms described in the plates for the *Report* can be classified as iconic signs as well. De Bry's illusionistic trees, for instance, unlike the word *tree* (which belongs to Peirce's category of the "symbol"), share with their object the qualities of roundness, of having branches, etc.

While the plates for the *Report* may be full of iconic signs, the individual lines that make up those icons function as indexes. An index is the physical trace that leads us directly to its source, and for this reason it bears a stronger connection to its object than does the icon: as Peirce defines it, the index is "really and in its individual existence connected with the individual object."[9] The concept is in fact much older than Peirce, extending as far back as Augustine, who in the fourth century AD first distingished between conventional signs and natural signs *(signa naturalia),* the latter being the equivalent of the index. For Augustine and others ever since, smoke as a sign of the fire to which it is physically linked has served as one of the chief examples of a natural sign.[10] The lines that constitute de Bry's engraved smoke are also, I would suggest, noteworthy indexical signs—not as signs of fire, of course, but as visible traces of the engraver's hand and of the difficult process of pushing the burin into a resistant metal plate while at the same time turning that plate against the burin (a bespectacled engraver is engaged in this activity at the far right of the engraver's workshop in the final plate of van der Straet's *Nova reperta;* see Figure 3). Like the tracks of an animal (Augustine's other example of a natural sign), the engraved line bears an indexical relation to the activity that produced it.[11]

While all the engraved lines of the *Report* necessarily include an indexical dimension, the lines of the smoke seem to be a special case, for unlike the other lines in the engravings, they advertise their indexicality. Since the lines of the smoke fall somewhat short of representing a discrete form and instead mimic through their movements and patterns the motions of smoke, we cannot read these lines *as smoke* without also reading them *as lines* and therefore as indexes of the engraver's labor. Thus, another way of understanding the tension between the representational aims and the ornamental qualities of the engraved line is to view it as a tension between the iconicity of delineated form and the indexicality of the line itself. It is precisely this semiotic ambivalence that specialist engravers such as Goltzius, who knew how closely early modern audiences were attuned to the engraver's subtle manipulations of line, exploited in their reproductive engravings. In the case of the *Report,* this ambivalence, so apparent in de Bry's smoke, can offer valuable insight into the conditions of representing the New World around 1590.

Reading Smoke

How might we take this ambivalence seriously and yet at the same time read de Bry's smoke *as smoke,* thus situating it firmly within the horizon of possibilities of what the smoke of a New World campfire could signify for a European audience at the end of the sixteenth century? One such context for reading de Bry's smoke may be found in early modern prints and drawings treating the subjects of witchcraft and magic. The smoke in *Their manner of prainge* invites comparison, for example, with the turbulent, chaotic play of line in prints like Hans Baldung's chiaroscuro woodcut of the *Witches' Sabbath* (1510), perhaps the first single-leaf woodcut to treat this subject (Figure 29).[12] In Baldung's woodcut, smoke fumes into the sky from the pots of witches who are seated on the ground. The smoke suggests the transformative magic that makes possible such diabolical wonders as a witch who takes a backward flight on a goat, while it also calls to mind the commonly held belief that the demons summoned by witches were composed of condensed air.[13] In the airy disturbances of Baldung's *Witches Sabbath* and in related drawings by the same artist, as well as in works by other sixteenth- and seventeenth-century artists who treat similar subject matter,[14] the wild, undulating, and often elegant graphic line, tied to no specific representational duties, becomes an effective means for figuring precisely that which refuses figuration in witchcraft: the unseen forces within the air that are the source of the witch's power and the object of her conjurations.

There is good reason for considering de Bry's engraving alongside such images as Baldung's *Witches Sabbath.* The link between early modern attitudes toward witches and American Indians is well established.[15] Distant as they were from the revealed word of scripture, natives of the New World were thought by Europeans to be particularly susceptible to demonic influences, while their figures of spiritual authority were often specifically singled out as witches and conjurors. Jean de Léry, for example, upon observing a religious rite in Brazil during which shamans shake *maracas* and blow tobacco smoke on the participants, had no hesitation in referring to the event as a "witches sabbath."[16] The *Report* offers a similar assessment of an Algonquian medicine man who is the subject of a plate by Gijsbert van Veen titled *The Coniuerer* (Figure 30). According to the caption, "They haue comonlye coniurers or iuglers which vse strange gestures, and often contrarie to nature in their enchantments: For they be verye familiar with deuils, of whome they enquier what their enemys doe, or other suche

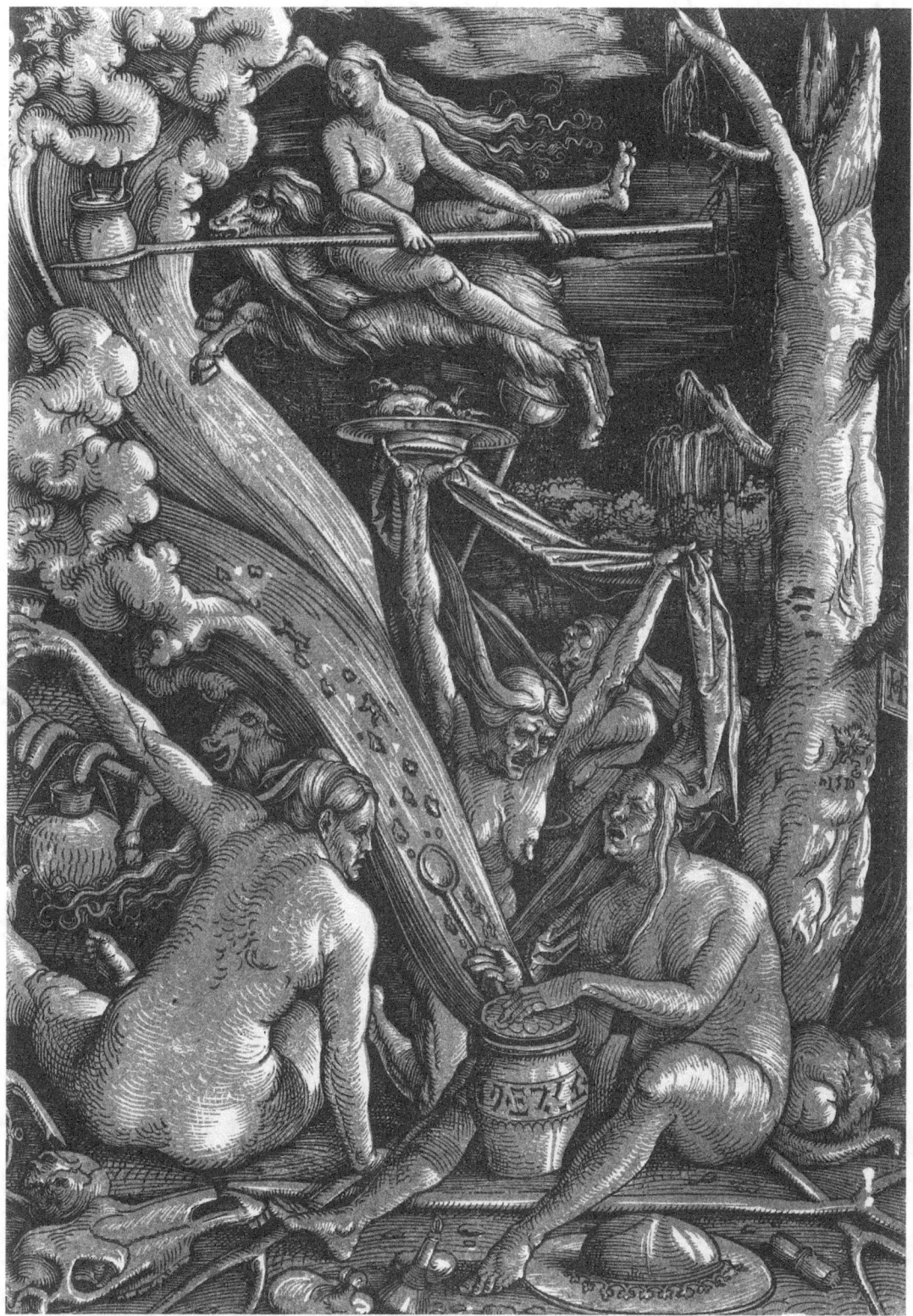

Figure 29. Hans Baldung, *Witches' Sabbath*, chiaroscuro woodcut, 1510. Copyright Trustees of The British Museum.

thinges."[17] In White's original watercolor, this figure is actually labeled the "flyer," a word that suggests the shaman's capacity for flight between earthly and spiritual realms.[18] The altered title that appears in the *Report,* however, with the aid of Harriot's caption, would have been more immediately digestible to an audience steeped in popular reports of witchcraft and magic.

Around the time of the *Report's* publication, an engraving by Crispijn de Passe titled *Saturn and His Children* explicitly makes a pictorial connection between the American Indian and the witch (Figure 31). The print, which belongs to a series of seven engravings of the planetary gods and their children based on drawings by Martin de Vos, shows Saturn riding in a chariot through his zodiacal house. Below him are those who fall under his influence, a motley crew that consists entirely of witches, magicians, and Indians, the latter engaging in a variety of activities, including mining and, in the right foreground, a cannibal feast. The smoke that rises from the savages' barbecue is echoed on the left-hand side of the sheet in a scene of sorcery in which three witches are borne aloft by the smoke produced by their own black rites.[19] For early modern viewers, such associations between the practices of witches and those of American Indians would carry over easily to de Bry's scene of ritualistic incantation around a smoking fire.

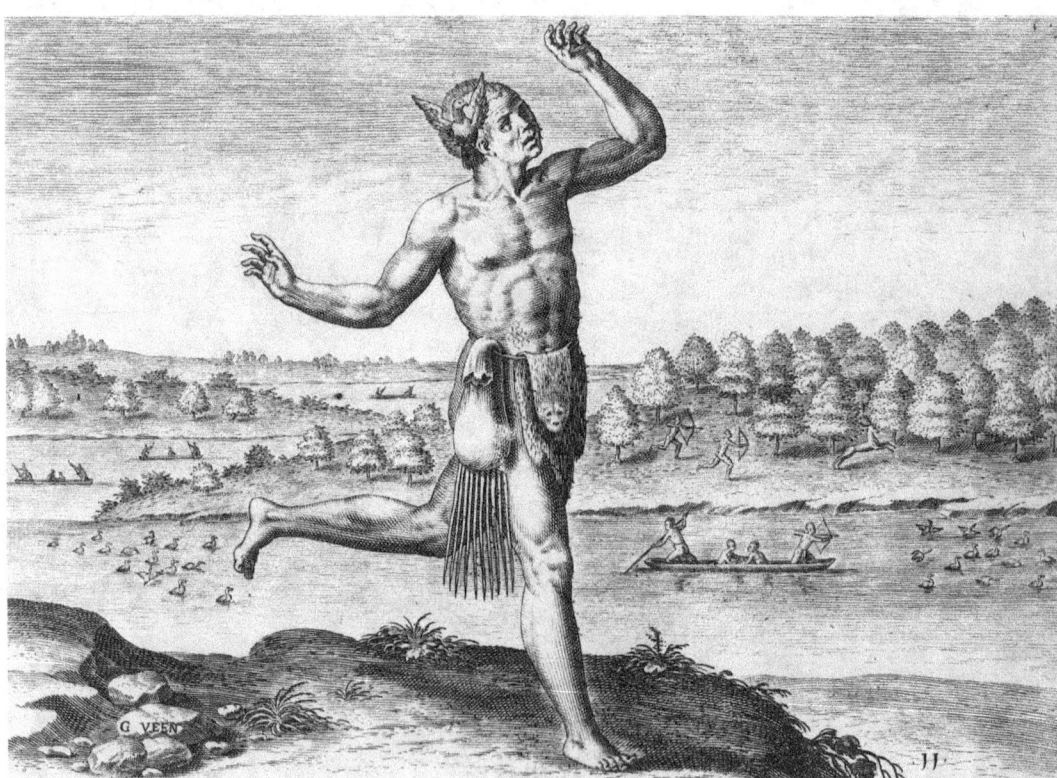

Figure 30. Gijsbert van Veen after John White, *The Coniuerer,* from *A Briefe and True Report.* Courtesy and with permission of British Library G.6837.

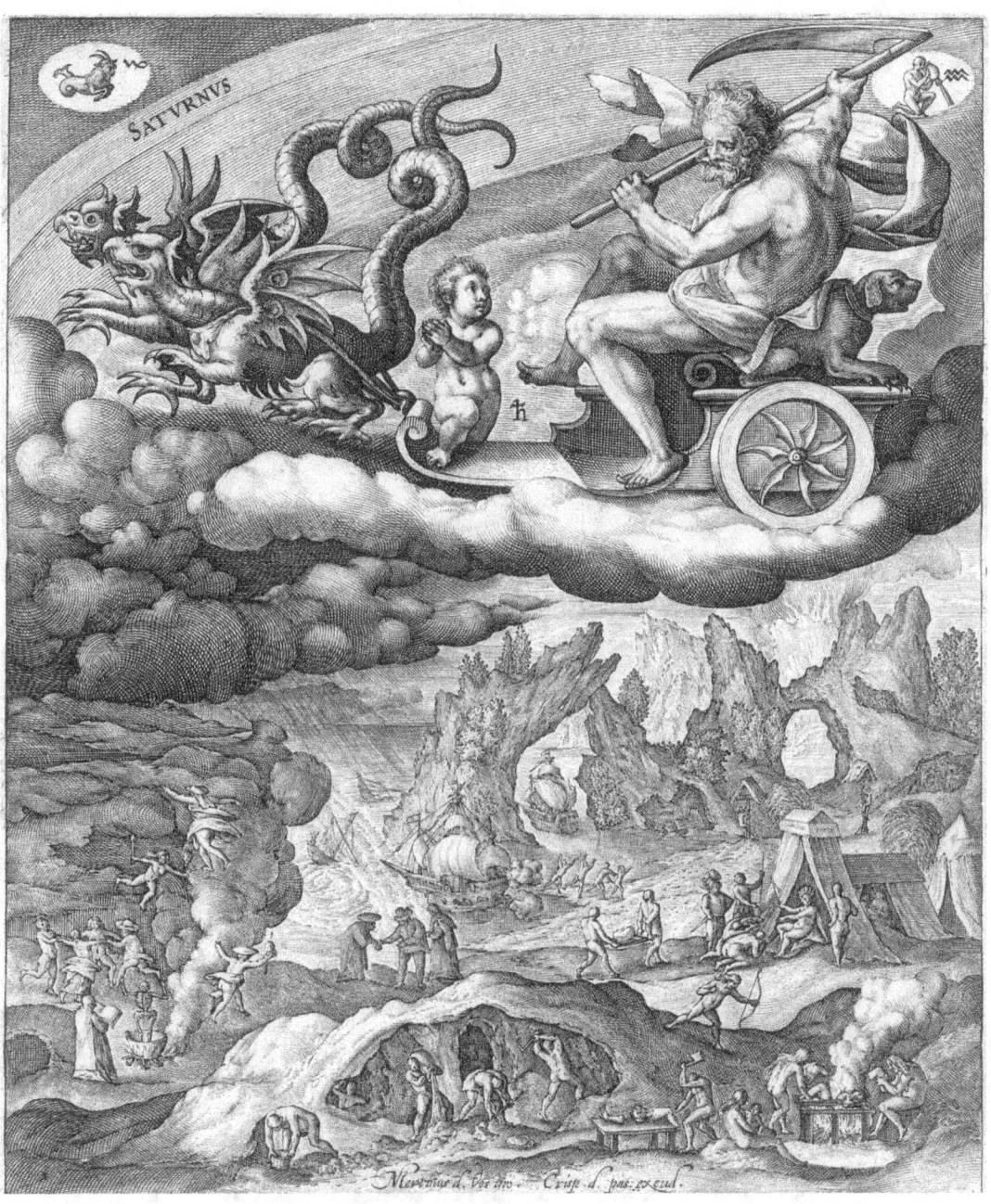

Figure 31. Crispijn de Passe after Martin de Vos, *Saturn and His Children,* from *The Seven Planets,* late sixteenth century. Rijksmuseum, Amsterdam.

The smoke we see rising in the midst of this possibly demonic ritual would not, therefore, have been a neutral substance to the early modern viewer but a bearer, in a very literal sense, of meaning, since it is precisely in such smoky perturbations of the air that demonic spirits were thought to assume visible form through the invocations of witches. Indeed, de Bry's smoke suggests, within a static and silent pictorial art, the very sounds produced by these figures who sit upon the ground with mouths open and rattles shaking. As they strike the air with their wandlike rattles, the smoke serves to carry their prayers to the inhabitants of the spirit world.[20] Heinrich Cornelius Agrippa, the most influential writer on magic during the sixteenth century, has this to say of the mediating role of the air in the practice of magic:

> [The air] immediately receives into itself the influences of all celestial bodies and then communicates them to the other Elements, as also to all mixed bodies. Also it receives into itself, as it were a divine looking-glass, the species of all things, as well natural as artificial, as also of all manner of speeches, and retains them; and carrying them with it, and entering into the bodies of men, and other animals, through their pores, makes an impression upon them, as well when they sleep as when they be awake, and affords matter for divers strange Dreams and Divinations.[21]

The work of the witch or the magician, then, was to manipulate the air in a manner that could call forth spirits. As Agrippa explains, "by certain vapors, exhaling from proper suffumigations, airy spirits are presently raised, as also thunderings and lightnings, and such like things."[22] Echoes of Agrippa, who was something of a Faustian figure in early modern Europe, were heard on the English stage just a few years after the publication of the *Report,* in words penned by Harriot's friend, Christopher Marlowe.[23] In the final act of *Dr. Faustus,* the doomed magus makes a plea to the stars to effect his own bodily translation through the medium of mist, cloud, and smoke:

> You stars that reigned at my nativity,
> Whose influence hath allotted death and hell,
> Now draw up Faustus like a foggy mist
> Into the entrails of yon laboring cloud,
> That when you vomit forth into the air,
> My limbs may issue from your smoky mouths,
> So that my soul may but ascend to heaven.[24]

Faust's description of a vaporous path to the heavens recalls de Passe's engraving, in which the abject progeny of the earth god—the bodies that occupy the fallen, saturnine world below—are tied to the stars through the medium of air. In its most exalted form, this medium is seen as the supportive cloud on which Saturn drives his chariot. This celestial cloud then merges with "laboring clouds" that spew rain over the gloomy terrain, and these storm clouds in turn, and almost imperceptibly, transform into the smoke produced by human sorcery. Like de Passe's smoke and clouds, de Bry's own surging smoke may be read as the visualization of the airy medium through which magicians and witches work their magic, the medium that unites the celestial with the earthly, that carries speech, that translates bodies and images (Agrippa's "species") and impresses them upon our senses. Through his smoke, de Bry lends to the suspect prayer of the savage, with its potentially demonic invocations, a kind of formless visibility.[25]

But even as de Bry's smoke leads us outward into the larger context of witchcraft and magic during the sixteenth century, this same context returns us to the engraver's lines, for the preoccupation with medium in the early modern literature on magic, witchcraft, and demonology can provide us, as it provided certain writers and artists, with a means of understanding the nature of the artist's involvement with his own materials.[26] The notion of a demonic manipulation of the air, for example, finds echoes both in the theory and practice of picture-making in the Renaissance, as in Leonardo's technique of *sfumato* (smokiness), which created an enhanced sense of illusion in his paintings by causing forms literally to merge with their surrounding atmosphere.[27] Understood in these terms, Leonardo's famous technique demonstrates the artist's "magical" ability to manipulate his medium. Similarly, one might well argue that Baldung's frenzied smoke offers a pictorial meditation on the idea of artistic creation as demonic possession. To be sure, one would be hard-pressed to argue that de Bry, in his ethnographic engravings for the *Report,* is chiefly concerned with the notion of the artist-as-magician. Nevertheless, as the charges of atheism, conjuring, and juggling made against the Raleigh circle (and Harriot, in particular) during the 1590s demonstrate, the ability to conjure the elements and the ability to conjure new worlds were not unrelated skills in the late sixteenth century.[28] And as we have just seen, Harriot and de Bry both belonged to a culture in which the witch, the magician, the demon, and the artist could all be conceived as manipulators of the same airy matter. It thus makes a good deal of sense that an engraver would choose to represent this medium—especially when it was stirred up by the prayers of New World savages—through a smoky display of his own art.

While the art and literature surrounding early modern magic and witchcraft can help us read de Bry's smoke, it is nevertheless important to recognize that de Bry does not *definitively* present this New World gathering as a scene of witchcraft: the burden is on the viewer to come to his or her own conclusion as to the specific nature of what Harriot in his caption identifies simply as a "strange custom." Again, Baldung's *Witches' Sabbath* provides a useful point of comparison. As Joseph Koerner points out, Baldung does not represent a Sabbath in which all of the deeds and implements of the witches have been named and accounted for. Instead the artist presents the viewer with the very problem of *knowing* witches and how they work their magic. The role of the audience is to make sense, as if we were ourselves inquisitors, out of ambiguous visual signs such as the sausage-like forms hanging over a pitchfork on the far left-hand side of the print, forms that might simply be sausages but could also be interpreted as signs of the symbolic castration that witches were thought to carry out on their male victims.[29] In this regard, the smoke functions critically in Baldung's print, for its formlessness suggests a meaning that has yet to materialize. De Bry's viewers are presented with a similar ambiguity (see Figure 23). For example, we do not and cannot know the precise nature of the prayers being spoken in *Their manner of prainge.* Other visual elements are similarly elusive. What, for example, might be the topic of conversation between the man and woman standing on the left, a pair that does not appear in White's original watercolor? The man gestures urgently but ambiguously at his companion, while she, just as ambiguously, points toward the fire. Perhaps the man is a figure of religious authority who attempts to use his influence to lure the woman into pagan worship. It is equally possible, however, that the man tries to dissuade the woman from participation in a rite toward which she seems to be drawn. After all, as de Bry makes clear at the beginning of the illustrated section of the *Report* with his engraving of the Fall (see Figure 11), it is a woman's natural weakness to surrender herself to diabolical temptations.

Perhaps one thing that can be said unambiguously about the meaning of *Their manner of prainge* is that it is a print about superstition, about prayer to false gods and irrational beliefs in the spiritual efficacy of mere ceremonial trappings (such as the rattles so carefully described by Harriot). It is therefore difficult to imagine that associations with witchcraft, on some level, would not have passed through the mind of any Protestant viewer who took a serious look at de Bry's image—even if this occurred only through association with "superstitious" Catholic ceremony, which was itself commonly linked to witchcraft.[30] But the connection with witchcraft must remain precisely at this level, the level of association. Whatever meanings are carried on the plumes of de Bry's smoke, they remain unresolved. We would do best to approach this smoke in the way Gaston Bachelard asks us to approach the poetic imagery of wind, clouds, flight, and the like: not as fully formed poetic images, but as means of figuring the mobility of the imagination.[31] De Bry's smoke may be understood, in similar terms, as a strategy for pictorializing the interpretive process.

This leads to yet a third possibility for reading that curious pair standing to the left, a reading that would trump both interpretations presented above. For before these figures occupy any specific roles within an imagined narrative, they are simply *interpreters* of the event to which they bear witness. As such, they thematize the central problematic of the print: the translation of vision into knowledge. As the woman points and looks toward the fire, she carries out the work of vision, and more specifically a carnal vision, as this female figure is, like many of the women depicted in de Bry's engravings for the *Report,* displayed as an object of male desire, her seminude body turned toward the viewer and thus presented for *his* visual consumption. The rhetorical gesture of the man, on the other hand, is turned away from the primary object of vision (the scene of prayer) as he seeks to engage his companion with his words, to translate her seeing into his knowing. Such is the (gendered) interpretive process rehearsed inside the picture by these figures and outside the picture by de Bry's viewer. What is crucial to recognize about this process is how it hinges on that viewer, a viewer who is hailed by the image as a subject capable of producing meaning out of so much visual matter, a subject who can translate the materiality of the engraver's medium—a materiality that reaches its most raw state in the formlessness of the smoke—into something meaningful. Into a scene of witchcraft, perhaps; and perhaps into other meanings.

The Beholder's Share

My own reading of de Bry's smoke, which has attempted to tie *Their manner of praige* into a specific cultural and historical moment's concerns with magic, witchcraft, and medium, in the end turns out to be inconclusive, for in a sense we are back where we started: with the individual viewer before the work, and the problem of determining the meaning of engraved lines that seem to resist all attempts to do so. So let us turn for the moment from the smoke itself to the viewer whose task is to make sense of it. What conclusions might we draw about this interpretive subject? As I have just suggested, we can certainly say it is a male subject. We can further say it is an *acquisitive* male subject, one who is invited to take an *interest* in the "virgin" land represented in the images and text of the *Report*. As Harriot writes in his initial address to the reader, this book has been published so that "you may generally know & learne what the countrey is, & thervpon consider how your dealing therein if it proceede, may returne you profit and gaine; bee it either by inhabitting & planting or otherwise in furthering thereof."[32]

Indeed, de Bry presents himself as a model for this subject, for he too is an investor in the Virginia enterprise, a businessman who declares no less than three times in the *Report* that this book and its illustrations have been engraved, printed, and published at his "owne chardges."[33] As indexes of the artist—pictorial equivalents to the alphabetical letters (de Bry's *TB*) at the bottom of the plate—the lines of de Bry's smoke serve as a declaration of this investment. Following them back to their producer, we arrive at a subject who is not so much a demonically inspired artist as an astute engraver-publisher whose authority resides in his financial and artisanal investment in copper plates and the printing press. But even as it foregrounds the engraver as the chief interested subject of the *Report*, de Bry's smoke also produces the viewer as an acquisitive subject, one who could potentially become a de Bry. The very purpose of the *Report*, after all, was to attract investors in the Virginia colony, investors who just might (like de Bry) make their own fortunes in the "marchantable commodity" of copper: "A hundred and fiftie miles into the maine," writes Harriot, "in two townes wee founde with the inhabitunts diuerse small plates of copper, that had beene made as wee vnderstood, by the inhabitantes that dwell farther into the countrey."[34] One such copper plate hangs around the neck of de Bry's *A cheiff Lorde of Roanoac,* as visual evidence of Virginia's riches (see Figure 4).

In contrast to the state-sponsored colonialism of Catholic Spain, the English effort to establish a colony in Virginia was to a large extent a commercial enterprise, one that depended for its success on generating financial interest among prospective investors and settlers—as Harriot attempts to do in the passage just quoted and as de Bry attempts to do in the engraving of *A cheiff Lorde of Roanoac*. And just as the Virginia colony can be seen as an early experiment in commercial colonialism, so too can de Bry's *America* (indeed a far more successful one). As Tom Cummins has argued, the nascent capitalism of Protestant Europe during the late sixteenth and early seventeenth centuries provides a critical context for our understanding of de Bry's *America* and of the role that visual images play in its thirteen volumes. De Bry's plates appealed to the viewer as particularized fragments of the New World, fragments detached from and indeed subversive of higher authorities (that of the crown, for example) that would supersede the authority of the individual viewer.[35] The illustrated plates for the *Report* served, like the plate around the neck of the cheiff Lord, as lures for investment in de Bry's New World enterprise; they "delighted the eye as they served the interests of capital."[36] The interpretation of de Bry's images, therefore, is not something that can be accomplished *for* the viewer. Belief in the image as an intercessor for a higher authority, after all, had been shattered by the Reformation's attack against religious images.[37] The work of interpretation now belonged to the anonymous individual in the marketplace, the potential investor.

As so much visual matter that has yet to be made meaningful, de Bry's smoke thus invites our interest as it hails us as the interpretive subjects who can discover the new world, invest in its opportunities, engrave our own names upon it—just as de Bry has done. This invitation becomes particularly apparent when we consider the smoke depicted in *Their seetheynge of their meate* and *The manner of makinge their boates,* plates that explicitly address the colonial possibilities of the New World by focusing on the productive activities of the Virginians (see Figures 25, 26). These images provide the viewer with evidence of the promising ingenuity for which both de Bry and Harriot praise the Virginians.[38] In the caption to *The manner of makinge their boates,* for example, Harriot writes: "The manner of makinge their boates in Virginia is verye wonderfull. For wheras they want Instruments of yron, or other like vnto ours, yet they knowe howe to make them as handsomelye."[39] The roiling smoke rising from between the two laborers in this image does not simply return us to the productive labor of the engraver; clearly it is a sign of the Indians' labor as well, a sign of the transformation they are working upon the world. This smoke suggests both the productivity of these Algonquians and their promise as a productive people. Thus the sign of de Bry's own investment in Virginia (the indexical lines of his smoke) is simultaneously the site of Virginia's potential *as* an investment. The outcome of this investment, however—like the smoke itself and like the response of the viewer—cannot be determined. The significance of the image is not the message it delivers but the kind of subject it constructs precisely through its deferral of a message. De Bry's smoke is the image of this deferral.

Smoke and /Cloud/

I have addressed some of the ways in which a contemporary audience might have received de Bry's smoke. While I have tried not to leap too quickly to particular meanings, while I have argued that the engraver's smoke may indeed be understood as a deferral of meaning, I have nevertheless focused my investigation on the viewer's impulse to find a content, a depth, within this surface play of lines. I have suggested that somewhere behind or within this smoke we might catch a glimpse of the airy prayers of the Virginians, of invisible demonic forms, of the artist's and perhaps most importantly the viewer's subjectivities. But at this point it is worth recalling Ruskin's caution that although meaning is certainly desirable, "first we must be ornamental." In the following paragraphs I will try to be more ornamental, by which I mean that I will keep my attention more closely focused on the surface qualities of de Bry's engravings. My interest in the ornamental quality of the engraved line, however, is not an interest in the line as decoration, but in its status as a material signifier on the page, a signifier whose relation to other such marks is governed by a more or less formal set of rules. At stake in de Bry's smoke, as we will see, is not only the subject it addresses, but the very logic of a structure of representation, one that in this case purports to hold the New World within its grasp. It is a structure that depends on the amorphousness of smoke for its very possibility.

By *structure of representation* I mean the structure of representation itself; more specifically, I mean the structure of *illusionistic* representation, which early modern artists found in the rules of linear perspective. Through the regular application of these rules, artists established a system for making forms depicted on a two-dimensional surface appear very much like our optical experience of the world. What is critical to recognize about this system is precisely that it *is* a system, a set of representational rules for artificially constructing an illusion of the world; in no sense can perspective be reduced to a natural reflection of things as they are.[40] In his *Optics* of 1637, René Descartes argued along these lines when he claimed that our optical perceptions of objects do not in any strong sense of the word *resemble* those objects. Interestingly, he chose to make his point through the example of engraving:

> we must at least observe that there are no images that must resemble in every respect the objects they represent—for otherwise there would be no distinction between the object and its image—but that it is sufficient for them to resemble the objects in but a few ways, and even that their perfection frequently depends on their not resembling them as much as they might. For example, you can see that engravings, being made of nothing but a little ink placed here and there on the paper, represent to us forests, towns, men, and even battles and storms, even though, among an infinity of diverse qualities which they make us conceive in these objects, only in shape is there actually any resemblance. And even this resemblance is a very imperfect one, seeing that, on a completely flat surface, they represent to us bodies which are of different heights and distances, and even that following the rules of perspective, circles

are often better represented by ovals rather than by other circles; and squares by diamonds rather than by other squares; and so for all other shapes. So that often, in order to be more perfect as images and to represent an object better, they must not resemble it.[41]

It is important to note that for Descartes representation is premised on a certain distance between a picture and its depicted object. Historically speaking this is the distance that opens up with the decline of the medieval cult image and its bond of identity between the picture and the figure depicted. With the loss of that bond emerges a new kind of relationship, one based on likeness across a field of difference. It now becomes the artist's task to convince the viewer that even though the picture is fundamentally distinct from that which it portrays, this difference can nevertheless be concealed through the artist's powers of illusion.[42] However, as Descartes argues, securing this bond of likeness is not, or at best is only in part, a matter of making the image physically resemble its object; and in fact a good deal of distortion is necessary to effect a convincing likeness. As I noted earlier, De Bry's tree in *The manner of makinge their boates* is an iconic sign that shares a certain quality of roundness with a real tree; but its two-dimensional, pictorial roundness—two parallel contours bridged by a series of many shorter, curved hatches that are more or less perpendicular to the primary contours—is worlds apart from the tactile roundness of a tree we might encounter in the forest. Descartes wants us to understand that perception is not finally a question of knowing how images resemble their objects; rather, it is a question of knowing the rules by which images communicate to the mind "all the diverse qualities of the objects to which they refer."[43] And the chief rule or regulatory structure through which images communicate, the rule that prevents an engraving from becoming a distorted, haphazard jumble of meaningless marks, is the rule of perspective.

The scholarly literature on linear perspective is, to say the least, vast, and many aspects of perspective—particularly the question of how it might be made into the object of historical inquiry—have hardly been resolved.[44] On a practical and relatively uncontroversial level, however, we can define perspective as a technique for depicting objects and the intervals between them on a two-dimensional surface so that these objects appear to recede from view in a manner similar to our direct perceptual experience of the world. The degree to which perspective might or might not accurately reflect that experience is not my concern; I am interested in perspective only as a set of rules for the artist's practice. De Bry's employment of these rules in the *Report* is not rigorous—even at his most stridently perspectival, we will not find all orthogonals meeting at a single vanishing point on the horizon. But this is not to say that the rules of perspective, when not followed strictly, cease to regulate illusionistic representation. When all is said and done, it is still the perspective system, understood in the broadest sense, that secures the possibility of reference in de Bry's engravings. Perspective is the foundational visual paradigm of the *Report*—one so dominant, so naturalized, that we tend to forget its artificiality and feel it superfluous even to point out its presence in pictures such as de Bry's Algonquian village (Figure 32). Represented from a bird's-eye perspective, the architecture, crops, and human activities that make up *The Towne of Secota* are all carefully arranged and brought within the beholder's visual command through the logic of the perspectival grid. In another case, to be considered in more depth in the following chapter, an Algonquian tomb housing the corpses of dead chiefs is placed within a perspectival structure that subjects to the most rational scrutiny an idolatrous practice that would have been seen by its Protestant audience as the height of pagan irrationality (see Figure 45). In both instances it is the binary structure of the perspective system—its function as the rule of measurement that mediates between an individual viewing subject on the one hand, and the world as referent on the other—that constructs and maintains the ideological divide between a host of binaries crucial to the *Report's* coloniological project: self versus world, Europe versus America, rational versus irrational, civil versus savage.

These binary oppositions are not simply constructed by perspective, they are *delineated* by it. Perspective is a rule of *lines,* lines that measure space (orthogonals and transversals) and lines that trace borders separating bodies from the measurable space that surrounds them (contours). "Perspective," writes Giovanni Paolo Lomazzo in a 1598 English translation of the *Trattato dell'arte della pittura,* "(being subordinate to Geometry & as it were the daughter thereof) *is a science of visible lines:* So that the subject therof is *a visible line.*"[45] As a science of the line, linear perspective in effect codifies a standard myth of painting's origins. Recorded in Pliny and Quintilian, and retold frequently (in words and later in pictures) from Alberti through the Romantics, this story locates the origins of painting in an act of tracing an outline around a shadow.[46] Pliny's version, for example, tells the story of a Corinthian maid who traces the shadow of her lover on a wall. The story does not, to be sure, describe the origins of perspective per se, and indeed the simple tracing of a shadow betrays either ignorance or rejection of perspective's illusion of spatial recession. But we should remember that this classical story served as an account of origins, and for the early modern artist the tracing of a shadow constituted the essential first step toward the more elaborate linear system of perspective.[47]

During the eighteenth century, Pliny's version of the story became a popular subject for pictorial works. An important early example appears as the frontispiece for the second English edition of Charles-Alphonse Dufresnoy's *The Art of Painting* (1716) (Figure 33).[48] The designer and engraver of this work, Simon Gribelin—an artist who earlier had copied de Bry's engravings from the *Report* for an eighteenth-century account of Virginia[49]—pictures Cupid guiding the hand of the maid as she traces the outline of her lover's shadow. The frontispiece offers us an image of painting's primitive foundations through a medium particularly well suited to displaying those foundations; for the engraver, like the Corinthian maid, practices an art of the line. Engravings such as Gribelin's anticipate John Ruskin's notion that the most primitive of all the visual arts is engraving precisely because it is a *linear* art.[50] To a certain

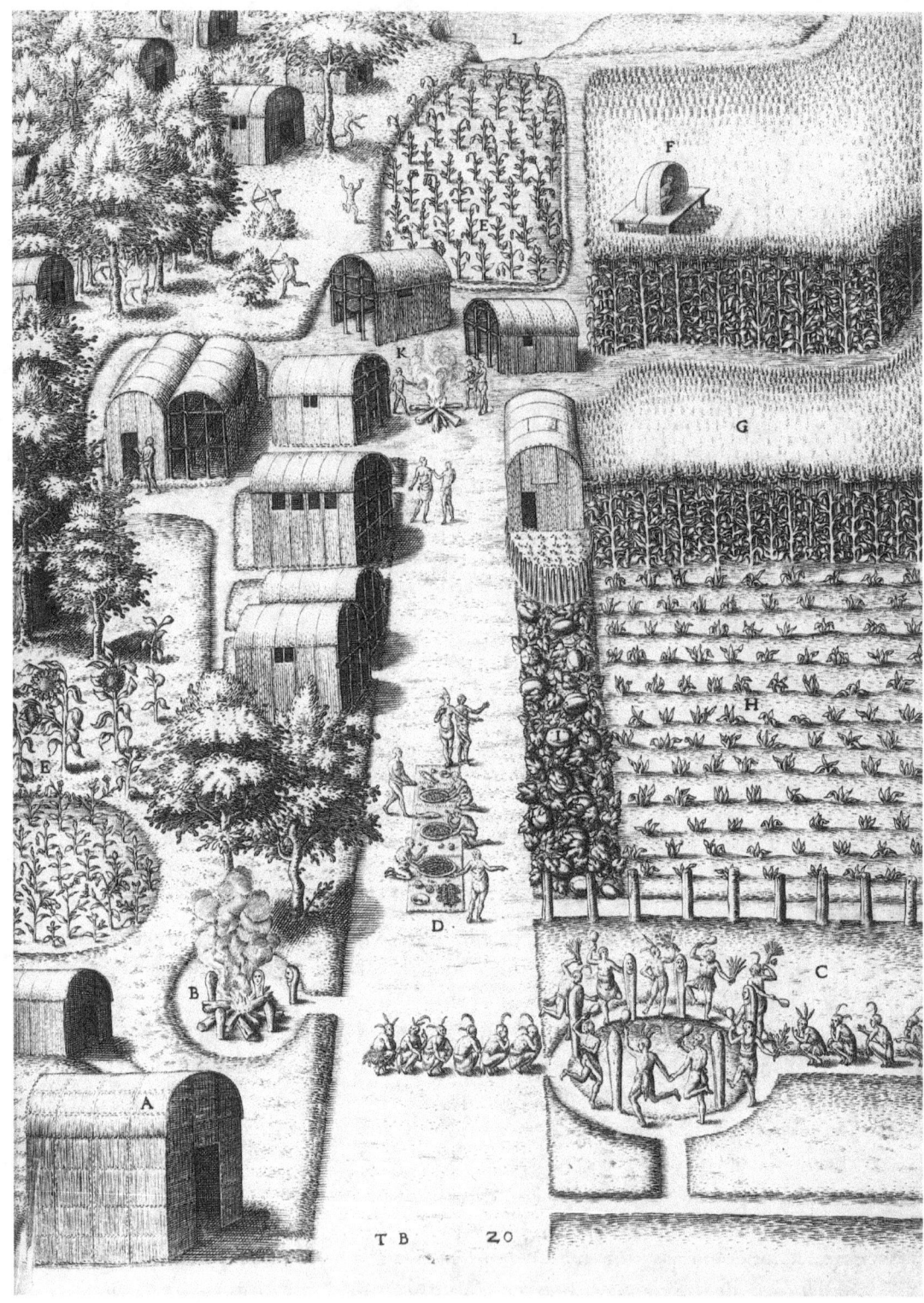

Figure 32. Theodor de Bry after John White, *The Towne of Secota*, from *A Briefe and True Report*. Courtesy and with permission of British Library G.6837.

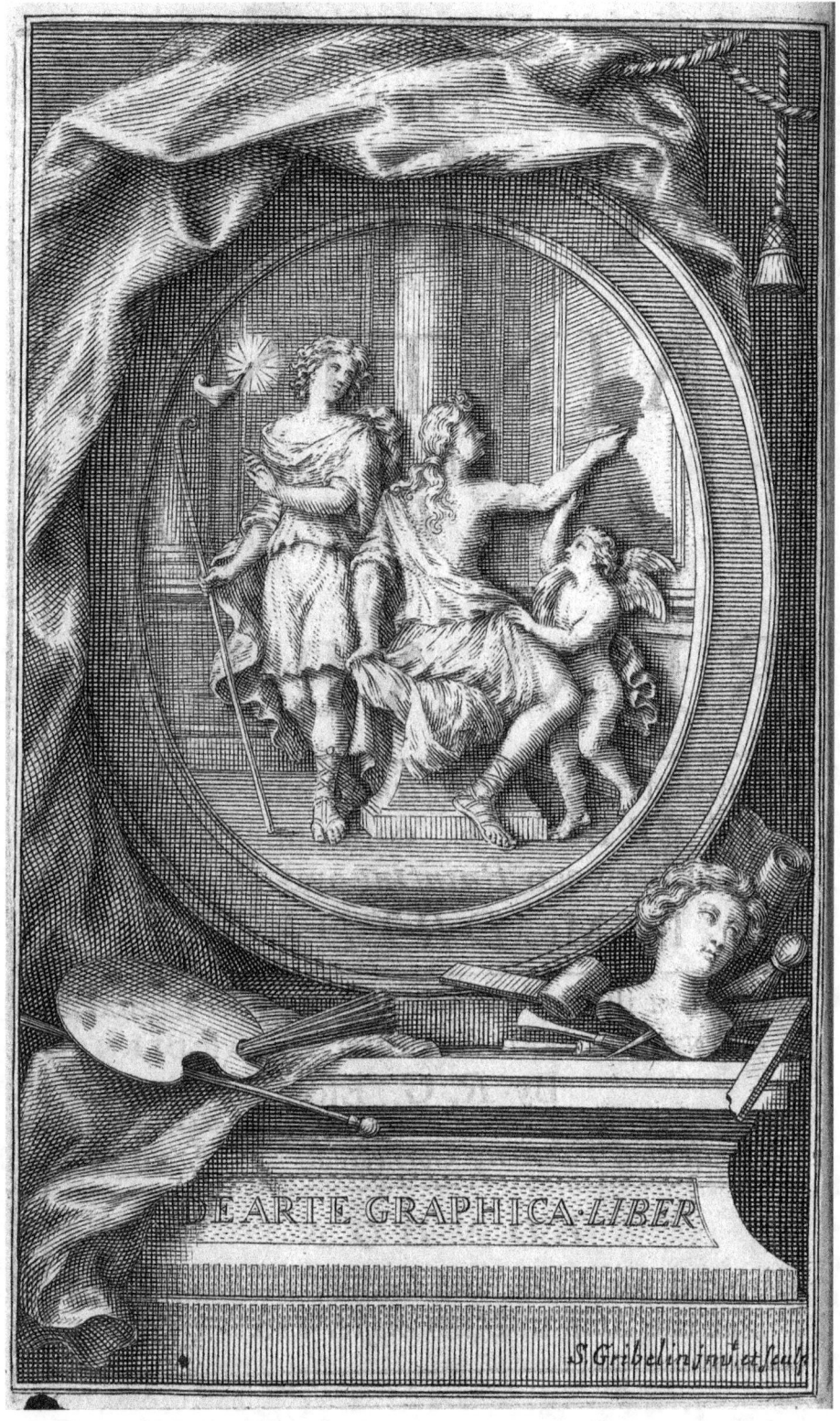

Figure 33. Simon Gribelin, frontispiece to Charles-Alphonse Dufresnoy, *The Art of Painting* (London, 1716). From the Collections of the University Libraries, University of Minnesota, Minneapolis.

extent this idea is implicit in the engraving of the tattooed Algonquian warrior discussed in the previous chapter, an image that should be read as a New World version of Gribelin's origin myth (see Figures 5, 16). As his stylus-like arrows meet the edge of his shoulder, this Virginian enacts a fantasy of self-origination through the tracing of his own contour; representation is born in an act of self-delineation by a tattooed savage who engraves his own flesh.[51] As both de Bry's and Gribelin's myths suggest, the effort to produce an illusion of the New World through engraving is a foundational exercise in circumscription.

But what of those more intangible aspects of the New World—the inscrutability of Native American religious practices, for instance, or the uncertain future of the Virginia colony as an object for investment? What of this deferred content that eluded the engraver's net of rationality, that could not be captured by an outline and set into measurable space, that could not, in short, be made to signify within the rules of the perspective system? I do not raise these questions to ask where in the engraving we might locate these unknowns: I have already suggested that the formlessness of de Bry's smoke provides a space for such projections and thus for the constitution of the viewer's own subjectivity. I ask these questions, rather, in order to begin considering the structural role that de Bry's smoke might play vis-à-vis the perspective system, for the kinds of ambiguous readings this smoke provokes—readings grounded in uncertainty, doubt, speculation—are precisely the kinds of meaning perspective will not admit. The formlessness of smoke serves as a negation of the perspective system: smoke is not any particular meaning but instead signifies all that cannot be contained by contours and orthogonals. By approaching de Bry's smoke in this way we can begin to grasp its semiotic function as the indefinable remainder of the perspective system (a function that must be understood as being prior to any attempt to *read* smoke). Smoke is the exception that defines the rule, the excluded term that makes it possible for perspective to cohere *as* a system. The concept that can help us account for de Bry's smoke, so conceived, is /cloud/.

In his *Theory of /Cloud/,* Hubert Damisch proposes a structuralist theory of visual representation in which the depiction of clouds in works of two-dimensional art has since the Renaissance played a constitutive role in the perspective system. By placing the word *cloud* between forward slashes, Damisch means to designate it as a signifier only, a pictorial graph isolated from any content a viewer might attach to it. Understood at this level, /cloud/ becomes a crucial term that establishes both the limits and the possibilities of generating meaning within perspectival representation. Damisch's theory is based on the basic semiological insight that meaning is produced through a system of exclusions. Perspective, in other words, can make meaning out of certain things—those that lend themselves to shape and contour, such as the architectural forms of canoes and tree trunks or the architectural form of the human body—but it can only define such elements because it excludes other things within the realm of visual experience that resist such codification, such as nebulous clouds and smoke. As Damisch writes, perspective can only know things that occupy a place and the contour of which can be defined by lines. But the sky does not occupy a place, and cannot be measured; and as for clouds, nor can their outlines be fixed or their shapes analyzed in terms of surfaces. A cloud belongs to the class of "bodies without surfaces," as Leonardo da Vinci was to put it, bodies that have no precise form or extremities and whose limits interpenetrate with those of other clouds.[52]

In the full passage cited by Damisch, Leonardo also notes that smoke belongs to this class of "bodies without surfaces."[53] Now clouds and smoke may not have definable surfaces, but the fact remains that they do appear quite frequently in Western art—and after all I am arguing that smoke takes up an inordinate portion of de Bry's plates in the *Report*. But the very regularity with which the motif occurs should alert us to the fact that more is at stake with clouds and smoke than their descriptive value. They carry out an essential semiotic function, establishing the limits on which representation is founded.

Precisely because of their critical role in marking the limits of signification, clouds became an important means for artists to point toward, while still refusing to depict, all that the new representational system of the Renaissance could not acknowledge. Dürer, for example, put them to work in the fifteen woodcuts of his *Apocalypse* (1498), an illustrated book de Bry would certainly have known and a work that in its introduction of /cloud/ into the new print medium stands as an important antecedent to de Bry's smoke. Based on the mystical imagery of the Book of Revelation, the *Apocalypse* addresses an impossible subject for the naturalistic artist: the unveiling of God's kingdom on earth. The novelty of Dürer's approach was to confront this challenge by "representing" God's invisible kingdom as the end of representation itself, as may be seen, for instance, in the way the artist depicts clouds in the *Vision of the Seven Candlesticks* (Figure 34). As Panofsky notes, the highly naturalistic candlesticks appear in perspective, supported by weight-bearing clouds. These same clouds, however, confound the logic of this very space as they "develop into what resembles vertical columns of smoke, weightless and unrestrained by the rules of perspective."[54] Dürer's smoky clouds thus affirm and at the same time deny rationalized space. Located at the cusp of the representational system, both defining that system's domain and resisting incorporation into its linear order, /cloud/ serves as a powerful means for Dürer to provide viewers access to the unrepresentable. For the first time in the history of Christian art, writes Damisch, the "the eruption of heaven on earth was conveyed, at the level of the system, by a rent in the very order of depiction, or representation."[55]

By the late sixteenth century the strategy introduced into the printed image by Dürer had become a common one. De Bry himself employs smoke as a means of opening a space of scriptural revelation within the representational image. In his depiction of Noah's sacrifice that serves as the frontispiece to the second book of *America* (1591), Noah kneels before his burnt offerings as plumes of smoke rise into the air and finally unfold into the tetragrammaton, the unpronounceable four letters of God's

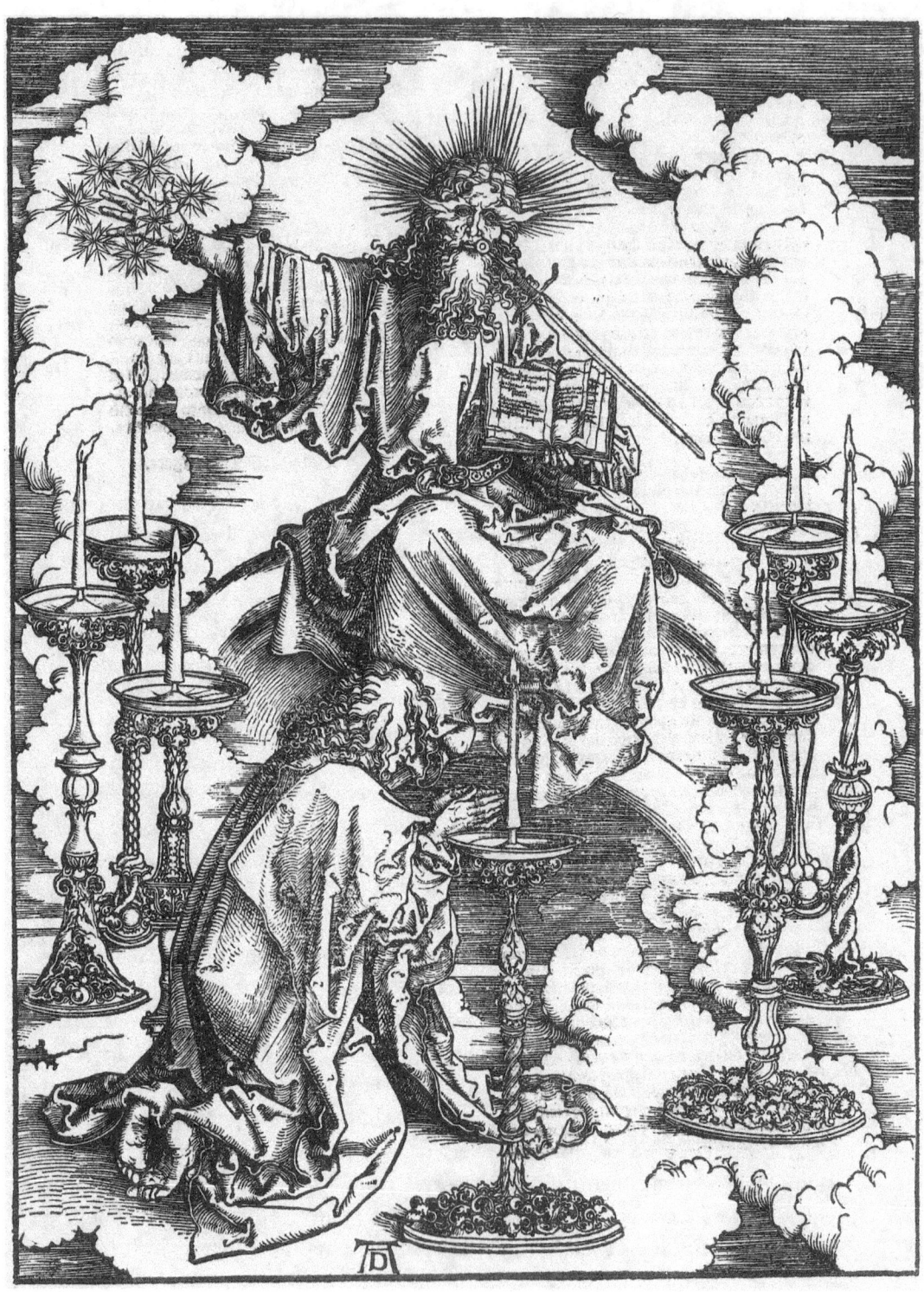

Figure 34. Albrecht Dürer, *Vision of the Seven Candlesticks,* from *The Apocalypse,* 1497–98. The Minneapolis Institute of Arts.

name (Figure 35). The spatial ambiguity of this column of smoke and its attendant rainbow (the sign of God's new covenant with Noah) designates an order of knowing that stands in stark contrast to the trail of naturalistically rendered animals that makes an orderly, two-by-two procession through perspectival space on the left-hand side of the print and to the architectural structures being built by Noah's sons on the right-hand side, structures that are critical in defining the perspectival space of the picture. More so than with Dürer, however, it is the materiality of the indexical lines of de Bry's smoke—tightly bunched, perfectly parallel, fastening our eyes on the linear patterns on the surface of the engraving even as the landscape recedes from view—that announces this disruption of perspective by the Word.

Coming on the heels of the Virginia plates, the engraving of Noah's sacrifice directly recalls the smoking fires of the Algonquians. The typical Protestant viewer would not, of course, have been likely to imagine the name of God rising from the Virginians' fires; but it is precisely the flexibility of /cloud/, its role as a structural element independent of any fixed iconography, that allows its significance to shift from context to context, from the heavenly to the demonic. In any case, I have not introduced Damisch's notion of /cloud/ for the sake of clarifying *what* de Bry's smoke might

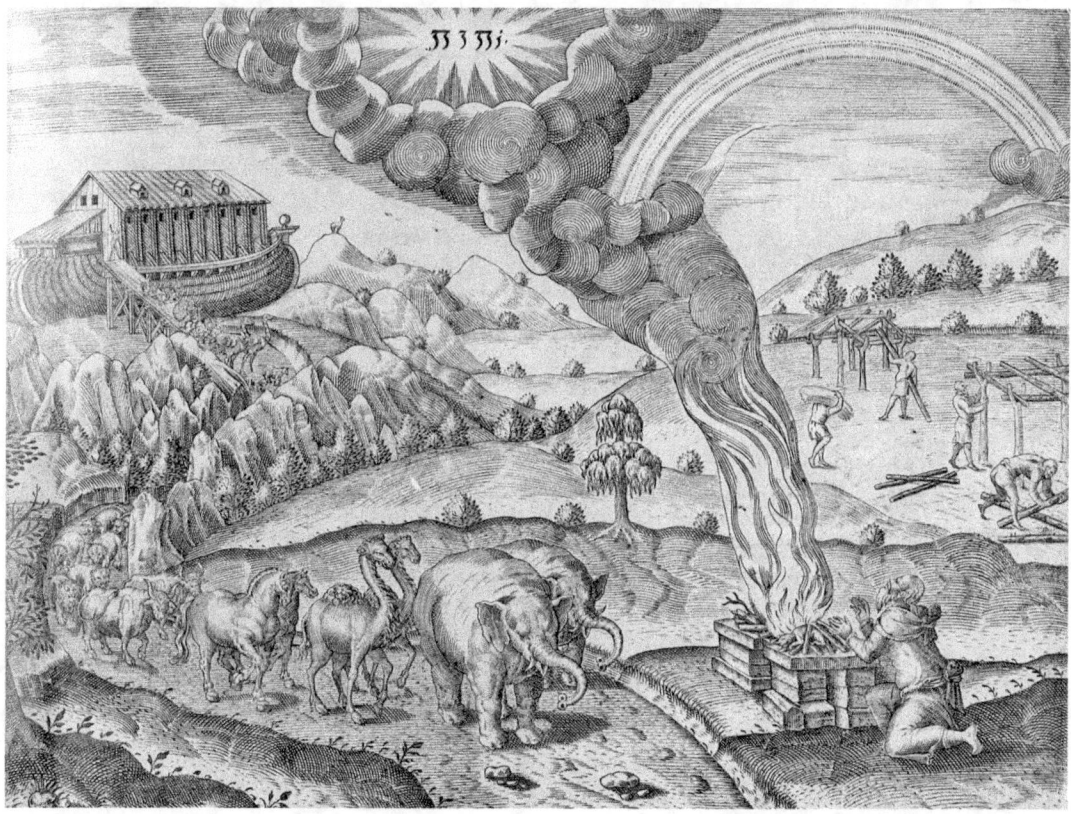

Figure 35. Theodor de Bry, *Noah's sacrifice,* frontispiece to *America,* part 2 (Frankfurt am Main, 1591). From the Collections of the University Libraries, University of Minnesota, Minneapolis.

signify but rather *how* it might signify. /Cloud/ allows us to situate the plates of the *Report* within a historical framework that operates, to use Damisch's phrase, "at the level of the system." What is at stake in de Bry's smoke, in other words, is the history of representation itself and its role in the work of New World discovery. Understood on a semiotic level, the billowing residue of the savage's fire is the residue of the representational system through which early modern Europe attempted to lay claim to an unknown land. It is therefore important in writing the history of Europe's pictorial response to the New World that we give this smoke its due, that we acknowledge the critical disruption in meaning that it marks. To do so is to understand that the cultural work of engraving the New World—the work of assimilating it line by line to the system of representation—was not only a matter of rendering that world visible, but also of marking the limits of its visibility.

Grotesques

Smoke is not the only visual element in the *Report* that marks these limits. In the margins of the text we come across another kind of linear ornament that recalls de Bry's smoke but belongs to a distinct ornamental tradition, one that emerged in fifteenth- and sixteenth-century Italy alongside Renaissance naturalism, and that indeed relies on that naturalism as the reference point for its subversive play. The tradition is that of grotesque ornament, and in the *Report* it takes the form of the printer's ornaments placed before and after sections of printed text (see Figures 37, 41, 42). Composed of hybrid beasts, disembodied faces, and a variety of vegetal and abstract patterns, these woodcut ornaments, a common feature of early modern books, are the sort of decorative, peripheral matter that readers are accustomed to passing over in printed books. We tend to look on such ornaments, if we choose to look on them at all, with an antiquarian's interest—as admirable, perhaps, for lending a certain aesthetic appeal to the text, and possibly as a means for attributing a book to a particular printer's workshop, but finally as a form of surface decoration that has nothing to tell us about the content of the book itself. But if we approach these grotesques with eyes conditioned by de Bry's smoke, they begin to take on a critical, defining role within the *Report*'s representational project. And because grotesques, unlike smoke, draw upon a sophisticated ornamental language tied to classical, medieval, and Renaissance visual traditions, they can lead us to a fuller understanding of how the ornamental remainder of the *Report* served a specifically *civilizing* function. By providing a locus for certain types of grotesque imagery that de Bry's audience identified with the savage, imagery that was opposed in fundamental ways to the carefully circumscribed world of illusionistic representation, de Bry's printer's ornaments confined "primitive" ways of seeing to the margins where, precisely as ornament, they could be emptied of significance.

To understand this civilizing work, it is necessary to understand something of the peculiar history and visual language of Renaissance grotesques. This form of ornament first became popular in the early sixteenth century, not long after the rediscovery around 1480 of Nero's Golden Palace and its decorative frescoes.[56] Dubbed *grotteschi* because they were found in the cave-like rooms, or grottos, of the partially buried palace, these ancient Roman frescoes were characterized by graceful symmetrical designs incorporating a wide variety of motifs—vegetable, animal, human, mythological, etc.—often combined into striking hybrids. While sixteenth-century Italian artists explored the possibilities of this new ornamental grammar in the form of wall and ceiling decoration, grotesques were quickly popularized across Europe through the printed image, first in works by Italian engravers and later by Northern European engravers like de Bry.[57] The first sheet of de Bry's *Grotisch fur alle Kunstler* displays features typical of Renaissance grotesques: a two-dimensional armature of festoons, vases, and rinceaux, the latter appearing here in the form of scrolling cornucopias; the employment of animal motifs, in this case, birds, monkeys, squirrels, and insects; the inclusion of masks or faces; and the incorporation of other ornamental traditions such as the strapwork designs that frame the three cartouches (see Figure 24).

Most mechanically reproduced grotesques, including de Bry's *Grotisch fur alle Kunstler,* were not conceived as prints for the collector but rather as source material for other artisans (de Bry calls them grotesques for "all artists" *[alle Kunstler]*), who incorporated the engraved designs into a variety of media: three of the most popular destinations for printed grotesques were metalwork, architectural decoration, and embroidery. De Bry's own designs were most likely intended for metalwork, although there is one documented case of his grotesques having served as models for seventeenth-century plasterwork decoration in a Scottish castle.[58] Another important application of printed grotesques was, of course, the printer's ornament. Whether it was de Bry or another artist who actually designed the ornaments for the *Report* is uncertain.[59] What we do know is that over the course of his career the engraver and publisher of this book put a good deal of effort into the design, engraving, and publication of grotesques. De Bry clearly took grotesque ornaments seriously, and perhaps therefore, as readers of de Bry's book, we should do the same.

Grotesques, as Randle Cotgrave defines them in his *Dictionarie of the French and English Tongves* (1611), are "Pictures wherein (as please the Painter) all kind of odde things are represented without anie peculiar sence, or meaning, but onely to feed the eye."[60] Taking grotesques seriously means taking seriously this senselessness.[61] Like de Bry's smoke, grotesques require us first to be ornamental, not simply for the sake of "feeding the eye" on their senseless play, but so that we might grasp the important cultural work grotesques performed precisely through this play. It was a work that involved incorporating elements from the wider culture, and in the process emptying them of "anie peculiar sence, or meaning." A strapwork grotesque designed by Marcus Gheeraerts and published in Antwerp by Philips Galle sometime in the last quarter of the sixteenth century can serve as a case in point (Figure 36). Titled *America,* the engraving puts on display exotic human and animal figures culled from a variety of sources, including two Inuits at the lower corners, based on watercolors by John White.[62] At the center of the design stands an allegorical figure of America, her

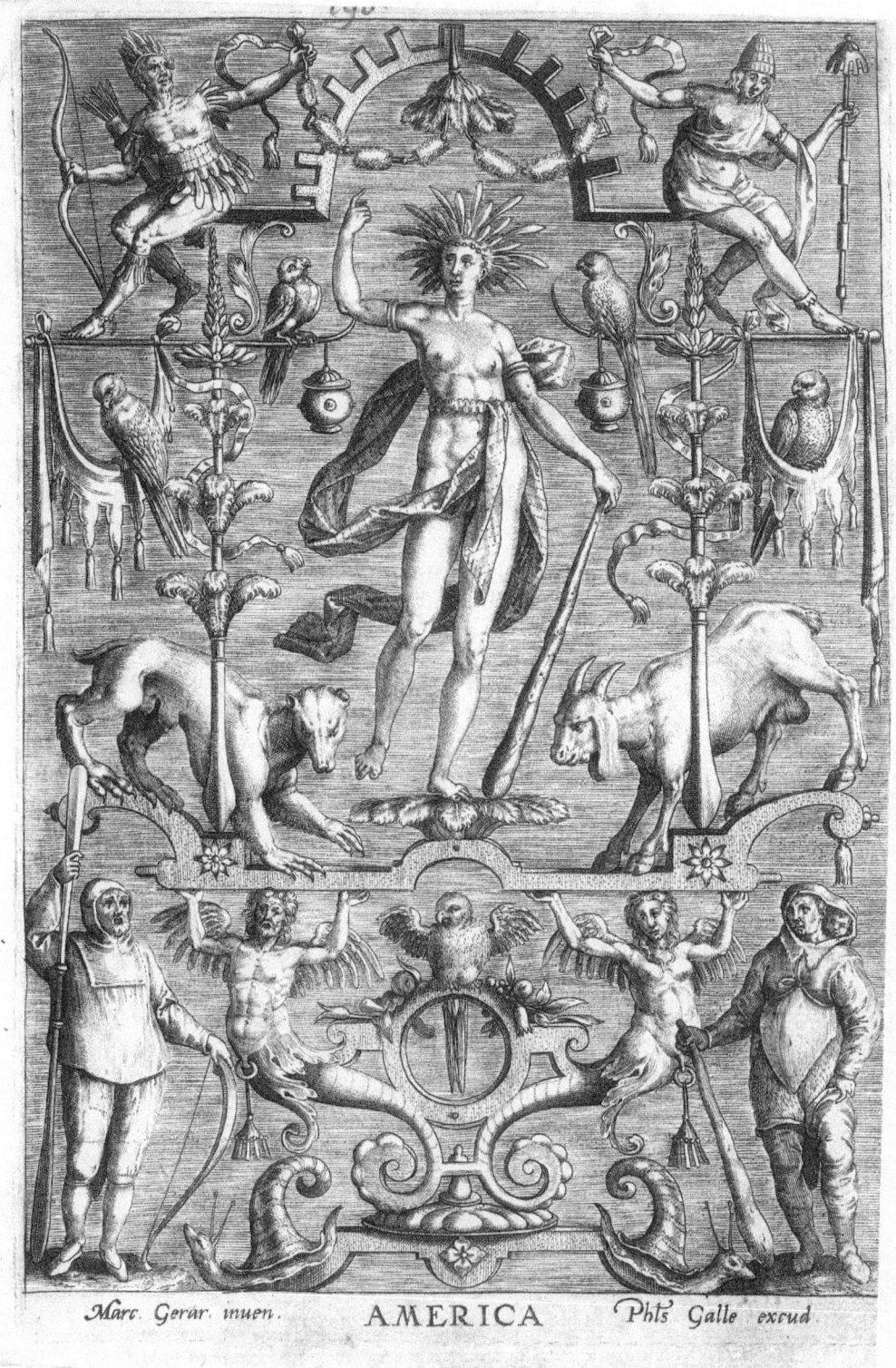

Marc. Gerar. inuen.　　AMERICA　　Phls Galle excud

Figure 36. Philips Galle after Marcus Gheeraerts, *America*, late sixteenth century. The Metropolitan Museum of Art,
Gift of the Estate of James Hazen Hyde, 1959 (59.654.55). Photograph from The Metropolitan Museum of Art;

right hand and index finger raised as if she were about to instruct the viewer in the meaning of the New World. Although the print is often labeled an allegory of America, it would be a mistake, as well as a futile interpretive exercise, to attempt to decipher a coherent allegorical message here. The irony (perhaps even the intentional joke) of America's tutorial gesture is that precisely because she is reduced to an element in an ornamental grotesque, she is unable to deliver on her promise. Within the ornamental world of grotesques—and this is why they proved to be particularly well suited to absorbing exotic elements—there is no pressure to name.[63] The domain of grotesques is an extralinguistic domain; as one scholar has recently put it, the grotesque "accomodates the things left over when the categories of language are exhausted; it is a defense against silence when other words have failed."[64] The failure of language before the wonder of the New World was a note regularly sounded in the sixteenth century, and grotesques offered an aesthetic mode uniquely adapted to preserving this experience; it was a mode for holding meaning—just as grotesques hold their gravity-defying figures—in suspension. In this sense, grotesques share a basic logic with the Renaissance collection, a logic wherein curious objects are accumulated not in order to classify the world according to familiar categories, but, to the contrary, in order to maintain its strangeness.[65]

One of grotesques' chief formal means for subverting the impulse to name and classify, and one of their most enduring features, is the hybrid. Grotesques are filled with chimeric forms such as the winged figures whose lower bodies fuse with scrolling strapwork at the base of Gheeraerts's design; the freedom to invent fantastical figures such as these made the practice of grotesques irresistible to many artists, while for others, from Vitruvius and Horace through counter-Reformation critics, it represented an unforgivable breach of decorum.[66] At any rate, whether it was seen in terms of the liberated imagination or as aesthetic violation, the grotesque hybrid insinuated itself throughout the ornamental margins of Renaissance culture. One hybrid element that appears regularly in grotesques, and that we find in a headpiece used on several pages of the *Report*, is the motif of the dolphin (Figure 37). As their tongues and tails merge into leafy tendrils and strapwork, these dolphins demonstrate the essential ambivalence of grotesques—the quality of being both one thing and another at the

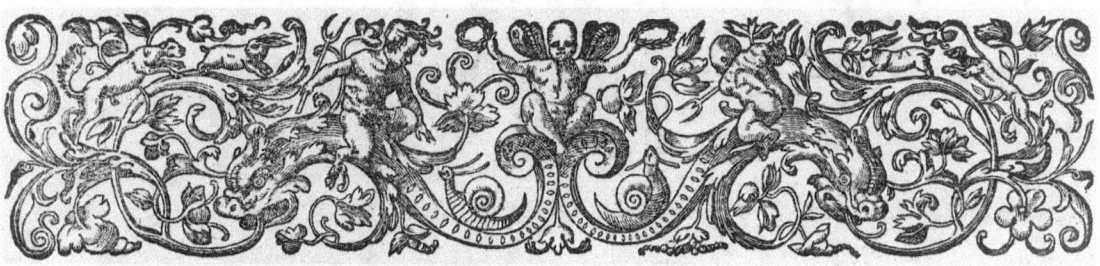

Figure 37. Headpiece, from *A Briefe and True Report*. Courtesy and with permission of British Library G.6837.

same time. Upon the back of one of the dolphins rides a young satyr (already a hybrid), holding a trident and apparently ready to take aim at the snail beneath him; but his wisps of hair, his trident, and his cloven hoof fuse with the surrounding vines—he is pure decoration. So while it is true that this ornament includes a hint of narrative content and while it is true that these dolphins, satyrs, and snails are on some level representational, the ambivalence of grotesques lies precisely in the way they raise the possibility of meaning, the possibility of figures in space carrying out actions, only to pull back and transform what we thought was a dolphin into acanthus scrolls, what looked like a snail hunt into linear decoration. All elements of grotesques are in this sense hybrids as they waver, like the lines of de Bry's smoke, in between ornamental and representational duties. Delighting in the confusion of categories, the printer's ornaments of the *Report* respond to a subversive impulse entirely foreign to the ethnographic function of de Bry's illustrated plates, in which the clear distinction among types is precisely the point.

However opposed in their essential visual logic, the grotesque ornaments and the representational plates of the Report are at the same time, by virtue of their opposition, inextricably linked. While grotesques often appear independently, they nevertheless must be understood—like their medieval counterparts, the drolleries of Gothic manuscripts—as a form of marginal art, an art that takes its meaning from its relation to a norm that, in its turn, is only conceivable in relation to its cast-off margins.[67] The norms that serve as the unavoidable points of reference for Renaissance grotesques are the conventions of naturalistic representation. According to André Chastel, grotesques depend on two laws: "the negation of space and the fusion of species." The "domain of grotesques," he writes, is "the antithesis of that of representation, whose rules are defined by the 'perspectival' vision of space and the distinction and characterization of types."[68] Chastel is here essentially repeating, in a more pictorial language and without a tone of condemnation, the classical Vitruvian position that grotesques are against nature: "Such things," writes Vitruvius, "neither are, nor can be, nor have been."[69] The pleasure of viewing grotesques is the pleasure of seeing the rules of naturalistic representation invoked, only to be flaunted: we take delight—safely within the confines of the margins—in watching a contour leave its appointed task of circumscribing a three-dimensional body and meander off to take up a new and purely decorative life in a scroll of foliage. Grotesques offer us a surreal world, a world of constant flux. It is not surprising therefore that sixteenth-century writers, when they undertook the difficult task of finding a language that could account for grotesques, chose to compare them to clouds.[70] Like clouds, grotesques are the airy, ethereal stuff of dreams, the leftovers of naturalism. In their own way, then, grotesques constitute a species of /cloud/: a nothing in themselves, they give birth to meaning elsewhere, in the spatial and taxonomical coherence of the perspective system.

Unlike clouds, however, grotesques incorporate a wide range of visual imagery, and in doing so they provide a fascinating commentary on just what it is that perspectival representation leaves behind in the ornamental margins. In these margins we find a world inhabited by primitive forms, irrational hybrids that remind us of a time when a more superstitious people invested visual images with supernatural force. Early modern commentators suggested as much when they drew connections between grotesques and indigenous art forms of the Americas, from the Franciscan Motolinía's assessment in the sixteenth century that "before [the Conquest], they [Mexican painters] knew how to paint only flowers, birds, and all kinds of grotesques, and if they painted a man or a horse, it was so ugly that it resembled a monster," to the Jesuit Lafitau writing in the early eighteenth century about the grotesque habits of the Iroquois. In one of the plates from *Customs of the American Indians* Lafitau places the figure of an American Indian, derived from one of de Bry's plates and ornamented with a false tail and horned headgear, alongside two satyrs derived from ancient monuments. In his text Lafitau compares Iroquois customs of bodily ornamentation to these antique hybrids with horns and tails who "have no reality and owe their existence only to the poets' imagination, to the hieroglyphic writing of the first times [i.e., grotesques], and the ignorance of later centuries."[71]

It was thus not only the antinaturalism of grotesques that provoked disapproval, but their proximity to the pagan/primitive. During the nineteenth century, this tendency to identify the marginal art of grotesques with a barbarous state of existence developed into a tendency to link ornamental forms *in general* with the most primitive art forms. Such evolutionary interpretations of ornament reached their apogee at the end of the century when Austrian architect Adolph Loos baldly stated that "The lower the cultural level of a people, the more extravagant it is with its ornament, its decoration. . . . To see decoration as a sign of superiority means to stand at the level of the Indians."[72] No one would have made the connection between savagery and ornament quite this explicitly and emphatically in early modern Europe, and Loos's views cannot, of course, be separated from the impact of evolutionary theory during the nineteenth century or from turn-of-the-century debates surrounding the decorative arts. Nevertheless, his comments do point us to a critical aspect of the ornamental grotesque: we must take seriously the possibility that in the grotesques decorating the margins of the *Report* de Bry's Protestant viewers would have found traces of a primitive visual vocabulary, remnants—now absorbed into the most sophisticated of ornamental styles—of a pagan past from which these viewers felt themselves increasingly distant. The *Report,* after all, is a book that seeks to create this distance, going so far as to draw a direct link between the savages of Virginia and those of a British past.

One of the crucial markers of this primitive condition beyond which the viewer has presumably progressed, a marker found in both the printer's ornaments of the *Report* and on the bodies of de Bry's British savages, is the apotropaic face. In the final section of the *Report,* de Bry presents us with his collection of ancient Picts and Britons who "haue bin in times past as sauuage as those of Virginia." The first of these savages, and the most fearsome of the group, is a Pict whose body is painted from shoulders to ankles with monstrous hybrids of all sorts (Figure 38). Located on his

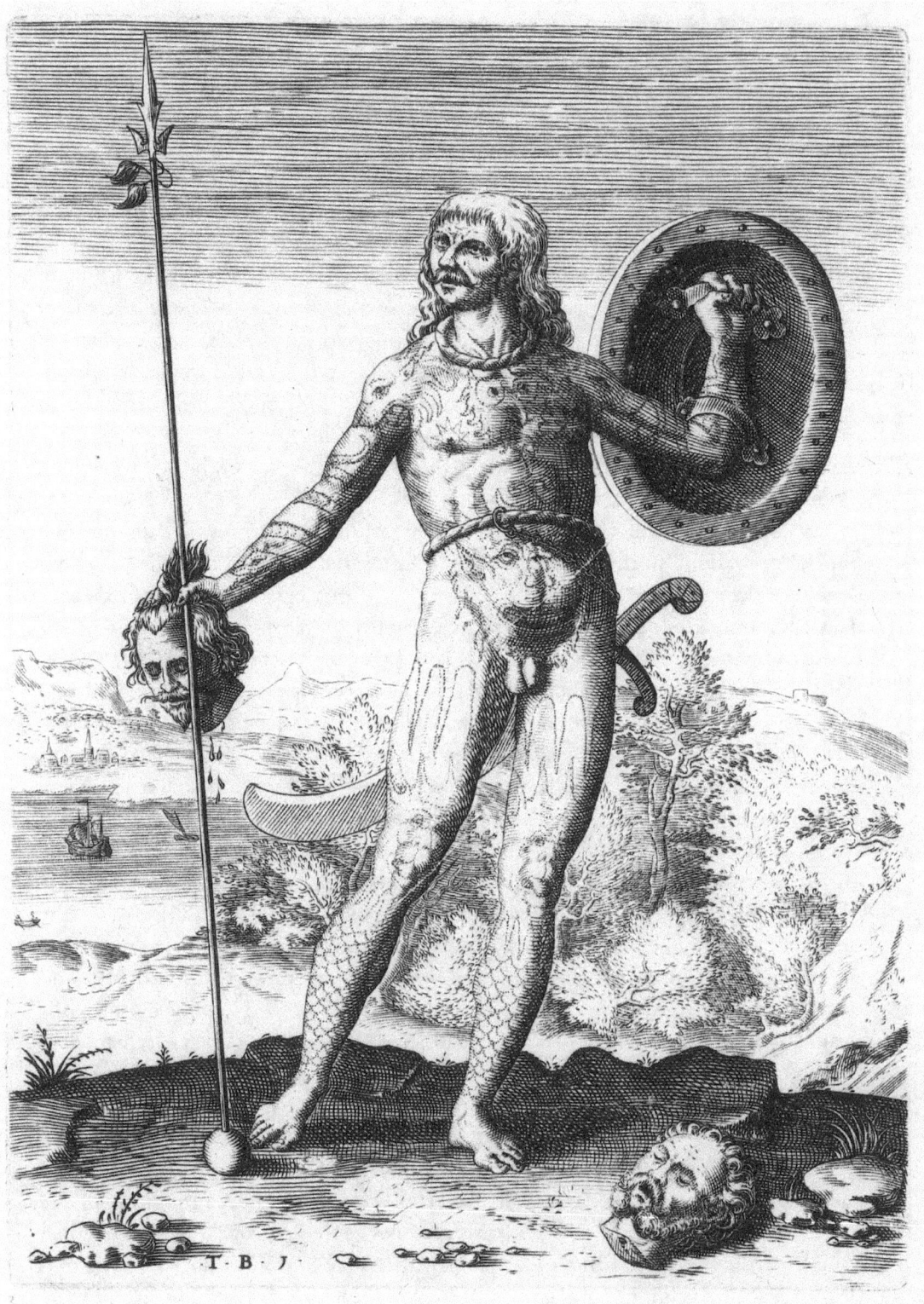

Figure 38. Theodor de Bry after John White, *The trvve picture of one Picte,* from *A Briefe and True Report.* Courtesy and with permission of British Library G.6837.

chest, belly, shoulders, and knees are grotesque faces whose purpose must have been recognized by early modern viewers as a means of magical protection against enemies. Harriot describes the Pict's bodily ornamentation in the caption:

> In tymes past the Pictes, habitans of one part of great Bretainne, which is nowe nammed England, wear sauuages, and did paint all their bodye after the maner followinge. . . . vppon their breast wear painted the head of som birde, ant about the pappes as yet waere beames of the sune, vppon the bellye sum feerefull and monstreus face, spreedinge the beames verye fare vppon the thighes. Vppon the tow knees som faces of lion, and vppon their leggs as yt hath been shelles of fish. Vppon their Shoulders griffones heades, and then they hath serpents abowt their armes.[73]

The description reads like a formula for designers of grotesques. In de Bry's engraving, which is based on an even more striking watercolor by White (Figure 39), the savage body itself becomes a grotesque, as its limbs and appendages merge with and emerge from the fantastical creatures painted on its surface. The two heads on the Pict's torso, which include an owl (traditionally a creature of ill omen) and a diabolical lion's head, fulfill the function of the protective gorgon heads commonly found on both ancient and Renaissance armor.[74] Indeed the Pict's grotesque bodily ornament seems to be derived from fifteenth- and sixteenth-century designs for fanciful, theatrically inspired armor, like that which protects the body of Carlo Crivelli's *St. George* (1472; Figure 40); and it is entirely possible that White based the design of his own figure on theatrical armor from the Elizabethan theater.[75] For the Pict, however, the absence of actual armor suggests that painted flesh has itself become a defensive shield, a form of protection, through the efficacy of the image alone, against the Pict's enemies.

But it is also essential to recognize that in leaving the printer's ornament and entering the realm of representation the grotesque takes on an entirely new significance. The tail, for instance, that hangs from the backside of de Bry's tattooed warrior, its point of attachment just hidden from view by the quiver, may exhibit some of the playfulness of the ornamental grotesque hybrid but its most basic function in the illustration is to identify this figure with a primitive state that plays loosely with distinctions between the human and nonhuman (see Figure 5). In this "true picture" of a Virginian, where we must have meaning, the subversiveness of grotesque ornament is contained—its potential threat to the perspective system is defeated—by means of its objectification. In this case and in the case of the decorated Pict, the grotesque is primitivized as a quality of the savage for the simple reason that the savage mind is itself supposed to be grotesque, that is to say, irrational and invested in the magical rather than in the representational power of the image. And so the savage paints his body with terrible faces, imagining that they help him in battle and protect him from his enemies. "When they go to battel," Harriot writes of the Virginians, with whom we are expected to compare the grotesque Pict, "they peynt their bodyes in the most terible manner that thei can deuise."[76]

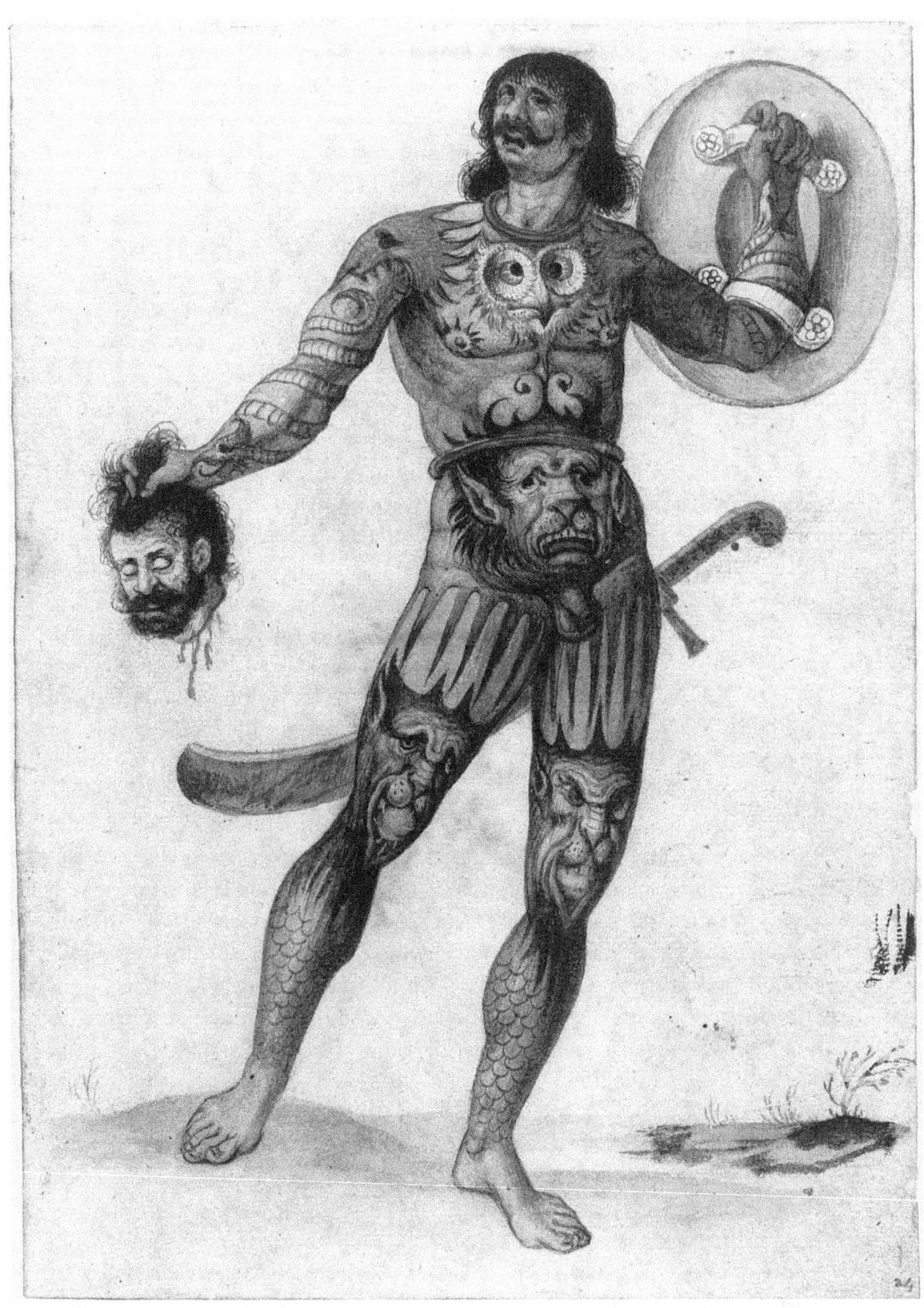

Figure 39. John White, *Pictish Man,* watercolor on paper, c. 1585. Copyright Trustees of The British Museum.

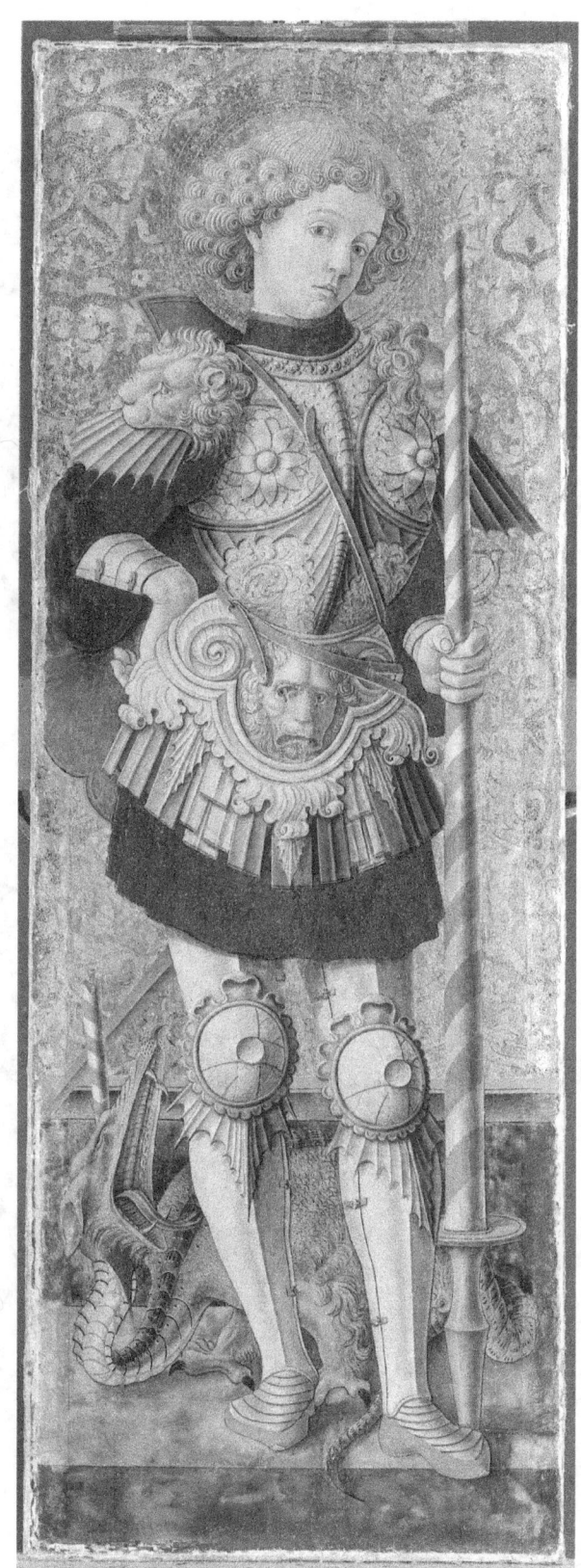

Figure 40. Carlo Crivelli, *St. George,*
tempera on wood, 1472. The
Metropolitan Museum of Art,
Rogers Fund, 1905 (05.41.2).

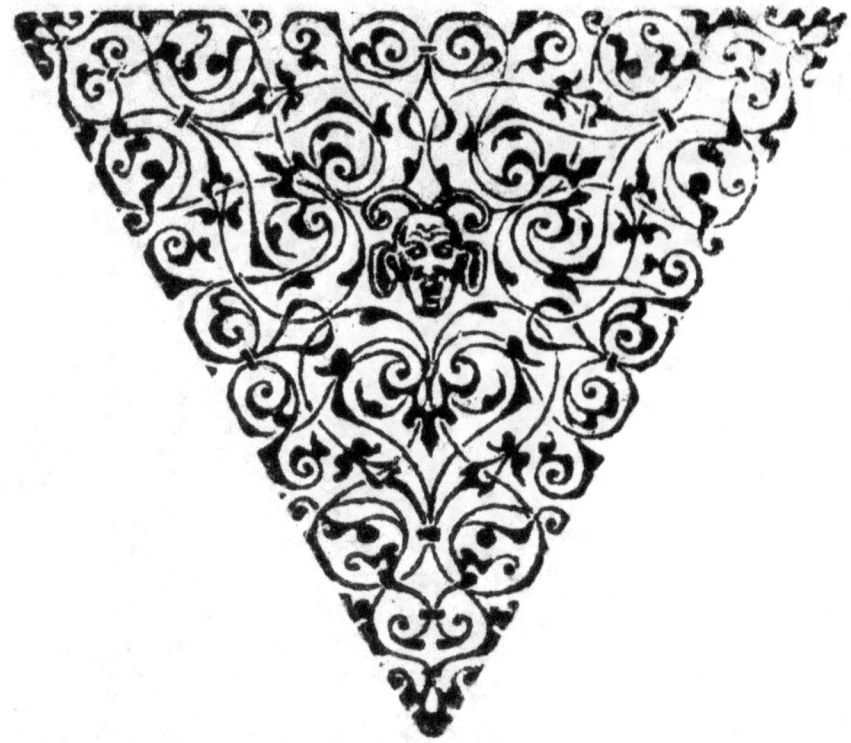

Figure 41. Tailpiece, from *A Briefe and True Report*. Courtesy and with permission of British Library G.6837.

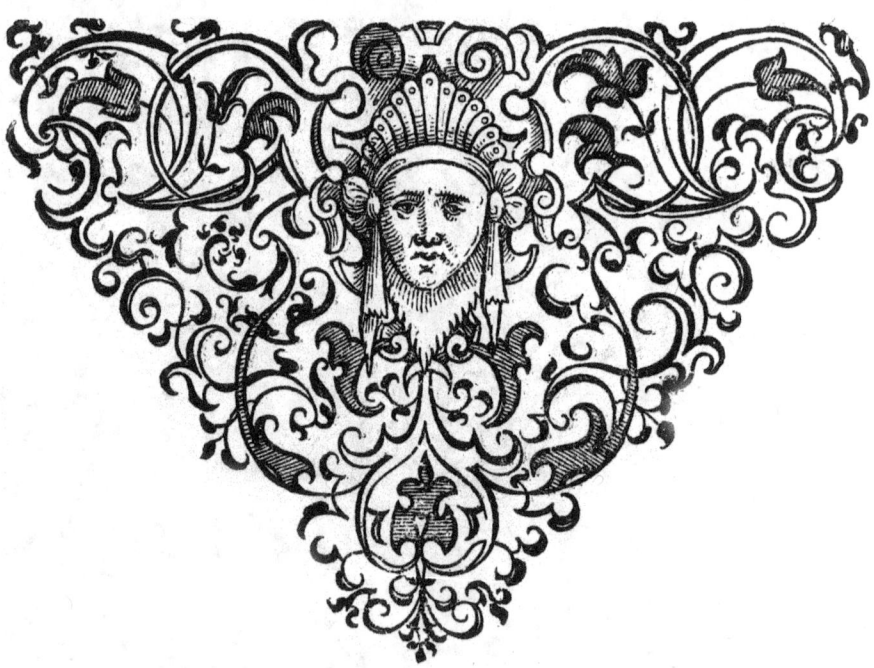

Figure 42. Tailpiece, from *A Briefe and True Report*. Courtesy and with permission of British Library G.6837.

On the page opposite de Bry's Pict, a grotesque printer's ornament—a tailpiece consisting of a tiny, scowling gargoyle surrounded by delightful arabesques—stares us in the face (Figure 41). Through the Middle Ages, gargoyles quite openly served, like the faces on the Pict, as protective images. The juxtaposition of this ornamental gargoyle and the Pict's bodily grotesques is therefore of some interest as an implicit commentary on the meaning (or meaninglessness) of grotesques, and it would seem to confirm Ernst Gombrich's argument that medieval drolleries and Renaissance grotesques display the vestiges of the apotropaic image.[77] We encounter a similar situation with another tailpiece, one that along with the gargoyle tailpiece is employed numerous times throughout the Report (Figure 42). At the center of this slightly larger ornament is a head surmounted by a crown of stylized palmettes, a common motif in Renaissance grotesques (de Bry often includes such heads in his grotesque designs) and one that was originally inspired by the apotropaic antefixes placed along the roofs of Etruscan temples.[78] Incorporated into grotesques, such motifs preserve the memory of the image whose function is, in Gombrich's phrase, one of "protective animation"; but of course there is little possibility of the gargoyle's face being taken seriously by the viewer in the way the Pict seems to take his own grotesques seriously. Within the pictorial arts of a civilized and Protestant society, products of human fancy are not, or at least are not supposed to be, animated by supernatural forces. Grotesques thus migrate from their central role among savages and pagans into the domain of pure ornament, where they cannot by definition have "anie peculiar sence, or meaning."

Still, the juxtaposition of these two pictorial instances of the grotesque, even if they occupy antithetical pictorial orders, should give us cause to wonder: How distant is the grotesque face that decorates the page from the grotesque face that protects the body? What would constitute the line between the *containment* of the magical image within the margins and the *survival* of pagan magic within the pages of a printed, Protestant text? This is an impossible line to draw because containment and survival are two sides of the same coin: the printer's ornaments banish magic to the peripheries while at the same time serving as the living trace of that same magic. And so even as it is being civilized this grotesque remainder continues to mark the possibility of an alternative relation to the image. Indeed one can imagine without too much difficulty how protective animation might operate just below the surface of the *Report*. De Bry's tailpiece, after all, performs a function not unlike the grotesques of the Pict, insofar as de Bry finds himself in a publishing situation where he is in need of his own protective devices. As we saw in the previous chapter, de Bry attempts to shield himself from counterfeiters with the apotropaic claim that "dyuers secret marks lye hiddin in my pictures, which wil breede Confusion vnless they bee well obserued."[79] The statement grows out of a publisher's anxiety about protecting his investment after it is released to a public over which he has no control. The condition I mentioned earlier—that of publishing for an open market in which meaning itself was largely a production of the reader—raised fundamental difficulties for printers, publishers, and authors who wished to maintain authority over their texts and images. It is not, therefore, entirely unreasonable to think of a printer's ornament, a mark of identity and even owner-ship,[80] as an image carrying the memory of a magical function, a function that a pub-lisher could not and perhaps would not want to make so fully *other* that its apotropaic power was no longer accessible.

The *Report*'s grotesque printer's ornaments return us, finally, to de Bry's smoke, which can itself be understood as an irruption of the grotesque within the book's representational plates. The pictorial logic of grotesques is by no means limited to imagery that explicitly adopts a conventional ornamental vocabulary. Ruskin, for in-stance, found it in the monumental works of Michelangelo, in which the grotesque "is stealing forth continually in a strange and spectral way, lurking in folds of raiment and knots of wild hair, and mountainous confusions of crabby limb and cloudy drap-ery" (one thinks of the complex twists and coils of beard and fabric in the *Moses*).[81] Perhaps it is even possible, as it was in the case of the printer's ornaments, to observe a vestigial magic in de Bry's clouds of grotesque smoke. As I have already argued, an early modern viewer would have been predisposed to see the convoluted lines of de Bry's smoky burin work through the lens of magic and witchcraft, but we should not be too quick simply to displace this magic onto the superstitious practices of Europe's others. As recent scholarship on the anthropology of art has suggested, orna-mental complexity functions across cultures as a "technology of enchantment."[82] Alfred Gell in particular has demonstrated how decorative patterns can serve as a means of producing confusion in viewers who find themselves unable to bring logi-cal organization to their visual field, as in Gell's example of the ornate linear designs carved on Trobriand canoe prow-boards. Used for Kula trading (a system of ceremo-nial exchange of valuables), these prow-boards are intended to bewilder the trading partners and thus make them willing to part with their most prized items. For Gell, however, the most important aspect of the viewers' response is not their actual psy-chological confusion (which is mild) but the fact that this confusion then leads the viewer to imagine a magical power emanating from the ornamented object itself. As Gell writes, "the canoe-board is not dazzling as a physical object, but as a display of artistry explicable only in magical terms, something which has been produced by magical means."[83]

While it is commonplace within the language of art history to speak of the mag-ical skill of the virtuosic artist, Gell's anthropology shows us how we might take such metaphorical language literally. Through their power to index the hand of the artist, the ornamental lines of de Bry's smoke are, no less than the linear designs on Trobriand prow-boards, capable of holding us under their spell.[84] Linear confusion, moreover, both historically within Europe and across diverse cultures, has performed an apotro-paic function. The multiplication of twisting and turning lines in ancient ornament, for example, could serve as a means of confounding demons and malevolent spirits. In general, practices of multiplication, ornamental and otherwise, that emphasize in-determinability and confusion have been shown to be a surprisingly durable means of guarding against evil.[85] The goal in such practices is to multiply individual elements and patterns in order to "breede Confusion" (to borrow de Bry's own phrase for his engraved marks) in one's enemies. Perhaps a good candidate for de Bry's protective secret marks, then, is his smoke, with its confusing lines. These indexical markers of the engraver's own labor and authority bear a trace of a type of image we tend not to link to the practice of early modern engraving but that perhaps deserves more attention than it receives: the magical image that stares back, that refuses admittance by warding off potentially evil or envious eyes.

I do not wish, however, to press the point too hard. At the beginning of this chapter, I set the goal of arriving at an understanding of the kind of disruption presented by de Bry's smoke. This disruption, as we have seen, is the making visible of representation's remainder; it does not, however, involve the *naming* of that remainder, which should itself be understood as a kind of void, a space in which we are invited to imagine that which cannot be circumscribed by the engraver's lines, that which cannot be "said" within the order of representation. And so, while I have ended with an apotropaic reading of de Bry's smoke, it is by no means intended to be a definitive reading of a grotesque imagery fundamentally opposed to definition. Indeed, the apotraism of de Bry's smoke is precisely *not* named as such; it is instead the *savage's* ornamental marks that are seen as magical and superstitious within the emergent ethnology of the *Report.* In contrast, the magic of de Bry's ornamental smoke can only exist below the surface as a nameless element, the savage leftover of a representational system that dreams of its own civility. Rather than attempting to name de Bry's smoke, I have therefore offered certain concepts that foreground ambivalence and indeterminability and thus prove useful for talking around the unnamable—magic and witchcraft, /cloud/, the grotesque. If we choose to see this smoke for what it is—which is, finally, nothing but pure line, a spiraling and shapeless materiality—then we can begin to understand the fundamental importance of a nameless pictorial element in the early visual representation of the New World. De Bry's project needed this element, indeed *produced* it as representation's formless by-product; produced it, in other words, as smoke.

3. Flatness and Protuberance
Reforming the Image in Protestant Print Culture

Images are almost as antient as Religion itself; nor is it in the least surprizing they
should be so, since the Origin of them is owing to the Weakness of the human Mind,
which not being able to fix its Attention long on Objects purely spiritual, turns by
insensible Degrees towards Matter, and endeavours to make the Object of its
Adoration palpable, if we may be allowed the Expression, to itself.

—*The Ceremonies and Religious Customs of the
Various Nations of the Known World*

They put their faith in a thing shaped like a pumpkin.

—Hans Staden, *The True History and Description of a Country of Savages*

This chapter will explore the place of the idol in early modern ethnography. Specifically, my concern is with engraved representations of image worship within a project,
both descriptive and comparative, that aspired to make Native American religion into
an object of scientific inquiry. The issues at stake in this investigation will ultimately
hinge on the body of Christ, for the problem that body presented to an early modern
scientific culture gripped by a Calvinist antimaterialism was the problem of religion's
visibility.

"In the Middle Ages," writes Gerhart Ladner, "the central tenet of Christian theology was also the greatest justification of Christian art. It was the Incarnation which
made religious art legitimate."[1] The fact that an invisible God had assumed human
form meant that he could be accessed through the senses, chiefly the sense of sight.
To be sure, the risk of lapsing into idol worship was by no means ignored during the
Christian Middle Ages, and medieval attitudes toward idolatry as well as the impact
of those attitudes on image-making practices have their own complex history.[2] Nevertheless, artists of the Middle Ages managed to produce countless religious images,
both sculptural and two-dimensional, as they steered a middle course between their
desire for sacred images and the strictures of the Decalogue. During the sixteenth
century in England and in northern Europe, however, the incarnational logic of the

87

late Middle Ages, with its emphasis on sensual access to God, gave way to a Protestant emphasis on the purity of the Word. The production of religious images declined in reformed regions of Europe; in England they largely disappeared.[3] One type of image we do encounter more frequently in Protestant culture, however, is the type of image published by Theodor de Bry in 1590, which might loosely be termed the "ethnographic" image. A more secular form of representation, the ethnographic image reflects a growing interest in cataloging and describing the various customs and manners of an expanding world. Religion itself fell under those customs and manners, so that even as the religious image recedes from view, we witness more images, and particularly printed images, describing religions.

My present concern is with the ethnographic image that takes the idol and idol worship as its subject matter. Through what strategies, and with what success, was the *ethnographic* image capable of framing the *religious* image as an object of empirical inquiry?[4] How did a Protestant intellectual community (I shall be concerned specifically with a Calvinist community composed of English Protestant and Huguenot authors) make a central, troubling fact of its own unreformed past into the object of a visual anthropology? Perhaps the simplest way to illustrate these questions would be to consider a late medieval object of devotion, such as the Sudarium of Veronica as engraved by the Master of the Playing Cards, alongside an ethnographic image of the early Enlightenment intended to expose Catholic idolatry, such as the *Representation of two famous Shrouds* by Bernard Picart (Figures 43, 44). Here we have two similar images—one alleged to bear the imprint of Christ's face, the other of his whole body—that are diametrically opposed in meaning: one is held up as religious truth; the other as a religious deception. Did the conditions of viewing the image of Christ change so radically between the fifteenth and eighteenth centuries that nothing of the sacred remains in Picart's "secular" engraving? My contention is that a desire for the presence of Christ's body, the original motive for viewing religious images such as the Sudarium, is not entirely banished from the image *of* religion. A longing for that body remains; indeed that longing is still at the very core of ethnographic looking within Protestant visual culture.

My focus, once again, will be an engraving by de Bry first published in Harriot's *Report*. Toward the end of the *Report*'s catalog of the "true pictures and fashions" of the Virginians is a plate titled *The Tombe of their Werowans or Cheiff Lordes* (Figure 45). The image, based on one of White's surviving watercolors, presents a supremely rationalized space in which we witness the Virginians' custom of preserving and paying homage to the bodies of their deceased leaders. The scene is completely contained within a large, vaulted architectural shell, a gridded pattern of wooden supports visible on its interior walls. The outer shell, in turn, contains a second structure, an enclosed scaffold supported by ten wooden posts. Matting that should form a fourth wall to this inner sanctum has been folded back over the roof in order to display to us the secrets enclosed within. We look into the elevated tomb as if we were stationed some twenty feet above the ground level of the outer vault, a space that, judging from the height of the scaffold (nine to ten feet high, according to Harriot), rises to approximately forty feet. From this commanding position we see nine emaciated and foreshortened bodies lined up neatly across the scaffold and leading us into the depths of the tomb. As the caption on the opposite page explains, these bodies are quite literally skin and bones:

> they cutt all the flesh cleane from the bones, which the[y] drye in the sonne, and well dryed the[y] inclose in Matts, and place at their feete. Then their bones (remaininge still fastened together with the ligaments whole and vncorrupted) are couered again with leather, and their carcase fashioned as yf their flesh wear not taken away. They lapp eache corps in his owne skinne . . . and lay yt in his order by the corpses of the other cheef lordes.[5]

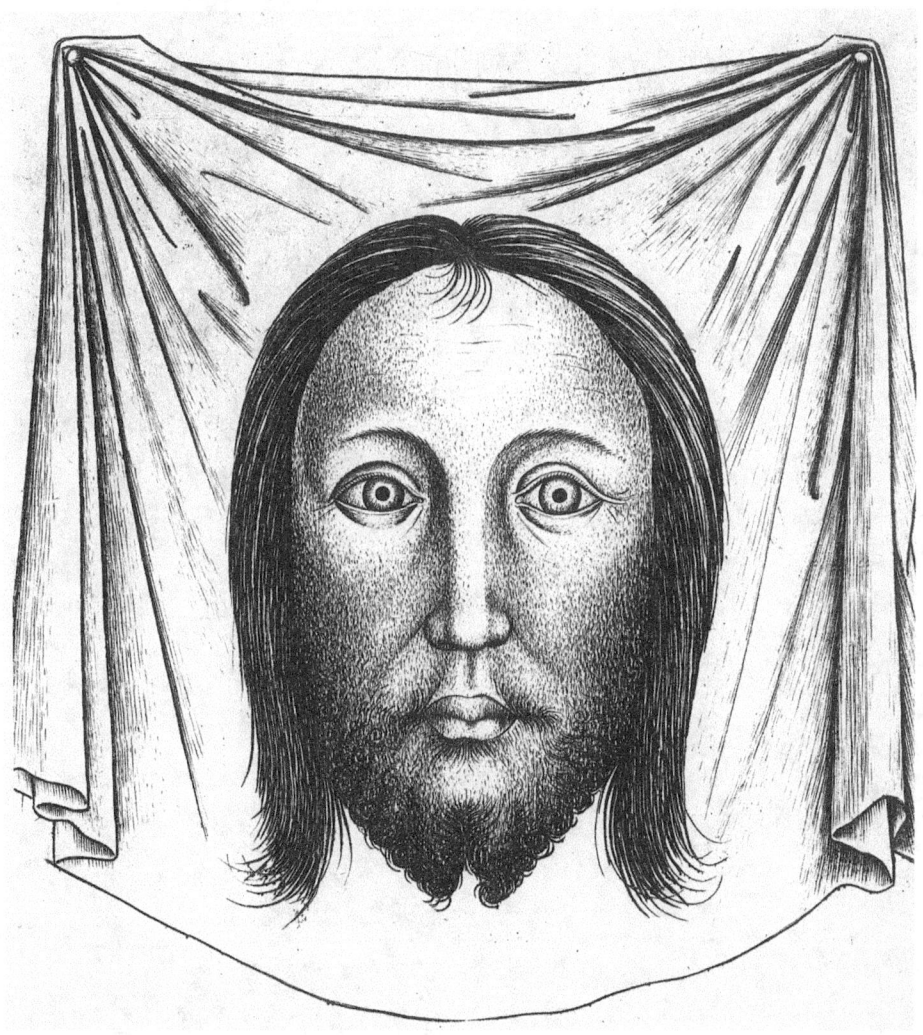

Figure 43. Master of the Playing Cards, *Sudarium*, c. 1440. Germanisches Nationalmuseum, Nuremberg.

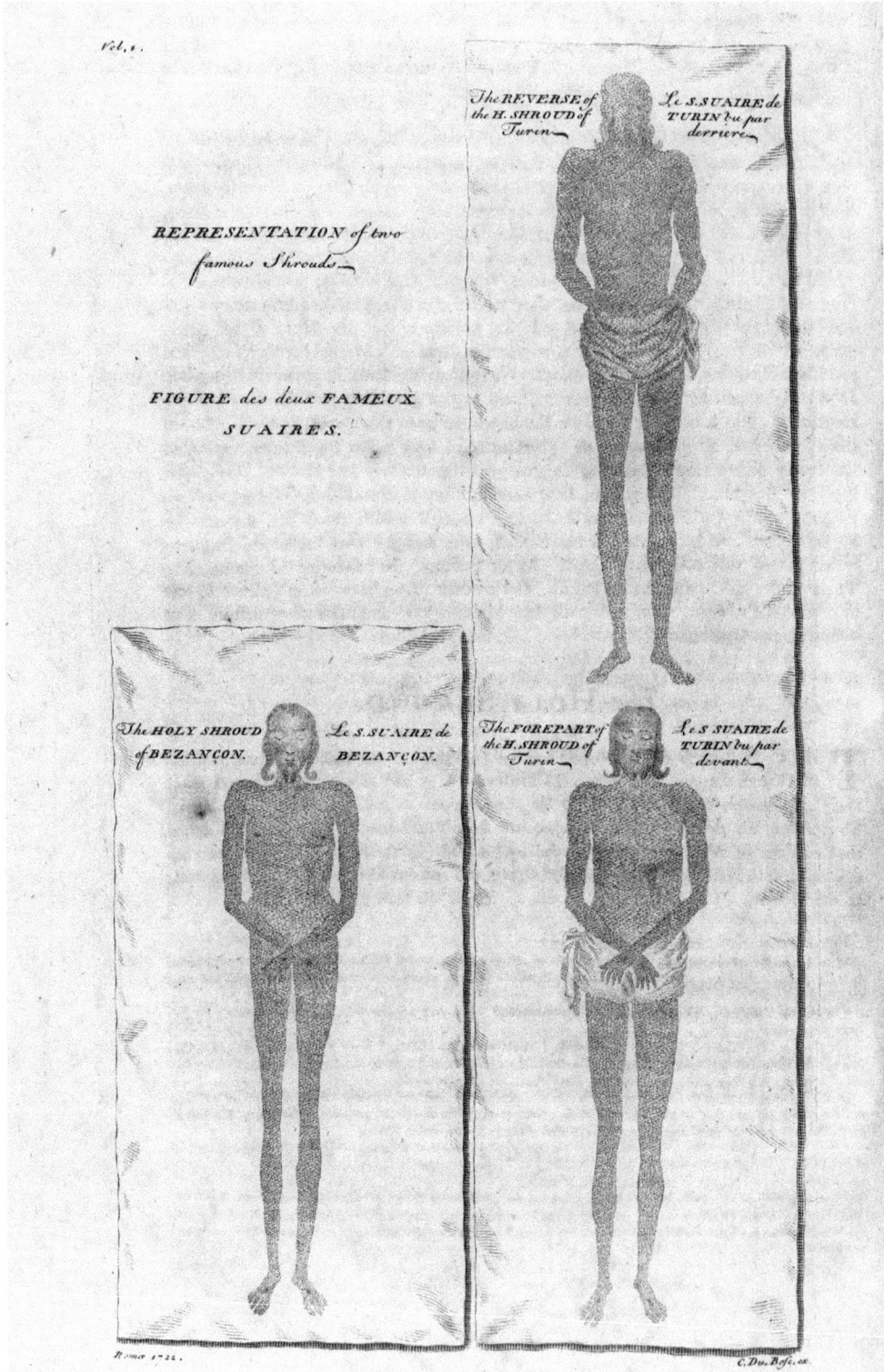

Figure 44. Bernard Picart, *Representation of two famous Shrouds,* from *The Ceremonies and Religious Customs of the Various Nations of the Known World,* volume 1 (London, 1733). Courtesy and with permission of The Rare Book and Manuscript Library of the University of Illinois, Urbana-Champaign.

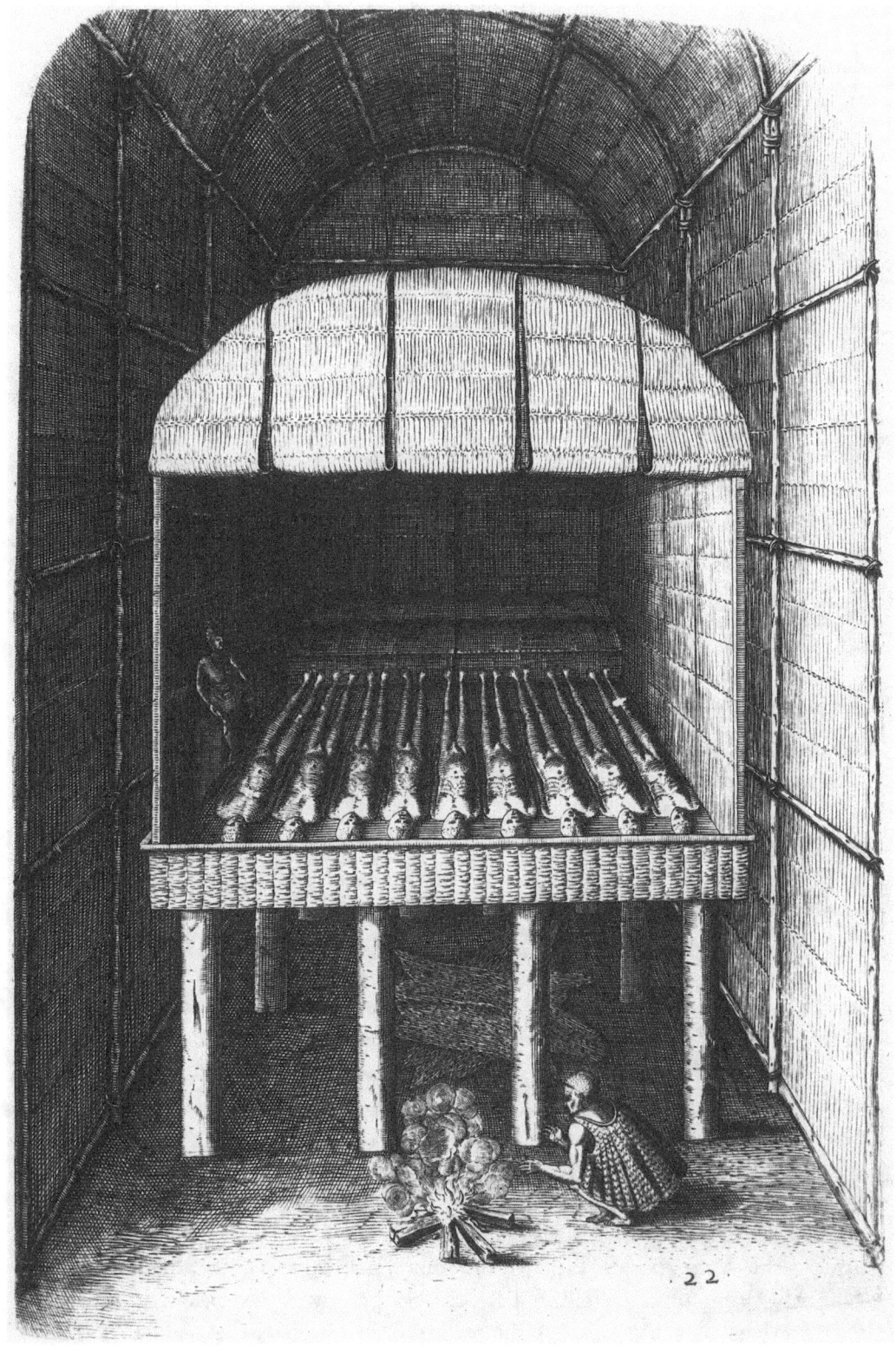

Figure 45. Theodor de Bry after John White, *The Tombe of their Werowans or Cheiff Lordes*, from *A Briefe and True Report*. Photograph courtesy of Edward E. Ayer Collection, The Newberry Library, Chicago.

On a ledge to the left of these bony relics sits an idol, a small, dark figure wearing a conical hat, hands on knees, looking out over the desiccated bodies. This is the Virginians' idol, Kiwasa, who they believe "doth kepe the dead bodyes of their cheefe lordes that nothinge may hurt them." Underneath the scaffold lay two deerskins, the bed of the resident priest. We see him crouching in the foreground before a small fire that sends up a modest cloud of smoke. Within this dim New World tomb the priest "Mumbleth his prayers nighte and day, and hath charge of the corpses."[6]

While the tomb would appear to be a private and protected space within the Virginians' society, de Bry's engraving is heavily invested in making this space transparent to the viewer. Everything has been bared to us: the obstructing fourth walls of both buildings have been removed and the most basic organizing structures—architectural, perspectival, even skeletal (the ribs of the corpses show through their skin)—have been rendered visible. Almost every line in the engraving that leads the eye into the pictorial space, from the wooden supports of the outer building to the bodies on the scaffold to the individual engraved lines themselves and excepting only the logs of the priest's fire and his deerskins, coincide with the orthogonals of the perspective structure. The effect is to reinforce the viewer's sense of transparency, the sense that the engraver, like the Virginians who prepare their chiefs' corpses, has stripped this mysterious, ritualistic space down to its barest bones. Nothing is permitted to stand as an impediment to a clear and distinct knowledge of New World religion.

The Tombe of their Werowans was one of the most widely copied and emulated of de Bry's engravings. Along with Harriot's verbal description, it is repeated, sometimes with creative improvisations, in a variety of travel accounts, atlases, and anthropological works of the sixteenth, seventeenth, and eighteenth centuries.[7] The engraving's popularity is surely due to the fact that it offers more than an isolated visual report on the New World; it displays a model for visual experience. Not only does it show us *what* can be seen in the depths of a Virginia tomb, it makes a powerful visual argument for *how* we should see this space. Indeed the skeletal structure of the tomb approaches the appearance of an instructional diagram, not unlike one of the plates from a 1653 perspective treatise by Abraham Bosse (Figure 46). In Bosse's engraving, which demonstrates how to construct the receding grid of a perspective construction on a flat and vertical surface, the perspectival viewer sits with his back to us before a self-projected linear diagram that would seem to provide the logical conclusion to de Bry's perspectivized bodies laid out on the raised platform. This schematic quality of de Bry's engraving made it readily adaptable to a variety of New World contexts, as when it was appropriated for a corner detail on John Smith's map of Virginia, engraved by William Hole in 1612 (Figure 47). Instead of holding the preserved corpses of dead chiefs, the space as depicted on Smith's map contains the Algonquian ruler Powhatan sitting on a scaffold in a Kiwasa-like pose, with text below informing us that "Powhatan held this state & fashion when Capt. Smith was deliuered to him prisoner." The perspectival viewer of de Bry's Virginia interior here becomes identified with John Smith himself in a legendary encounter of seventeenth-century English

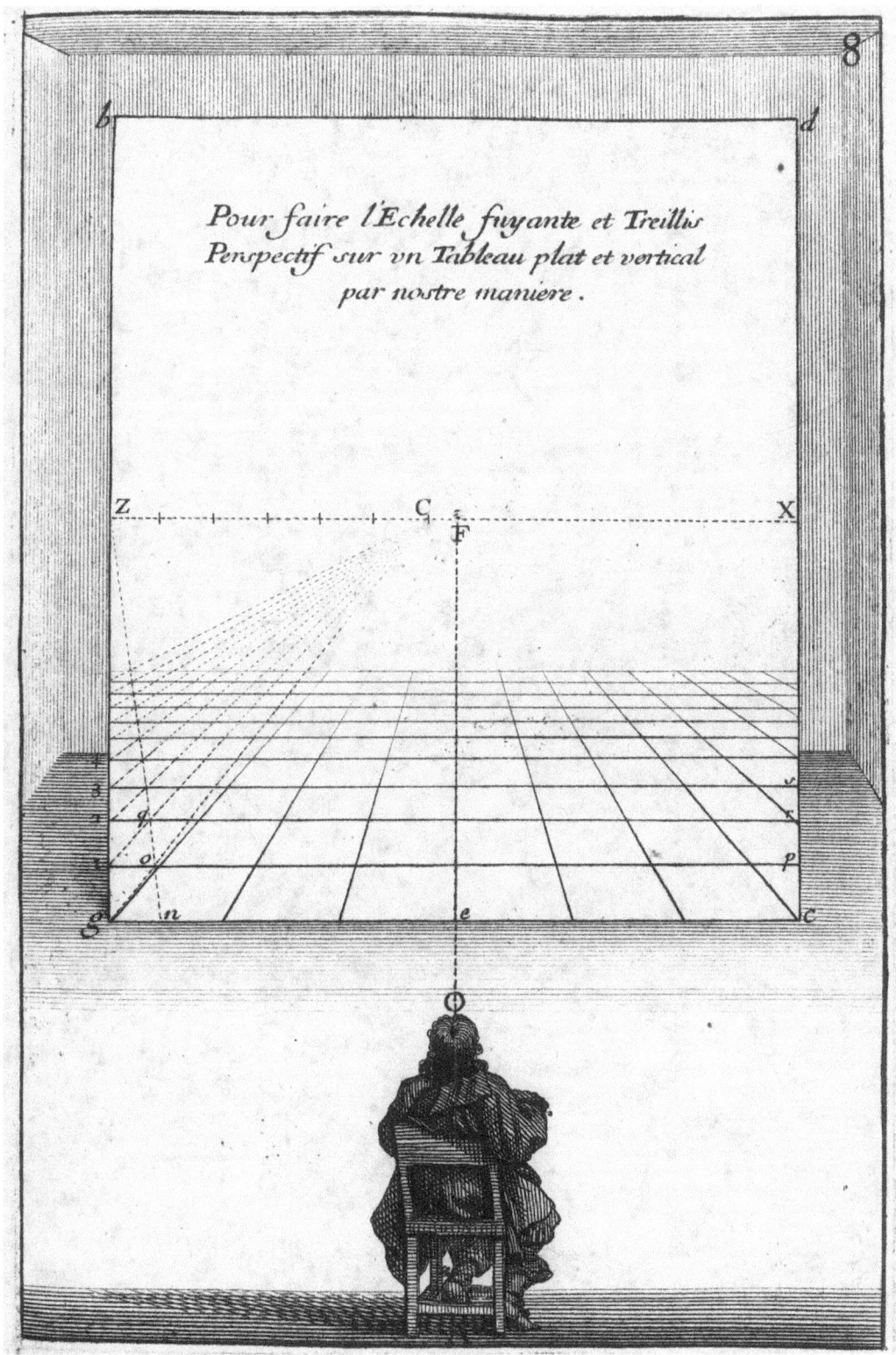

Figure 46. Plate 8 from Abraham Bosse, *Moyen universel de pratiquer la perspective* (Paris, 1653). Courtesy and with permission of The Rare Book and Manuscript Library of the University of Illinois, Urbana-Champaign.

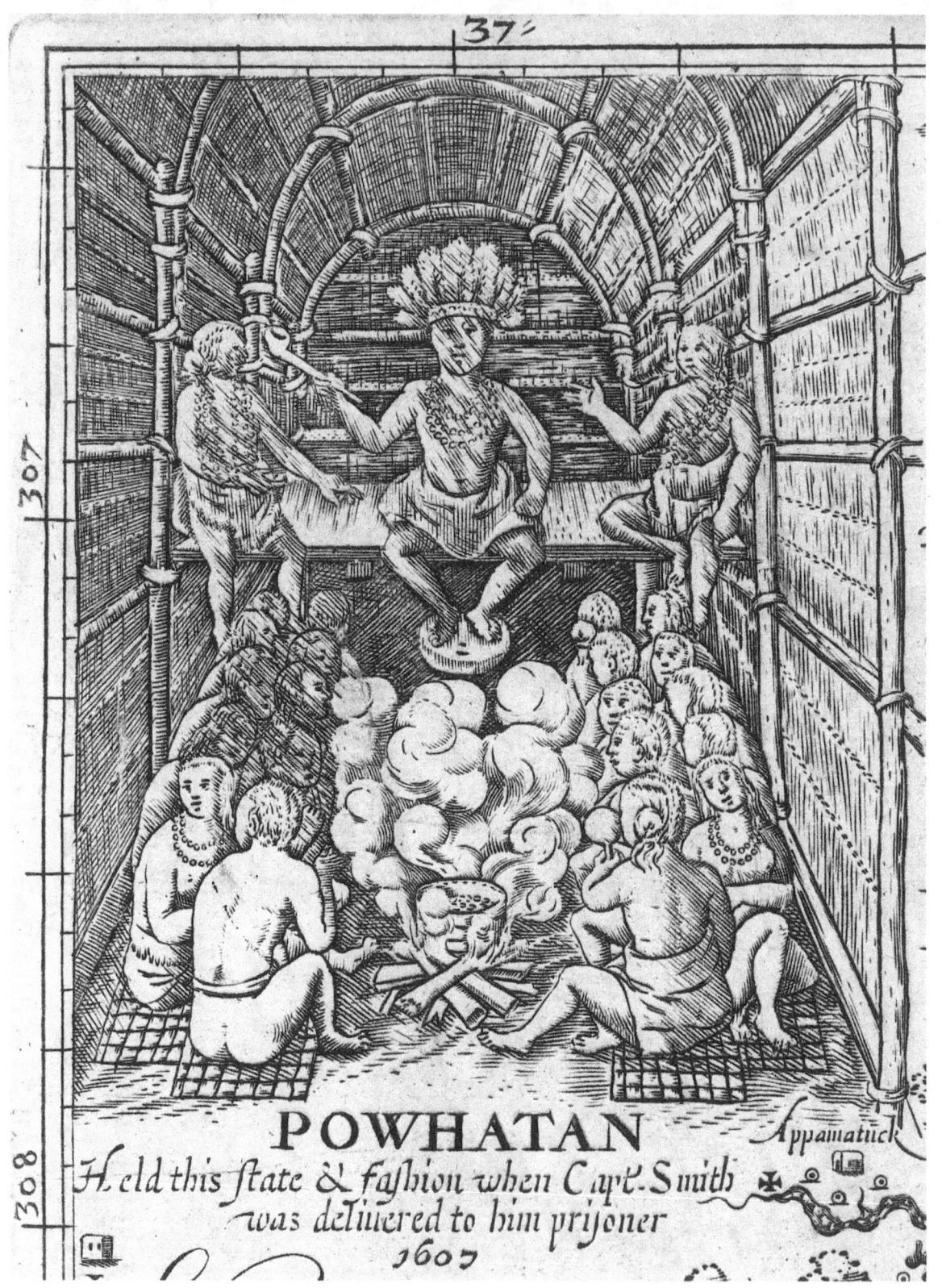

Figure 47. William Hole, map of Virginia (detail), from John Smith, *A Map of Virginia* (Oxford, 1612). Courtesy and with permission of British Library C.33.c.18.

travel literature.[8] Hole adopts the pictorial structure of de Bry's tomb because it serves as an effective framing device, one that would be repeated with some regularity in subsequent efforts to bring visual order to the New World.

For the most part, de Bry's engraving remained a space associated with efforts to describe American religious practices. One of the more faithful borrowings appears in an eighteenth-century text about which I will have a good deal more to say, *Cérémonies et coutumes religieuses de tous les peuples du monde*. Published by Amsterdam bookseller Jean Frédéric Bernard in seven large folio volumes between 1723 and 1737 and translated into English between 1733 and 1739 as *The Ceremonies and Religious Customs of the Various Nations of the Known World*, this encyclopedic account of the world's religions combines texts drawn from numerous authors with hundreds of plates designed by French Protestant engraver Bernard Picart (Picart's *Representation of two famous Shrouds* also appears in this book). Picart's *Tombs of the Virginian Monarchs*, based directly on de Bry's model and with few alterations outside a reversal of the composition, appears in the volume containing "the Ceremonies of the Idolatrous Nations" (Figure 48). For Picart and for nearly all the authors who appropriated de Bry's image for their own purposes, the chief visual attraction of this tomb seems to be its exemplarity as a space of New World idolatry.

Picart's use of de Bry's image is a particularly interesting case because it appears in a text that is at once an important anthropological work (a seminal text in the history of comparative religion) and a work that, like the *Report* almost a century and a half earlier, offers a distinctly *Protestant* perspective on New World religion. Indeed while the various authors, artists, and editors who appropriated de Bry's engraving certainly valued *The Tombe of their Werowans* as a means of rationally framing the religious practices of the New World, their treatments of this image are also of interest for the extent to which they mingle the scientific objectives of a nascent ethnology with a Calvinist suspicion of images. It was, after all, only in the recent past that the reformed circles that produced texts such as the *Report* and the *Ceremonies* ceased to pray to the sacred images of their Catholic past. In the sixteenth and seventeenth centuries, iconoclasts were still in the midst of destroying such objects. It is not at all unlikely that the dark, vaulted space of de Bry's *The Tombe of their Werowans*, containing a wooden idol and the preserved bodies of deceased ancestors, would have conjured up in the minds of its early viewers distant memories of the church crypts of pre-Reformation Europe, the types of spaces where the saints' cults had venerated the relics of *their* ancestors.[9] Any attempt to account for this representation of an Algonquian religious custom must therefore come to terms with Protestant Europe's relationship to the materiality of the sacred image. As we shall see, however distant de Bry's engraving may seem from the idol, however much it may insist on its capacity to achieve a rational perspective on the base matter that holds the savage idolater in its thrall, the ethnographic print and the idol are in the end both images. For their audiences, the difference between the two could therefore only be a difference of degree, not of kind.

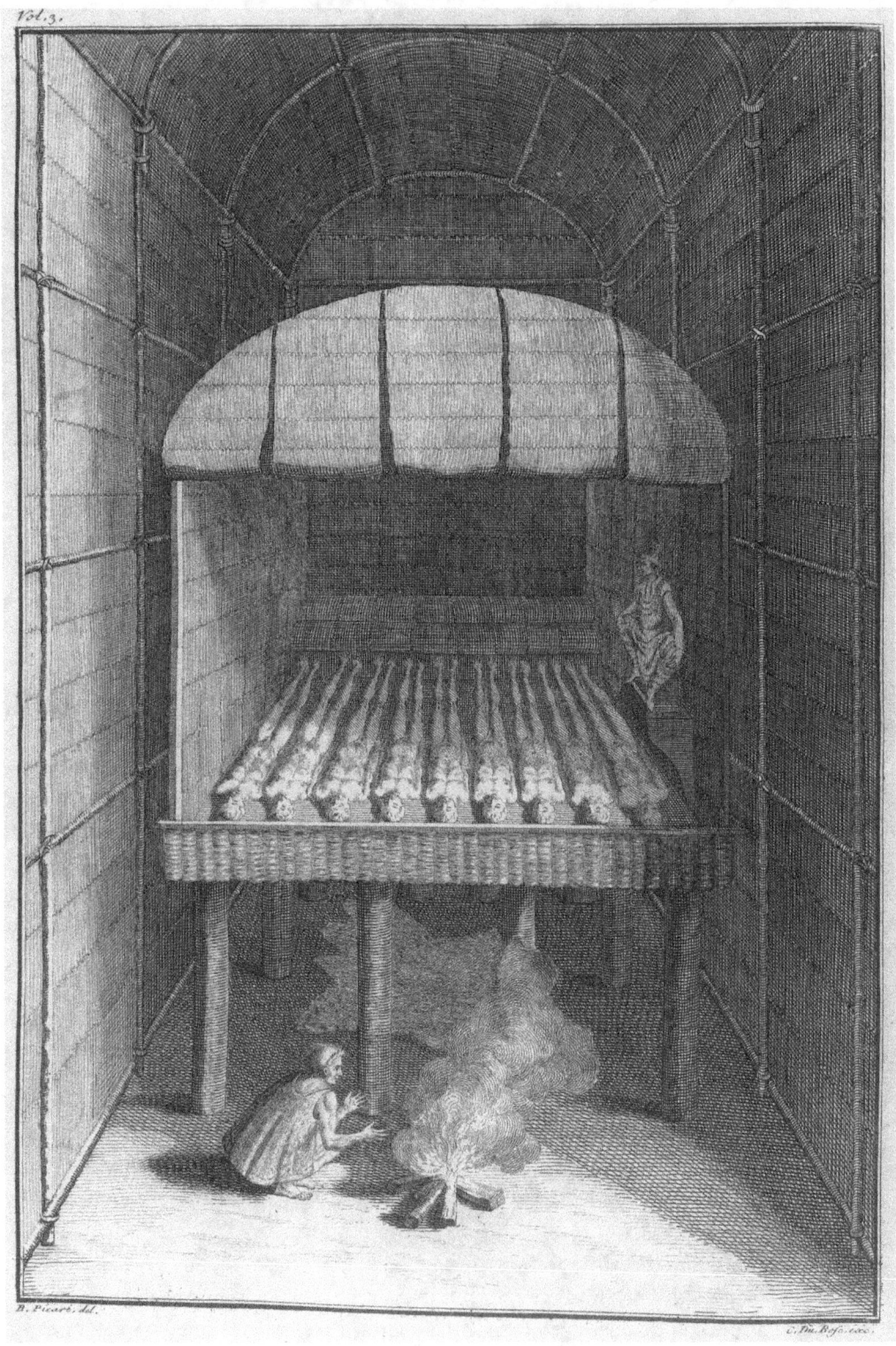

B. Picart. del.

C. Du. Bosse. exc.

Figure 48. Bernard Picart, *Tombs of the Virginian Monarchs,* from *The Ceremonies and Religious Customs of the Various Nations of the Known World,* volume 3 (London, 1734). Courtesy and with permission of The Rare Book and Manuscript Library of the University of Illinois, Urbana-Champaign.

Sculpture and Print

It is the sculpted image, and particularly the figure sculpted in the round, that has throughout the history of the monotheistic religions been the type of image most closely associated with idolatry.[10] Unlike a painting or engraving that consists of illusions on a flat surface, sculpture involves a certain equation between the living presence of the individual portrayed and the actual materials—the wood, stone, plaster, bronze, wax, etc.—from which the work is crafted. Such lifelike images have always exerted a strong hold over viewers, especially when considered to be animated by divinity, as in the case of the cult statues of pagan antiquity or in the case of the Algonquians' idol Kiwasa. In the Christian West, a fear of idolatry put a halt to the production of monumental sculpture at the end of antiquity, but the cult statue was reintroduced in Europe during the twelfth century, and soon came to play a critical role in devotional practice.[11] Three-dimensional images—cult statues of Christ, the Virgin and saints, as well as the reliquaries to which these images were intimately related—seemed to their audiences uniquely capable of playing host to the sacred figures of the Church. Even earthly donors could attain a special relation to the divine through the realization of their own likeness in the round. Aby Warburg, always attuned to the survival of pagan forms in Western art, noted in his 1902 essay on "The Art of Portraiture and the Florentine Bourgeoisie" the almost magical power of the life-sized wax votive figures that hung from the vaults of the church of Santissima Annunziata. Despite the radical differences between the "magical fetishism of the waxwork cult" described by Warburg, which lasted into the seventeenth century in Florence, and the Algonquians' preservation of the corpses of their deceased chiefs, both societies shared a belief in the spiritual efficacy of the three-dimensional figure, both sought to preserve a living spirit within "the palpable form of a human image."[12]

For Protestant iconoclasts, however, such palpable images—particularly in the form of the cult image—constituted idols in their most overt and dangerous form. As the author of the Elizabethan "An Homily against Peril of Idolatry, and Superfluous Decking of Churches" wrote around 1560, the most perilous image, the kind most capable of provoking the worship of a mere piece of wood, is the "one dumb idol or image standing by itself."[13] Flat images, on the other hand, such as pictures hung on walls or stained glass windows, were deemed less dangerous because they did not attempt to approach through a three-dimensional medium the conditions of life itself, and so they were less likely to be worshiped.[14] I will return to the Reformation's distinction between round and flat images, but at this point it is worth noting that the distinction is by no means a clear one—the flatness of religious paintings, after all, did not save them from destruction at the hands of iconoclasts. Just as Warburg found a survival of the waxwork effigy in fifteenth-century portrait frescoes, with their "comparatively discreet attempt to come closer to the Divine through a painted simulacrum," so the apparent difference in medium between sculpted images and printed images should not blind us to the ways in which early modern viewers might have responded to the flat print in a rather "sculptural" fashion.[15]

From the earliest years of printmaking in the fifteenth century, the new relief and intaglio processes may profitably be understood through their relationship to sculpture. Both new printmaking processes were introduced in Europe during a period that saw profound changes in the methods of producing images as well as in habits of response, as the "era of images" gave way to the "era of art."[16] One general development we can trace through this complex historical process, which is critical to an understanding of the early history of prints, is a shift in the concept of the image from one centered on religious sculpture, the efficacy of which was tied directly to its tactile presence, to one centered on a two-dimensional image that showcased the artist's ability to simulate the viewer's optical experience of the world.[17] Fifteenth-century devotional prints, such as the Sudarium of the Master of the Playing Cards, would seem to belong to this latter category: hardly a "literal" presentation of divinity, Christ's face appears to the viewer as a pictorial illusion composed of lines creating patterns of light and dark across a flat surface (see Figure 43). Yet the print's surface is not entirely flat. Like any intaglio print, it is in fact a work executed in relief. The lines that compose the Sudarium, because they were forced into the recessed lines of the copper plate when the paper was damp, actually stand out very slightly above the surrounding paper. The copper plate whose impression the paper received is itself a work of sculpture. Pushing his burin into the plate, the *sculptor*—the Latin term commonly used during the early modern period to designate both engravers and sculptors[18]—prepared his matrix by removing material from a flat surface, producing a tactile surface that was able to carry out its reproductive work only by virtue of its existence in three dimensions.

The extremely low relief of the print and the shallow digging involved in the plate's production may seem trivial reasons for calling an engraving a work of "sculpture." The printmaker, after all, ultimately relies on the same techniques of optical illusion as the draftsman or painter, and whatever sculptural qualities the plate and print might possess are a far cry from the kind of sculptural presence possessed by the cult statue. But as Charles Talbot has argued, the materiality of early devotional prints is likely to have had important implications for their audiences. Talbot points out that the intaglio print functions like a seal, a fact that lent the print a symbolic and even mysterious authority:

> Since the print had pressed against the form-giving object, some invisible quantity of that former presence might be thought to remain attached to the impression. This phenomenon is akin to the meaning of touch in certain other situations. Authority and rank were conferred with gestures of touching, and clothing could acquire the status of a sacred relic when it had been worn by a saint.[19]

The impression takes on the authority of the original through its literal contact with the mold, a contact that is indexed by the shallow relief of the print itself. If we have any doubts about the weight that such a model of authority might have carried for the fifteenth-century viewer, we need only consider the subject matter of the Master of the Playing Cards' print. The Sudarium, the most holy of Christian relics, was created through the contact of Christ's face with the flat surface of Veronica's cloth; it thus stands as the exemplary instance of the process that produced the devotional print itself.[20] More than a pictorial representation of an absent body, this engraving is wedded, through the materiality of the sculptural process that brought it into existence, to the sacred body of Christ.[21]

The special authority residing in the sculptural aspects of the print's production extends well beyond the early years of printmaking. William MacGregor has recently made a strong argument that intaglio printmaking provided early modern psychological philosophers with powerful metaphors for framing the invisible processes of human cognition: sensory perception was regularly imagined in terms of the *engraving* and *imprinting* of images on the mind.[22] Such metaphors in turn had implications for the way audiences responded to prints. John Evelyn, a great collector of prints and a strong proponent of their use for educational purposes, called for the inclusion of prints in texts for students: "what a Treasury of excellent things might by this expedient be conveyed, and impressed into the *waxen Tables* and Imaginations of *children.*"[23] This tactile language of impressing knowledge on the mind provides a way of understanding the authority of an engraving like Picart's *Representation of two famous Shrouds* (see Figure 44). To be sure, the reception of Picart's ethnographic print would have been quite different from the reception of the Master of the Playing Cards' fifteenth-century devotional print. The miracle of Christ's divine impression could not have provided the controlling metaphor in Picart's case: the multiplication of "unique" shrouds (we witness two here: the shroud of Besançon to the left, and to the right, both recto and verso of the shroud of Turin) suggests that the power of these particular relics is more superstition than miracle. At the same time, it is not difficult to imagine how an eighteenth-century viewer's internalization of the cognitive metaphors of engraving and imprinting could have activated this image with a different kind of presence, a presence that reaches out, as it were, to impress its disenchanting message on the receptive imagination of the viewer.

If we want to understand the kinds of authority that could attach to early modern prints, from the Master of Playing Cards to Bernard Picart, we cannot therefore overlook the print's special status as a two-dimensional object created through and bearing the traces of a sculptural process. Early modern viewers did not overlook this fact, as suggested by the very title of Evelyn's treatise on engraving, the first book to give serious attention to the history of this medium. Evelyn's *Sculptura, or the History, and Art of Chalcography and Engraving in Copper* (1662) begins with an extended discussion, in the taxing prose of a seventeenth-century antiquarian, of the history of sculpture and the technical terminology that has been used since antiquity to account for its various types. These opening pages serve to demonstrate how engraving is in the strongest sense a form of the sculptor's art, "an *Art which takes away all that is superfluous of the Subject matter, reducing it to that Forme or Body, which was design'd in the Idea of the Artist.*"[24] While engraving, of course, cannot be classified as a sculptural work in the round like the cult statue, its early modern practitioners and collectors still considered it to belong to the same art form that had catalyzed the Reformation's controversy over religious images in the first place (as an art that grew out of the goldsmith's trade, engraving had also been directly involved in the gilding of cult statues and reliquaries).[25] This physical substance of the intaglio print—of the impressed page itself and of the carved metal matrix that produces the impression—is often overlooked by art historians in favor of its more obvious pictorial and reproductive qualities. I would here like to make a case for taking seriously the engraving's tactile nature, for engaging with its physical presence in the way de Bry shows *A cheiff Lorde of Roanoac* engaging with his own blank copper plate: as the kind of object that, by virtue of its irreducible materiality, might even be hung around the neck as a "token of authoritye" (see Figure 4).

In the following pages I will consider how the pictorial technique discussed in the previous chapter in relation to the ornamental lines of de Bry's smoke—that is, the technique of linear, or artificial, perspective—was employed by de Bry and later engravers as a means for coming to terms with the sculptural matter of the "flat" image. If the print, as I have suggested, was something more than a flat, passive surface carrying a representation, if it was an active sculptural presence that could be conceived as *impressing* its authority on the viewer, then perspective offered a powerful optical means for containing that (potentially dangerous) materiality. A useful set of terms for understanding the relationship between sculptural and perspectival approaches to the image is provided by the opposing categories of tactile and optical perception, formulated in the late nineteenth century by the Viennese art historian Alois Riegl. In the tactile or "near" image, the literal presence of the object's surface immediately before the viewer, a presence verifiable by the sense of touch, confirms the external reality of the object. Insofar as sculptural objects insist upon the impenetrability of their surfaces, they reaffirm these objective, tactile qualities. The pilgrim who reaches out to touch a statue of the Virgin, for example, does so in the belief that the reality of the image—or, to use a more medieval term, its lifelikeness—inheres in the solidity of the wood itself. Even a print, when conceived as an objective surface that stamps its message on the beholder's mind, retains certain qualities of the tactile image. Perspective, on the other hand, is a technique that negates tactile qualities; it denies the integrity of the surface by flattening it and treating it as a window. The perspectival image belongs to Riegl's optical or distant image, in which the illusion of depth distances the beholder from the external reality of the object; the object's reality now lies in subjective experience.[26]

For Riegl, writing at the turn of the century, the history of Western civilization could be understood as a developmental process of transcending the tactile qualities of the visual image. He associated tactility above all with antiquity, when "the ultimate goal of the visual arts . . . was the representation of external objects as clear material entities," and Riegl saw the development of art in the West as a progression from the tactile to the optical, from near vision to distant vision, from the isolated material object to perceptual qualities of mind.[27] We can, indeed, detect an earlier form of this civilizing narrative within de Bry's own engravings, in which the art of the savage is shown to be an art of fundamentally tactile values, as demonstrated by the tattoo rased into the Algonquian warrior's flesh or the raw plate of copper hanging from the neck of the Virginia chief, or in the sculptural presence of the idol Kiwasa who is in fact pictured independently in a second plate from the *Report,* stationed within the opening of a circular hut and looking very much like a Christian cult image within its shrine (Figure 49). This is the type of sculptural matter that exercised Protestant authors and artists. By means of their ethnographic prints (always partly tactile images themselves), they attempted to subject this matter to a *distant* vision.

As demonstrated in de Bry's engraving of the tomb, the technique of perspective was one of the chief optical resources for managing the tactile matter of the New World. In modifying his engraving from White's original watercolor drawing, de Bry clearly made a choice to emphasize its perspectival structure (Figure 50). The addition of the second building that encloses the tomb considerably reinforces the perspectival recession already suggested by the preserved bodies—bodies that in de Bry's version

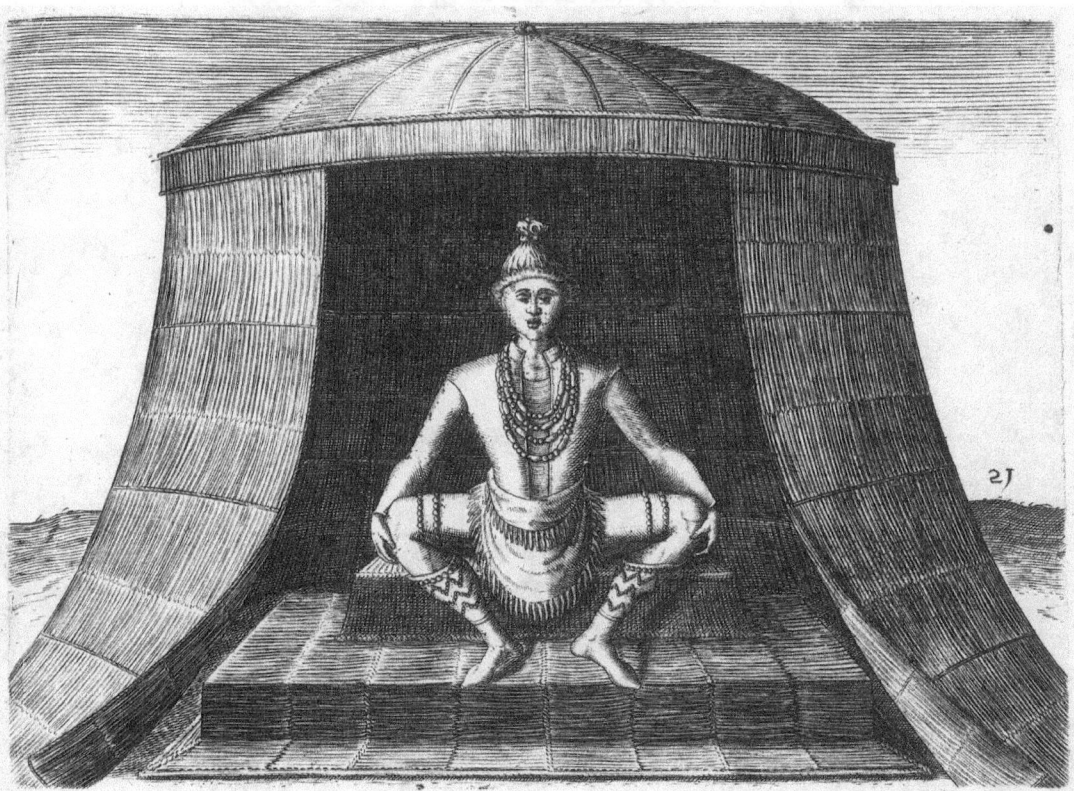

Figure 49. Theodor de Bry, *Ther Idol Kiwasa,* from *A Briefe and True Report.* Courtesy and with permission of British Library G.6837.

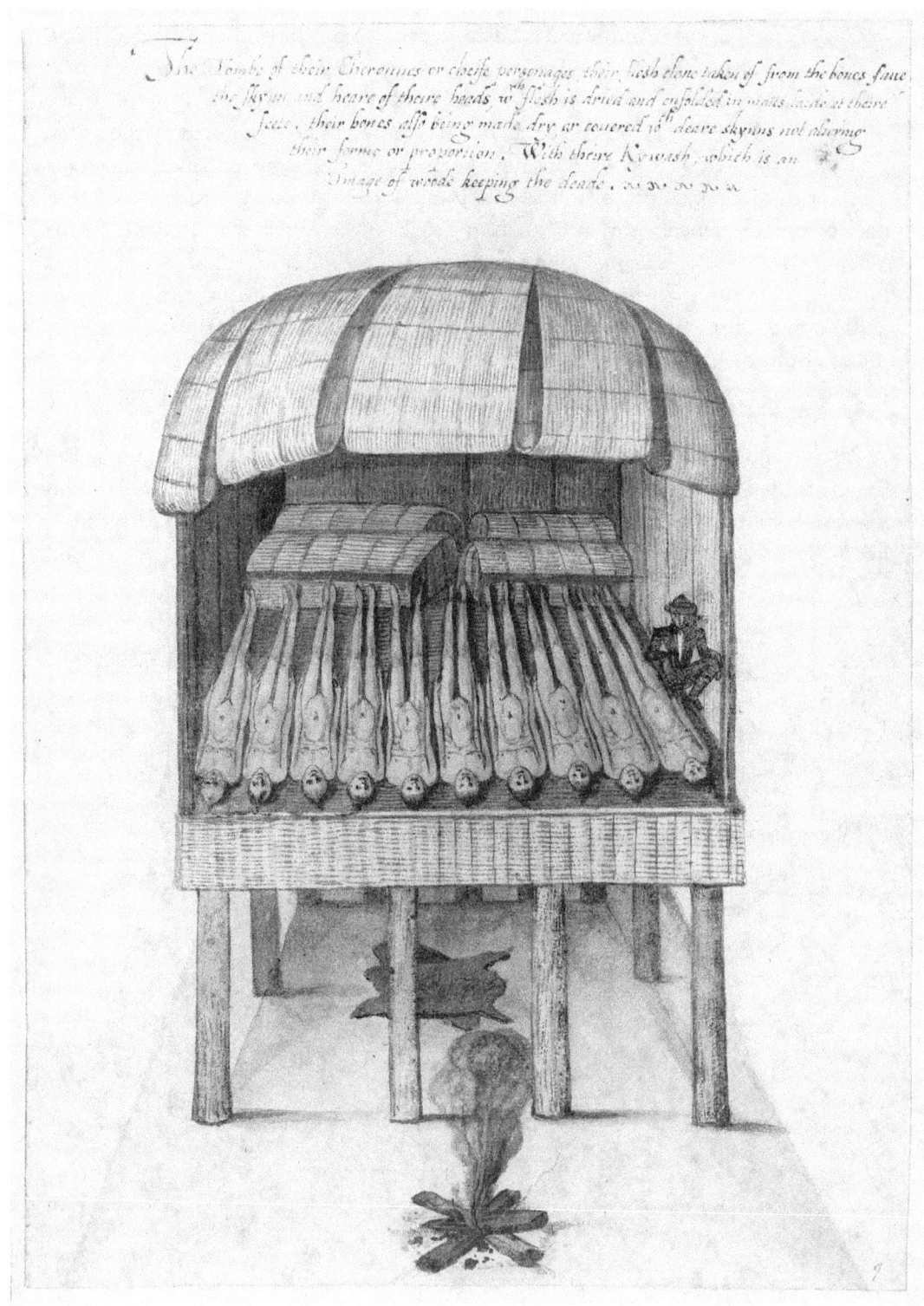

The Tombe of their Cherounes or cheiffe personages, their flesh clene taken of from the bones saue the skyn and heare of theire heads, w[ch] flesh is dried and enfolded in mates laide at theire feete. their bones also being made dry ar couered wth deare skynns not alterinc their forme or proporcion. With theire Kewash, which is an Image of woode keeping the deade.

Figure 50. John White, *The Tombe of their Cherounes*, watercolor on paper, c. 1585. Copyright Trustees of The British Museum.

even more closely approximate the receding orthogonals of a systematic perspectival construction.[28] The engraving's optical severity has the effect of distancing viewers from the tomb and its contents, as well as from the tactile presence of the page itself, for de Bry's insistent deployment of linear perspective desiccates his image, as if he were emptying it of all its sculptural substance.

The Unreformed Savage

Because of its strident perspectivism, de Bry's *The Tombe of their Werowans*, more than any other plate in the *Report*, directly involves the viewer as a constitutive factor in the making of New World knowledge. As viewers, we are invited to imagine ourselves within the situation that Bosse's engraving makes explicit, a situation characterized by a rigid and distancing geometry of vision that has its origin in a single subject's point of view (see Figure 46). How, then, might we historicize this subject position? In other words, if de Bry's engraving offers a perspective on Algonquian religious practice, then *whose* perspective is it? Although any attempt to answer such questions can hardly serve as an adequate historical accounting for de Bry's image (it is precisely the stability of this subject that I will be putting into question), nevertheless it must serve, by virtue of the engraving's perspectival structure, as an essential starting point. In previous chapters we have encountered two different types of viewing subject in the *Report*: in the first chapter I argued for the importance of a literate subject; in the second chapter I considered de Bry's smoke in relation to an acquisitive subject. De Bry's perspectival tomb presents us with yet a third point of view, that of the reformed subject.

As a Walloon from Spanish-ruled Liège who joined the thriving community of religious exiles in Frankfurt, de Bry belonged socially and intellectually to a staunchly Protestant, anti-Catholic world. The entirety of de Bry's *America*—begun in 1590 with the *Report* and continued by de Bry and his sons until the publication of the thirteenth volume in 1634—has been described by Daniel Defert as "the Protestant codex of the New World."[29] While it holds an important place in the history of the visual ethnography of America, it must also be understood as a massive piece of anti-Spanish, anti-Catholic propaganda, a "machine de guerre," as Michèle Duchet has called it, in the struggle for religious and political dominance in both the New World and the Old World.[30] For de Bry, the idol had a critical role to play in this struggle. Throughout the illustrations for *America*, we are encouraged to make the implicit connection between the idolatry practiced by Indians—the subject of numerous engravings—and Catholic idolatry. In other words, in our assessment of de Bry's engravings we must take into account the Reformation's repudiation of Catholic religious imagery, for this most visual of the early publications on the New World is also the most thoroughly *anti*visual.

Episodes of idolatry are constantly appearing throughout de Bry's work. De Bry's title pages, for example, often showcase an idol at top center. The "thing shaped like a pumpkin" mentioned by Hans Staden in the second epigraph to this chapter

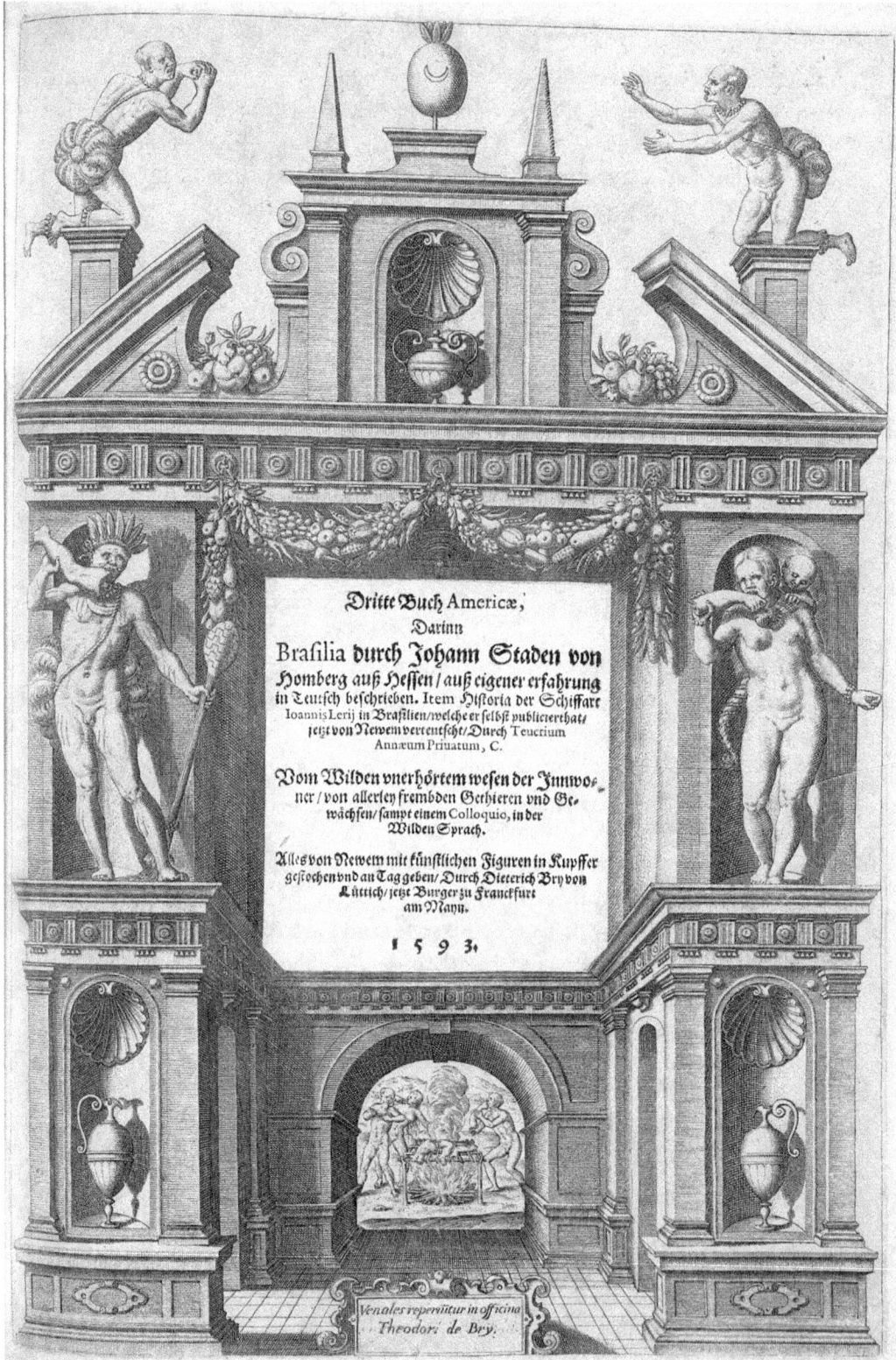

Figure 51. Theodor de Bry, title page for *America,* part 3 (Frankfurt am Main, 1593). From the Collections of the University Libraries, University of Minnesota, Minneapolis.

is pictured at the top of the title page to part 3 (1592), which features Hans Staden's and Jean de Léry's accounts of their experiences among the Tupinamba of Brazil (Figure 51). Such images would have been among de Bry's best known to a late sixteenth- or early seventeenth-century public, since title pages would have been issued as single sheets and used as advertisements for the complete volumes. Many individual illustrations also treat the subject of idolatry. In part 2 we find a New World version of the well-known episode of idolatry from the Old Testament, the worshiping of the golden calf in Exodus, with Florida Indians now playing the role of the Jews, and the calf masquerading as a sacred stag (Figure 52). De Bry's linking of American and Catholic idolatry is at its most explicit in an engraving from part 1 titled *Their danses which they vse att their hyghe feastes,* in which Virginia Indians perform an idolatrous dance around a ring marked by a number of anthropomorphic posts (Figure 53). The scene is somewhat modified from White's version, which the artist describes as "A Ceremony in their prayers wth strange iesturs and songs dansing abowt posts carued on the topps lyke mens faces."[31] But when the image is appropriated by de Bry, the accompanying text tells us that the Indians dance about "certayne posts carued with heads *like to the faces of Nonnes couered with theyr vayles*" (my italics), and indeed de Bry's posts actually assume a nunlike appearance. In a curious reversal of roles—attributable, perhaps, to a reformed sense of humor—Old World idolaters become New World idols.

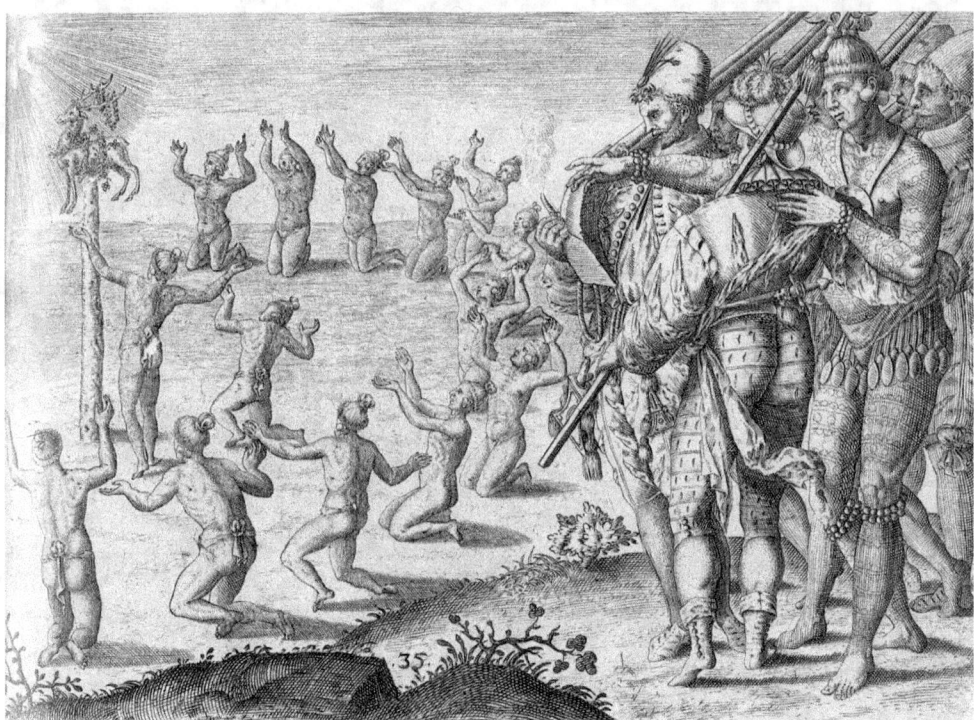

Figure 52. Theodor de Bry after Jacques Le Moyne, *Their Solemn Ritual in Consecrating a Deerskin to the Sun,* from *America,* part 2. From the Collections of the University Libraries, University of Minnesota, Minneapolis.

In the *Report,* the central idol is the figure called Kiwasa (or Kywash, in White's original drawing). In White's collection, this idol appears only in the picture of the tomb, but in de Bry's illustrations for the *Report* it appears no less than three times: in *The Tombe of their Werowans,* in its own plate titled *Ther Idol Kiwasa,* and at the top center of the title page (see Figures 9, 45, 49). As it appears on the title page where its placement reflects its position of priority within the Algonquian social structure, and as it appears in its own plate, this figure is de Bry's own improvisation on the small idol in White's tomb (neither the title page nor the separate plate has a precedent in White's surviving collection).[32] As it appears within *The Tombe of their Werowans,* Kiwasa assumes a role in an idolatrous ritual carried out by the crouching priest, a figure who does not appear in White's watercolor and who serves to link the scene more directly to Catholic practice as he "mumbleth his prayers" below the corpses like a Catholic priest "mumbling" in Latin. The presence of the priest demonstrates that the tomb is not simply a site for the preservation of the dead (a conclusion

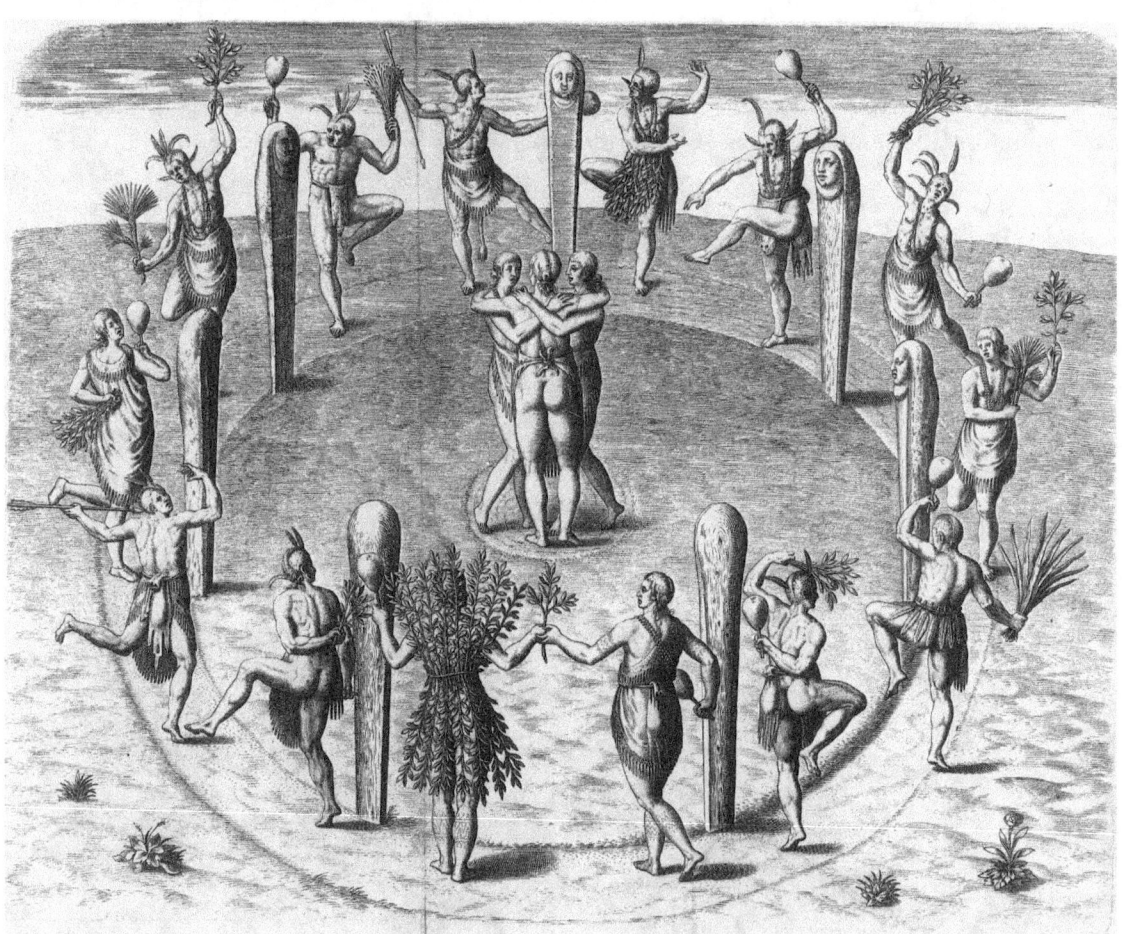

Figure 53. Theodor de Bry after John White, *Their danses which they vse att their hyghe feastes,* from *A Briefe and True Report.* Courtesy and with permission of British Library G.6837.

one might reach with regard to White's image, which includes no live figures), but also for idolatrous worship, not only of the wooden idol Kiwasa but also of the dead bodies themselves. "Thes poore soules," we are told in the caption, "are thus instructed by nature to reuerence their princes euen after their death."[33]

By strategically placing Kiwasa throughout the illustrations for the *Report,* de Bry makes it the centerpiece of Algonquian society. On the opening page of the book, the viewer is made aware that this New World society is based on a superstitious investment in an object that, we soon learn, is merely "carued of woode." From the very beginning it is apparent that the reading and viewing of this early work of North American ethnography will be an act of spiritual self-policing, as one comes to recognize in the practice of the savage precisely what must be banished from the practice of one's own faith. "To be a Protestant," notes historian Margaret Aston, "imposed on each individual this inescapable thought: Have I a right belief of God? Or are my thoughts idolatrous? To know God was to know his enemy, the Antichrist within, to be acquainted with the iniquitous sin of idolatry."[34] We can begin to see where the representation of American Indians and the practice of one's own faith could overlap in de Bry's world: to observe and record the idolatry of the Americans, to acquaint oneself with their "papist" practices, was to exercise just the sort of vigilance that made one a good Christian.[35]

Understood in its Protestant context, then, *The Tomb of their Werowans* reads as the perspectival projection of a reformed subject who can only imagine idolatry at a distance, as a practice that characterizes the *other's* relation to the image. But however insistent de Bry's perspective may be in its distancing of the beholder from idolatrous desires, perspective remains, as Panofsky wrote in his classic essay on the subject, a "two-edged sword":

> Perspective creates distance between human beings and things . . .; but then in turn it abolishes this distance by, in a sense, drawing this world of things, an autonomous world confronting the individual, into the eye. . . . Thus the history of perspective may be understood with equal justice as a triumph of the distancing and objectifying sense of the real, and as a triumph of the distance-denying human struggle for control; it is as much a consolidation and systematization of the external world, as an extension of the domain of the self.[36]

We can certainly take exception to the totalizing and triumphant quality of Panofsky's view of perspective. Despite his demonstration that there is neither a subjective nor objective position from which one might evaluate perspective, Panofsky never went so far as to make a claim for the complete relativism of perspective; instead, he understood it to symbolize a transcendent cultural totality, a Renaissance weltanschauung in which an autonomous self and world emerged simultaneously.[37] Nevertheless, there is a great deal of value in Panofsky's description of perspective as a fundamentally dialectical practice, because it offers us a way out of the mistake of simply subjectifying perspective and thus reading the image of the tomb as the symbol of a unified Protestant subject, or objectifying it and thus treating de Bry's engraving as an expression of a Renaissance sense of the real. Indeed, Panofsky's passage lends itself to a profitable misreading, one that would interpret the two-edged sword of perspective in terms of a radical *uncertainty* that threatens to dissolve the coherence both of the subject and its reality. Panofsky's formulation gestures (unintentionally, to be sure) toward the opening of a rift within the humanist subject of Renaissance perspective, making this subject, as Hubert Damisch has put it, "anything but 'humanist.'"[38] The reformed subject of de Bry's Virginia tomb, in other words, turns out not to be a unified cultural totality at all but a fundamental *problem* of representation. It is a divided subject who, like the seated viewer of Bosse's diagram, coolly distances himself from the world in order to subject that world to his own rational authority, but who at the same time seeks to abolish this distance by subjecting *himself* to the materiality of the world, with all its threatening idols staring back at him.[39]

In de Bry's engraving, the desire of the subject to control his world, to make it an extension of the self through a perspectival projection, is translated into a reformed subject's spiritual need to contain the idol, the deeply felt need of a self-policing Calvinist conscience. It is thus both an assertion of control over and a *reaction against* the matter of the world. De Bry's engraving asks the viewer to participate in a Protestant self's unfinished struggle to control its own unreformed past by distancing that past, by opening up a rational space between the viewing subject and a troubling sacred body that—because the Reformation could not do away with the doctrine of the Incarnation—is always on the verge of reappearing and abolishing any coherent distinction between self and other. Christ's body, I suggest, continues to lurk in the shadows of this Virginia tomb in the same "darke corners" where, as Harriot writes, the idols of the Virginians "shew terrible."[40] But before I turn to the question of specifically where we might locate Christ's body in this image, let me first consider two eighteenth-century texts that reproduce de Bry's tomb and offer insight into how at the beginning of the Enlightenment an increasingly scientific attitude toward religion continued to struggle with the visible matter of religion.

The Matter of Religion

For early modern viewers, de Bry's engraving, popularized by the numerous editions of the *Report* published between 1590 and 1634, made his perspectival tomb synonymous with Virginia itself. But it was not until the publication of two texts in the early eighteenth century, Robert Beverley's *History and Present State of Virginia* (1705) and Jean Frédéric Bernard's *The Ceremonies and Religious Customs of the Various Nations of the Known World* (originally published 1723–43), that the engraving was brought into the service of a project we can recognize as self-consciously empirical in its approach. Beverley was a Virginia-born Englishman who was proud of the taste for simplicity and directness his colonial life had instilled in him. He notes in his preface: "I am an

Indian, and don't pretend to be exact in my Language: But I hope the Plainness of my Dress, will give [the reader] the kinder Impressions of my Honesty, which is what I pretend to."[41] Beverley's invocation of the Indian as the paradigm of natural, unornamented thought (by no means a consistent attitude on the author's part) establishes the tone of cool rationality that in the author's opinion sets *History and Present State of Virginia* apart from the clearly biased accounts of Virginia that had appeared during the previous century: it is "for the Information of Mankind" that Beverley writes, not "for the Benefit of the Bookseller."[42] And to prove that his book is based on firsthand visual evidence and is not the product of his own invention, he illustrates the ethnographic section of his book, titled "The Native Indians, Their Religion, Laws, and Customs, in War and Peace," with pictures: "I have been the more concise in my account of this harmless people, because I have inserted several Figures, which I hope have both supplied the defect of Words, and render'd the Descriptions more clear."[43] All but one of his fourteen plates appear in the third part of *History and Present State of Virginia,* which considers "The Native Indians, their Religion, Laws, and Customs, in War and Peace" and which offers the author's observations on the Indians with whom he had contact throughout his life. The engraver of the plates was Simon Gribelin, a French Protestant refugee who worked in London during the early eighteenth century and who based his designs on de Bry's plates from the *Report* (Beverley makes no mention of the fact that these plates were derived from an earlier source).[44] One of these engravings represents the familiar tomb, which in Gribelin's version is even more orderly and clean in its perspectival construction than in de Bry's version (Figure 54).

History and Present State of Virginia was particularly popular in its French translation, *Histoire de la Virginie:* before it went through even a second edition in English, it went through four editions in French, with an audience composed primarily of Huguenot exiles living in the Netherlands.[45] The third French edition, published in 1718, was issued in Amsterdam by Jean Frédéric Bernard, who five years later issued the first volume of the *Ceremonies,* with engravings executed by the workshop of Picart.[46] In the volume on the "idolatrous nations," Bernard in fact draws heavily on Beverley's text as a source of information on Algonquian idolatry, while Picart, as we have seen, returns to de Bry's *The Tombe of their Werowans* in order to picture a space for this idolatry.

Amsterdam provided a conducive climate for the publication of these critiques of American religious practices, since it was at the center of what has been called the Radical Enlightenment, an intellectual movement of the early eighteenth century that was both republican and secularizing in spirit.[47] Bernard and Picart participated directly (and Beverley and Gribelin indirectly through their publishers) in a vibrant community of Protestant refugees in the Dutch city, and in their massive account of the world's religious institutions they contributed to an important early phase of the Enlightenment critique of religion. In this regard, the Protestant spirit of a text like the *Ceremonies* is more liberal than that of de Bry's *America,* which must be understood in the context of the intense, and intensely doctrinal, religious conflicts of the sixteenth and early seventeenth centuries. Nevertheless, the same antimaterialism we

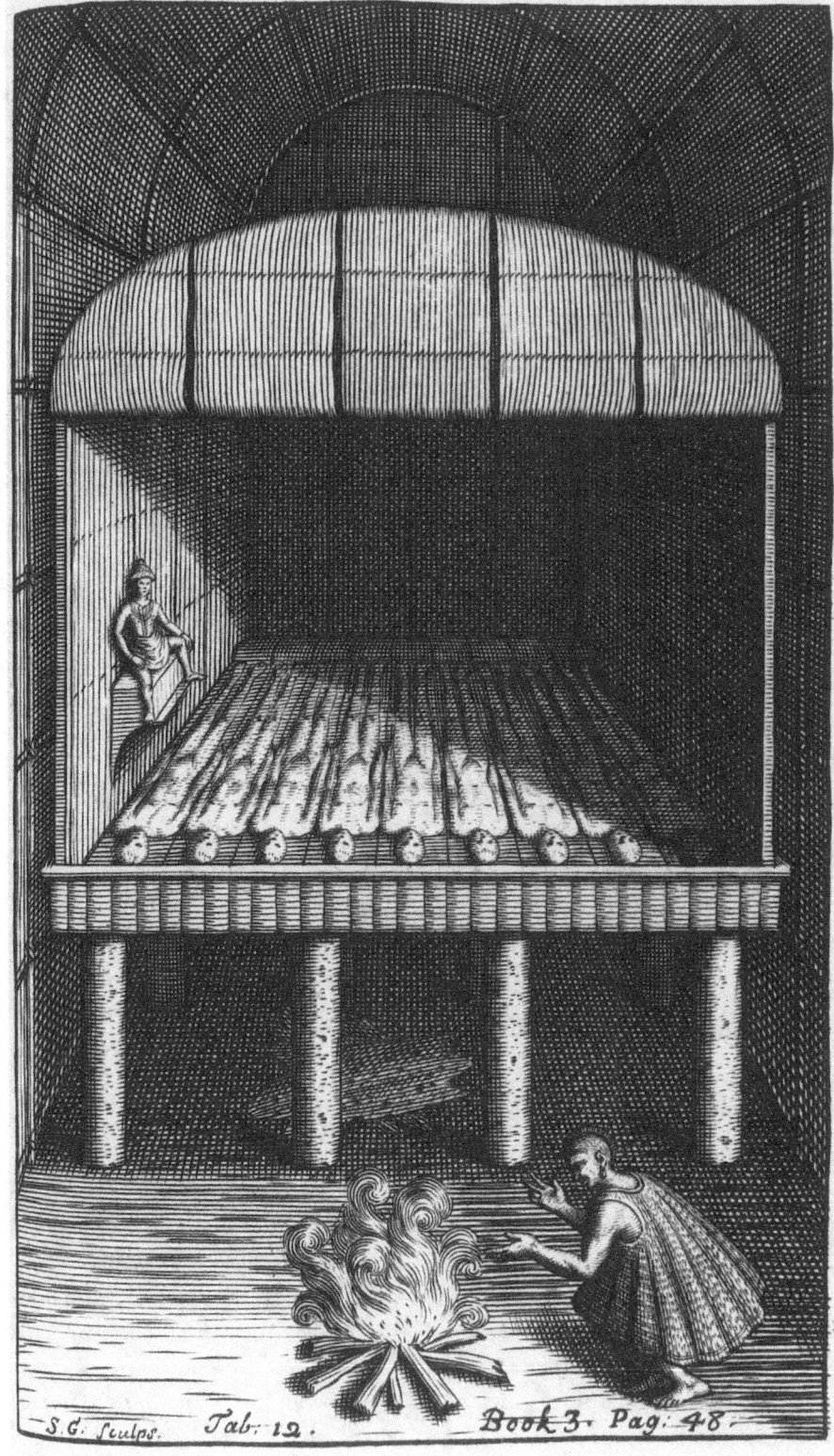

Figure 54. Simon Gribelin, *The Burial of the Kings,* from Beverley, *The History and Present State of Virginia* (London, 1705). Courtesy and with permission of The Rare Book and Manuscript Library of the University of Illinois, Urbana-Champaign.

encountered in de Bry continues to inform the production of knowledge about New World religion in these influential Protestant works of the early Enlightenment.

Beverley and Bernard's interest in representing the idol grows out of a shared pre-occupation with religious matter. For both, the idolatry of the Virginians—their worshiping of a wooden idol and the preserved bodies of dead "kings"—is a problem of the materiality of religion. As the author of one of the introductory essays of the *Ceremonies* writes: "Happy are they who can raise their Minds to what is most sublime and mysterious in Religion, and leave the material Part to vulgar and abject Souls! but few, alas! very few there are of the former. Some Men cannot, and others will not part with their sensual Notions."[48] It is that very failure of the masses to depart from a base religious materialism that makes an ethnographic project such as the *Ceremonies* possible in the first place, for its ambition is to record in essays and images all the various customs and practices that a stubborn sensuality had caused mankind to build up around religion. We witness here the beginnings of an anthropology of religion, a relativizing approach to faith in which no belief system—not even Protestantism, the subject of volumes 5 and 6 of Bernard's *Ceremonies*—is above the rule of science.

If Bernard's purpose is to collect and compare religious matter, Beverley's chapter on the religion, laws, and customs of the Virginians is more a field-worker's effort to lay bare the base materialism of American religion. Beverley is always uncovering deceptions, and more than once he narrates an episode in which the consummately rational author, confronted with a piece of Indian superstition, divests it of its mystery and presents it to the world as so much tangible, trivial matter. Beverley recounts, for example, an adventure in which, while the Indian priests and worshipers are occupied briefly on business elsewhere, he sneaks into their temple, or *Quioccasan*, "the inside of which, they never suffer any *English* Man to see." At the back of the temple, in a "dismal dark" place "cut off by a Partition of very close Mats," the author discovers a wooden idol, which he investigates with a scientist's detachment. This experiment is finally brought to an end when, "having spent about an hour in this enquiry, we fear'd . . . that if we staid longer, we might be caught offering an affront to their Superstition."[49] Yet Beverley returns with visual proof of what he has witnessed, for following his story he includes the "Figure of their Idol, which was taken by an exact Drawer in the country" (the identity of this "exact drawer" is left ambiguous). He refers to a plate labeled *Idol call'd. Okeè, Quióccos, or Kiwasà* (Figure 55). Gribelin has clearly created this composition by combining two of de Bry's plates: the engraving of the tomb and the engraving of *Ther Idol Kiwasa* (see Figures 45, 49). The result is a version of the Algonquians' idol (a "dumb" piece of wood "which those poor people are taught to worship with a devout Ignorance") that is no longer simply framed by an enclosed space, as in de Bry's plate, but is now clearly *contained* by that space. In plates like this, with the New World idol situated securely at the back of its perspectival temple, readers of Beverley's and Bernard's texts were presented with an exemplary space onto which they could project the matter that was essential to a scientific approach to religion.

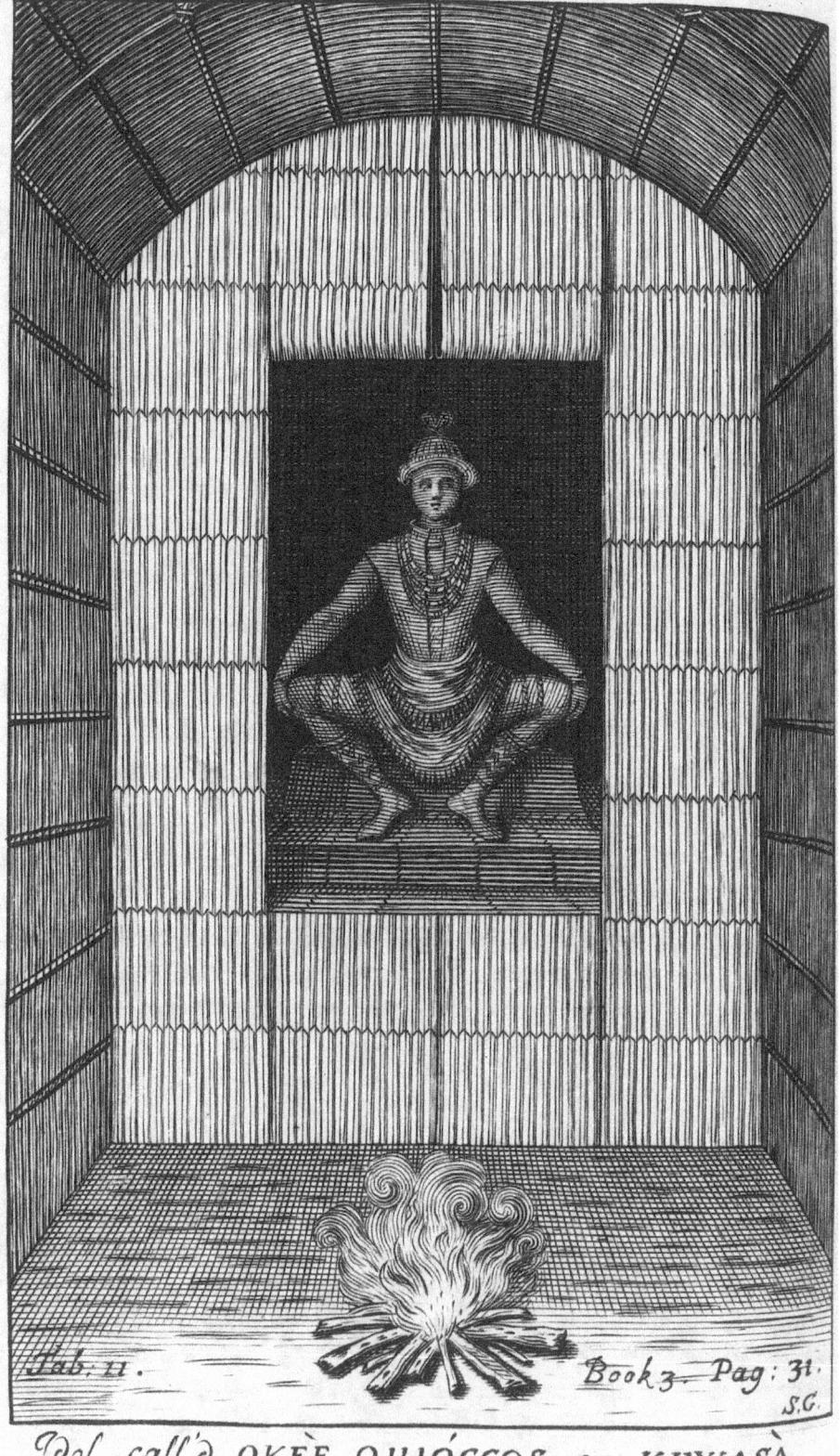

Idol call'd, OKÈE, QUIÓCCOS, or KIWASÀ.

Figure 55. Simon Gribelin, *Their Idol in his Tabernacle*, from *The History and Present State of Virginia*. Courtesy and with permission of The Rare Book and Manuscript Library of the University of Illinois, Urbana-Champaign.

Yet to say that religion has been systematically and spatially materialized in these eighteenth-century works is not to say that the authors' attitudes toward religion have been fully secularized. For even as Enlightenment ethnography reduces all religions to the same material level, it remains deeply indebted to the Reformation attitudes toward idolatry that we encountered in de Bry. Idolatry was itself a problem of the materiality of religion, one that troubled Protestant divines throughout the sixteenth and seventeenth centuries. Indeed, scholars have located the intellectual origins of the Enlightenment's objectification of religion in the writings of seventeenth-century Calvinist theologians in England, which in text after text explore the nature of the Reformation's central sin.[50] In his *Antidote against Idolatry* (1669), Cambridge theologian Henry More defines idolatry as "a very sore and grievous Disease of the Soul, vilely debasing her, and sinking her into *Sensuality* and *Materiality,* keeping her at a vast Distance from the true Sense and right Knowledge of God, and leaving her more liable to bodily Lusts."[51] By the late seventeenth century this Calvinist impulse to know the true, immaterial nature of divinity by knowing its opposite began to spark an interest in the comparative study of religions—that is, in the treatment of the various religions of the world as so many material practices. Being a good Protestant, after all, was not unlike being a good empiricist: both required one to be always on the lookout for sensuality and materiality in religion. Those who failed to elevate themselves above the material may have been damned in the eyes of the elect, but they were also good objects for scientific inquiry. In this way a Calvinist antimaterialism eventually succeeded in rationalizing religion by embodying it; by making it, for example, into a matter of wooden objects and preserved corpses contained within an illusionistic space.[52]

Vision and the Origin of Idolatry

One important aspect of this rationalization of religion was the need to account for how idols had come into being in the first place: *why* did people worship wooden statues and decaying relics rather than the true, invisible God? In their efforts to answer this question, early speculators on the origins of idolatry, such as English deist Charles Blount, transformed a central element of seventeenth-century Calvinist thought, anticlericalism, into a full-fledged historical theory about the birth of idolatry. The result was the imposture theory, which held that an elite "Sacerdotal Order" was responsible for imposing, out of its own self-interest, "absurd and impious Tenents concerning God and Religion, withdrawing [the people] as well from the use of their Reason." These are Blount's words from his *Great Is Diana of the Ephesians: Or, the Original of Idolatry* (1680), in which the author knits together the imposture theory with euhemerist ideas, according to which idolatry began in the gradual deification of dead princes and heroes. The result is an account of idolatry's primitive origins that would seem to explain all the essential elements of our image of the Algonquian tomb—deceiving priest, dead kings, and wooden idol alike:

This Idol being therefore at first worshipped only in commemoration of some *Hero,* or gallant Person as his Effigies, grew in time to be by Posterity revered as a God; and as his courage or prudence in his life-time, was conducive to the grandeur and glory of his Subjects, so they thought being dead, he was no less able to assist them; with which expectation they paid frequent Vows, Prayers and Sacrifices unto him, such as were ordain'd by their Priests.[53]

For both Beverley and Bernard, the image of the Algonquian tomb stands as the visual proof for Blount's theory. Both authors filter their discussion of idolatry through the figure of the priest crouched in the foreground before his sacred fire: "A Priest watches Day and Night in this Mausolæum by a lighted Fire," the text corresponding to Picart's plate informs us, "and 'tis there that he acquits himself of some pious Duties which he imagines affect the Deceas'd in some Measure. If he himself does not give Credit to it, 'tis certain he imposes the Belief of it upon the People."[54] Beverley reveals his own adherence to this notion of pernicious priestly influence in his recounting of a conversation he once had with an Indian. Having stopped at the house of an Englishman while traveling, Beverley encounters a native of the region and sits with him before the fire, offering him "plenty of strong Cyder" in the hope it will make him "open-hearted." Beverley, who has himself explored the Indians' temple and examined their idol, then begins to interrogate his new acquaintance:

> I then asked him concerning the Image, which they Worship in their *Quioccasan;* and assur'd him, that it was a dead insensible Log, equipt with a bundle of Clouts, a meer helpless thing made by Men, that could neither hear, see, nor speak; and that such a stupid thing could no ways hurt, or help them. To this he answer'd very unwillingly, and with much hesitation; However, he at last deliver'd himself in these broken and imperfect sentences; *It is the Priests—they make the people believe, and—* ——Here he paus'd a little, and then repeated to me that *it was the Priests*——and then gave me hopes that he wou'd have said something more, but a qualm crost his Conscience, and hinder'd him from making any farther Confession.[55]

The priest, then, is a key figure in the image of the tomb as it appears in the *History and Present State of Virginia* and the *Ceremonies.* Crouching within a gloomy temple interior before a smoking fire, he continues to suggest a link between Catholicism and New World idolatry, as in de Bry's version. But for Beverley and Bernard the priest has also become something more than this. He has become a figure with enormous explanatory power in an emerging science of religion, a figure whose deceptions have for the entire history of mankind clouded the common people's vision, leading them to make an irrational investment in the power of mere matter.

We, the viewers of the Algonquian tomb, share with Beverley a position of superiority over the savage idolater: unlike the confused and fearful Indian whom Beverley interviews, we see the priest for what he is—a fraud. We "see," in other words, in a way that the savage fails to see. With eyes fixed only upon visible matter, the savage is a slave to his sense of sight. Enlightenment attitudes toward religion are in this sense characterized not only by a strong antimaterialism, but also by a tendency toward the denigration of the chief sense through which matter is perceived. "As invisible spiritual intelligence is an object too refined for vulgar apprehension," writes David Hume in his *Natural History of Religion* (1757), "men naturally affix it to some sensible representation."[56] That vulgar apprehension, which was specifically a visual apprehension, was thought by many eighteenth-century writers on religion to be particularly pronounced in primitive humanity and, indeed, to be the very source of idolatrous worship. According to David Hartley in his *Observations on Man* (1749), "Idolatry, heathenish and popish, has made a much quicker and more extensive progress in the world on account of the stability and vividness of visible impressions and ideas, and the difficulty, obscurity, and changeable nature, of abstract notions. And image-worship seems even to have been derived in great measure from this source."[57] Hartley and Hume both imply that enlightenment (something that, Hume believed, few were capable of achieving) requires a progression from the visual and idolatrous to the abstract and intellectual; we must rise above our sense of sight. But while this denigration of vision, this equation of sight and barbarism, is one central aspect of an Enlightenment approach to religion, we also associate the Enlightenment with its celebration of vision. Here, of course, we must distinguish between qualities of vision—that is, between an abstract or enlightened vision equated with reason, and the savage's vision, which is purely material and focused on base things and is therefore susceptible to priestly deceptions.

The central visual problem of the image of the Algonquian tomb is precisely the differentiation between these two qualities of vision. On the one hand, as an image of *idolatry,* the engraving is deeply invested in transcending the visual conditions of the New World—the kind of primitive conditions under which humans fall into the worship of images. The viewer's perspective on idolatry, a perspective that dematerializes the picture surface while distancing the viewer from the objects represented on it, is in this sense one that aspires to what Hume calls "invisible spiritual intelligence." Seen in this light, in which the viewer assumes a disembodied perspective on religion, the image demonstrates the tendency within Enlightenment thought to assume a metaphorical identification between the rational point of view of subjective consciousness and the literal viewpoint of linear perspective.[58] On the other hand, as a material image, a tactile object in its own right, the engraving shares with the idol an inevitable appeal to the "vulgar apprehension" of the viewer. The failure to achieve a disembodied perspective on New World idolatry is, after all, a possibility we must entertain, for as we learned from the *Ceremonies,* there are, alas, few who *can* "raise their Minds to what is most sublime and mysterious in Religion." And the adoption of a perspectival viewpoint is no guarantee of success in this effort. Indeed, Descartes himself never adopted perspective as a metaphor for the *cogito* precisely because, as a practice of picture-making, it is grounded in a necessarily *embodied* viewer who is fully subject to sensory deceptions.[59] Our perspectival image thus raises the pressing question of how one can materialize the idol as the object of ethnographic inquiry and at the same time raise the mind above that matter. Should we take the engraving's insistence on visual control as a successful metaphor for a disembodied rationality? Or is that insistence perhaps best understood as the demonstration of a frustrated need—a need made all the more urgent by the chosen subject matter of idolatry and by the materiality of the print itself—to create a point of view that would somehow escape the influence of figures such as this cunning priest (a version perhaps of the "evil genius" of Descartes's *Meditations*) who would deceive our senses?

If, then, in its effort to put to rest any doubts about the viewer's distance from idolatry, the overinscribed perspective of the tomb in fact raises such doubts, then these should perhaps be attributed to the same Protestant fear of a return to unreformed Christianity that we first saw in de Bry and that was still alive and well in Enlightenment ethnography.[60] In Beverley's *History and Present State of Virginia,* this fear takes the form of a fierce anti-Catholicism: "No bigotted Pilgrim," the author writes, "appears more zealous, or strains his Devotion more at the Shrine, than these believing *Indians* do, in their Idolatrous Adorations. Neither do the most refin'd Catholicks undergo their pennance with so much submission as these poor Pagans do the severities, which their Priests inflict upon them."[61] The urgency of this anti-Catholicism, an urgency that parallels that of Gribelin's perspective, may be explained by something the Protestant viewer would have found uncomfortably familiar about the sacred bodies in the Indian tomb, something that is part of Protestant belief and "idolatrous" Catholicism alike—the belief in an immaterial God who, in order to redeem mankind, *became flesh.* Christ's body, or rather the ever-present possibility of that body's return in the form of an idol, is the matter that troubles this ethnographic image. It is the religious matter that the viewer of this image, despite his or her most determined efforts, cannot entirely displace onto the New World.

In the *Ceremonies* we even come across Christ's body explicitly, as the object of Catholic superstition, in the plate titled *Representation of two famous Shrouds* (see Figure 44). Like the preserved bodies in the image of the tomb, this preserved image of Christ's body is presented as just one more deception, as evidence of a failure of Catholics to raise their minds above matter. Christ's image is in this case embodied, made into an ethnographic object, precisely to show that it is an *error* to embody Christ. We have arrived again at the central question of this chapter: how can the image have it both ways? How can the viewer gaze upon an engraved depiction of an embodied Christ (however flat and insubstantial that embodiment may appear on the shrouds) and at the same time raise the mind above that body? The perspectival viewer of the tomb, as that image is presented in the texts of Beverley and Bernard, is encouraged to make the metaphorical leap into enlightenment. But this is also a metaphorical leap *out* of a very old visual problem, a problem of idolatry, incarnation, and visual form that reaches back at least to medieval Christianity and that, in spite of its sublimation by Enlightenment ethnography, still informs the production of perspectival knowledge of New World religion during the eighteenth century.

The Return of the Unreformed

The Biblical underpinning of the Reformation's concern with the idol and its visual form was the second commandment: "Thou shalt not make unto thee any grauen Image, or any likenesse of any thing that is in heauen aboue, or that is in the earth beneath, or that is in the water under the earth."[62] This sentence of the Decalogue received a renewed emphasis during the Reformation, assuming independent status as a commandment, whereas previously it had been treated as a gloss on the first commandment, "Thou shalt haue no other Gods before me." In England, Protestant theologians returned again and again to the prohibition of images and specifically to the interpretation of *graven image* (*pesel* in Hebrew; *sculptile* in the vulgate) in their tireless efforts to determine which uses of images should be considered legitimate and which illegitimate.[63] But they never settled on any one rule for determining what did or did not constitute a graven image. Indeed, Protestants were presented with a confusing array of guidelines and proscriptions for policing their visual behavior. These included considerations of the place where viewing took place, the subject matter of the image, and its visual form.

One of the primary distinctions between image types was between those images that were accorded religious worship *(latria)* and which were therefore proscribed, and those that were accorded only civil worship *(dulia)*. It was a distinction based on quality of worship, and this quality was in turn determined by the location of that worship. According to the prominent Elizabethan theologian William Perkins, author of *A Reformed Catholike* (1598): "Wee acknowledge the ciuill vse of images as freely and truly as the Church of Rome doth. By *ciuill vse* I understand, that vse which is made of them in the common societies of men, out of the appointed places of the solemne worshippe of God."[64] Another important issue was the subject matter of the image: certain subjects were considered more legitimate than others. God the Father, for example, could never be represented by a mere image; a portrait, however, might be acceptable, or even a historical subject from the Bible—but only so long as they were painted, as Perkins notes, "in priuate places."[65] Thomas Tenison, author of *Of Idolatry* (1678) and Archbishop of Canterbury at the time Beverley published his *History and Present State of Virginia,* explicitly gives license to subject matter that would seem to include the images of Algonquian idolatry in Beverley's and Bernard's texts: "it is not unlawful to carve or paint the Images of false gods, by way of story, or in order to the exposing of them in the particulars in which they are ridiculous."[66] The fact that theologians such as Perkins and Tenison felt they needed to justify in this fashion what images *could* be made suggests that there was something that was still troubling about such secular imagery, even if the image was intended to show what false belief looks like. So seriously did these writers take the prohibition of images in the Decalogue that they began with a general assumption that all images were by their very nature potential idols.[67]

Finally, there was an effort to distinguish between image types based on their formal properties, which is an approach I would like to consider in more detail. The primary distinction—one that is not too distant from Riegl's distinction between tactile and optical images—was between the "protuberant" image and the "flat" or "depressed" representation, categories that were invoked not so much to establish any certain rules as to what was and was not idolatry, but more as a kind of barometer that could test the danger of idolatry present in any given image. Perhaps the fullest expression in England on this matter is found in Henry Hammond's *Of Idolatry* of 1646:

> you may first observe some considerable difference between the two sorts of *resemblances,* which have been usuall among men. Some *extantes, corporeall* figures standing out, . . . statues, *graven images;* others onely *representations,* or *pictures, painted* on windows, tables, chalices, &c. The former of these were most used by (because fittest for the turns of) the Heathens, being by them (through the commodiousnesse and advantage of their bodily shapes) conceived to be more capable of animation by those gods of which they were the resemblances. . . . The other *pictures* which are called *dimissae, depressae,* a *plain painting* on a table, &c. without any *protuberancy,* or *bunching,* were not by the *Gentiles* thought so capable of receiving that *animation.* The distinction is *Maimons;* the first he calleth . . . *the protuberant image,* the other . . . the *depresse,* either drawn on a table in *colours,* saith he, or weaved in *hangings.* The former of these and not the latter, was it which was so strictly forbidden the *Jews.*[68]

The same or similar types of distinctions are found in other treatises. Tenison, for example, makes the distinction in terms of images of "presence" (images that include the "Statues of the Heathen," which, like the protuberant image, were thought to be divinely animated) and images of "representation" (simple likenesses that are the rough equivalent of what are for Hammond "onely *representations,* or *pictures*").[69]

The distinction between the protuberant and depressed image is as old as Jewish law, and Hammond cites the famed Jewish philosopher of the twelfth century, Maimonides (Moses ben Maimon), who in his monumental codification of Jewish law and tradition, the *Mishneh Torah,* made just these distinctions. During the seventeenth century, Maimonides's work experienced a revival in Holland, where it was translated widely by Protestant Hebraists. The specific work to which Hammond refers is a translation by Dionysius Vossius of a section of the *Mishneh Torah* regarding Jewish relations with gentiles, and particularly the problem of idolatry, which Vossius titled *De idololatria* (1641).[70] While Maimonides's contrast of the protuberant and depressed image goes back to the Jewish response to pagan cult statues, the Reformation revival of this terminology—especially as it was incorporated into treatises on idolatry such as Hammond's—must be understood in relation to the reintroduction of the cult statue into Christian worship during the twelfth century. For it was precisely this cult statue that the Reformation reacted against so harshly: these were the protuberant objects of Catholic idolatry that had formed the chief targets of iconoclasts throughout England and the Continent. While *De idololatria* was published after most of the image-breaking during the Reformation had already taken place, it does seem to have provided theologians such as Hammond and Tenison with a vocabulary that could articulate, after the fact, just why those statues had posed such a threat.[71]

It is a vocabulary that may therefore help us understand the threat that New World idolatry posed within Protestant ethnography. Specifically, it allows us to re-think the solution that the image of the tomb offers to the problem of picturing idolatry. The pictorial strategy of placing the idol in perspective and thus opening a distance between the enlightened subject and the idol (the very distance that the idol itself, as an image of spiritual *presence,* would close) may be understood as a kind of *flattening* of the protuberant idol. Both perspective and flattening are strategies of dis-tancing, of removing the threat of the idol, and in the image of the Algonquian tomb the perspectival grid is imposed as a kind of flattening response to that threat.

Indeed, perspectival construction is better than a simple flattening; it is more like a *depressing* of the idol, because it creates an optical illusion in which the idol spatially recedes from the viewer's immediate presence. And this, too, has its parallel in the formal classifications of a pre-perspectival world, for recessed images were comparable to, and perhaps even more acceptable than, flat ones. As Hammond notes, again with reference to Maimonides, "a *ring* that hath for a *seal* the figure of a Man, if it be *gib-bous,* or swelling out, is not itself lawfull to be *worne,* but yet it is *lawfull to seal* with it, because the *impression,* in that case, is *hollow,* not swelling out, and on the other side if the seal be *depresse,* or *hollow,* it is lawfull to *weare,* but not to seal with it."[72] In a very literal sense, the less matter in the image, the less presence it has, and the less presence it has, the less danger it poses to what Hume called the "vulgar apprehension" of mankind. The carved intaglio plate is a perfect instance of the kind of image that, by Maimonides's lights, would be acceptable, since it is in a very literal sense a hol-low seal created through the subtractive process of removing metal from a plate. The impression of this metallic seal, on the other hand, is somewhat more dangerous, for it is gibbous—it stands out on the page. And however slight that danger, however minor the protuberance of the engraver's lines may be, the print nevertheless retains the physical substance of an impression, and we have seen how closely early modern viewers were attuned to the sculptural qualities of printed images. Perspective speaks directly to this materiality because, through optical means, it returns the depressed quality of the intaglio plate to the final impression, thus mitigating its tactile presence. In the case of the perspectivized tomb, it is the *appearance* of hollowness, the illusion of empty space between the viewer and the scene of idolatry, that makes the priest with his corpses and idol seem safely distant in the elsewhere of the New World, far from anxious Calvinist consciences.

I am suggesting, in other words, the existence of a certain homology—at least insofar as seventeenth-century Protestant aesthetics and the Enlightenment anthro-pology of religion are concerned—between the depressed image of Jewish tradition on the one hand, and, on the other, what Panofsky called perspective's "distancing and objectifying sense of the real" and what Riegl called, speaking in more general terms, the "distant image." The categories of the protuberant and the depressed invoked by seventeenth-century Protestant treatises on idolatry constitute an important *subtext* to the optical, perspectival viewing of the idol during the eighteenth-century. This should not be too surprising, for as we have seen, the fascination of Beverley and Bernard's texts with the New World idol was fueled by a certain discomfort with, and a consequent need to achieve a certain distance from, an unreformed past—a past full of protuberant cult statues. Thus, although we link the notion of the depressed image with Jewish tradition and medieval Christianity, and although we associate the perspectival image with modernity, there are nevertheless shared concerns here that have been overlooked in our need to find fundamental breaks between the medieval and the modern.

Those shared concerns center on the body of Christ. The Christian belief that God had assumed a visual, material form in his Son provided the ultimate justification for the medieval cult statue and indeed for all medieval religious representation. But while the *doctrine* of the Incarnation remained at the core of Protestant belief, the Reformation retreated from the incarnational thinking that since the late Middle Ages had legitimized the making of protuberant religious images.[73] In their retreat from the materiality of the Christian past, Protestant theologians such as Hammond found a critical tool for articulating their antimaterialism in the notion of the depressed image; and, similarly, Enlightenment authorities on the idolatry of savages found a means for exercising their antimaterialism in the assumption of a perspectival point of view. In the latter case, however, despite the apparent distance of the eighteenth-century ethnographic image from the cult statue, the sacred body remains potentially present in a way that belies the image's appearance of hollowness. This is because the perspectival attitude toward protuberant forms is an inherently ambivalent one, one that requires us to qualify our notion of the perspectival image as an exemplary depressed image. To understand exactly what sort of qualification is needed and in what way Christ's irrepressible body might still lurk within our perspectival image of New World idolatry, we must consider the historical relationship between perspective and incarnational thinking.

Tenison points us in the direction of perspective's uncertain relationship with Christ's body with an interesting caveat about the flat image. He first notes, like Hammond, that there is less danger in images "especially if they be flat Pictures, not Protuberant Statues," but he then continues:

> nor Pictures which the Artist hath expressed with roundness. The worse and the more flat the work is, the less danger there is of its abuse. *Titian* hath painted the Virgin and the Child Jesus so very roundly, that (as Sir *Henry Wotton* a very good judg both of the pictures and dispositions of men, saith of it) a man knows not whether to call it a piece of Sculpture or Picture.[74]

In other words, a flat picture is best when its figures do not *seem* protuberant, which is as much as to say when they are not perspectivally foreshortened. For while perspective can indeed appear to distance bodies, as in the image of the Virginia tomb, it can equally appear to bring those bodies closer, abolishing their distance from the beholder and thus making them seem *more* present. Sir Henry Wotton, upon whose visual astuteness Tenison relies, describes the roundness of Italian pictures in his *Elements of Architecture,* in which he in fact shows great admiration for the ability of Italian painters to employ shadow in such a way that a figure in a picture could appear to have the material presence of a sculpture.[75] During the Italian Renaissance the chief purpose of perspective had not been to represent a hollow spatial continuum at all, but to provide fictive, three-dimensional settings for enhancing the roundness, or *rilievo,* of figures.[76] Indeed, Alberti, who codified painter's perspective in the fifteenth century, wrote that the function of the painter is "to describe with lines and to tint with colour on whatever panel or wall is given him similar observed planes of any body so that at a certain distance and in a certain position from the centre *they appear in relief, seem to have mass and to be lifelike*" (my italics).[77] For Tenison, however, the lifelikeness of simulated relief is troubling because it promotes the abuse of religious images. And Tenison is right on the mark insofar as he recognizes the tendency toward protuberant bodies in Italian pictures as originating out of desire for sacred presence. The perspectival foreshortening of the body was not employed by Italian Renaissance artists as a means of rationalizing religion, but it was often employed as a means of bringing sacred bodies into the presence of the viewer, bodies such as Christ's and the Virgin's. Because the bodies in our Algonquian tomb bear a material relation to their Renaissance predecessors, the place of the foreshortened body within the history of perspective deserves some further consideration.

The bodies in the tomb exemplify the type of extreme perspectival foreshortening that preoccupied artists, especially those with a special concern for perspectival problems, since the fifteenth century. The reclining figure was a problem of such interest, I would suggest, because of the challenge it posed to artists: this was nothing less than the challenge of reconciling the abstract mathematics of perspective with the corporeal matter of the world. In the reclining figure, the line that is the primary axis of the vertical, standing body is collapsed onto the orthogonal—that is, onto the horizontal line that recedes at ground level toward the vanishing point and that defines perspectival space. To foreshorten perfectly the human figure is therefore to reconcile the matter of the body with the idealized visual field of perspective. For fifteenth- and sixteenth-century artists this had been a challenge of practical interest primarily in religious art; during the later sixteenth and seventeenth centuries, when illustrated perspective manuals began to appear with more frequency, it became increasingly a subject of theoretical interest as perspectivists sought more rigorously to envelop bodies within a homogenous spatial continuum.[78] Jan Vredeman de Vries's 1605 perspective manual, for example, includes plates that attempt to work out just this problem (Figure 56). A single reclining figure lies on a table within a vaulted architectural space, and despite the open door to the right, the figure appears (much like the bodies in the New World tomb) to be locked firmly within the perspective construction of the hollow room. Another instance of the reclining figure appears in an earlier manuscript known as the *Codex Huygens,* a sixteenth-century treatise on perspective based on the work of Leonardo da Vinci (Figure 57). Below his diagram, the author of the *Codex Huygens* gives us some indication of the fame that the depiction of the reclining figure could bring to practitioners of perspective: "Those painters who have left in their work some representations of a body stretched out on the ground and extending its soles towards the spectator have acquired the name of great perspectivists with the mob, they have earned much honour and praise, and they have remained a byword for many centuries."[79] The author's comment that these artists have appealed mainly to the mob *(volgo)* should not be taken as a criticism of this perspectival problem itself, but rather as an expression of impatience with artists who failed to live up to the highest standards of mathematical rigor.

His frustration is not without justification. As Robert Smith has shown, in depictions of the sharply foreshortened figure by Italian Renaissance artists, "natural vision" wins out over correct perspective. The classic example of this is Andrea Mantegna's *Dead Christ,* a painting that, even though Christ's proportions seem naturally or intuitively correct, is well known for its lapses in perspective (Figure 58).[80] For Mantegna, an interest in pictorially realizing the corporeal volume of the human form—specifically Christ's form—takes precedence over a strict adherence to the rules of perspective, and this seems to be just the attitude that irritates the author of the *Codex Huygens.* But it is not a poor grasp of perspectival theory that is responsible for the appearance of Mantegna's painting; rather, it is a different set of pictorial priorities. For Italian Renaissance artists the primary goal in foreshortening the human figure was not to contain that figure within a mathematically correct space, but to bring the sacred body as fully as possible into the viewer's space. Although Mantegna's *Dead Christ* should hardly be taken as typical of all Renaissance foreshortened bodies (the *Codex Huygens,* after all, belongs to this period), I do take it to be exemplary of a basic difference in pictorial sensibility between the kind of foreshortening practiced by Mantegna and that practiced by the eighteenth-century Protestant engravers Gribelin and Picart. During the Italian Renaissance, the perspectival foreshortening of sacred figures must be understood, like the cult statue of the late Middle Ages, in relation to incarnational thinking. Renaissance painters responded to the incarnational theology of the period, a theology that was focused not on the purity of the Word but on the Word made flesh in Christ.[81] Behind Mantegna's painting is a desire to materialize the faith of his viewers. The *Dead Christ* does not insist on the rationality of the space in which Christ is contained, but on the presence of his body, which indeed seems *not* to be fully contained by pictorial space as it protrudes into the world of the spectator. Mantegna's painting may be flat, but in its insistence on its roundness it is the kind of flatness that will later trouble Protestant theologians like Thomas Tenison.[82]

How unlike Mantegna's protuberant Christ are the withered corpses of our American kings. The incarnated body is precisely what this ethnographic image does *not* want. Its foreshortened figures are in effect a dematerialization of Mantegna's Christ. With their flesh removed—"They pick all the Flesh off from the Bones as clean as

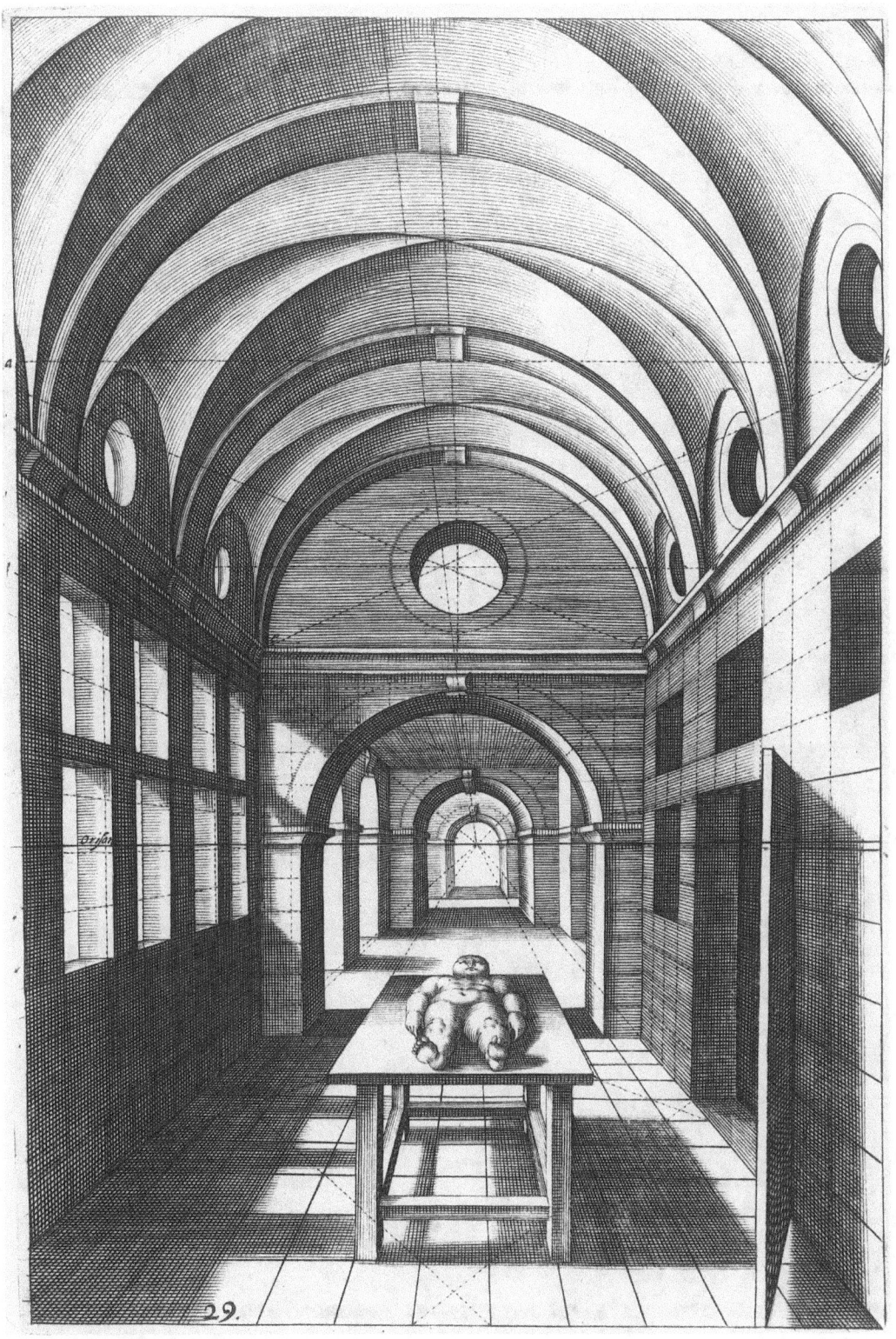

Figure 56. Henrik Hondius, Plate 29 from Jan Vredeman de Vries, *Perspective* (The Hague, 1604–5). Courtesy and with permission of The Rare Book and Manuscript Library of the University of Illinois, Urbana-Champaign.

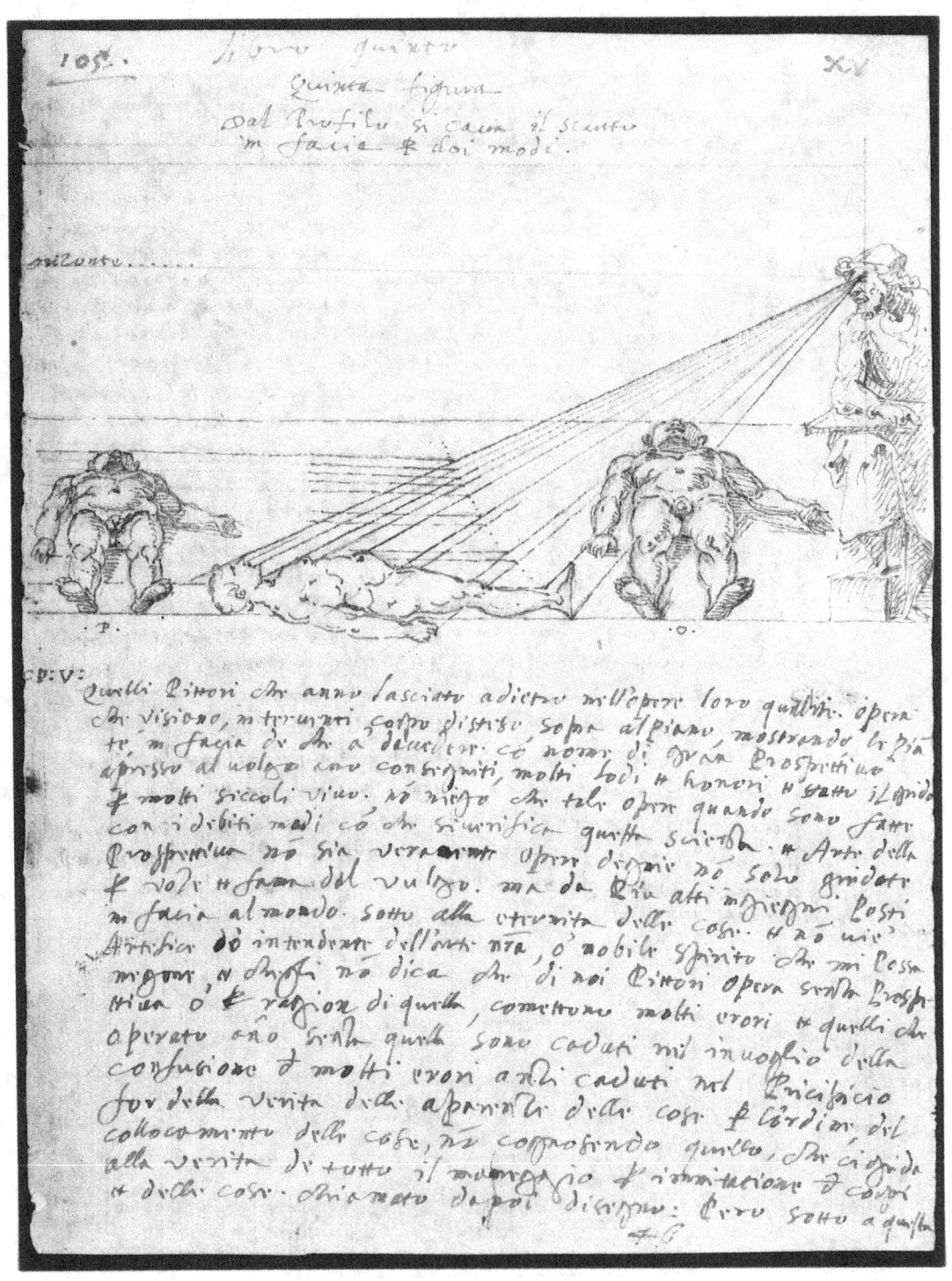

possible"[83]—and lacking any signs of sexuality, these bodies have lost the substance of bodies: dead, empty, and asexual, they map easily into the bare bones of the tomb's perspective as so many bodily orthogonals (an effect that is particularly pronounced in Gribelin's version of the image). Another dematerializing move is the multiplication of bodies, which appear as so many converging lines insisting on their recession, rather than as a single body insisting on its protuberance. We might think of this image as a diagrammatic reaction to that earlier perspectival body; it is an effort to *contain* that body within a supremely rationalized architectural perspective, as the plate from de Vries's treatise seems so completely to contain the diminutive reclining figure within its rigorously constructed space. Or, to consider the tomb once again alongside the plate from Bosse's treatise, it appears that Gribelin and Picart, in giving us the matter of American religion, would also like to slough off the matter of the world (including the viewer's body) on their way to creating a mental schema, the disembodied image of perspectival thought itself (see Figure 46).

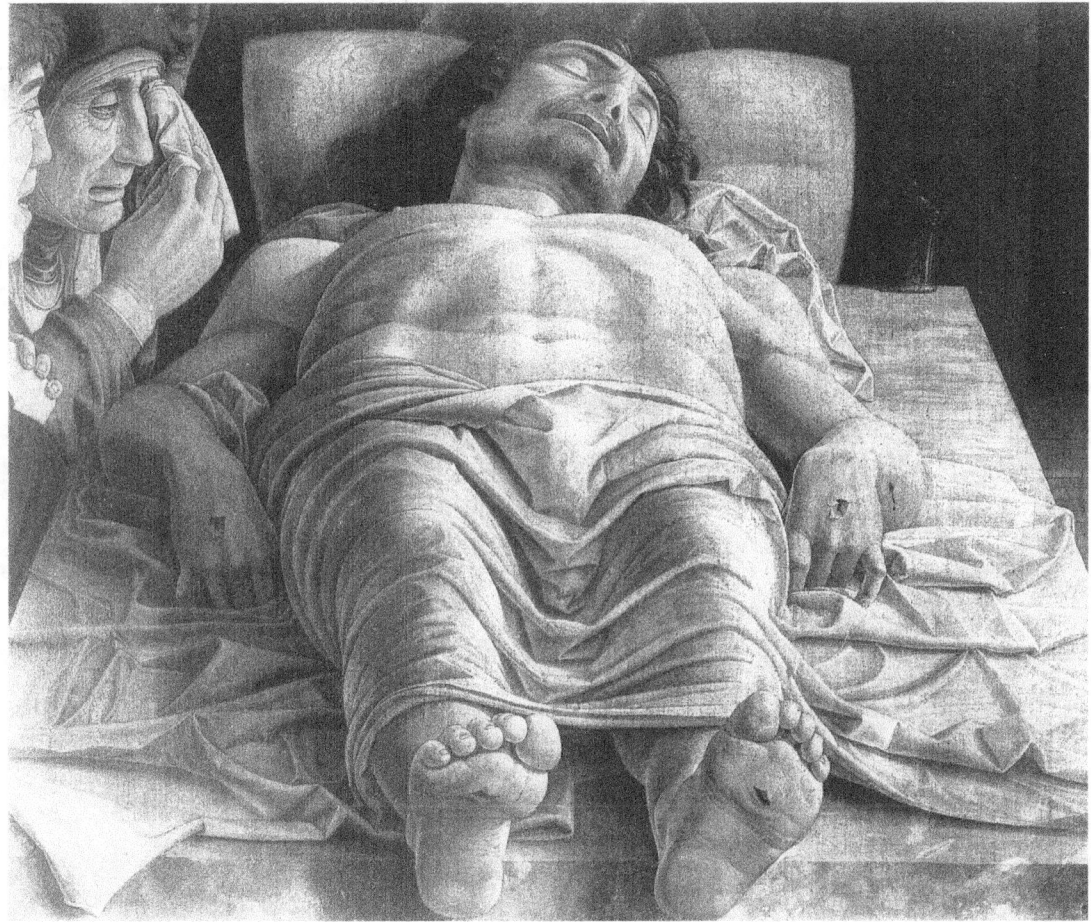

Figure 58. Andrea Mantegna, *Dead Christ,* tempera on canvas, before 1506. Milan, Pinacoteca di Brera. Courtesy and with permission of the Italian Ministry of Artistic and Cultural Heritage.

My reading of the engraving of the Virginia tomb has centered on two competing impulses: one to materialize religion, to realize the religious customs of the world as the visual objects of an empirical science; the other to dematerialize it, to remove the sacred body as far as possible (almost to the point of annihilation) from the viewer's presence. And as I have argued, the need for this dematerialization of religious matter arises from its troubling proximity to Protestant belief, a proximity that is bound up with the very history of perspective itself. As Leo Steinberg has argued about paintings such as Mantegna's *Dead Christ,* the materialization of divinity is exactly what the *Renaissance* artist was seeking: "Lifelikeness posed no threat, because these Renaissance artists regarded the godhead in the person of Jesus as too self-evident to be dimmed by his manhood."[84] This presence of God in mere matter is exactly what was no longer self-evident to a reformed Catholic of the seventeenth or eighteenth century—it was something to be sublimated in one's own faith; recorded, studied, and criticized in the religions of others. But even if no longer self-evident, that unreformed content continues to haunt the "enlightened" subject of eighteenth-century ethnography. The engravings of the Virginia tomb in Beverley's *History and Present State of Virginia* and Bernard's *Ceremonies* insist so strongly on their perspectival structure, on depressing their protuberant subject matter, because viewers knew at some level that this struggle toward an empirical knowledge of American religion depended on—indeed, by virtue of its embodiment in the form of intaglio prints, was *constituted by*—a *desire* for the tactile, sculptural image. The perspectivally foreshortened human figure can thus serve as a kind of object lesson for understanding the Protestant ethnographic image. For like that foreshortened body so deeply rooted in the embodiment of the sacred, the countless graven images that fill early modern ethnographic texts inevitably appealed to a base sensuality and materiality in the viewer that could easily become, if not properly distanced, a desire for the body of Christ.

4. The Art of Scratch
Wood Engraving and Picture-Writing in the 1880s

It is not easy to be done with a civilization of the hand.

—Roland Barthes, "The Plates of the Encyclopedia"

Consider two reproductions, both published in American periodicals within twenty-five years of each another. The first, John White's watercolor drawing of *The Flyer,* was reproduced in *Century Magazine* in 1882 in the first of a series of articles on colonial American history by historian and novelist Edward Eggleston (Figure 59). The second, a drawing by the same artist titled *One of their Religious men,* was reproduced in *Putnam's Monthly* in 1907 in the article "Governor John White: Painter and Virginian Pioneer," which was written by British art historian and poet Laurence Binyon (Figure 60). Both images convey similar visual information. Both strive for a photographic accuracy that reproduces even the smallest details of the original, down to the artist's handwriting. Eggleston and Binyon wanted to provide their audiences with the real thing; that is, with faithful reproductions of a watercolor collection that, after having been lost for almost three centuries, had been rediscovered in 1865 by American book collector Henry Stevens, and promptly sold to the British Museum.[1] By providing the American public for the first time with accurate reproductions of these eyewitness visual records of sixteenth-century Virginia, *Century* and *Putnam's* were making up for centuries of degraded copies.[2] Beginning with de Bry's engravings in 1590, which in Eggleston's words reproduced White's watercolors "with only moderate accuracy," White's "authentic" vision of early Virginia had grown more and more mediated, more and more distant from its viewers.[3] Popular nineteenth-century works on American Indians included reproductions removed two and even three times from White's originals.[4] In the plates that appeared in *Century* and *Putnam's,* a direct link to one of the earliest English encounters with native America became available once again. The

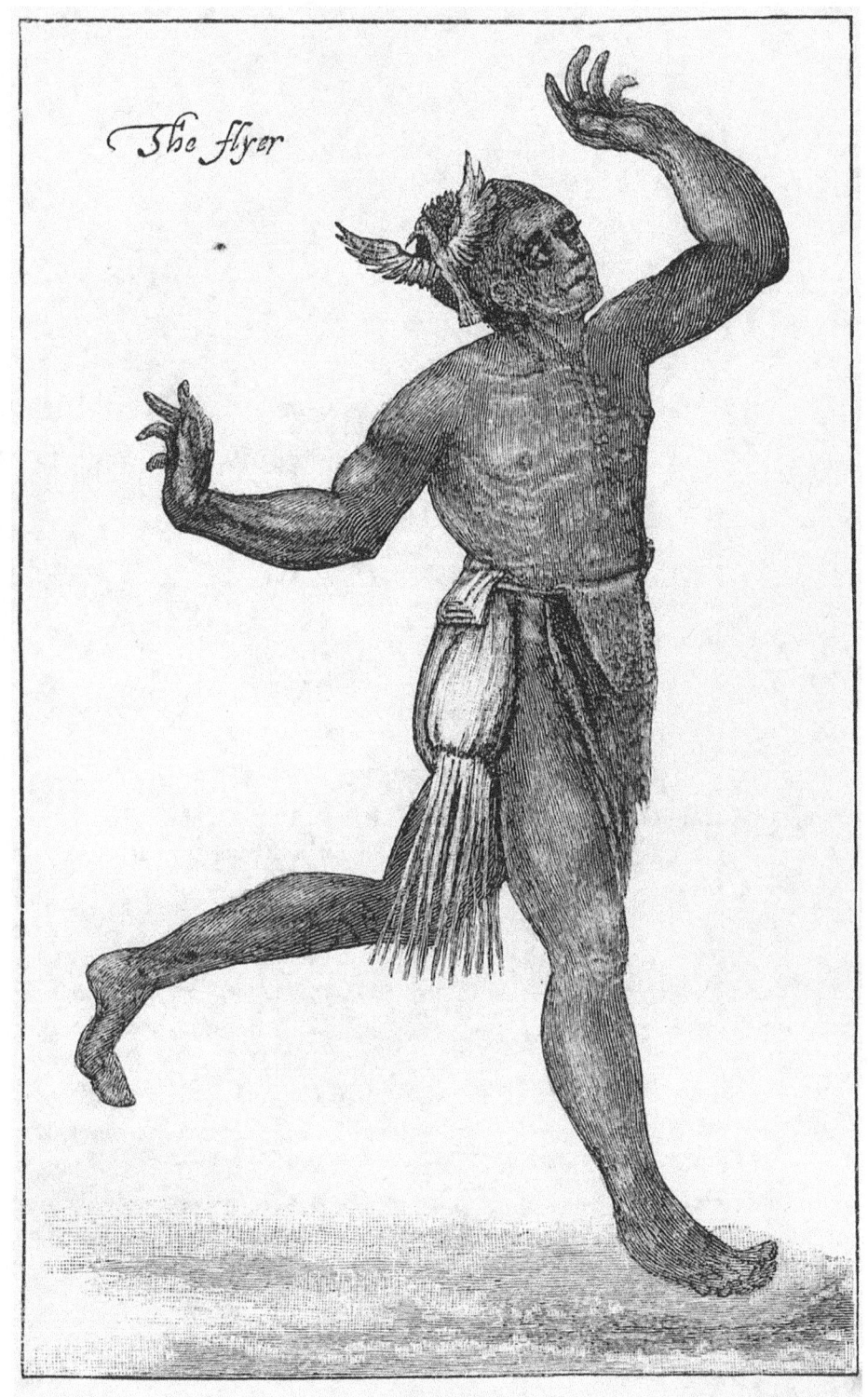

The flyer

AN INDIAN CONJURER. (FROM JOHN WHITE'S ORIGINAL DRAWING, NOW IN THE BRITISH MUSEUM.)

Figure 59. John White, *The Flyer,* wood engraving, *Century* (November 1882). From the Collections of the University Libraries, University of Minnesota, Minneapolis.

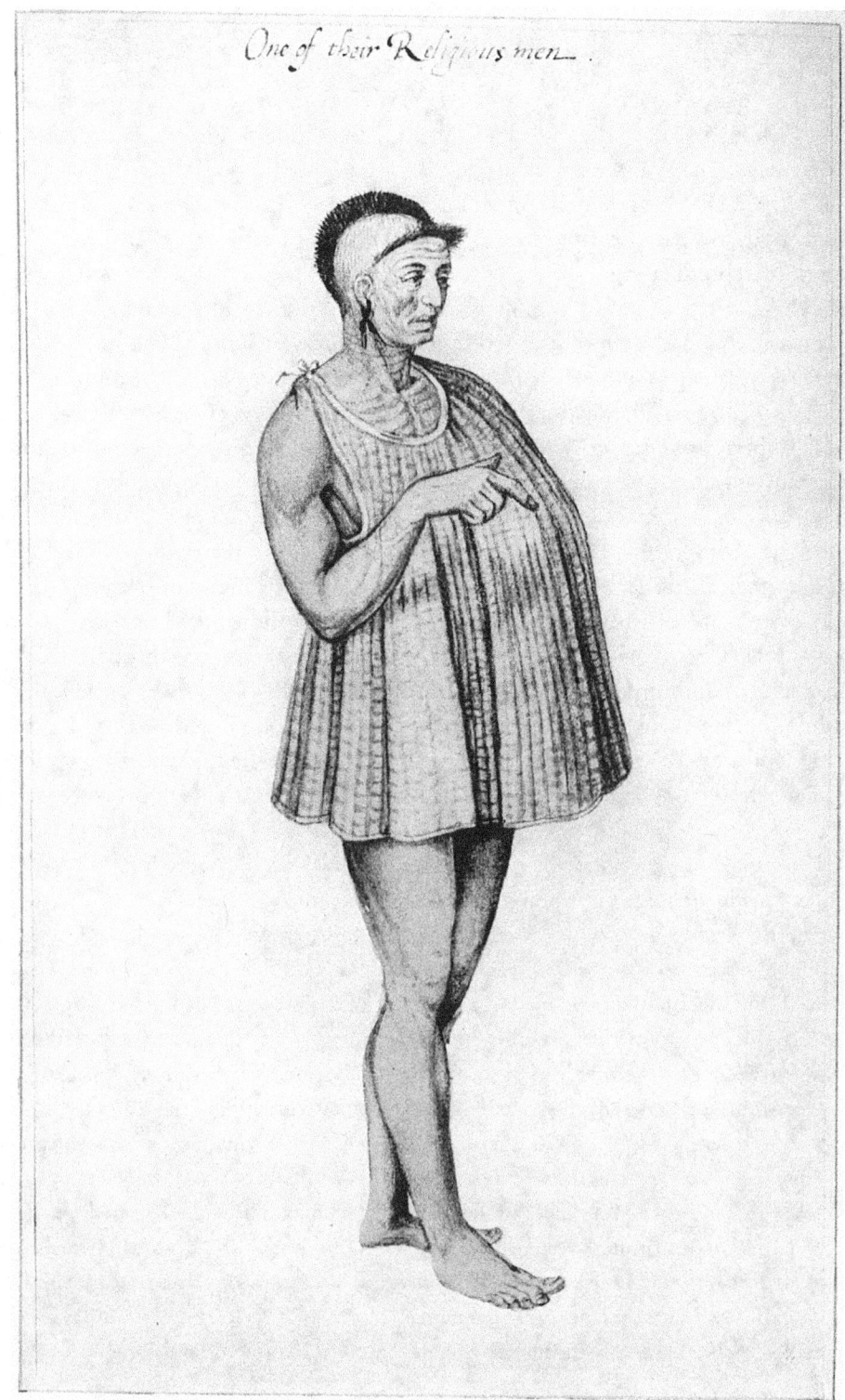

Figure 60. John White, *One of their Religious men,* halftone, *Putnam's Monthly* (July 1907). From the Collections of the University Libraries, University of Minnesota, Minneapolis.

new reproductions of *The Flyer* and *One of their Religious men*—in contrast to the same two figures as they are reproduced in an 1840 edition of Picart's *Ceremonies* (Figure 61)—allow us, as Binyon writes, "to see with our own eyes."[5]

Yet there is also an important difference between the two reproductions. Even though both are based on photographs of White's originals and even though both attempt to reproduce those originals as accurately as possible, the reproductive processes differed considerably: the plate from *Century* is a wood engraving based on a photograph that had been transferred to a wood block, while the plate from *Putnam's* is not an engraving at all but a halftone reproduction made entirely through a photomechanical process. The distinction seems relatively minor, more a technical matter than a properly art-historical one. Yet some rather large claims have been made for the significance of this transition from handmade reproductions to photomechanical processes. As William Ivins has argued, it was only during the latter part of the nineteenth century, as photographic reproductions became more common, that the viewing public began to realize that there was indeed an important difference between original works of art ("the brush marks, the chisel strokes, and the worked textures, the sum totals of which are actually the works of art") and the syntax or code through which the reproduction communicates the original to the viewer.[6] For Ivins the emergence of the halftone process during the 1890s and early 1900s as the preferred method for reproducing works of art was an event of singular importance precisely because it allowed the viewer to see the hand of the original artist rather than the hand of the engraver:

> The great importance of the half-tone lay in its syntactical difference from the older hand made processes of printing pictures in printer's ink. In the old processes, the report started by a syntactical analysis of the thing seen, which was followed by its symbolic statement in the language of drawn lines. This translation was then translated into the very different analysis and syntax of the process. The lines and dots in the old reports were not only insistent in claiming visual attention, but they, their character, and their symbolism of statement, had been determined more by the two super-imposed analyses and syntaxes than by the particularities of the thing seen. In the improved half-tone process there was no preliminary syntactical analysis of the thing seen into lines and dots, and the ruled lines and dots of the process had fallen below the threshold of normal vision. . . . At last men had discovered a way to make visual reports in printer's ink without syntax, and without the distorting analyses of form that syntax necessitated. Today we are so accustomed to this that we think little of it, but it represents one of the most amazing discoveries that man has ever made—a cheap and easy means of symbolic communication without syntax.[7]

While Ivins's faith in the transparency of the halftone has been criticized, there is no question that in very important ways the halftone did offer "the particularities of the thing seen" in unprecedented fashion.[8] And because of the invisibility of its syntax, it *seemed* transparent, as if the original were speaking for itself rather than through an

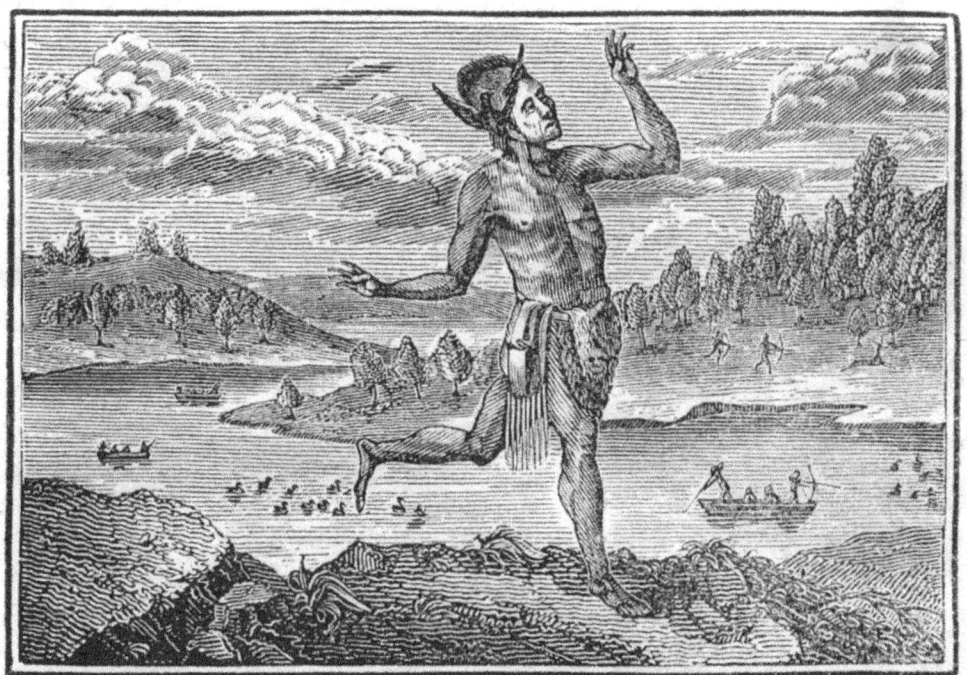

Virginia Magician. p. 563.

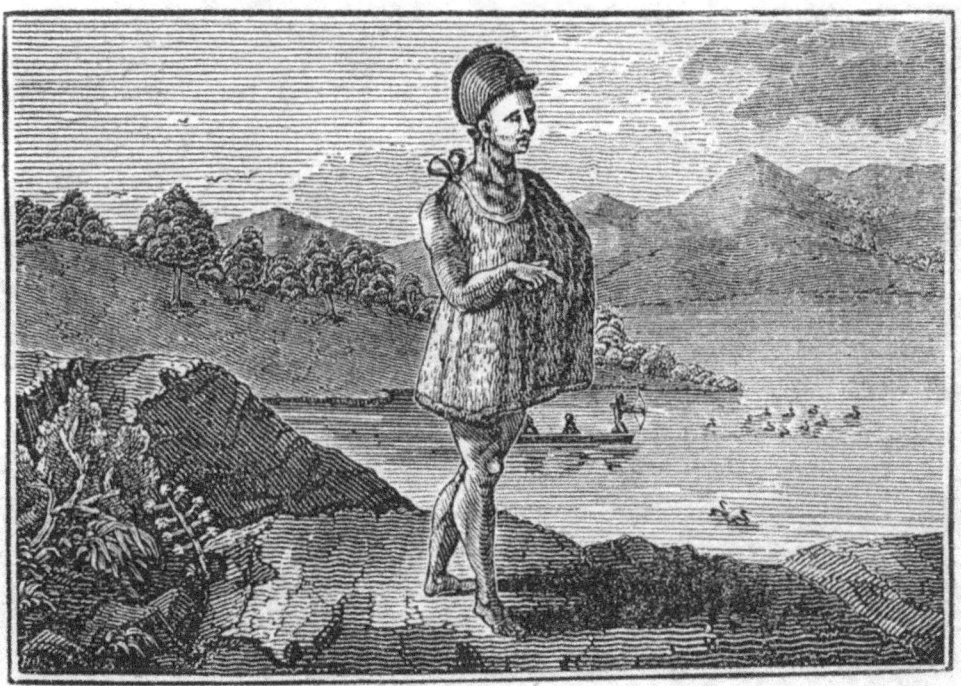

Virginia Priest. p. 563.

Figure 61. *Virginia Magician* and *Virginia Priest,* from Charles A. Goodrich, *Religious Ceremonies and Customs, or the Forms of Worship Practised by the Several Nations of the Known World* (Louisville, 1840). DeWitt Wallace Library, Macalester College, St. Paul, Minnesota.

intervening process. The halftones of White's watercolors in *Putnam's* made viewers feel that they were seeing with their own eyes what Binyon called the "handiwork of White." Indeed, halftone reproduction and other photographic processes, because of their value in reporting detailed information about pictorial surfaces, have played a crucial role in shaping the discipline of art history as it is practiced today.[9] As André Malraux wrote in *Museum without Walls* (1967), "For the past hundred years, (if we except the activities of specialists), the history of art has been the history of that which can be photographed."[10]

The concern of this chapter, however, is not photomechanical reproduction but the "old reports" that immediately preceded the halftone and that were effectively put to rest by the new method during the 1890s.[11] Those old reports are exemplified by *The Flyer* and the other fifteen reproductions of White's Virginia images that appeared in 1882 and 1883 in three of Eggleston's articles for *Century*.[12] When we begin to examine *The Flyer* closely, we see that its codes are indeed *not* below the threshold of vision; the image resolves not into the thing itself but into a pattern of hundreds of very thin parallel lines, into a *syntax,* the visible sign of a wood engraver's concentrated efforts with his tools. These lines convey a good deal of visual information about White's watercolor, but at the same time they tell us about the labor of reproducing that watercolor—about the intricacy and perhaps even the monotony of that labor. During the 1880s, just prior to the triumph of the halftone, wood engraving had been the preferred method for reproducing works of art, and this was particularly true for *Century,* a magazine famous for the quality of its wood engravings. But for all of their skill, *Century's* engravers faced a dilemma that would disappear with the introduction of the halftone: if there was indeed an important difference between the message of the original and the syntax through which that message was communicated to the viewer, then what was to be done with the insistently present, insistently interfering, insistently *material* lines of the engraver? How were the makers and viewers of reproductions to negotiate between the engraver's visible syntax and the desire for an unmediated visual experience of the original?

Our own habits of seeing, trained by photography and its rhetoric of transparency, have made it easy to overlook the significance of the wood engraver's lines.[13] Yet those lines were the subject of frequent, sometimes urgent discussion both in America and in England during the late nineteenth century. I would like to make a case for the importance of *not* overlooking those lines, of coming to terms with their materiality. The engraver's lines were implicated in the most basic processes of producing meaning within the illustrated press of the late nineteenth century. In the busy, tedious lines of the reproductive wood engravers of the 1880s, as we shall see, the labor of making civilization out of a savage past—the labor of *evolving*—is made visible.

The Author's Hand

The reproduction of John White's watercolors in *Century* during the 1880s offers an interesting parallel to their reproduction three hundred years earlier in the *Report.* In both cases the authors explicitly point out that the engravings were copied directly from the eyewitness accounts by White, and that the reproductions have been faithful to the originals. However, while de Bry and Harriot were seeking the true pictures and fashions of a people still unknown to Europeans in 1590, Eggleston sought a somewhat different type of authenticity. For Eggleston and his readers, White's images provided access not to a living present but to a distant past, to the moment of American colonization and, thus, to borrow the title of the article in which Eggleston first reproduced White's images, to the "Beginnings of a Nation." Before we turn to the wood engraver's lines, then, it is worth considering in more detail the kind of value a late nineteenth-century audience might have placed on a new reproductive project based directly on these unique visual records of the moment of England's encounter with the New World.

After White's collection was sold to the British Museum in 1866 it remained in relative obscurity until, in 1880, Eggleston came across it while conducting research for his history of colonial America. These watercolors, Eggleston believed, were surely the original images used by de Bry for the *Report's* copper-plate engravings. As such, they were extremely valuable documents for a historian who insisted on the authenticity of his sources. In his thirteen articles on colonial America published in *Century* between 1882 and 1890, Eggleston was careful to draw directly from sources "contemporaneous, or nearly so, with the events narrated."[14] In the spirit of one his chief influences, nineteenth-century French historian Augustin Thierry, Eggleston sought to write a history based not on authorities who lived long after the actual events, but on the original sources themselves.[15] "Too often," wrote British historian James Gairdner in an 1880 article on historical sources, "especially in our own generation, the most popular and attractive historians have sought rather to supersede this reference to original authors, and have produced works which are rather a barrier to block up the way of true historic study than a real help."[16] It was not only in his reliance on original texts that Eggleston sought to break this barrier, but in his use of illustrations as well. As one of *Century's* editorialists noted in 1885 in reference to the images used in Eggleston's historical series: "A great amount of pains has been expended to insure the authenticity and veracity of these cuts; it is, indeed, intended to make them as valuable for historic purposes as the text itself."[17] The claim recalls the words of de Bry himself in the *Report,* in which he points out his "ernest paynes in grauinge the pictures . . . in Copper, seeing yt is a matter of noe small importance."[18] During the nineteenth century as during the sixteenth, the authority of the documentary project rests on the care, and indeed the *pain,* that the engraver takes in reproducing authentic sources.

After the publication of his articles, Eggleston continued efforts to ensure their "authenticity and veracity." This involved the deattribution of a collection in the British Museum that an earlier scholar had assigned to John White. During the early eighteenth century, Hans Sloane, the great collector, natural historian, and founder of the British Museum, acquired a collection of images he believed were White's originals. The volume containing these drawings includes an inscription in Sloane's hand:

> The originall draughts of yᵉ habits, towns customs &c of the West Indians, and of the plants birds fishes &c found in Groenland, Virginia, Guiana &c by Mʳ. John White who was a Painter & accompanied Sʳ. Walter Ralegh in his voyag. See the preface to the first part of America of Theodore de Bry or the description of Virginia where some of these draughts are curiously cutt by that Graver.[19]

Sloane clearly believed he had found the source for de Bry's famous engravings. But the authorship of the drawings, while a subject of interest for Sloane on account of the influence de Bry's work continued to exert during the eighteenth century, was nevertheless secondary to their scientific value. The drawings comprise one of the several so-called "Sloane albums" in the British Museum, albums in which images were collected more for the sake of the natural-history subjects they recorded than for the fame of the artists who produced them.[20] Sloane and other members of the British scientific community drew upon these images as so many specimens. Mark Catesby, for instance, without ever bothering to acknowledge White, copied seven natural-history subjects for his *Natural History of Carolina, Florida, and the Bahama Islands* (1731–43).[21] For Catesby and Sloane, as for de Bry before them, *John White* was essentially an empty name, a label that could be conveniently attached to an important set of watercolor drawings but a name that was finally less important than the curious subject matter of the drawings themselves.

Eggleston, in contrast, invested a great deal in the authority of White's name, and it was therefore a matter of some importance to show that Sloane had incorrectly attributed the drawings in the Sloane album. In a letter to the *Nation* in 1891, Eggleston was the first to argue against that attribution. Sloane's drawings, he claimed, were merely "early and rather clumsy copies." The true originals were in the collection that Henry Stevens had sold to the museum. Eggleston based his conclusions on his own skills as a connoisseur. He had compared the two sets of drawings and decided that only the recently purchased collection showed the quality and accuracy we might expect from a skilled artist who had seen his American subjects firsthand. And even though that collection included no actual signature, it showed a stylistic unity that pointed to a single author. Both the maps and figures, Eggleston wrote, are "by the same hand . . . , and that hand is presumably White's. The correspondence between the handwriting and the execution of the map [of the southern Atlantic coast] and the figures shows that they are by the same clever artist."[22]

For Eggleston, all of White's images were signed by the artist in the sense that any work of art that comes under the scrutiny of the connoisseur betrays the hand of its producer. I would suggest, moreover, that *The Flyer* stands out from the other drawings reproduced in *Century* as a signature piece, indeed as a kind of self-portrait. During the 1880s, a decade that saw the popularization of scientific connoisseurship through the influence of Giovanni Morelli, even insignificant details in a painting, such as the way the artist draws hands and ears, began to be treated as the signature of the artist in question. As Morelli writes, "every important painter has, so to speak, a type of hand and ear peculiar to himself," an observation that he demonstrated in the illustrations to his *Italian Painters* (Figure 62).[23] In an important respect, then, the hands that *The Flyer* so prominently displays—flaunts even—*are* John White's hands, insofar as they are executed in a manner in which only John White could have executed them: with an elegant, mannered curving and twisting of the fingers that can also be found in the more modestly arranged hands of White's other figures. The flourishes of the shaman's fingers, furthermore, echo the italic flourishes of White's writerly hand as seen in the text at the top left corner of *The Flyer*. When considered from the connoisseur's point of view, this image in its unabashed display of the artist's hand would seem to confirm Eggleston's argument that both handwriting and execution point to the identity of the artist. *The Flyer* is, moreover, the first of White's figures that appears in *Century*, and to the immediate right of the image we have Eggleston's introduction of John White himself, artist and governor, as if there were indeed a special correspondence between *The Flyer* and its producer. Both,

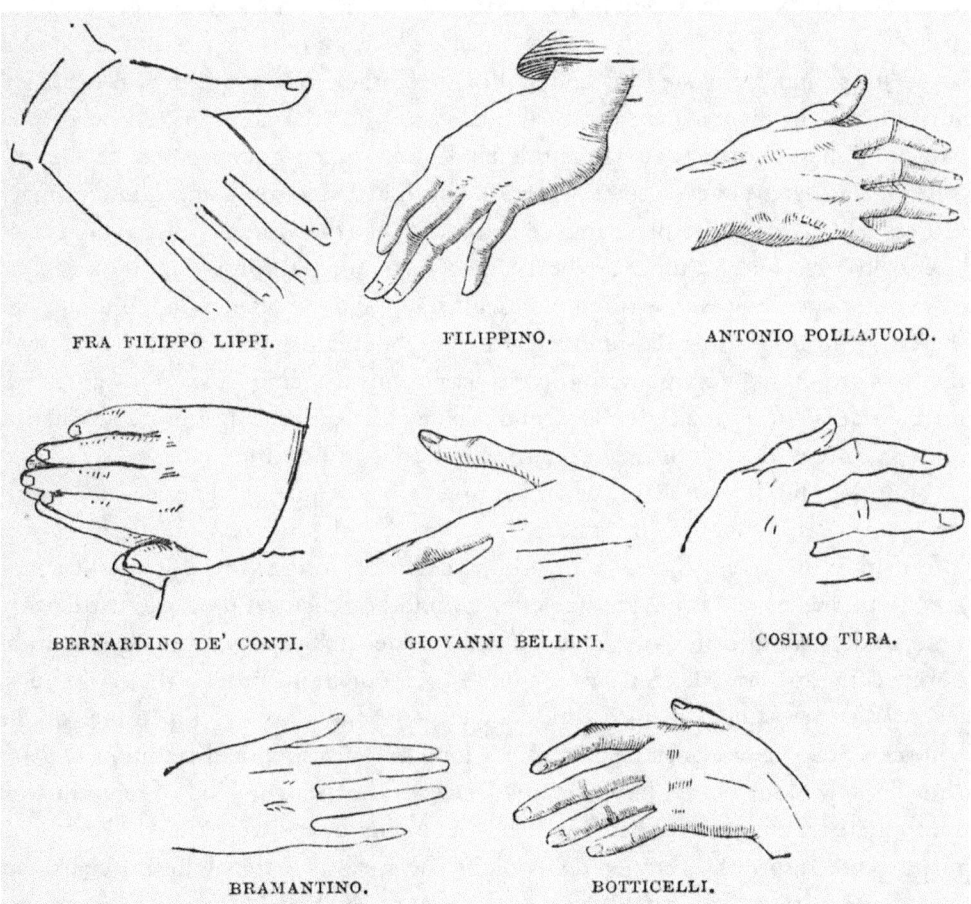

Figure 62. *Typical Hands,* from Giovanni Morelli, *Italian Painters* (London, 1892–93). From the Collections of the University Libraries, University of Minnesota, Minneapolis.

after all, are exemplary go-betweens, interpreters whose task is to translate between worlds. In the Flyer's case, this translation is carried out through the gesticulations of winglike hands that interpret between spirit and human worlds; in White's case, it is the deft hand of the clever artist that interprets for posterity the moment of New World encounter.[24]

Hardly an empty name, John White became the referent of his collection when it was reproduced in *Century*. One might even argue that the artist's name became his collection's *primary* referent. For while the illustrations of White's watercolors may have been intended to provide historical evidence in support of Eggleston's narrative—while they may have been considered "as valuable for historic purposes as the text itself"[25]—the only evidence they clearly contribute to Eggleston's history of early America is evidence of their own authenticity. Remarkably, Eggleston offers no commentary at all on his reproductions. In the case of *The Flyer*, as with the other reproductions of White's images, we are provided only with captions that offer a brief title—AN INDIAN CONJURER—followed by a statement of authenticity—"FROM JOHN WHITE'S ORIGINAL DRAWING, NOW IN THE BRITISH MUSEUM." The historical value of the image is realized when it returns us, self-reflexively, to the hand of its producer.

With so much invested in the hand of the author (nothing less than historical authenticity, in this case), a great deal hinged on the accurate transmission of that hand to a mass audience. As far as the hand of a writer was concerned, that transmission was relatively easy, since a historian such as Eggleston could quote primary sources in *Century*'s letterpress and be confident that the writer's words would have essentially the same meaning as they had in their original form. The transmission of visual images, however, was more difficult. Photography offered one solution, but there was no means of mass-producing actual photographs on the same page with the letterpress. The halftone was not yet a feasible option, since it was only at experimental stages during the early 1880s, and existing photomechanical processes such as photogravure were prohibitively expensive and difficult to print.[26]

But even by the late 1880s, when halftones were frequently appearing in American periodicals, they were not universally accepted as the best way to transmit visual information. In *Century*'s case, a lingering attachment to the syntax of an older process, wood engraving, made the transition to photomechanical processes particularly slow. Under the editorship of Richard Watson Gilder (1881–1909), the magazine stubbornly clung to and defended this method of reproduction through the early 1900s, when other magazines had turned to the cheaper though less artful halftone. Unlike halftones, wood engravings belonged to a long and distinguished tradition that included the work of Dürer, Holbein, and Bewick. This was the kind of reproduction appropriate for a magazine that saw itself as a beacon for the arts. Under Gilder, *Century* became "a sort of illustrated textbook on the arts," as Arthur John has characterized it, and because Gilder believed that to cultivate good taste among his readers was to cultivate good morals, he sought reproductions of the highest quality—the kind one could remove from the magazine and hang on the wall.[27] Therefore, through a "great amount of pains" and at great expense, Gilder brought his readers the best wood engravings of the so-called New School. Gilder valued their reproductions over half-tones because the syntax of the wood engraver was like the brushstroke of the artist it reproduced: it held a capacity to influence taste and shape morals. The problem with the halftone, noted an 1890 editorial in *Century,* was that, unlike the engraver, "it cannot interpret tones; it cannot think."[28]

Yet the halftone did offer one thing that wood engravings, it seemed to some, could not offer—objectivity; and objectivity had its own kind of morality. As viewers became increasingly attuned to the difference between the message of the original work and the syntax of the engraving, the accurate reproduction of that original with as little interference as possible became a moral imperative. Lorraine Daston and Peter Galison have termed this moralizing pursuit *mechanical objectivity,* and it was sought with particular zeal in scientific illustration during the late nineteenth and early twentieth centuries.[29] Mechanical objectivity, as the phrase suggests, was grounded in photography and photomechanical forms of reproduction: it was premised on the elimination of the fallible human hand from the reproductive process.[30] Its morality was not one of accuracy (halftones, after all, failed to reproduce certain qualities of the original, as wood engravers were always pointing out); rather, it was a morality of self-restraint, of not presuming to judge what viewers should be left to judge for themselves. But it was not only scientists who sought mechanical objectivity; it was pursued by the reproductive wood engravers of *Century* as well. Even as the New School of wood engravers celebrated their status as fine artists, they celebrated the objectivity of their methods as well. Aided by the use of photography-on-the-block, members of this school sought something close to photographic veracity in their reproductions: "Exactly to reproduce," wrote engraver John Davis, "that is the present aim of the engraver on wood."[31] Yet in reproducing works of art, the wood engraver inevitably left his own mark. He worked with a visible syntax that advertised his subjectivity. There was, then, a fundamental ambiguity, both epistemological and moral, in the lines of the New School engraver. Should these lines be flaunted or suppressed? Should the engraver be an artist or a machine?

It was partly this ambiguity surrounding the subjectivity/objectivity of the chief reproductive method of the 1880s that made it a frequent topic of discussion in the popular press. During this decade, numerous articles and editorials on both the practice and history of wood engraving appeared in *Century* and in *Century's* chief competitor, *Harper's New Monthly Magazine.* Two magazine issues, flanking either end of the decade, allow us to see the most prominent wood engravers of the period wrestling with these questions in their own words: the February 1880 issue of *Harper's,* which includes a "Symposium of Wood-Engravers" expressing their views on the New School and its objectives, and the August 1889 issue of *Century,* with a series of articles by engravers on "Originality in Wood-Engraving," "Painter-Engraving," and "The New School of Engraving." The latter series stresses the treatment of wood engraving as a fine art, similar in status to etching, for with the rising popularity of the halftone the outlook for wood engraving as a method of reproduction was growing less certain. The same John Davis who in "A Symposium of Wood-Engravers" claimed that the aim of wood engraving was "exactly to reproduce," declared in his 1889 article, "Let art be your master."[32]

    Harper's "A Symposium of Wood-Engravers," in contrast, calls attention to the objectivity of the New School by pitting its leading members—chief among them Timothy Cole, *Century's* star reproductive engraver—against William J. Linton, the leading practitioner of an older school of wood engraving and the author of an 1879 article in *Atlantic Monthly* that had rather viciously attacked one of Cole's engravings for *Century.* For Linton, the integrity of the engraver's line was everything: "Every line of an engraving ought to have a meaning."[33] An engraving from William Cullen Bryant's *The Song of the Sower,* based on a drawing by W. J. Hennessy, demonstrates

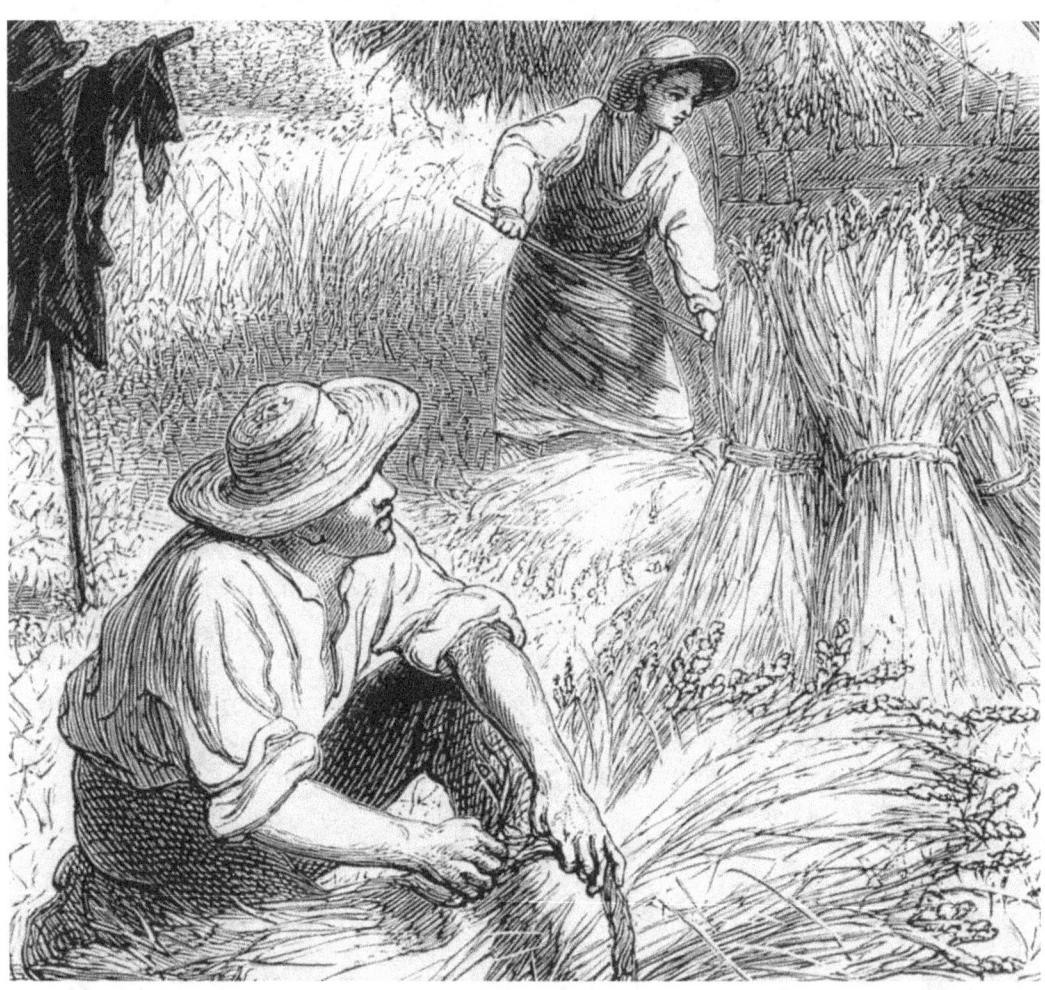

Figure 63. William J. Linton, *The song of him who binds the grain* (detail), wood engraving, from William Cullen Bryant, *The Song of the Sower* (New York, 1871). From the Collections of the University Libraries, University of Minnesota, Minneapolis.

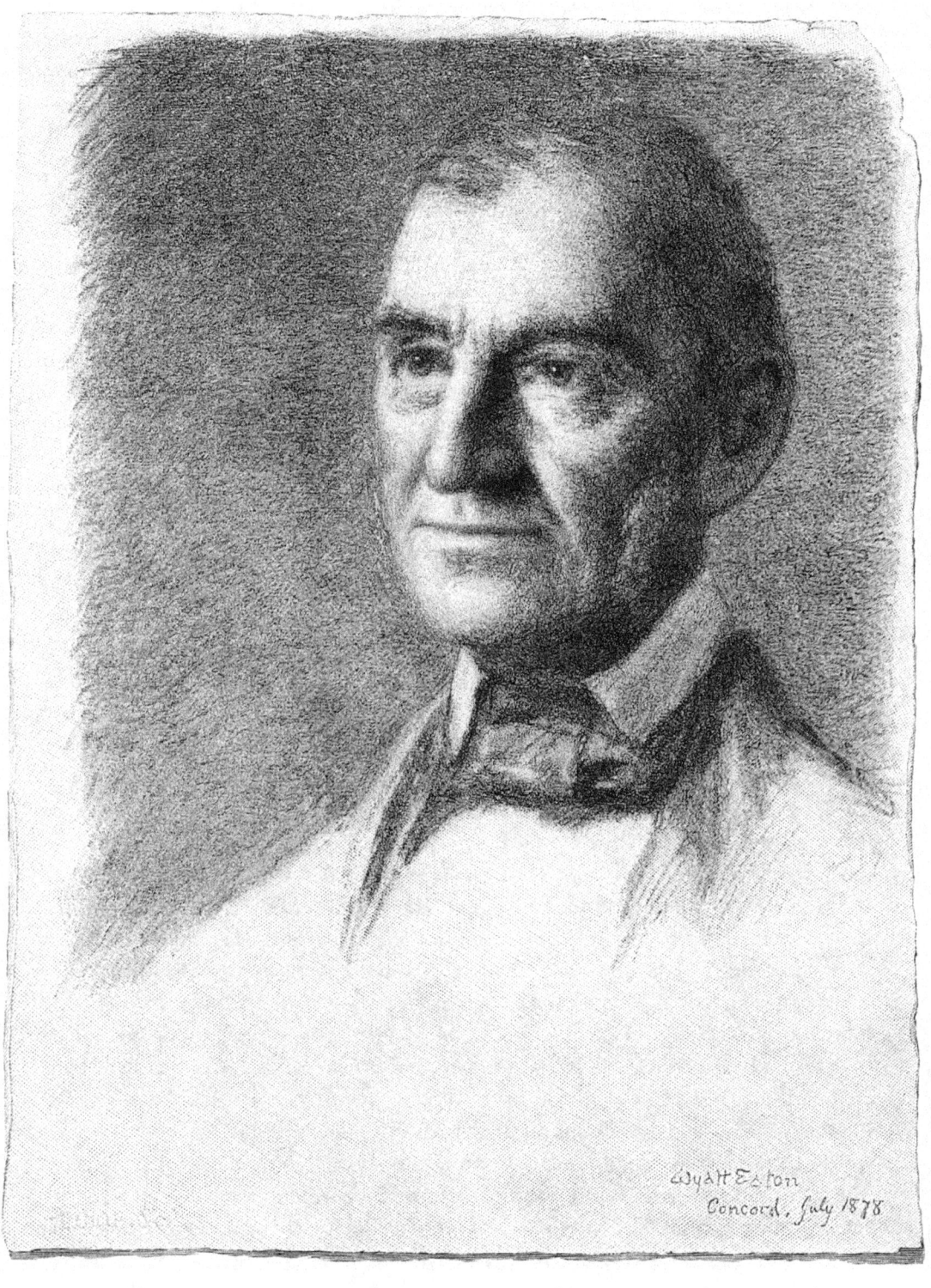

Figure 64. Timothy Cole after Wyatt Eaton, portrait of Ralph Waldo Emerson, wood engraving, *Scribner's Monthly* (February 1879). From the Collections of the University Libraries, University of Minnesota, Minneapolis.

the method favored by Linton, in which each line stands out from the others and declares its purpose: there is no mistaking this image for anything other than a wood engraving (Figure 63). The problem with engravings like Cole's head of Ralph Waldo Emerson, after a drawing by Wyatt Eaton, was that forms are "hidden under a minuteness of weakest line that muddies everything"[34] (Figure 64). In reproducing the effect of another medium (Eaton's crayon) rather than foregrounding the engraver's line, Cole showed himself to be capable of producing "marvels of microscopic mechanism," but he fell short, in Linton's view, of producing art.[35] Cole responded with the charge that Linton's lines were more about the engraver than the work being reproduced: "it would seem natural that when seeing an engraving of a drawing you should recognize the artist first and not the engraver: 'Drawn by So-and-so, engraved by So-and-so.' But when looking at an engraving of Mr. Linton's you say instinctively, 'Engraved by So-and-so, drawn by So-and-so'—just reversing the order." The same note was struck by most of the New School participants in *Harper's* "A Symposium of Wood-Engravers": they claimed that Linton "preserves and protrudes himself," or that "Mr. Linton's engravings always suggest Mr. Linton."[36] Yet in spite of this criticism of Linton's failure to subordinate his own hand to that of the artist being reproduced, the New School engravers continued to appeal to the subjective authority of their own lines. They saw themselves at once as true artists and perfect machines. Whether we judge them as successful in this is beside the point: I am not interested in accepting their debate on its own terms; that is, as a debate of artistic subjectivity versus mechanical objectivity. Rather, I would like to explore the particular quality of labor that occurs between those two idealized poles of art and technology, a quality of labor that somehow resides in or is symbolized by those minute lines that struggle to be two things at once: the hand of an engraver and the hand of another artist.

John Ruskin, author of the most penetrating analysis of wood engraving to be published during the latter half of the nineteenth century, was deeply concerned about that labor. In *Ariadne Florentina: Six Lectures on Wood and Metal Engraving*, delivered at Oxford in 1872 and published in several editions before the end of the century, Ruskin insisted on the absolute priority of the *production* of the engraving over what we might term its "consumption," that is, its dissemination to a mass audience. For Ruskin the value of an engraving lies in what it tells us about its own making. Like Ivins, who penned *Prints and Visual Communication* some eighty years after Ruskin gave his Oxford lectures, Ruskin was acutely attuned to the indexical quality of the engraved line. But while Ivins found this line to be a distracting feature of engraving that ultimately had to disappear in order for printed reproductions to reach their true potential of visual communication without syntax, Ruskin believed the engraver's line to be saturated with vital meaning. In Ruskin's writings, there is a moral significance to the engraved line that yokes it to a broader cultural and, indeed, agricultural value. The instrument with which the engraver works, Ruskin points out, is a "solid ploughshare." He includes a picture of this tool in his book, to demonstrate its plowlike form, and declares that engraving is in fact a form of plowing: "to engrave is, in final strictness, 'to decorate a surface with furrows.' . . . A ploughed field is the purest type of such art" (Figure 65).[37]

It is this elemental quality of engraving that is at the basis of Ruskin's deep investment in the art. For Ruskin the engraver carries a heavy moral burden, and indeed we can hear echoes of de Bry's "nuls sans soucy"—now transposed into the earthy rhetoric of England's back-to-the-land movement—in Ruskin's writings on this subject. From Ruskin's point of view, the engraver cannot be without care because his art is a species of husbandry, and it is the engraver's duty always to be tending to his block, taking care not to harm it with unnecessary or misguided labor. And because the furrows of the engraver will always carry a message about his labor, he can never get away with artificial effects that stray beyond the intrinsic qualities of the medium: "Look,—all the world,—look for evermore, says the foolish engraver; see what a fool I have been! How many lines I have laid for nothing!"[38] In his lecture on "The Technics of Wood Engraving," Ruskin finds an "immortal" expression of the engraver's labor in a woodcut from Hans Holbein's *Dance of Death,* an image he calls *The Last Furrow* (Figure 66). George Woodberry, author of a two-part "The History of Wood-Engraving" that appeared in *Harper's* in 1882 and was clearly written under Ruskin's influence, essentially summed up Ruskin's views on Holbein's print for the readers of American illustrated magazines: "Every line has its work to do, has its meaning, which it expresses perfectly, easily, and economically, without waste of labor or ineffectual effort," and for this reason Woodberry called Holbein's *The Last Furrow* "the greatest work of

The instrument with which the substance, whether of the wood or steel, is cut away, is the same. It is a solid ploughshare, which, instead of throwing the earth aside, throws it up and out, producing at first a simple ravine, or furrow, in the wood or metal, which you can widen by another cut, or extend by successive cuts. This (Fig. 3) is the general shape of the solid ploughshare:

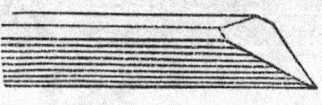

Fig. 3

but it is of course made sharper or blunter at pleasure. The furrow produced is at first the wedge-shaped or cuneiform ravine, already so much dwelt upon in my lectures on Greek sculpture.[3]

Figure 65. Figure 3 from John Ruskin, *Ariadne Florentina* (Sunnyside, Orpington, Kent, 1876). From the Collections of the University Libraries, University of Minnesota, Minneapolis.

art in the older manner, if not the greatest in any manner."[39] For Woodberry as for
Ruskin, the greatness of Holbein's woodcut lies in its demonstration of the engraver's
labor, a demonstration seen not only in Holbein's actual lines but in his subject matter, plowing, "the purest type" of engraving.[40]

For Ruskin, the actual process of engraving is, like the tilling of the earth, sacro-
sanct. Thus he never allows his audience to forget the materiality of his subject. In his
first lecture, he arrives at the most material of definitions: "Engraving, then, is in brief
terms, the Art of Scratch. It is essentially the cutting into a solid substance for the sake

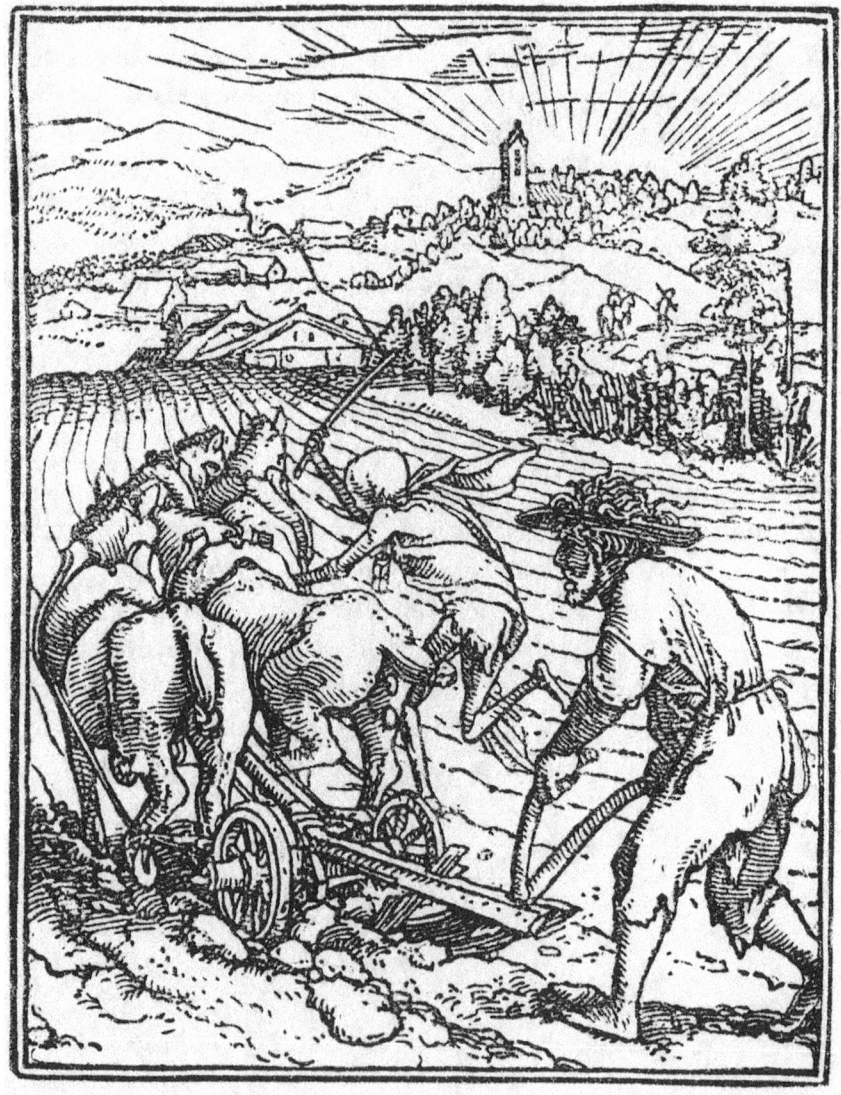

Fig. 4

Figure 66. Hans Holbein, *The Last Furrow*, Figure 4 from *Ariadne Florentina*. From the Collections of the University
Libraries, University of Minnesota, Minneapolis.

of making your ideas as permanent as possible,—graven with an iron pen in the Rock for ever."[41] The *end* of engraving, to be sure, is to express something immaterial—thought itself; but for Ruskin the engraver's intellect must never be separated from the hand: "every day shows me more and more the importance of the Hand."[42] Linda Austin has argued that there is something biblical resembling a Judeo-Christian ethics of self-mortification in the way Ruskin values labor in his later works.[43] Holbein's *The Last Furrow* is an exemplary image in this regard, for even as Death drives the team of horses and the plowman to their end, the ragged laborer stoically suffers through his lot; it is an image that weaves together engraving, plowing, and self-sacrifice. This message of labor and suffering serves, in effect, as a protest against the consumerist orientation of a magazine like *Harper's,* in which the woodcut was reproduced with Woodberry's article. Holbein's scratches, permanent and immutable, were for Ruskin opposed to the whims of a mass audience that desired more and more images while holding little or no regard for the process of engraving itself. As the photograph, which carries no message about the labor behind its production, quite literally became the basis of wood engraving, reproductive engravers for illustrated magazines multiplied and concealed their lines in their attempt to imitate the surface effects of original works. Photography, along with this "foolish" engraving it encouraged, represented a threat to individual labor and to the moral value of the artist's hand in society. For a reviewer in *Atlantic Monthly,* Ruskin's *Ariadne Florentina* made a case for the lasting value of engraving "in the face of the various chemical and mechanical processes which seem to be rendering the art obsolete."[44] We have seen *Century's* engravers struggling with this dilemma, trying to balance the competing claims of production and reproduction, but Ruskin was unequivocal in his views: "*Permanence,* you observe, is the object, not multiplicability;—that is quite an accidental, sometimes not even a desirable, attribute of engraving."[45]

It would be easy to align Ruskin with an engraver like William Linton.[46] Certainly his aesthetic priorities were in many ways opposed to those of New School engravers like John Davis, who claimed that "the engraver's business is to put a picture in such a shape that it can be indefinitely multiplied."[47] But *Ariadne Florentina* offers more than a program for a particular school of engraving. Ruskin's deep concern with the materiality of graphic representation helps us to look at *all* engravings, including those of *Century,* through the fundamental problem of labor. Indeed, I would suggest that *The Flyer* and the thousands of wood engravings that ornament the pages of *Century* throughout the 1880s, in addition to the writings on the nature and objectives of wood engraving that one encounters over the same period, raise a basic Ruskinian question: What kind of labor is behind the engraver's scratch?

We have begun to answer this question simply by recognizing that this labor is deeply conflicted. On the one hand, in the face of the demands of mass culture, the engraver's scratch tends toward its own self-effacement. "Every day the urge grows stronger to get hold of an object at close range in an image, or, better, in a facsimile, a reproduction," wrote Walter Benjamin.[48] Responding to this urge, the audience of

Century, along with its engravers, did their best to see through and suppress the syntaxes of image-making in order to bring themselves closer to the "real thing."[49] On the other hand, even as reproductive engravers attempted to meet this demand, they continued to appeal to the aura of inimitability that attached to the unique scratch. In 1889 Elbridge Kingsley, one of the chief representatives of the New School, wrote in *Century* that the wood engraver's "personality is bound to show itself in some shape, giving change and variety in contrast with that of another. He cannot get rid of his method any more than of his handwriting."[50] Simply because it is the visible evidence of an individual's labor, the engraved line, even that of the New School engraver, must be understood as a kind of signature, just as John White's handwriting and execution had served for Eggleston as incontrovertible evidence for the self-identification of artist and work. Let us pursue the question of the engraver's labor, then, by considering the scratch-as-signature.

During the 1880s the editors of *Century* peppered the pages of their magazine with scratched signatures of all kinds. An 1882 article on the life and work of Thomas Bewick (1753–1828), who was widely recognized at the time as the father of modern wood-engraving methods, presents Bewick's own signature-scratch (Figure 67). In this small engraving, which originally appeared on a receipt Bewick gave to purchasers

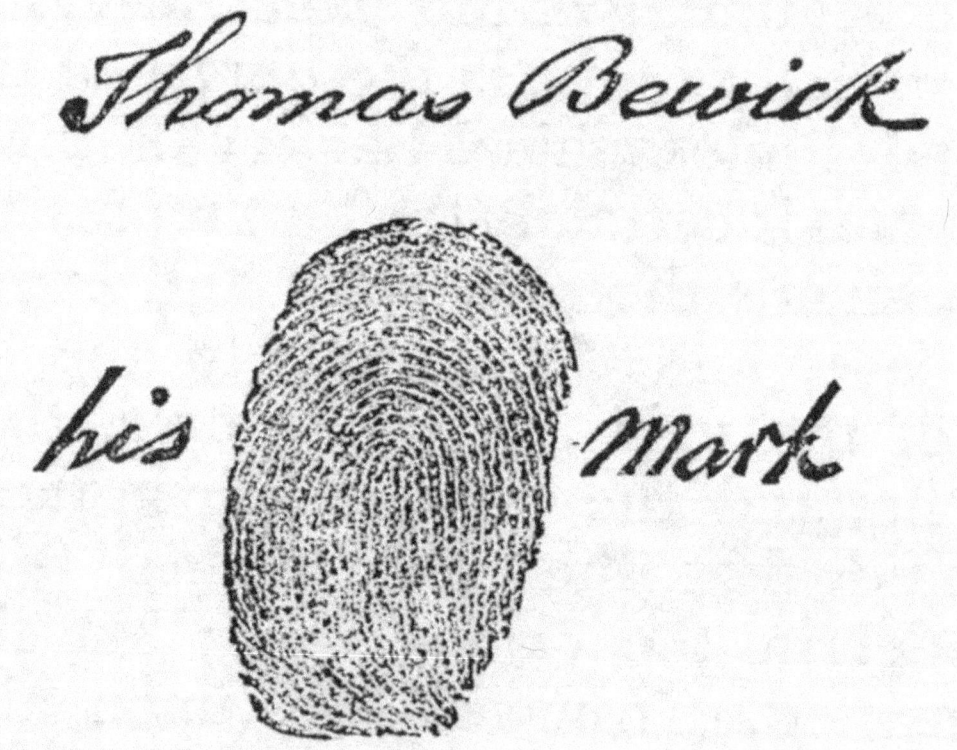

Figure 67. Thomas Bewick, *Bewick's Thumb-Mark, Century* (September 1882). From the Collections of the University Libraries, University of Minnesota, Minneapolis.

of his illustrated *Fables of Aesop* (1818) and which is reproduced as the final illustration of the *Century* article, the artist combines his engraved thumbprint with his signature.[51] On either side of the thumbprint, Bewick engraves the words "his" and "mark," as if to say: "Thomas Bewick his 'thumb' mark." Thus we have the most self-reflexive of wood engravings: a "print" by the most famous wood engraver of the eighteenth and nineteenth centuries reproducing his "hand" as both handwriting and literally as an impression from his hand. Moreover, the series of parallel white-and-black lines that constitute Bewick's engraved thumbprint demonstrates the trademark white-line technique first developed by this artist and used by his followers, including the New School engravers (*The Flyer* is a textbook demonstration of the use of white line). These signature lines of Bewick's thumbprint may also be found throughout the preceding pages of the article in the lines that make up numerous other prints by Bewick, as if the making of every engraving was in a sense the making of the artist's fingerprint. Appearing in *Century* and reproduced by *Century's* wood engravers, Bewick's mark has significance for the work of the New School engraver. The linking of the engraver's lines with his actual signature serves as a general declaration, in opposition to the consumerist urge to erase the mark, that to scratch a line upon a surface is to call

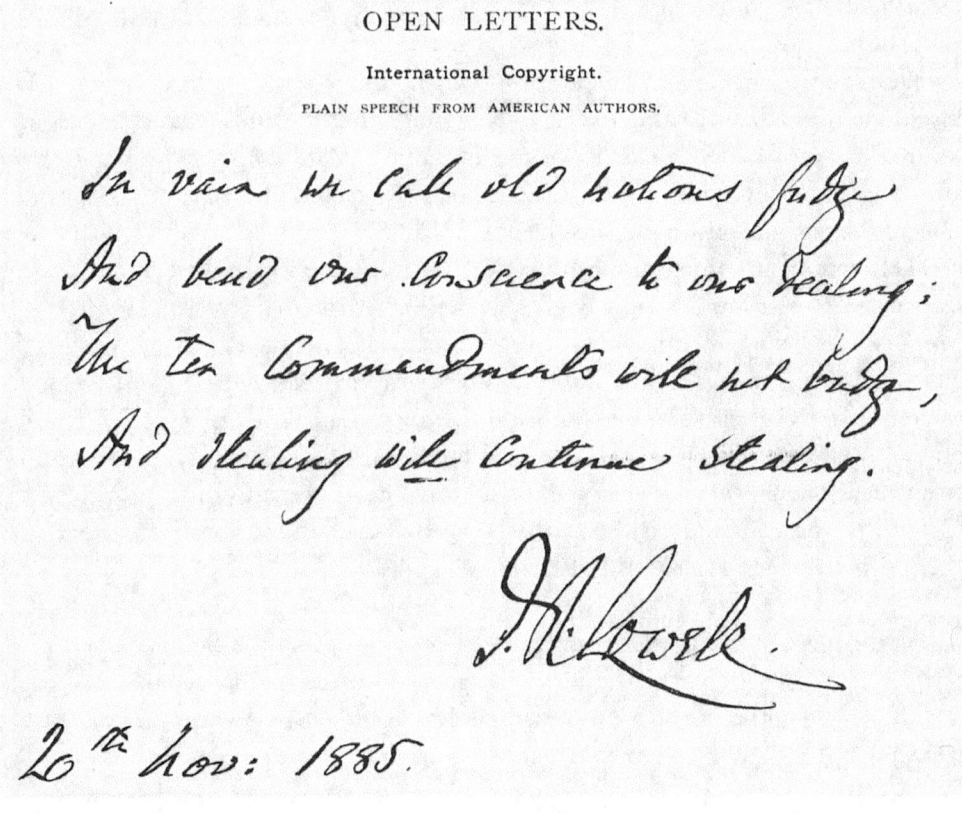

Figure 68. James Russell Lowell, handwritten poem, *Century* (February 1886). From the Collections of the University Libraries, University of Minnesota, Minneapolis.

attention to the hand of the wood engraver (although we should not forget that in making this facsimile of Bewick's signature, one of *Century's* engravers was indeed erasing his own hand).

It was a regular practice in *Century* to reproduce actual signatures with wood engravings, and Bewick's thumbmark provides a touchstone against which we can view all the other engraved signatures, letters, and poems that appear throughout the magazine. To take just one example, consider the handwritten verses by James Russell Lowell that appear in the February 1886 issue at the beginning of a series of open letters on the question of international copyright (Figure 68). Many of *Century's* authors, including Edward Eggleston, spoke out in support of an international copyright law that would protect American authors from cheap foreign competition.[52] Lowell's scratches serve as a defense of the very concept of copyright: they are authentic marks that lead us back to the hand that produced them. The dissemination of the author's labor through the mass media is met by the reclamation of that labor under the sign of the scratch. And scratch this is indeed—chicken scratch. Lowell's handwriting is practically illegible. But that very illegibility strengthens the claim of authorship. Unrecognizable scrawls and scratches are opaque; their meaning is available to their producer but to no one else, and in this sense they are the very opposite of the mass media's rationalized letterpress.

The printing of illegible signatures was so common in *Century* that in the February 1882 issue a mock advertisement for *Maskwell's Compendium* poked fun at it. "The illegibility of the handwriting of our public men," the ad claims, "has been a source of great concern and inconvenience to thousands." With *Maskwell's Compendium*, anyone could easily transform their indecipherable scratch into elegant penmanship. One of the testimonials to the effectiveness of Mr. Maskwell's method—which makes a characteristic late nineteenth-century link between the scratch and the American Indian—comes from the Ugh! Ugh! Agency in Arizona. There, *Maskwell's Compendium* was being recommended "to the Indians of this Agency as the most useful aid to the acquisition of a clear and beautiful style of penmanship."[53] The suggestion, of course, is that there is something primitive about bad handwriting when it is not masked well by an acquired hand. Indeed for Ruskin the scratch is the most primitive of marks. In *Ariadne Florentina,* Ruskin divides artists into three provinces: the Colourists, the Chiaroscurists, and the Delineators. The Delineators are the first of the provinces. They begin, writes Ruskin:

> in the primitive work of races insensible alike to shade and to colour, and nearly devoid of thought and of sentiment, but gradually developing into both. Now as the design is primitive, so are the means likely to be primitive. A line is the simplest work of art you can produce. What are the simplest means you can produce it with? A Cumberland lead pencil is a work of art in itself, quite a nineteenth-century machine. Pen and ink are complex and scholarly; and even chalk or charcoal not always handy. But the primitive line, the first and last, generally the best of lines, is

that which you have elementary faculty of at your fingers' ends, and which kittens can draw as well as you—the scratch.[54]

The simple, primordial line scratched into a solid substance. The viewer of such a scratch is returned not only to the subject that originated it, but to the primitive foundations of subjectivity from which a civilization of thought and sentiment "gradually develop[s]." The latter phrase is a critical one, for it suggests that the engraver's scratches are not stable—they are not entirely primitive nor are they entirely civilized, but are always gradually developing from one to the other. In the following pages we will consider further the primitive qualities of the scratch, and in what respects civilization in the 1880s was gradually developing from them.

Picture-Writing

Appearing in the May 1885 issue of *Century* is a brief article by the artist George de Forest Brush. Titled "An Artist among the Indians," the piece includes a full-page engraved reproduction of Brush's *The Picture-Writer* (Figure 69). As Brush notes, his picture "is supposed to be a scene in the interior of a Mandan lodge."[55] The center of the picture is occupied by three figures. Two are young, rather lethargic-looking men,

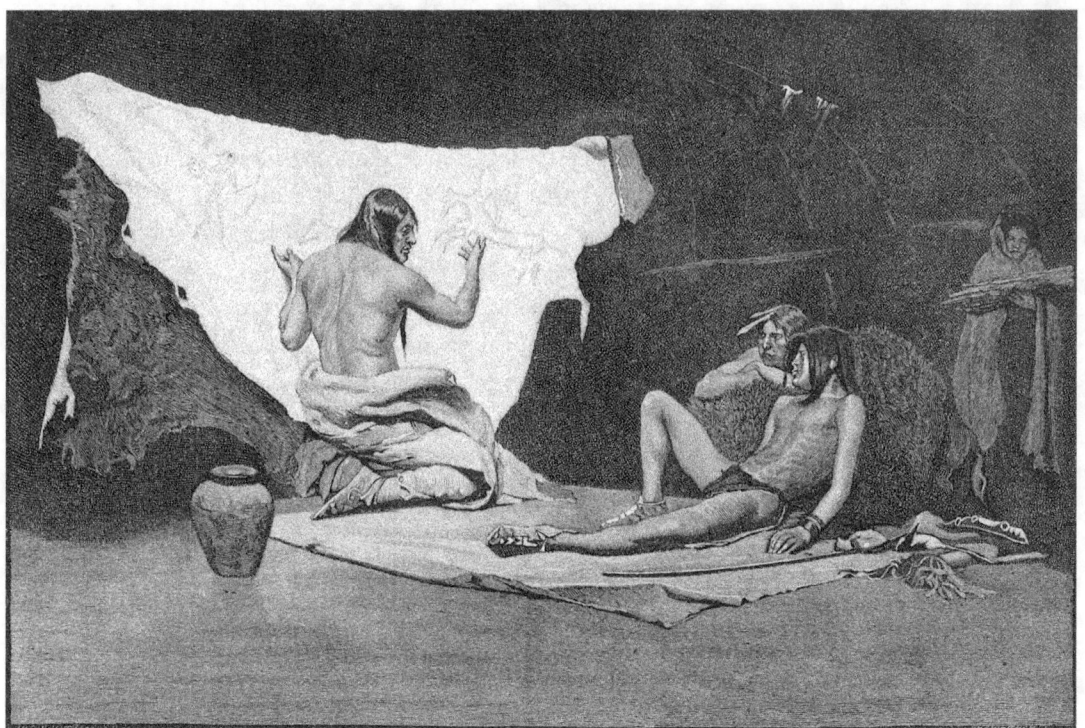

Figure 69. George de Forest Brush, *The Picture-Writer*, wood engraving by J. H. E. Whitney, *Century* (May 1885). From the Collections of the University Libraries, University of Minnesota, Minneapolis.

one of whom is clearly a quotation of Michelangelo's *Creation of Adam* from the ceiling of the Sistine Chapel. The men appear to be listening—whether with boredom or rapt attention is unclear—to the broad-backed figure who kneels before a hanging buffalo skin. This man, also a quotation of a figure from the Sistine ceiling, the *Libyan Sibyl,* is surely the picture-writer referred to in the title of the work, although he is not in fact engaged in the act of picture-writing, but instead appears to be explaining to the young men the significance of the pictographic characters outlined on the skin. He is perhaps loosely based on the famed Mandan chief, Mah-to-toh-pa, whose buffalo robe displaying his war exploits is discussed at length in George Catlin's *Letters and Notes on the Manners, Customs, and Conditions of the North American Indians,* first published in 1841.[56] We can make out three of the characters on the buffalo skin: a human figure with bow and shield at left, the head of a horse that is just visible above the man's left shoulder, and a horse and rider to the right. Here we witness something close to what Ruskin must have had in mind when referring to "the primitive work of races insensible alike to shade and to colour." Readers of *Century,* as we shall see, would have easily assimilated the Mandan chief's pictographs to an evolutionary framework in which Native American forms of visual communication are to be understood as modern survivals of the primitive scratch, precisely the sort of scratch in which the engraver's line (if we are to follow Ruskin) has its origins.

But the pictographs of Brush's picture-writer offer us more than a nineteenth-century lesson in the origins of engraving, for in marking the origins of Ruskin's primitive School of Delineators, these marks return us to the origins of *all* art-making, including the art of painting. That is to say, *The Picture-Writer,* a painting in which we observe an artist whose orientation before a vertical surface of representation rehearses that of Brush himself as he painted the picture, offers a window into the historical origins of Brush's own practice as a teller of stories and a conveyor of messages through the painting of pictures. Brush himself seems perfectly aware of this parallel between the picture-writer and his own work as a painter. In the accompanying article, he writes that he has no interest in filling his paintings of Indian subjects with gratuitous antiquarian details: "I do not care to represent them in any curious habits which could not be comprehended by us; I am interested in those habits and deeds in which we have feelings in common."[57] The point of sympathy in this picture would seem to be a common feeling for artistic production.

The Picture-Writer may thus be understood as Brush's own variation on the iconography of the origins of painting. As we saw in the second chapter, the most common story in this tradition, which reached the height of its popularity in printed and painted works of the late eighteenth and early nineteenth centuries, involves the Corinthian maid who preserves the image of her lover by tracing his shadow upon a wall (see Figure 33). Brush, however, replaces this classical myth of painting's origins with a new myth, one that engages contemporary evolutionary thought by implying a progression from a savage form of picture-making (Native American picture-writing) to a civilized form of picture-making (picturing Native Americans). What makes Brush's painting civilized is the artist's civilizing touch—the authority of his hand, a hand trained in Europe and underwritten by the greatest hand known to the civilized world: Michelangelo's. *The Picture-Writer,* then, represents an evolution culminating in Brush himself. Just as the Mandan picture-writer edifies the young men through his story (the painting, incidentally, later assumed the title *The Picture-Writer's Story*), so Brush edifies his viewers by giving them the story of art; that is, the story of an art-historical evolution from the picture-writing of savages to Michelangelo to an American master of the late nineteenth century.

There are perhaps other narratives one might read into Brush's painting; I prefer this evolutionary narrative because it is so strongly reinforced by the magazine in which the painting was first reproduced. As a self-consciously *American* magazine of the arts, *Century* was committed to bringing America, and more specifically American artists, into the mainstream of an artistic evolution that had begun with the picture-writing of savages, achieved its first glory in Greece, and was reborn in fifteenth-century Italy. Seen through the lens of *Century's* nationalism and its social evolutionism, America was the next step in this march of civilization. As Charles Waldstein wrote in his 1886 essay on "The Lesson of Greek Art," Americans are "the Magna Græcians of the West."[58] Through articles such as Waldstein's and through larger series such as the Old Masters Series and the American Masters Series, *Century* carried out its civilizing mission by educating its audience in the proper appreciation of art and its development through time.[59] This project of edification involved the reproduction of many works of art. From Gilder's assumption of editorship in 1881 through the early 1900s, *Century* published, as no magazine had before, wood engravings of innumerable monuments of art history from ancient Greece to nineteenth-century America. Through these images readers were to learn the story of the progress of civilization. *The Picture-Writer,* with its message about the evolution of the American artist, may be seen in this regard as a kind of program statement for *Century Magazine.*

What of the first stage of this evolution then? What of picture-writing and its role in the evolution of culture? Brush's interest in picture-writing was hardly unique. It was part of a wide, late nineteenth-century interest in the picture-writing of American Indians, a subject discussed and illustrated with some frequency in the periodical literature of the time and in anthropological publications as well. But while Brush implies that picture-writing stands at the historical origins of painting, it was of interest particularly for the insight it offered into the history of *writing.* The nineteenth century's foremost authority on picture-writing was Garrick Mallery, whose 800-page study titled "Picture-Writing of the American Indians" was published as the 1888–89 *Report of the Bureau of Ethnology.* Picture-writing was worthy of the ethnologist's attention because, as Mallery wrote, it represents "a phase in the evolution of human culture. As the invention of alphabetic writing is admitted to be the great step marking the change from barbarism to civilization, the history of its earlier development must be valuable."[60] Although, as Mallery notes, it is the lack of alphabetical writing that distinguishes the savage from civilized society, the savage at the same time possesses his own version of writing—a pictorial writing—that in fact *links* him to the civilized world of letters through a continuous chain of cultural development.

Mallery's approach to picture-writing is indebted to the evolutionary anthropology that emerged during the last third of the nineteenth century. This school of thought posited that primitive society and civilized society alike belonged to a single overarching phenomenon called *culture,* the history of which it was the evolutionist's task to trace. Edward Tylor's landmark work of evolutionary anthropology, *Primitive Culture,* published in 1871, opens with a definitive statement on the relationship between culture and evolution. "Culture or Civilization," Tylor begins, "taken in its wide ethnographic sense, is that complex whole which includes knowledge, belief, art, morals, law, custom, and any other capabilities and habits acquired by man as a member of society."[61] Culture, in other words, is not bound to any one practice or set of practices in the sense that the early modern notion of civility was based on the individual's mastery of certain outward bodily behaviors and practices such as table manners or handwriting.[62] Instead, Tylor's "culture," while necessarily manifested in the physical evidence of specific social practices, was an idealized category (a complex whole) that made it possible to grasp the unity of human history under a single concept. On the one hand, as Tylor notes, the notion of culture suggests uniformity: like the laws of nature, the laws of culture never change. On the other hand, there are "various grades" of culture, and these "may be regarded as stages of development

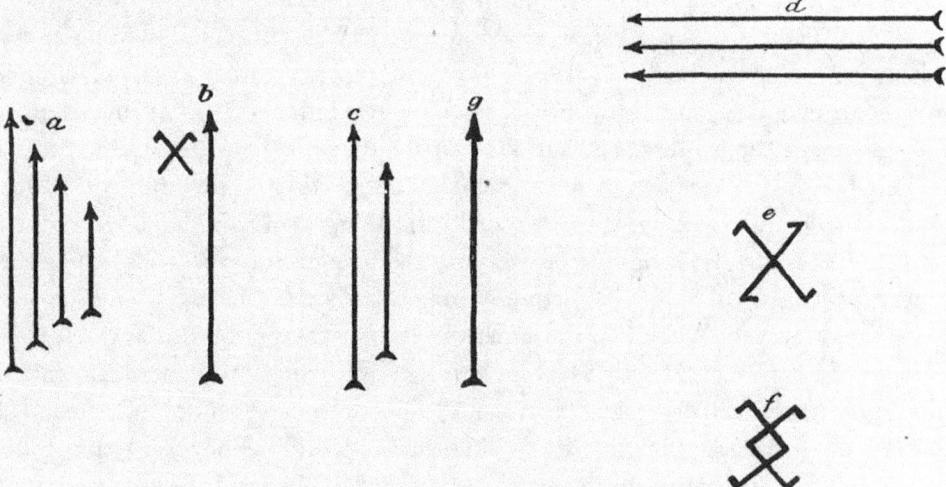

Figure 70. *Virginian Tattoo Designs,* after Theodor de Bry, from Garrick Mallery, *Picture-Writing of the American Indians* (Washington, D.C., 1893). From the Collections of the University Libraries, University of Minnesota, Minneapolis.

or evolution, each the outcome of previous history, and about to do its proper part in shaping the history of the future."[63] Thus while the laws of culture remain uniform, the complex whole progresses through time.

This notion of human culture as the product of an evolutionary process that operates free of supernatural causation and according to its own internal laws marks a fundamentally different way of thinking about savage life than what had preceded it. We cannot, of course, take on the history of anthropological thought here, but we can compare Mallery's evolutionary treatment of picture-writing to Theodor de Bry's treatment of the tattoo as discussed in the first chapter. Indeed we have a specific occasion to do so, for Mallery reproduces de Bry's tattoos in "Picture-Writing of the American Indians" (Figure 70). During the sixteenth century, the chief distinction between savage and civilized society had been—as for Mallery in the nineteenth century—the distinction between those who lacked the technology of alphabetical writing and those who possessed it: America "is so new, such a child," wrote Montaigne, "that we are still teaching it its ABC."[64] But when de Bry indexed the tattoos of the Virginians with his alphabetical letters, his goal was not to suggest an evolutionary connection between the two forms of symbolic communication. Neither de Bry nor Harriot offer their thoughts on the relationship between tattoos and letters, but when we encounter sixteenth-century commentary on the marks produced by American Indians, there is little interest in what they might share with civilized writing practices. José de Acosta devotes a whole chapter of his *Natural and Moral History of the Indies* (1590) to demonstrating the dissimilarity between Native American sign systems and alphabetical writing, and he concludes definitively that "no Nation of the Indies discovered in our time, hath had the vse of letters and writings, but of the other two sortes, images and figures."[65] In the final analysis, images and letters were of two different "sortes." This is not to say there was in fact nothing shared between the two, and the argument of my first chapter is that they share a great deal. But in a society that looked for causation not in the laws of cultural evolution but in the Word of God, made manifest in the letters of scripture, the American Indian's lack of letters could be understood only in terms of radical difference. Mallery, in contrast, like Brush, who approaches his Native American subjects out of interest "in those habits and deeds in which we have feelings in common,"[66] encourages his readers to recognize a continuity between the culture of tattoos and the culture of letters. When he reproduces de Bry's tattoos in his chapter on "Totems, Titles, and Names," the logic of the evolutionary argument places the tattoos and the alphabetical letters that index them at the opposite poles of a shared cultural history. Mallery emphasizes this fundamental connectedness by dissociating the tattoo from the body of de Bry's Alonquian man. In "Picure-Writing of the American Indians," the Virginia tattoos have been fully assimilated to the civilized page; coextensive with their surrounding text, they are to be understood as a distinct stage on the developmental path toward phonetic writing.

Picture-writing thus played an important role in the work of nineteenth-century ethnologists such as Mallery and Tylor who sought to demonstrate an evolutionary

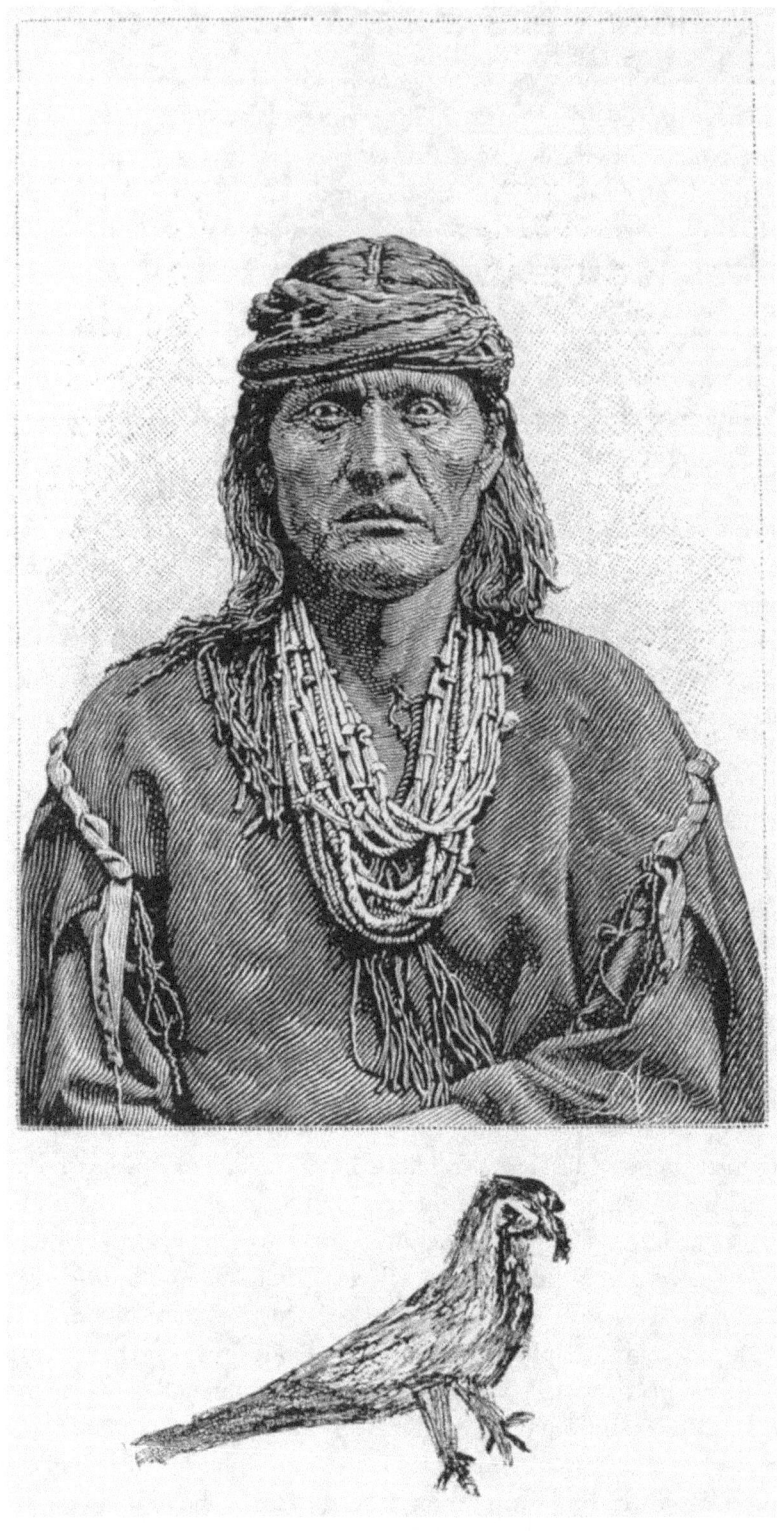

Figure 71. *Portrait and Autograph of Pa-lo-wah-ti-wa, Governor of Zuñi, or Head Political Chief, Clan of the Macaws,* wood engraving after photograph by John K. Hillers, *Century* (August 1882). From the Collections of the University Libraries, University of Minnesota, Minneapolis.

continuum in human culture. It also made its way into the popular ethnology of *Century*, in which illustrations of picture-writing provided readers with the opportunity to piece together their own evolutionary narratives. Consider the portraits of several Zuñi men that appear in an 1882 *Century* article by Sylvester Baxter titled "An Aboriginal Pilgrimage" (Figure 71).[67] The article tells the story of Frank Hamilton Cushing and a delegation of six Zuñi Indians who accompanied the famous anthropologist to the eastern United States after Cushing had completed two years of fieldwork in New Mexico.[68] The engraved portraits of these notable Indians each include an "autograph," following a standard model for the frontispiece portraits of prominent men and women that appeared in *Century* throughout the 1880s. This same issue of *Century*, for instance, begins with a portrait of Richard Wagner that includes the composer's signature; similarly, Cole's frontispiece portrait of Emerson is followed on the facing page by a brief poem, written and signed in a hand nearly as difficult to read as Lowell's. The Zuñi autographs, however, are not typical signatures. While they do indeed display the "hands" of their authors, these hands appear as picture-writing. Below the portrait of Pa-lo-wah-ti-wa, governor of Zuñi, for example, is a rudely sketched bird signifying that he belongs to the Clan of the Macaws. Here, in the pre-alphabetic picture-autograph, *Century*'s readers could bear witness to the primitive origins of Wagner's, Emerson's, and Lowell's signatures.

Following the appearance of "An Aboriginal Pilgrimage," *Century* published a series of three articles by Cushing relating his experiences in New Mexico, titled "My Adventures in Zuñi" and illustrated by Henry Farny.[69] Like the autographed portraits in Baxter's article, Farny's illustrations display an interest in picture-writing. In *Zuñi Weaving*, Farny transforms a photograph by John K. Hillers of a solitary Hopi weaver into an atmospheric scene of Zuñi daily life (Figure 72).[70] Of Farny's many additions to Hillers's image, the most important for our purposes are the pictographic characters—a deer, a bird with a snake in its beak, etc.—that the artist scratched into the picture at far left. Farny's embellishment of Hillers's photograph is suggestive, for it serves as a declaration that this is what Indians can be expected to do: they scratch pictures on adobe walls. Elsewhere, in his portrait of *Pa-lo-wah-ti-wa, Governor of Zuñi*, Farny offers his own take on picture-writing as a stage in the evolution of culture (Figure 73). Of particular interest are the various marks that surround the governor's profile. It is unclear whether the scrawl directly below that profile is part of the mimetic representation above it or is its own symbolic form of communication. It appears to be another form of the governor's signature, his mark, produced in imitation of alphabetical writing but forming no real characters. One recalls the famous "Writing Lesson" in Claude Lévi-Strauss' *Tristes Tropiques*, when, mimicking the note-taking anthropologist, the Nambikwara chief takes pencil and paper but produces only "unintelligible scribbling."[71] Such marks are the most primitive of lines, the first, faltering steps toward the representation of ideas. As such they serve as a prelude to the two linear designs at the top left of Farny's picture: the national seal of the Zuñi and the governor's macaw. Both these designs appeared, inscribed in a savage hand, in "An Aboriginal Pilgrimage" (see Figure 71 for the governor's macaw). But Farny refines the earlier versions, cleans them up, as if to emphasize their evolutionary distance from the illegible scratch at the bottom of the portrait. Although we are still at the level of the picture, we have now progressed into a picture-*writing* capable of communicating ideas such as *nation* and *clan*. Finally, at lower right, Farny's own alphabetical signature, along with his mark—an *O* with a dot in the center, like a bull's-eye—designates the artist who has produced this meditation on culture. Considered together the various marks on the portrait suggest an evolution of the signature from scratches to picture-writing to letters. Packed into Farny's little portrait is the whole story of the artist's gradual development.

On the one hand, this evolutionary approach to picture-writing, articulated by ethnologists and explored visually by *Century*'s illustrators, had the effect of raising the savage's pictures up to the level of writing: Pa-lo-wah-ti-wa is not all that different

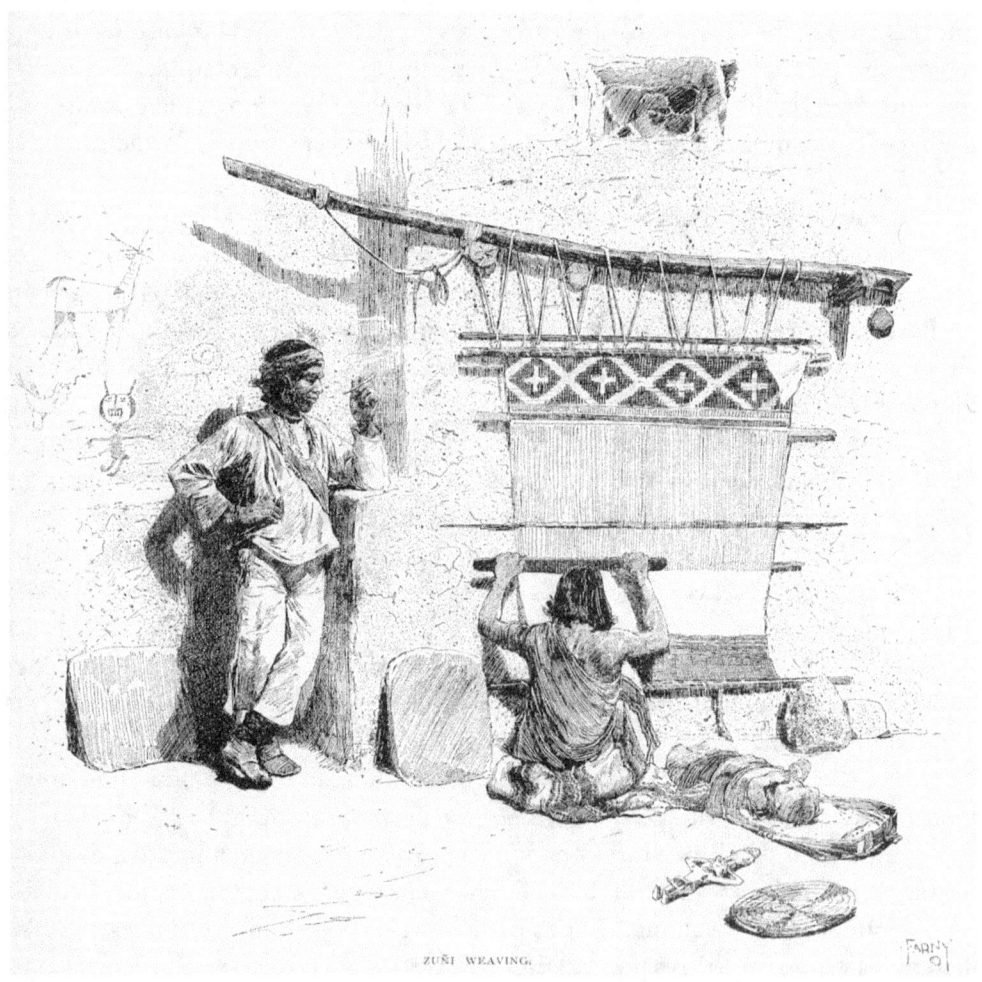

Figure 72. Henry Farny, *Zuñi Weaving, Century* (February 1883). From the Collections of the University Libraries, University of Minnesota, Minneapolis.

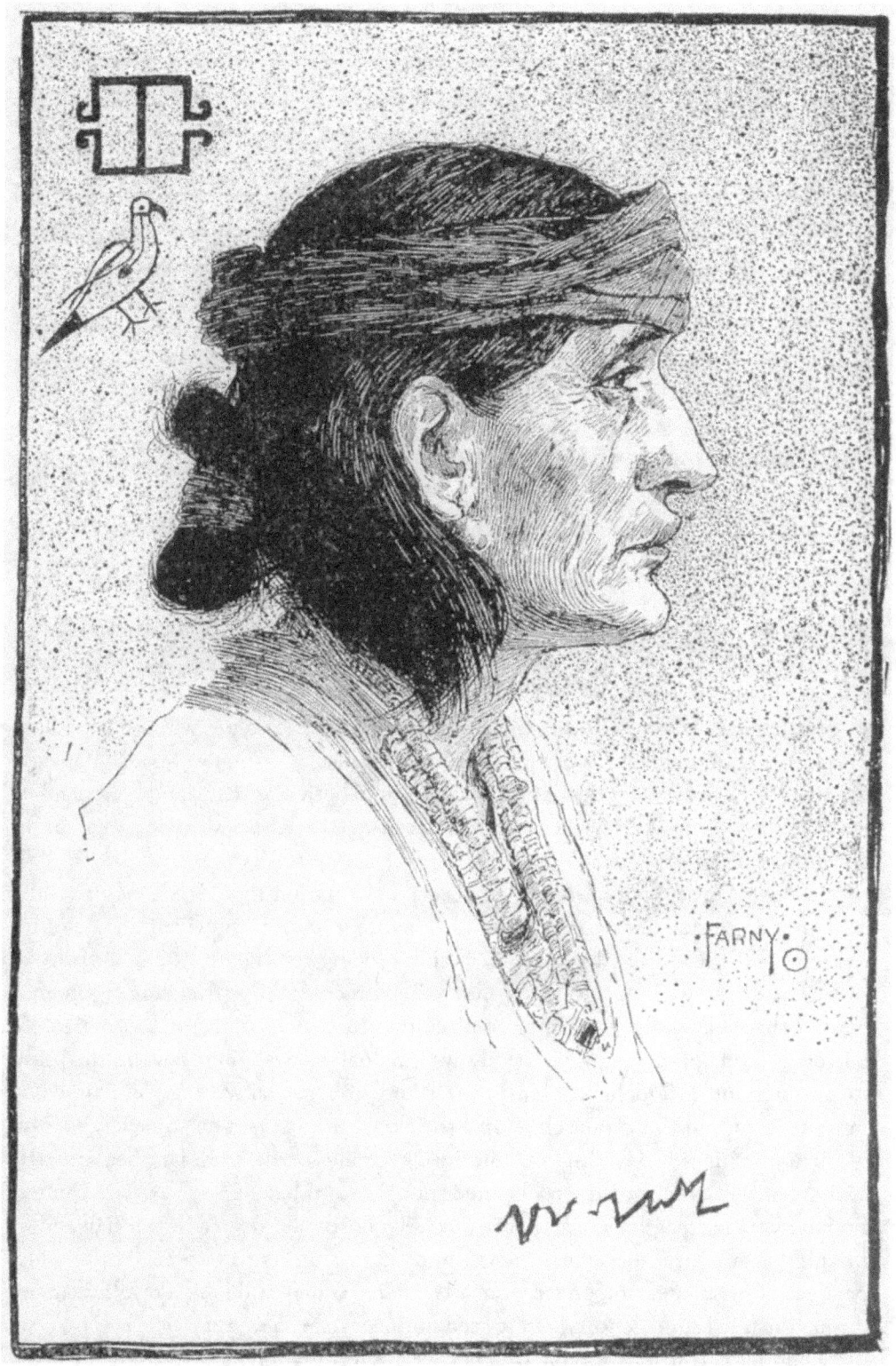

Figure 73. Henry Farny, *Pa-lo-wah-ti-wa, Governor of Zuñi, Century* (December 1882). From the Collections of the University Libraries, University of Minnesota, Minneapolis.

from Wagner and Emerson, for he too is capable of writing his name. On the other hand, this elevation in status of the savage's signs had its converse, for it helped bring the writing of the civilized world—like the signatures of Wagner, Emerson, Lowell, and Farny—down to the level of the picture. That is to say, the return to the origins of writing in *picture*-writing helped set an alphabetic civilization on firmly pictorial foundations.[72] Garrick Mallery and Edward Tylor both argued that these pictorial foundations should be considered prior even to the emergence of human speech. Language, they claimed, began not with the uttering of sounds but with the eyes; it began with a soundless language of physical gestures that eventually acquired a permanent form with the development of picture-writing. This interest in the visual origins of writing pervades both the anthropological and the paleographic literature of the period. In an essay on "Picture-Writing and Word-Writing," Tylor claims that the continued use of Roman numerals and other forms of pictorial communication "show that even in the midst of the highest European civilization, the spirit of the earliest and rudest form of writing is not yet quite extinct."[73] Indeed, the alphabet itself was proof of that. As magazine articles on the history of writing noted, some letters still betray their pictorial origins. In a *Harper's* article published in 1873, William Hayes Ward noted that the letter *O* retains the round form of an eye, its original pictorial symbol in the Phoenician alphabet; while Oxford Assyriologist A. H. Sayce, who published two articles on the origin of writing in *Living Age* during the 1880s, claimed that the letter *K* "resembles very remarkably the long sleeved glove with only a thumb which appears in the Hittite [hieroglyphic] inscriptions."[74] When we write we are also drawing, as *Century's* reproductions of handwriting, both alphabetic and pictographic, make so clear. After all, as Mallery reminds his reader, the Greek word *graphein* means both to write and to draw.

In this pictorial civilization of the 1880s, a civilization in which a picture could be a kind of writing and writing a kind of picture, evolution provided a logic of interpretation. If readers and viewers were always being returned to the materiality of the letter, to its visual opacity, then they were also constantly struggling to progress beyond that primitive, pictorial stage of culture, to evolve from matter to idea. To borrow Ruskin's phraseology, we are always "gradually developing" beyond the primitive scratch into "thought and sentiment." And alphabetical writing still marked an important stage in this evolution. While the alphabet remained on some level a form of picture-writing, it nevertheless continued to stand as the boundary between savagery and civilization because it liberated thought from having any *necessary* connection to pictures. In alphabetical writing, the relationship between a drawn sign and its meaning is arbitrary; thought becomes, or at least is on its way to becoming, independent of the matter of representation. The letter *O* may still look like a human eye during the nineteenth century, but it need not refer to an eye. Reading, then, is an act of evolution, and it matters not whether we are reading letters or reading a picture such as Brush's or Farny's. To read such pictures is to be left not with a picture but with a powerful *idea*—the idea of evolution and of the transcendence of mere pictures.

Over-Illustrating

Century was governed by this logic of interpretation in which every act of reception rehearses the evolution from savagery to civilization, from picture to idea. I noted earlier that in the effort to tell the story of civilization's progress, *Century* published countless engraved reproductions. Insofar as reproductions like *The Picture-Writer* are material images, unreclaimed by thought, they must be understood as a kind of picture-writing that still awaited "evolution" into discourse.[75] Although *Century's* mission was nominally to bring civilization to America through its engravings, that mission may equally be seen as one of civilizing those very reproductions. In an article on "The Graphic Art" published in *Scribner's Monthly* in 1872 (*Scribner's* changed its name to *Century* in 1881), Benson J. Lossing wrote that "engravings form the literature of the unlettered—a literature almost as old as human society."[76] Through this pictorial "literature of the unlettered," *Century's* readers were constantly being returned to the origins of culture in picture-writing precisely so that they could evolve beyond these conditions.

Richard Watson Gilder, writing in 1897, articulated exactly this logic in criticizing what he saw as the current overabundance of printed matter. Gilder was appalled by the sheer volume of writing and illustration that was appearing on the market at the end of the century, and by what he considered the low quality of most of it. While *Century* had long been putting great expense into time-consuming wood engravings, other magazines were concerned only with printing cheap halftones as fast as possible and without discrimination. And there seemed to be no end to the glut of words and images. "It might at first be thought," writes Gilder, "that the power to print must exceed the material for printing. But it has become evident that the quantity of matter that may be printed is quite sufficient to keep the presses going; it is only in quality that there is any deficiency. The material for record is inexhaustible." The time was at hand, Gilder feared, that consumption would rule, and the press, instead of trying to edify its audience, would merely be a supplier for vulgar appetites. After this happens, he concludes, "we shall all begin again, and the art of selecting from the world's thought and doings what is really worthy of record and worthy of examination will once more be exalted among men."[77] The descent into a barbaric materialism would be followed by the ascent, once again, into civilization. This is the logic according to which *Century* had operated all along. The magazine's civilizing mission was to be forever beginning again, producing a vast amount of pictorial matter in order to evolve beyond it. This is *Century's* evolutionary cycle.

Gilder's concerns about overproduction belong to a wider late nineteenth-century concern with a phenomenon that writers of the time labeled "over-illustration." As Neil Harris has shown, this criticism was closely tied to the emergence of the halftone in the 1890s and early 1900s and to the attendant proliferation of magazine illustration.[78] Yet the complaints, which focused on the pernicious ways in which pictures were causing readers' minds to stray from the letterpress, had already begun in the 1880s. Perhaps the fullest meditation on the matter during that decade came in 1884 from journalist Charles T. Congdon, writing in the *North American Review*. Congdon's article, titled "Over-Illustration," is clearly indebted to the Enlightenment tendency, discussed in the previous chapter, to associate sensual experience, and particularly visual experience, with savage forms of existence. For Congdon, reading should occur in an abstract realm; pictures serve only to return us to mankind's infancy in ancient temples and tombs, where people scratched on the walls "the great unprinted book of human life." Images are a crutch for the weak of mind: the better the text, the less it needs pictorial embellishment. Congdon admits that engravings had improved in quality in recent years, and he even singles out *Century* and grants that its prints "are almost all that could be desired of the kind—well-drawn, well-engraved, and admirably printed. They are instructive, and for those who will not think, they help the text." Even *Century*'s engravings, the best engravings, are a hindrance to the mind's ascension into the rarefied air of true thought. It was not just poor illustrations that troubled Congdon, but a whole "system of illustration"—a system with *Century* at the forefront—that was "aboriginal and savage, if not childish."[79] An editorialist for the *Nation,* writing in 1893, reaffirmed Congdon's arguments. He could not understand how some regard "the increasing fondness for labor-saving and thought-saving 'graphic representation,' as a part of the progress of civilization. To us, on the contrary, it has always appeared as a distinct reversion to barbarism, being nothing more nor less than a recurrence to the picture-writing and sign-language of savages."[80]

Such protests were hardly subversive of the system of illustration, however: the treatment of the growing number of magazine illustrations as a form of savage picture-writing was, as we have seen, a prelude to an evolution from material marks into immaterial thought. And although Gilder himself was at the forefront of protests against overproduction, his own magazine in fact reveled in its capacity to produce printed matter. No magazine at the end of the nineteenth century was more mechanized, more capable of printing more engravings in less time, than *Century.* Much of this was due to the magazine's master printer, Theodore Low De Vinne. The foremost printer of his day and on the cutting edge of printing technology, De Vinne wrote a number of articles for *Century* on the history of printing methods and on current practices. The illustrations for his 1890 article on "The Printing of *The Century*" delight in the productivity of his presses. In a scene in *Century*'s mailing room, for example, workers are dwarfed by towering stacks of magazines (Figure 74). The sheer volume of matter is impressive—indeed almost oppressive, particularly in the case of the man in the right foreground who, straining to pull his massive load of periodicals, trudges forward with eyes thoughtlessly on the floor. Perhaps this is the look of a mind burdened by too many pictures. Another illustration from the same article, *Store-Room for Woodcuts and Designs,* looks like Congdon's worst nightmare (Figure 75). Here countless woodblocks recede into infinity: the pictorial matter for publication is truly, as Gilder observed, inexhaustible.

Century's engravers owed a great deal to De Vinne's technological advancements in printing. Thanks to his methods it was possible to print the minute lines characteristic of the New School's work. In his *Ariadne Florentina* lectures, Ruskin had complained about the poor quality of the wood engravings in the popular press. Instead of relying on the simple, straightforward line—Holbein's line—engravers for newspapers and periodicals were trying to satisfy the masses by giving them special effects of light and shade; they were trying to do things with their lines that wood engravers should not and could not do. De Vinne believed Ruskin had spoken too soon. Although English writers had "oracularly declared that the province of engraving on wood was limited to the delineation of form only; . . . that it was presumptuous for an engraver on wood to attempt any serious deviation from the outline style of Dürer and Holbein," they had done so only because they were not yet aware of all the technological improvements that would come about between 1870 and 1890.[81] New steam-powered presses made it possible to print finely engraved blocks with a precision and in quantities never before imagined. We are left to make the doubtful conclusion that, had Ruskin been writing in 1890, or even in 1880, rather than 1873, he would have embraced these new machines along with the lines of the New School engravers.[82] What De Vinne did not take into consideration was the critique of consumer society implicit in Ruskin's critique of popular engraving practices, practices that were in Ruskin's view "enslaved to the ghastly service of catching the last gleams in the glued eyes of the daily more bestial English mob."[83] Too much concern with multiplicability, with meeting the vulgar demands of the mob, risked returning the engraver's scratches to the primitive conditions from which they first emerged.

It was because he wished to preserve the engraver's hand from the corrupting influences of mass culture that Ruskin deemed multiplicability to be an accidental

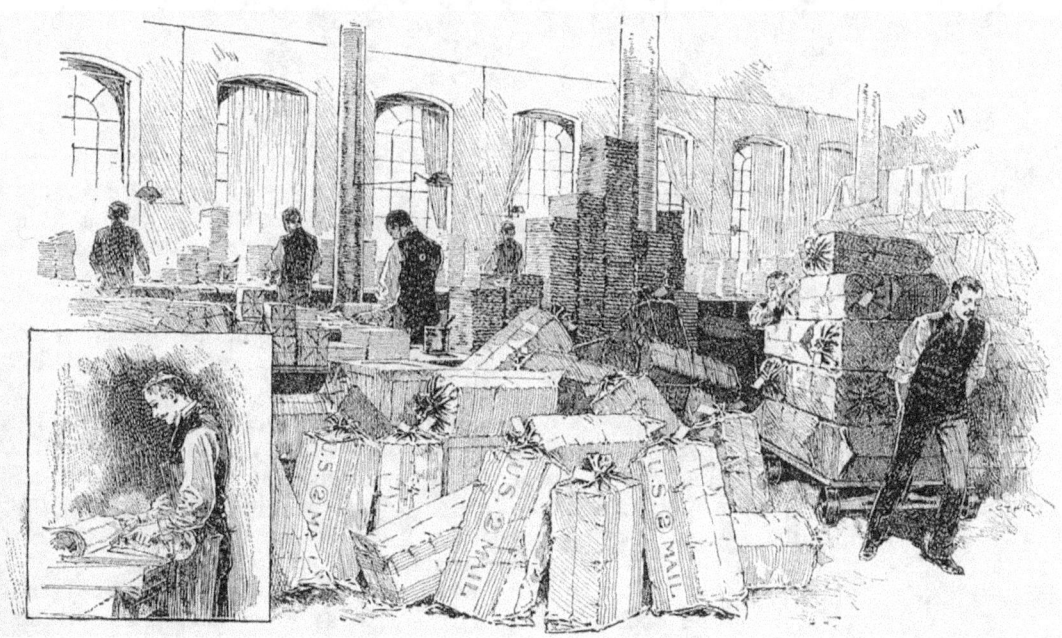

Figure 74. *In the Mailing Room, Century* (November 1890). From the Collections of the University Libraries, University of Minnesota, Minneapolis.

quality of engraving. For De Vinne, however, whose job was to disseminate the product of the engraver's labor among hundreds of thousands of consumers, multiplicability was everything. In 1880 *Scribner's* published two articles by De Vinne on "The Growth of Wood-Cut Printing" that, in their concern with multiplication, form a counterpart to Woodberry's articles that appeared in *Harper's* two years later.[84] While Woodberry's Ruskinian treatment of wood engraving is concerned above all with a history of the engraver's hand, De Vinne's articles, as well as his illustrations, are devoted to multiplicability. Perhaps the most striking feature of the articles is a series of ten illustrations of printing presses that traces an evolution from the handpresses of the sixteenth-century to the steam-powered cylinder presses used by De Vinne to print wood engravings. To follow this episode in the history of technical illustration is to see the fallible human hand gradually give way to the machine.

We begin in 1520 in a room full of exertion (Figure 76). A facsimile print of a sixteenth-century woodcut shows a small room with only three workers, a space in which we might imagine Holbein, in consultation with his woodcutter and printer, watching the *Dance of Death* appear one sheet at a time through an expenditure of human labor. It is the type of printing that William Morris sought to revive in the 1890s at the Kelmscott Press, the type of printing that would have made John Ruskin happy.

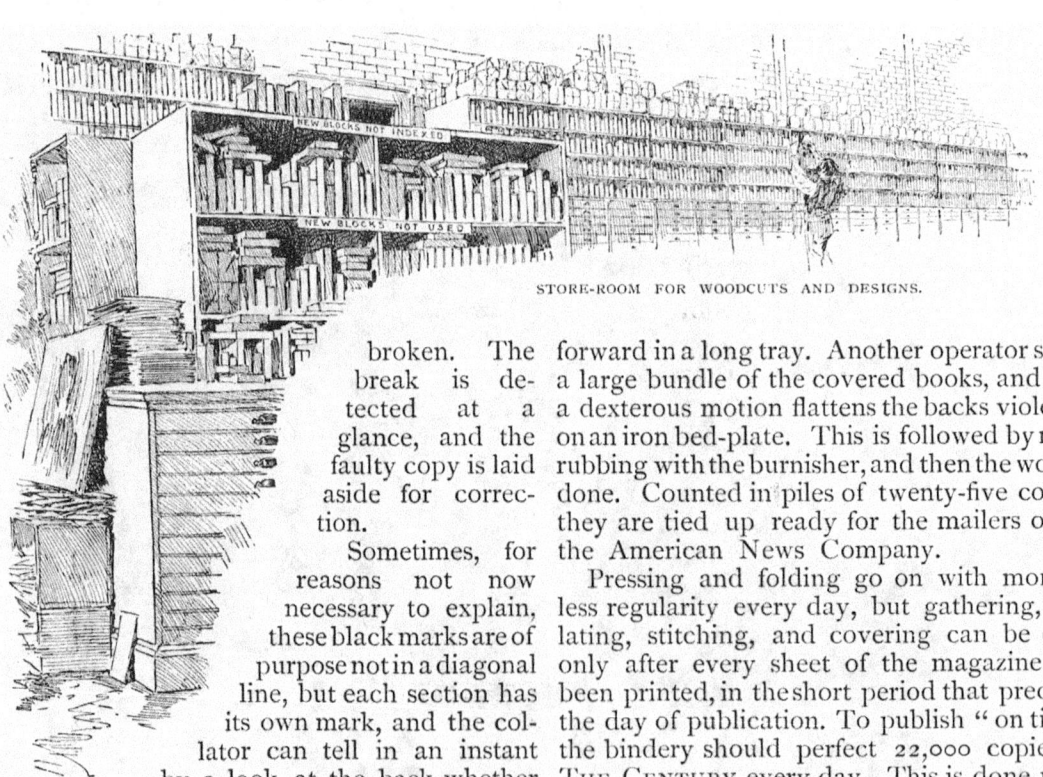

STORE-ROOM FOR WOODCUTS AND DESIGNS.

broken. The break is detected at a glance, and the faulty copy is laid aside for correction.

Sometimes, for reasons not now necessary to explain, these black marks are of purpose not in a diagonal line, but each section has its own mark, and the collator can tell in an instant by a look at the back whether

forward in a long tray. Another operator s a large bundle of the covered books, and a dexterous motion flattens the backs viol on an iron bed-plate. This is followed by i rubbing with the burnisher, and then the wc done. Counted in piles of twenty-five co they are tied up ready for the mailers o the American News Company.

Pressing and folding go on with moi less regularity every day, but gathering, lating, stitching, and covering can be only after every sheet of the magazine been printed, in the short period that prec the day of publication. To publish " on ti the bindery should perfect 22,000 copie THE CENTURY every day. This is done i

Figure 75. *Store-Room for Woodcuts and Designs, Century* (November 1890). From the Collections of the University Libraries, University of Minnesota, Minneapolis.

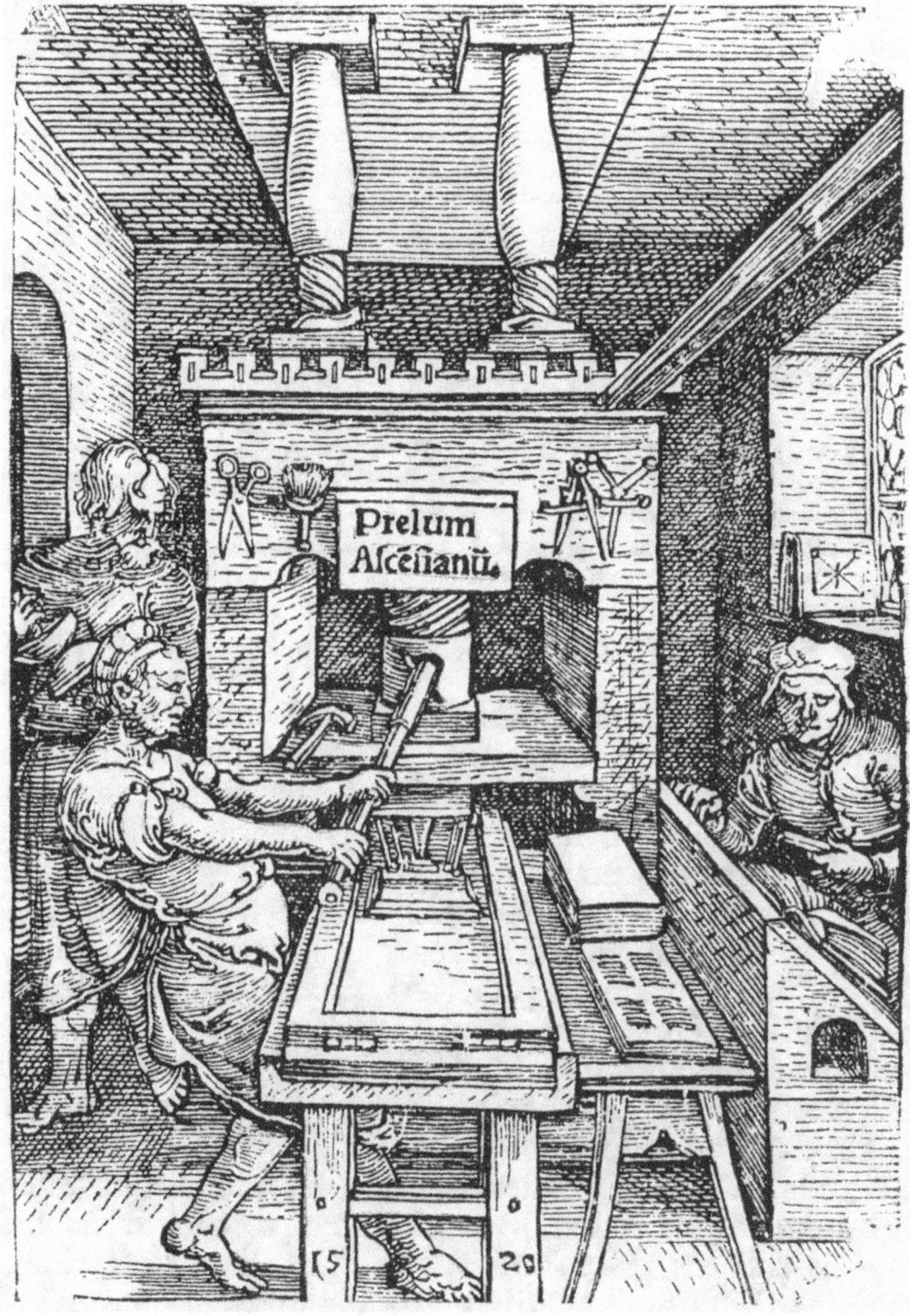

Figure 76. *The Hand-Press of the Sixteenth Century, Scribner's Monthly* (April 1880). From the Collections of the University Libraries, University of Minnesota, Minneapolis.

By the time we get to the end of the second article and to the latest steam-powered presses, however, there are no more signs of human labor at all (Figure 77). The press stands in glorious isolation, looking rather like a locomotive prepared to move of its own accord. The work of the individual hand in engraving belongs now to a different world, the world of the engraver alone with his art, far from the mechanical roar of the modern press. The final image in the series gives us a close-up view of the stop-cylinder press in action, as it demonstrates De Vinne's system of overlays for printing wood engravings (Figure 78). Here we will finally see what the press has been up to in its four hundred years of evolution. Out of this engine we might expect the future of engraving to emerge. But what emerges is unintelligible visual matter, a hieroglyphics of geometric shapes. We are looking at the overlays, of course, which were the cut-out layers of paper that the printer attached to the cylinder in order to achieve proper pressure in the printing of wood engravings: a "tedious method," De Vinne admits, but necessary if one is to obtain a "satisfactory result."[85] And as De Vinne assures us, the eventual results will indeed make pictorial sense; they will be the kind of engravings for which *Scribner's* and *Century* were known. But this illustration does not, in fact, give us that coherence; it offers visual fragments that De Vinne's evolutionary narrative of the press must then resolve into a meaning. And for this reason the illustration is suggestive, for it articulates visually the condition feared by so many critics that a single-minded pursuit of quantity was primitivizing the popular press through the indiscriminate production of undigested visual material. In *The Overlays Fixed on the*

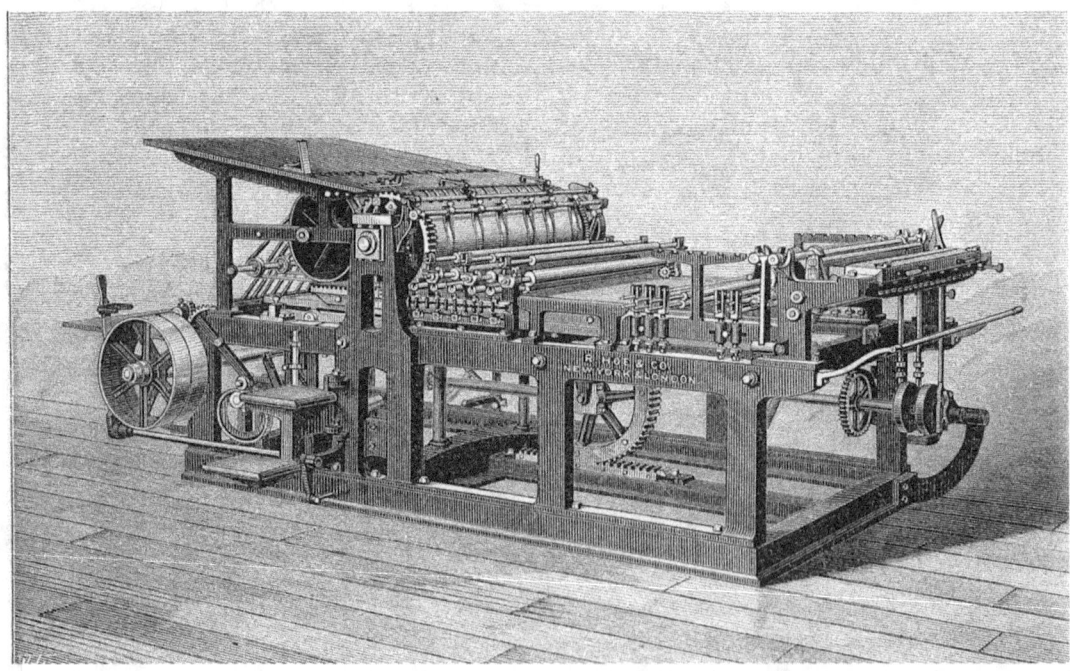

Figure 77. *Stop-Cylinder Printing Machine, Scribner's Monthly* (May 1880). From the Collections of the University Libraries, University of Minnesota, Minneapolis.

Cylinder, De Vinne's press, the most advanced technology around for the multiplication of images in 1880, appears as a machine for picture-writing.

As the illustration of overlays and the critics of over-illustration both suggest, the engravings that appear throughout *Century* should not be considered (as the rhetoric of the magazine itself would have it) as the fully civilized culmination of an evolutionary narrative of art. Such meanings arrive through acts of reception: through the reception of the image by the text surrounding it, through the reception of a viewer who negotiates between text and image, and through the reception of the engraver, who, after all, is a viewer whose act of reception can be read in his lines. It is therefore important that when we look at the reproductions of White's watercolors published in *Century* in the 1880s, we resist the temptation to normalize their meaning by treating them as the products of an authoritative hand, as Eggleston would have us do; that is, as evidence of an early American encounter cohering under the sign of the author. Indeed, their incoherence represents a condition not unlike that of the Renaissance collection.[86] The threat that magazine illustrations posed to critics of over-illustration was the threat of a reversion to that prelinguistic collection, the threat of winding up with an article or book that was more a cabinet of curiosities than a meaningful story.

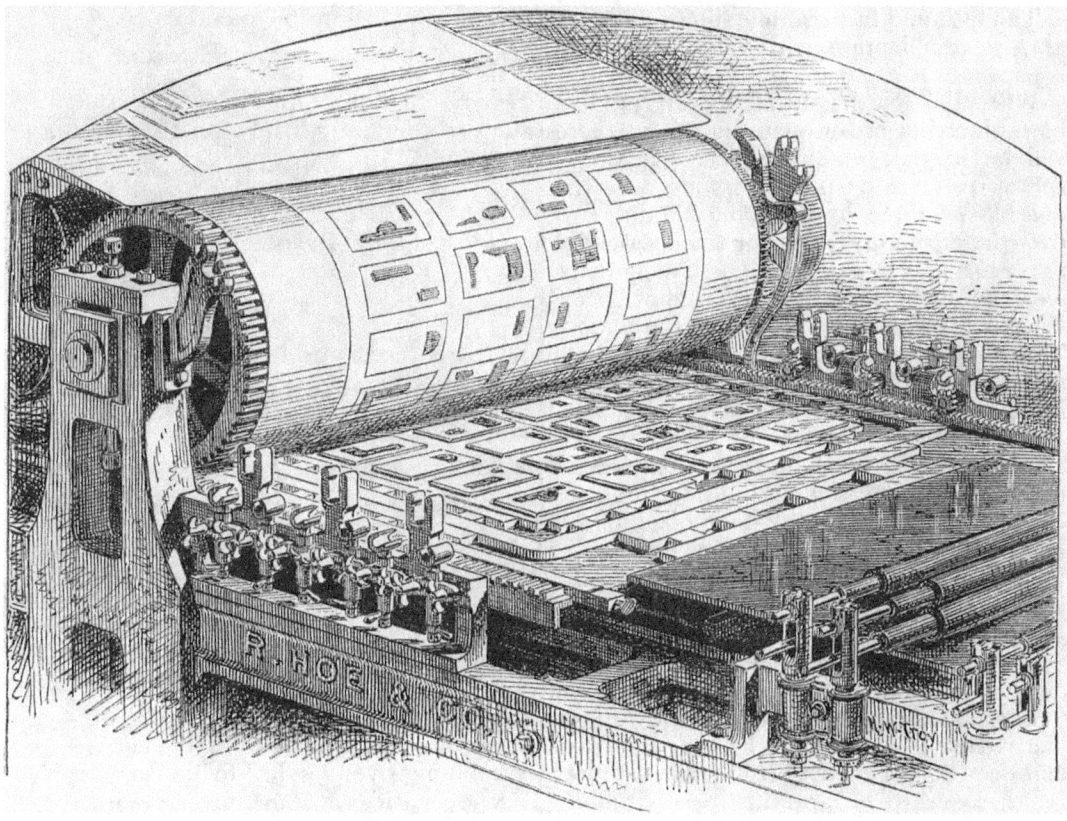

Figure 78. *The Overlays Fixed on the Cylinder, Scribner's Monthly* (May 1880). From the Collections of the University Libraries, University of Minnesota, Minneapolis.

For the nineteenth century, the condition of the Renaissance collection became a distinctly *primitive* condition, a condition of over-illustration to be feared and avoided, and the civilizing of which was one of the important rituals of the late nineteenth-century press.

Engraving, Evolving

My earlier comments on *The Picture-Writer* treated it as Brush's production; my reading of its evolutionary story about the artist's civilizing hand was contingent on our assumption that the reproduction is capable of giving us that hand. But what happens to the picture's story when we begin to treat it as an *engraving* composed of hundreds of lines that do their best to imitate the photograph from which the engraver worked? After all, the name of that engraver, J. H. E. [John Henry Ellsworth] Whitney, appears below the reproduction quite prominently, even before Brush's name. Whitney's lines, moreover, the constitutive marks of a picture about the making and interpreting of marks, would have been particularly visible to an audience not yet familiar with the halftone. This was an audience accustomed to encountering discussions and debates about the proper syntax of wood engraving in *Century* and in other illustrated magazines of the time. Where, then, do Whitney's scratches fit into the picture?

It should be evident by now that there are two poles that largely determine what we might call the playing field for reproductive engraving during the 1880s. On one side are its primitive aspects, the scratches and picture-writing that began on the walls of temples and tombs or in a Mandan lodge, which constitute the first step of cultural evolution. It is from this savage condition that the engraver, or any artist for that matter, gradually develops into thought and sentiment. On the other side is the artist and his civilized hand—the hand of a George de Forest Brush, for instance. It is the reproductive engraver's task to reproduce this hand as a camera would, and in so doing, to efface himself. It is also the reproductive engraver's deepest desire to become such a hand himself. Where, then, do the engraver's lines fit within this playing field? I would suggest that they have no comfortable niche, that they represent a troubling *in between.* The reproductive engraver's lines are condemned to be always approaching or growing more distant from one or the other of these idealized poles: neither author nor savage, neither hand nor machine, they are forever developing. They are what Bruno Latour has called "hybrids," belonging to none of the sacred categories of modernity (in this case, categories such as "the author," "the savage," "art," and "science"), but performing the real work of constituting those categories.[87] As such, the lines of the New School engraver have an important story to tell about the labor of evolving at the end of the nineteenth century.

Ruskin offers insights into this labor. As the writer and anthropologist Andrew Lang noted in an 1884 essay on "The Art of Savages," Ruskin's artistic views are intimately tied up with those of the savage. Taking the aestheticist's view that art ought to be disinterested, Lang begins his essay with a critique of Ruskin:

"Avoid Coleridge, he is *useless*," says Mr. Ruskin. Why should the poetry of Coleridge be useful? The question may interest the critic, but we are only concerned with Mr. Ruskin here, for one reason. His disparagement of Coleridge as "useless" is a survival of the belief that art should be "useful." This is the savage's view of art.[88]   .

For Ruskin, art is tied materially to the circumstances of production and consumption, and it does not—cannot—exist anywhere but within those conditions precisely because it is *made* of those conditions. To misrecognize this fact, to ignore the material conditions of art-making, is therefore not only an aesthetic mistake but a grave social and moral mistake as well. This view of art, as Lang observes, is what ties Ruskin irrevocably to the savage. The savage is concerned with the utility of art because savage art is tied by necessity to the exigent circumstances of savage life. Ruskin and the savage are both locked in an aesthetic materialism: for both, art must always be firmly rooted in worldly matter; for both, art is irreducibly tactile. Thus the distance between past and present, savage and civilized, can never be absolute. For Ruskin, art can never really *be* civilized; that is, it can never transcend its material conditions. Rather, it is always *becoming* civilized, gradually developing beyond the primitive line. Hence the importance of the engraver, that founding member of the School of Delineators, because his line more than any other shows the savage origins from which the artist is always engaged in the labor of evolving. Ruskin has much to teach us about how to interpret the wood engravings that appeared in *Century* during the 1880s, engravings such as *The Picture-Writer* and *The Flyer,* for he forces us, as he forced his contemporaries, to read into the engraver's lines the very processes of producing civilization.

And what specifically do the lines of the New School engravers finally have to tell us about these processes? They tell an ambiguous story; and how could it be otherwise in the case of these engravers who argued that their lines were both unique signatures and exact copies? One thing we can say is that their lines indicate a great deal of exacting, minute, even tedious labor. The laying on of line after line, slavishly in imitation of a hand and a method that did not belong to the engraver himself, was not self-evidently noble work in the eyes of critics such as Ruskin and Linton. Ruskin illustrates in *Ariadne Florentina,* for example, some of the intricate crosshatch work of engravers for the popular press, work he thought had no proper place in the wood engraver's art (Figure 79). In his lecture, delivered only seven years after the conclusion of the American Civil War, Ruskin goes so far as to suggest a connection between consumer culture's exploitation of the engraver's labor and the only recently abolished exploitation of slave labor in the United States. "Now calculate," Ruskin writes,

—or think enough to feel the impossibility of calculating—the number of woodcuts used daily for our popular prints, and how many men are night and day cutting 1050 square holes to the square inch, as the occupation of their manly life. And Mrs. Beecher Stowe and the North Americans fancy they have abolished slavery![89]

Of course we could take De Vinne's side and argue that the work of the New School engravers represents something more sophisticated than the kind of work Ruskin was criticizing. In *Century* we see wood engraving realizing possibilities never dreamed of before. We see true virtuosity. Yet virtuosity, as William Ivins suggests, can also be tedious. Ivins has no kind words for "the trivial, boring, and empty virtuosity of engraving over a photographic basis, that was, so short a time ago, the much vaunted characteristic of the American school of wood-engraving."[90] Whether the critic is a Ruskin or a Linton defending an older school of engraving, or an Ivins defending the halftone process against the engravers it replaced, there is something embarrassing— to art and to civilization itself—about the busy, labor-intensive lines that make up *The Picture-Writer* and *The Flyer*. Those lines raised the troubling possibility that the labor of evolution was *not* a one-way street that progresses from the picture-writing of the savage to the civilized hand of the artist; they suggest instead that the labor of producing civilization *could* be tedious work, that it was the work of civilizing an inexhaustible supply of printed matter, of constantly struggling to emerge from the primitive conditions of an over-illustrated press. Here, finally, is the difference between Eggleston's engraving of *The Flyer* and Binyon's halftone: in the reproductive syntax of Eggleston's version we can *see* the labor of evolving from the picture-writing of the savage. And in seeing that labor, we can read a story about the illustrated magazine in the 1880s and the endless work of manufacturing civilization.

97. Now I take up *Punch*, at his best. The whole of the left side of John Bull's waistcoat—the shadow on his knee-breeches and greatcoat—the whole of the Lord Chancellor's gown, and of John Bull's and Sir Peter Teazle's complexions, are worked with finished precision of cross-hatching. These have indeed some purpose in their texture; but in the most wanton and gratuitous way, the wall below the window is cross-hatched too, and that not with a double, but a treble line (Fig. 4).

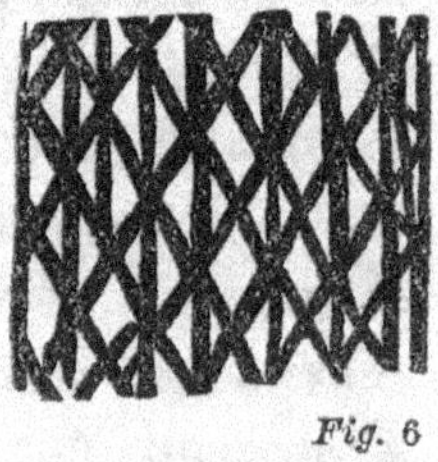

Fig. 6

There are about thirty of these columns, with thirty-five interstices each : approximately, 1050—certainly not fewer— interstices to be deliberately cut clear, to get that two inches square of shadow.

Figure 79. Figure 6 from *Ariadne Florentina*. From the Collections of the University Libraries, University of Minnesota, Minneapolis.

Notes

Introduction

1. I will often use the terms *ethnography* and *ethnographic* to refer, anachronistically, to early modern efforts to describe American Indians. The images and texts I examine in the first three chapters were produced between 1590 and the 1730s, whereas the word *ethnography,* according to the *Oxford English Dictionary,* first appeared in English in the 1830s. I use this term to refer to what were during the early modern period largely untheorized modes of classification and description, generally referred to at the time as the study of customs, manners, or habits. I use modern terminology not to suggest sharp boundaries between diverse descriptive practices—nor between the realms of the sacred and the profane—at a time when such boundaries were very much in-the-making, but to keep in sight the role that early modern efforts to describe customs and manners played in the formation of modern disciplinary categories.

2. Jean de Léry, *History of a Voyage to the Land of Brazil, Otherwise Called America,* trans. Janet Whatley (Berkeley: University of California Press, 1990), 62.

3. Throughout this book I will regularly use the word "savage" (usually without quotation marks, for the reader's sake) because it is a word favored by the authors I discuss. I do not use the word as an implicit endorsement of their ideas about the indigenous peoples of the Americas but rather to put those very ideas under critical scrutiny.

4. Francis Bacon, *A Selection of His Works,* ed. Sidney Warhaft (New York: Odyssey Press, 1965), 323.

5. See Peter Parshall, "Imago Contrafacta: Images and Facts in the Northern Renaissance," *Art History* 16 (December 1993): 554–79; and Claudia Swan, "Ad Vivum, Naer Het Leven, from the Life: Defining a Mode of Representation," *Word & Image* 11 (October–December 1995): 353–72. On the dominance of a descriptive mode of picturing in northern Europe during the early modern period, see Svetlana Alpers, *The Art of Describing: Dutch Art in the Seventeenth Century* (Chicago: University of Chicago Press, 1983).

6. Léry, *History of a Voyage,* lx. Sancerre, in the events following the St. Bartholomew's Day Massacre, was besieged in 1573 by royal Catholic forces. Léry, who lived through this

siege, published an account of it the following year: *Histoire memorable de la ville de Sancerre* (1574).

7. For an analysis of the visual rhetoric of Léry's woodcuts, see Claire Farago, "Jean de Léry's Anatomy Lesson: The Persuasive Power of Word and Image in Framing the Ethnographic Subject," in *European Iconography East and West,* ed. György E. Szönyi (Leiden: E. J. Brill, 1996), 109–27.

8. Michel de Certeau, "Writing vs. Time: History and Anthropology in the Works of Lafitau," *Yale French Studies* 59 (1980): 40.

9. The album of White's drawings in the British Museum's Department of Prints and Drawings includes approximately seventy-five watercolors, including eighteen ethnographic works. The surviving set of watercolors is probably one of several such sets that White made based on a much larger body of work that has not survived. The authoritative studies of White's body of work are Paul Hulton and David Beers Quinn, *The American Drawings of John White, 1577–1590,* 2 vols. (London: Trustees of the British Museum, 1964); and Paul Hulton, *America 1585: The Complete Drawings of John White* (Chapel Hill: University of North Carolina Press, 1984).

10. The book was first published unillustrated in 1588 in London.

11. Theodor de Bry in Thomas Harriot, *A Briefe and True Report of the New Found Land of Virginia: The Complete 1590 Theodor de Bry Edition* (New York: Dover Publications, 1972), 41.

12. On the de Brys' concern with reaching a wide readership with their travel accounts, see Michiel van Groesen, "A First Popularisation of Travel Literature: On the Methods and Intentions of the De Bry Travel Collection (1590–1634)," *Dutch Crossing* 25 (Summer 2001): 103–31.

13. Thomas Jefferson to John Adams, June 11, 1812, *The Adams-Jefferson Letters: The Complete Correspondence between Thomas Jefferson and Abigail and John Adams,* vol. 2, ed. Lester J. Cappon (Chapel Hill: University of North Carolina Press, 1959), 306.

14. Certainly the most influential study (focusing on Harriot's text for the *Report* but not the de Bry engravings) is Stephen Greenblatt's "Invisible Bullets," which appears in Greenblatt, *Shakespearean Negotiations: The Circulation of Social Energy in Renaissance England* (Berkeley: University of California Press, 1988), 21–65. Other readings that address Harriot's text and its illustrations include Mary C. Fuller, *Voyages in Print: English Travel to America, 1576–1624* (Cambridge: Cambridge University Press, 1995), 38–54; Eric Cheyfitz, *The Poetics of Imperialism: Translation and Colonization from the Tempest to Tarzan,* 2nd ed. (Philadelphia: University of Pennsylvania Press, 1997), 175–213; and Shannon Miller, *Invested with Meaning: The Raleigh Circle in the New World* (Philadelphia: University of Pennsylvania Press, 1998), 114–52. The most thoughtful and sustained interpretations of the de Bry engravings in the *Report* are Daniel Defert, "Collections et nations au XVIe siècle," *L'Amérique de Théodore de Bry: Une collection de voyages protestante du XVIe siècle,* ed. Michèle Duchet (Paris: Editions du centre national de la recherche scientifique, 1987), 47–67; and Mary Baine Campbell, *Wonder and Science: Imagining Worlds in Early Modern Europe* (Ithaca, N.Y.: Cornell University Press, 1999), 51–67.

15. James Clifford, *The Predicament of Culture: Twentieth-century Ethnography, Literature, and Art* (Cambridge, Mass.: Harvard University Press, 1988), 14–15.

16. Bernadette Bucher, *Icon and Conquest: A Structural Analysis of the Illustrations of De Bry's Great Voyages,* trans. Basia Miller Gulati (Chicago: University of Chicago Press, 1981), xv–xvi.

17. Tom Conley is the only commentator on de Bry's engravings I am aware of who has seriously considered how particular modes of representation (engraving, perspective)

are themselves implicated in de Bry's broader project of representing the encounter. In a series of brief but suggestive readings of de Bry's illustrations for his 1598 edition of Bartolomé de Las Casas' *Brevísima relación,* Conley reflects on the relationship between de Bry's engravings of Spanish violence and the violence of representation itself. See Tom Conley, "De Bry's Las Casas," in *Amerindian Images and the Legacy of Columbus,* ed. René Jara and Nicholas Spadaccini (Minneapolis: University of Minnesota Press, 1992), 103–31.

18. This translation of the Latin caption to *America,* as well as the translation of the caption to *Sculptura in æs* that follows, are provided in Bern Dibner, *"New Discoveries": The Sciences, Inventions, and Discoveries of the Middle Ages and the Renaissance as Represented in 24 Engravings Issued in the Early 1580s by Stradanus* (Norwalk, Conn.: Burndy Library, 1953).

19. Recent commentary on van der Straet's *America* includes Michel de Certeau, *The Writing of History,* trans. Tom Conley (New York: Columbia University Press, 1988), xxv–xxvii; Peter Hulme, *Colonial Encounters: Europe and the Native Caribbean, 1492–1797* (London: Methuen, 1986), 1–12 passim; Louis Montrose, "The Work of Gender in the Discourse of Discovery," *Representations* 33 (Winter 1991): 1–41; José Rabasa, *Inventing America: Spanish Historiography and the Formation of Eurocentrism* (Norman: University of Oklahoma Press, 1993), 23–48; Tom Conley, *The Self-Made Map: Cartographic Writing in Early Modern France* (Minneapolis: University of Minnesota Press, 1996), 305–9; Benjamin Schmidt, *Innocence Abroad: The Dutch Imagination and the New World, 1570–1670* (Cambridge: Cambridge University Press, 2001), 129–33; and Michael J. Schreffler, "Vespucci Rediscovers America: The Pictorial Rhetoric of Cannibalism in Early Modern Culture," *Art History* 28 (June 2005): 295–310. For more general discussion of van der Straet's *Nova reperta,* see Michel N. Benisovich, "The Drawings of Stradanus (Jan van der Straeten) in the Cooper Union Museum for the Arts of Decoration, New York," *Art Bulletin* 38 (December 1956): 249–51; Jean-Claude Margolin, "Á propos des Nova Reperta de Stradan," in *Esthétiques de la nouveauté à la renaissance,* ed. François Laroque and Franck Lessay (Paris: Presses de la Sorbonne Nouvelle, 2001), 1–28; and Alice Bonner McGinty, "Stradanus (Jan van der Straet): His Role in the Visual Communication of Renaissance Discoveries, Technologies, and Values" (PhD diss., Tufts University, 1974).

20. De Certeau, *The Writing of History,* xxv.

21. Michiel van Groesen notes the friendly relationship between de Bry and Philips Galle, and speculates that de Bry may well have worked for the prominent engraver (Michiel van Groesen, "De Bry and Antwerp, 1577–1585: A Formative Period," in *Inszenierte Welten/Staging New Worlds,* ed. Susanna Burghartz (Basel: Schwabe Verlag, 2004), 35.

22. Norbert Elias, *The Civilizing Process: The History of Manners and State Formation and Civilization,* trans. Edmund Jephcott (Oxford: Blackwell, 1994). As will become clear in the course of this book, the art of engraving was at best an ambivalent ally of the civilizing process. For a study of the complex and ambivalent role that technology played within Renaissance humanism, see Jessica Wolfe, *Humanism, Machinery, and Renaissance Literature* (Cambridge: Cambridge University Press, 2004).

23. Georgius Agricola, *De re metallica,* trans. Herbert Clark Hoover and Lou Henry Hoover (New York: Dover Publications, 1950), xxv.

24. De Bry in Harriot, *Briefe and True Report,* 41. De Bry's remarks on the Virginians' lack of metals also call to mind the words of Gonzalo in Shakespeare's *The Tempest.* Drawing upon golden-age imagery that since Columbus had frequently been applied to the Americas, Shakespeare has Gonzalo imagine an ideal commonwealth on the enchanted island where there is "no use of metal" (II.i.154).

25. Harriot, *Briefe and True Report,* 50.

26. Michael Adas has compellingly argued that Europeans' sense of their own technological superiority became a critical means for distinguishing their own civilization from "savage" societies. But as both Adas and Joyce Chaplin have argued, this sense was by no means fully developed during the sixteenth and seventeenth centuries. See Michael Adas, *Machines as the Measure of Men: Science, Technology, and Ideologies of Western Dominance* (Ithaca, N.Y.: Cornell University Press, 1989); and Joyce Chaplin, *Subject Matter: Technology, the Body, and Science on the Anglo-American Frontier, 1500–1676* (Cambridge, Mass.: Harvard University Press, 2001). Chaplin has a tendency to overstate the claim that during the early phase of settlement Europeans believed themselves to share a "common humanity" with the indigenous peoples they encountered. For a cogent critique of Chaplin along these lines, see Benjamin Schmidt, "American Natural," *Reviews in American History* 30 (December 2002): 530–40.

27. Bacon, *Novum organum* (1620), bk. 1, aphorism 129, in *Works,* 373.

28. On body language in these images, see Karen Ordahl Kupperman, "Presentment of Civility: English Reading of American Self-Presentation in the Early Years of Colonization," *William and Mary Quarterly* 54 (January 1997): 193–228.

29. Harriot, *Briefe and True Report,* 27.

30. Joseph Koerner, "Hieronymus Bosch's World Picture," *Picturing Science, Producing Art,* ed. Caroline A. Jones and Peter Galison (New York: Routledge, 1998), 299. Also see chapter 3 of my book for further discussion of this idea.

31. Tom Conley's *Self-Made Map,* which addresses the mapping of the self in early modern France, is an extended and insightful discussion of the ways an early modern perspectival subject produced itself through new modes of visual and literary representation.

32. Peter Parshall, "Art and the Theater of Knowledge: The Origins of Print Collecting in Northern Europe," *Harvard University Art Museums Bulletin* 2 (Spring 1994): 28.

33. Bacon, *Novum organum,* bk. 1, aphorism 74, as quoted in Pamela H. Smith, *The Body of the Artisan: Art and Experience in the Scientific Revolution* (Chicago: University of Chicago Press, 2004), 232. Smith provides an excellent discussion of the central but problematic role of the mechanical arts in the new science. On the mechanical arts and the idea of scientific progress in the early modern period, see also Paolo Rossi, *Philosophy, Technology and the Arts in the Early Modern Era,* trans. Salvator Attanasio, ed. Benjamin Nelson (New York: Harper & Row, 1970).

34. William M. Ivins Jr., *Prints and Visual Communication* (Cambridge, Mass.: MIT Press, 1969), 3.

35. For a discussion of van der Straet's plate showing the invention of *Conspicilla* (spectacles) that similarly addresses the way this invention both corrects and perpetuates "the defects of human vision," see Wolfe, *Humanism, Machinery, and Renaissance Literature,* 169. It is also worth noting that, for the viewer leafing through the plates of *Nova reperta,* the man with a cane being carved by the engraver in *Sculptura in æs* might well recall the blind figure in the background of *Conspicilla* who walks with a dog and cane.

36. For an overview of key studies and problems in the materiality of print, especially in relation to printmaking, see Graham Larkin and Lisa Pon, "Introduction: The Materiality of Printed Words and Images," *Word & Image* 17 (January–June 2001): 1–6. This short essay introduces a special issue of *Word & Image* on the materiality of print in early modern Europe.

37. The notion of the savage as remainder is crucial to de Certeau's reading of Léry's *History of a Voyage.* Léry's writing leaves a remainder, "a waste that it produces through succeeding in doing what it does, but which comes as a by-product. This waste product of constructive thinking—its fallout and its repressed—will finally become the other" (de

Certeau, *The Writing of History,* 237). For de Certeau, this remainder takes the form of the speech of the Tupis, which writing cannot recover and which Léry must therefore leave in Brazil. My own understanding of this remainder is more grounded in base matter than intangible speech, and in this respect the remainder I address in *Engraving the Savage* has more in common with what Stephen Greenblatt has called the "problem of the leftover." Greenblatt identifies a persistent anxiety in early modern English literature that originates in a concern within eucharistic theology over what to do with the leftovers of the consecrated host. See Greenblatt's essay on "The Mousetrap" in Catherine Gallagher and Stephen Greenblatt, *Practicing New Historicism* (Chicago: University of Chicago Press, 2000), 136–62.

38. "Ralph Lane's Discourse on the First Colony," in David Beers Quinn, *The Roanoke Voyages 1584–1590: Documents to Illustrate the English Voyages to North America under the Patent Granted to Sir Walter Raleigh in 1584,* vol. 1 (New York: Dover Publications, 1991), 269–70.

39. Native copperworking in North America at the time of European contact was in fact quite sophisticated. Created through cold-working (i.e., the forging of cold metal through hammering procedures), native copper artifacts ranged from adornment items (hair ornaments, gorgets, beads, headdresses, ear spools, copper-covered masks) to ritual items (zoomorphic and anthropomorphic rattles and effigies) to spearheads and other ceremonial items such as axes, needles, and pins. See Kathleen L. Ehrhardt, *European Metals in Native Hands: Rethinking the Dynamics of Technological Change, 1640–1683* (Tuscaloosa: University of Alabama Press, 2005), 56–71.

40. On the use of copper and its value as a commodity in fifteenth- and sixteenth-century engraving workshops, see David Landau and Peter Parshall, *The Renaissance Print, 1470–1550* (New Haven, Conn.: Yale University Press, 1994), 23–27.

41. On the relationship between the geometric grid of cartography and ethnographic understanding in early modern Europe, see Valerie Traub, "Mapping the Global Body," in *Early Modern Visual Culture: Representation, Race, and Empire in Renaissance England,* ed. Peter Erickson and Clark Hulse (Philadelphia: University of Pennsylvania Press, 2000), 44–97.

42. These are some of the terms used in three important studies of this "concept": Roy Harvey Pearce, *Savagism and Civilization: A Study of the Indian and the American Mind* (Berkeley: University of California Press, 1988); Edward Dudley and Maximillian E. Novak, eds., *The Wild Man Within: An Image in Western Thought from the Renaissance to Romanticism* (Pittsburgh: University of Pittsburgh Press, 1972); and Olive Patricia Dickason, *The Myth of the Savage and the Beginnings of French Colonialism in the Americas* (Edmonton: University of Alberta Press, 1984).

43. See, for example, Joseph Roach, *Cities of the Dead: Circum-Atlantic Performance* (New York: Columbia University Press, 1996); and Serge Gruzinski, *The Mestizo Mind: The Intellectual Dynamics of Colonization and Globalization,* trans. Deke Dusinberre (New York: Routledge, 2002).

44. Alfred Gell, "The Technology of Enchantment and the Enchantment of Technology," in Gell, *The Art of Anthropology: Essays and Diagrams,* ed. Eric Hirsch (London: Athlone Press, 1999), 159–86.

1. Savage Marks

1. Harriot, *Briefe and True Report,* 75.

2. Mary B. Campbell, "The Illustrated Travel Book and the Birth of Ethnography: Part I of De Bry's *America,*" in *The Work of Dissimilitude: Essays from the Sixth Citadel*

Conference on Medieval and Renaissance Literature, ed. David G. Allen and Robert A. White (Newark: University of Delaware Press, 1992), 181. Also see Mary Baine Campbell, *Wonder and Science,* 57.

3. Michel de Certeau, *The Practice of Everyday Life,* trans. Steven F. Rendall (Berkeley: University of California Press, 1984), 140.

4. While original watercolors by John White exist for most of the engravings in the *Report,* no original survives for *The Marckes of sundrye of the Cheif mene of Virginia.* The engraving may therefore have been based on a lost original, or it may have been an invention of de Bry with the help of Harriot and/or White. I suspect the latter is the case, since the figure of this Algonquian man seems to be based on de Bry's engraving of *A weroan or great Lorde of Virginia* that appears earlier in the *Report.* It should also be noted that tattoo markings clearly related to those in *The Marckes of sundrye of the Cheif mene of Virginia* appear on the back of two foreground figures in John White's watercolor of dancing Indians.

5. See Panofsky, "Iconography and Iconology: An Introduction to the Study of Renaissance Art," *Meaning in the Visual Arts* (Chicago: University of Chicago Press, 1955), 26–54.

6. Elio Antonio de Nebrija, quoted in Walter D. Mignolo, *The Darker Side of the Renaissance: Literacy, Territoriality, and Colonization* (Ann Arbor: University of Michigan Press, 1995), 38.

7. Juliet Fleming, *Graffiti and the Writing Arts of Early Modern England* (Philadelphia: University of Pennsylvania Press, 2001), 46. Derrida proposes the idea of a "cultural graphology" in the chapter "Of Grammatology as a Positive Science," in *Of Grammatology,* trans. Gayatri Charavorty Spivak (Baltimore: Johns Hopkins University Press, 1976), 74–93. Jonathan Goldberg's *Writing Matter: From the Hands of the English Renaissance* (Stanford: Stanford University Press, 1990) and Fleming's *Graffiti and the Writing Arts* are both brilliant efforts toward the realization of this project in the context of Renaissance England.

8. As Joyce Chaplin's work suggests, an English audience might well be inclined to read the Algonquian warrior's longbow and arrows as a sign of a distinctly *English* virtue. Chaplin argues that during the sixteenth century the English were apt to recognize in the Indian's bow and arrow a savage nobility that could be identified, nostalgically, with Britain's own heroic past. See Chaplin, *Subject Matter,* 79–115.

9. For a detailed study of the iconography of difference in late medieval and early Renaissance Europe, see Ruth Mellinkoff, *Outcasts: Signs of Otherness in Northern European Art of the Late Middle Ages* (Berkeley: University of California Press, 1994).

10. Léry, *Histoire d'un voyage faict en la terre du Brésil,* ed. Jean-Claude Morisot (Geneva: Librairie Droz, 1975), 105. The English translation is mine.

11. See Hubert Damisch's critique of iconography in "Semiotics and Iconography," in *The Tell-Tale Sign: A Survey of Semiotics,* ed. Thomas A. Sebeok (Lisse, Holland: Peter de Ridder Press, 1975), 27–36.

12. For two useful models of conceptualizing these networks of mediation, see Bruno Latour, *We Have Never Been Modern* (Cambridge, Mass.: Harvard University Press, 1993); and Friedrich Kittler, *Discourse Networks: 1800/1900,* trans. Michael Metteer (Stanford: Stanford University Press, 1990).

13. W. J. T. Mitchell, *Picture Theory* (Chicago: University of Chicago Press, 1994), 48.

14. Joseph-François Lafitau, *Customs of the American Indians Compared with the Customs of Primitive Times,* trans. William N. Fenton and Elizabeth L. Moore, vol. 1 (Toronto: Champlain Society, 1974), 7.

15. Ibid., 7.

16. De Certeau, "Writing vs. Time."

17. Lafitau, *Customs of the American Indians,* 34. On Lafitau's illustrations, which include numerous figures taken from de Bry's engravings for the *Report,* see William C. Sturtevant, "The Sources of Lafitau's American Illustrations," in Lafitau, *Customs of the American Indians,* vol. 2, 271–97.

18. Michel Foucault, *The Order of Things: An Archaeology of the Human Sciences* (New York: Vintage Books, 1970), 56.

19. Lafitau's "system," de Certeau argues, "has no place in time or space. It is a non-lieu" (de Certeau, "Writing vs. Time," 53).

20. As Derrida observes, "Writing, sensible matter and artificial exteriority: a 'clothing.' It has sometimes been contested that speech clothed thought. . . . But has it ever been doubted that writing was the clothing of speech?" (Derrida, *Of Grammatology,* 35).

21. John Barrett, quoted in Goldberg, *Writing Matter,* 225.

22. There were those, however, who did locate the origins of writing with Adam and Eve, and some thought that Hebrew letters had been given to Adam directly by God. Saint Augustine implies as much in *The City of God,* book 18, chapter 38. As Derrida notes, Blaise de Vigenère also expressed this belief in his *Traité des chiffres ou secrètes manières d'escrire* (1586) (*Of Grammatology,* 76). William Kempe's beliefs, however, were more typical. In *The Education of Children* (1588), Kempe claims that the first letters were engraved on pillars by Seth and Enoch before the flood. Although Kempe admits there is no evidence of writing before this, he also shows that the reign of the alphabet is not necessarily dependent on the precise dating of the origins of writing: "No doubt these [pre-alphabetical] ages were adorned with such heroicall spirits and golden wittes, that they did conceive and keepe in minde without the helpe of letters a great deale better than the ages following could do: so that their letterlesse and unwritten doctrine did bring that fruite and commodities, which ours doth now being written" (*Four Tudor Books on Education,* ed. Robert David Pepper [Gainesville: Scholars' Facsimiles and Reprints, 1966], 191). Kempe does not speak of Adam and Eve's lack of writing as a deficiency, but instead argues that the earliest ages were already so thoroughly immersed in "unwritten doctrine" that they had no need of letters. So perfectly were they guided by the *logic* of the alphabet that they had no need for the writing practices that their descendents (including Kempe) would have to rely on. Various possible origins of the alphabet are discussed in the introductory text of de Brys' *Alphabeta et characteres* (1596), titled in the 1628 translation "A Discourse of the Diversity of Letters used by the diuers Nations in the world; the antiquity, manifold use and variety thereof, with exemplary descriptions of aboue threescore seuerall Alphabets, with other strange writings."

23. See Goldberg, *Writing Matter,* 207–22.

24. Harriot, *Briefe and True Report,* 25–26. Harriot's remarks are similar to those of José de Acosta, a Jesuit missionary in New Spain and author of the *Historia natural y moral de las Indias* (1590), translated by Edward Grimston in 1604: "Some learned men write, that all which the Indians make mention of, is not above 400 yeeres old, and whatsoever they speake of former ages, is but a confusion full of obscuritie, wherein we find no truth. The which may not seeme strange, they having no vse of bookes, or writing" (Father Joseph de Acosta, *The Natural and Moral History of the Indies,* trans. Edward Grimston, ed. Clements R. Markham [London: Hakluyt Society, 1880], 71). For a discussion of Acosta and the Spaniards' frustration with the Indians' lack of writing, see Anthony Pagden, *The Fall of Natural Man: The American Indian and the Origins of Comparative Ethnology,* 2nd ed. (Cambridge: Cambridge University Press, 1986), 186. De Certeau discusses the

opposition between European writing and native orality as a structuring principle of early ethnography in *The Writing of History,* 209–43.

25. Harriot, *Briefe and True Report,* 25.

26. Minimal evidence survives as to what Harriot's Algonquian alphabet might have looked like, though John Shirley has made an attempt at reconstructing it. See John W. Shirley, *Thomas Harriot: A Biography* (Oxford: Clarendon Press, 1983), 107–12.

27. See Johannes Fabian, *Time and the Other: How Anthropology Makes Its Object* (New York: Columbia University Press, 1983), 11–12 and 26. Several scholars have addressed the complex issues of historical time raised by de Bry's illustrations. See Mary Campbell, *Wonder and Science,* 51–67; Denise Albanese, *New Science, New World* (Durham: Duke University Press, 1996), 24–29; and Shannon Miller, *Invested with Meaning,* 56–69.

28. Pagden's thesis stated in the introduction to *The Fall of Natural Man* is worth quoting here: "[This book] begins with a fact: the discovery of American man; and it ends with a simple proposition: that for the cultural historian—who had inherited from the theologians that project which in the nineteenth century came to be 'anthropology'—differences in place may be identical to differences in time" (Pagden, *Fall of Natural Man,* 2).

29. On the role played by the figure of Time in Lafitau's image, see de Certeau, "Writing vs. Time," 57–60.

30. As Defert argues, this affirmation at the beginning of de Bry's series of New World images that "we are all sons of Adam and Eve" should also be understood in the political context of sixteenth-century debates regarding the return to a natural law. See Defert, "Collections et nations au XVIe siècle," 59–63.

31. For a discussion of such theories, see Margaret Hodgen, *Early Anthropology in the Sixteenth and Seventeenth Centuries* (Philadelphia: University of Pennsylvania Press, 1964); and Don Cameron Allen, *The Legend of Noah: Renaissance Rationalism in Art, Science, and Letters* (Urbana: University of Illinois Press, 1949), especially chapter 6, "The Migrations of Men and the Plantation of America."

32. Karen Ordahl Kupperman makes this observation in *Indians and English: Facing Off in Early America* (Ithaca: Cornell University Press, 2000), 51.

33. Thomas Nashe, "Pierce Penilesse his supplication to the devill," in *The Works of Thomas Nashe,* vol. 1, ed. Ronald B. McKerrow (New York: Barnes & Noble, 1966), 172. Nashe's statement may have inspired a similar accusation against Christopher Marlowe, another suspected atheist, which was the first item on a long list of charges made in 1593 by the spy Richard Baines. According to Baines, Marlowe claimed that "the Indians and many Authors of antiquity have assuredly writen of above 16 thousand yeares agone wher Adam is proved to have lived within 6 thowsand yeares" (quoted in Shirley, *Thomas Harriot,* 182). This accusation is of particular interest for its betrayal of something more than a mere fear of Indians *living* prior to biblical times, for it attributes Marlowe with saying that the Indians "have assuredly writen" before Adam. A preadamic Indian is a threat to an orthodox order of *writing,* an order in which all history is contained within the closure of the Word. For a discussion of Harriot's suspected atheism in relation to patterns of subversion and containment in the *Report,* see Greenblatt, *Shakespearean Negotiations,* 21–65. For a discussion of preadamitism in late sixteenth-century England and in early modern Europe more generally, see Philip C. Almond, *Adam and Eve in Seventeenth-century Thought* (Cambridge: Cambridge University Press, 1999), 49–57.

34. See note 26 for chapter 1.

35. John Aubrey, quoted in Shirley, *Thomas Harriot,* 107.

36. Acosta, *The Natural and Moral History of the Indies,* 396–97. For a discussion of the value that Acosta and other sixteenth-century Spanish historians placed on indigenous

scripts, see Jorge Cañizares-Esguerra, *How to Write the History of the New World: Histories, Epistemologies, and Identities in the Eighteenth-century Atlantic World* (Stanford: Stanford University Press, 2001), 63–92. For a discussion of the importance of Acosta's *History* in the development of comparative ethnology, see Pagden, *Fall of Natural Man,* chapter 7, "A programme for comparative ethnology (2): José de Acosta."

37. As an image that produces the savage as a blank page on which the viewer can write his/her own subjectivity, de Bry's engraving exemplifies de Certeau's definition of the operation of writing within the "scriptural economy," as set forth in *The Practice of Everyday Life:* "I designate as 'writing' the concrete activity that consists in constructing, on its own, blank space *(un espace propre)*—the page—a text that has power over the exteriority from which it has first been isolated . . . a space that delimits a place of production for the subject. It is a place where the ambiguities of the world have been exorcised" (134). For de Certeau reading van der Straet's *America* according to this same logic, see de Certeau, *The Writing of History,* xxv–xxvi.

38. Fleming, *Graffiti and the Writing Arts,* 79–112. Fleming analyzes the literary and visual culture of tattoos in early modern England, when antiquarians began to develop an interest in the tattooed bodies of their ancient British ancestors, such as those depicted by de Bry at the end of the *Report.* Fleming argues that "the tattooed ancestor stands for a barbarian past that is at once acknowledged and disavowed. That tattooing . . . is the fetish permitting this avowal-that-is-not-one explains, I think, the curious combination of levity and anxiety with which tattoos are treated in the antiquarian account, as they have been treated ever since" (106).

39. Johann Theodor de Bry, *Caracters and Diversitie of Letters Used by Divers Nations in the World; the Antiquity, Manifold Use and Varietie Thereof: With Exemplary Descriptions of Very Many Strang Alphabets* (Frankfurt am Main: John Nicol for William Fitzer, 1628), 5.

40. Though I will not address this issue here, it is also possible to consider the tattoo and other forms of nonalphabetic marking as forms of Derrida's "writing in the narrow sense." See Fleming's discussion of this issue in *Graffiti and the Writing Arts,* 115–18.

41. See Fleming, *Graffiti and the Writing Arts,* 90–91, for a fuller discussion of the language used to describe tattooing, and of its convergences with the language of writing.

42. The most detailed study of tattooing in Oceania is Alfred Gell, *Wrapping in Images: Tattooing in Polynesia* (Oxford: Clarendon Press, 1993). Also see Nicholas Thomas, Anna Cole, and Bronwen Douglas, eds., *Tattoo: Bodies, Art, and Exchange in the Pacific and the West* (Durham: Duke University Press, 2005). An important collection that focuses on tattooing in the West and that reassesses the notion that Western tattooing originates in the European encounter with Pacific cultures is Jane Caplan, ed., *Written on the Body: The Tattoo in European and American History* (Princeton: Princeton University Press, 2000).

43. On tattooing among North American Indians, see Steve Gilbert, ed., *Tattoo History: A Source Book* (New York: Juno Books, 2000), 88–98. On tattooing among southeastern Indians, see John R. Swanton, *The Indians of the Southeastern United States,* Bureau of American Ethnology Bulletin 137 (Washington, D.C.: Smithsonian Institution, 1946), 532–36; and Charles Hudson, *The Southeastern Indians* (Knoxville: University of Tennessee Press, 1976), 30–31, 203, 380.

44. John Hart, *An Orthographie* (Menston, England: Scolar Press, 1969), 1.

45. In marking their community of origin, the tattoos perform a genealogical function for the Algonquians. And as Derrida notes, "it is now known, thanks to unquestionable and abundant information, that the birth of writing (in the colloquial sense)

was nearly everywhere and most often linked to genealogical anxiety" (*Of Grammatology,* 124).

46. Gell formulates a "basic schema of tattooing" that provides a promising starting point for theorizing the tattoo as supplement. The tattoo, argues Gell, may be understood as a supplementary skin, "an extra skin, over the skin, a wrapping for the person which is not separate, but integral" (*Wrapping in Images,* 32).

47. Derrida, *Of Grammatology.* See in particular the chapter "The Violence of the Letter: From Lévi-Strauss to Rousseau," which is a reading of Claude Lévi-Strauss, "Writing Lesson," in *Tristes Tropiques,* trans. John Wightman and Doreen Wightman (New York: Penguin, 1992). Derrida's well-known chapter has been essential for my reading of de Bry.

48. Foster Watson, *Tudor School-Boy Life, the Dialogues of Juan Luis Vives* (London: Frank Cass & Co., 1970), 70. A loose translation of Vives's *Linguae latinae exercitatio* was made into English, French, and Italian, along with the original Latin, by M. Claudius Desainliens in his *Campo di fior, or else, the flourie field of foure languages* (London, 1583). See also Goldberg, who quotes this same passage from Watson's translation (*Writing Matter,* 63). In his chapter "The Violence of the Letter: Instruments of the Hand," which takes up issues of writing and violence raised in Derrida's similarly titled chapter in *Of Grammatology,* Goldberg analyzes the relationship between violence and writing pedagogy in early modern England.

49. Anthony Grafton and Lisa Jardine, *From Humanism to the Humanities: Education and the Liberal Arts in Fifteenth- and Sixteenth-century Europe* (London: Duckworth, 1986), xvi.

50. Elias discusses at length the influence of Erasmus's *De civilitate morum puerilium* (1530) on the development of the concept of *civilité.* See Elias, *The Civilizing Process,* especially part 2, "Civilization as a Specific Transformation of Human Behavior." Elias's general concern with manners is merged with a specific concern with writing and the letter in Goldberg's *Writing Matter,* in which many of the manuals to which I have referred are examined at length. Although I do not pursue the issue here, it is also crucial to note the fundamentally gendered dynamics through which humanist writing manuals promote the acquisition of a (beleaguered) masculine civility as the containment of an unruly femininity. As Barbara Correll writes of Erasmus's pedagogical works: "women function as an essential negative to be overcome by civilizing labors and education, a constructed threat . . . that motivates male students to inscribe themselves in cultural masculine structures of civility" (*The End of Conduct: Grobianus and the Renaissance Text of the Subject* [Ithaca: Cornell University Press, 1996], 64).

51. For a discussion on the humanist emphasis on the civilizing letter in the Spanish colonial context, primarily through the Latin and Castilian grammars of Nebrija, see Mignolo, *The Darker Side of the Renaissance,* chapter 1, "Nebrija in the New World: Renaissance Philosophy of Language and the Spread of Western Literacy." For an examination of how the general intellectual commitments of humanism—as opposed to its disciplinary emphasis on writing—shaped the ideology of the Roanoke enterprise and other early English colonial projects in America, see Andrew Fitzmaurice, *Humanism and America: An Intellectual History of English Colonisation, 1500–1625* (Cambridge: Cambridge University Press, 2003).

52. See Goldberg, *Writing Matter,* 28–40. Here Goldberg discusses Richard Mulcaster's *The First Part of the Elementarie* (1582), in which the author, who desires to set forth a proper grammar-school curriculum, can never get his topic "in hand" precisely because there is no single founding moment, in advance of all others, at which the illiterate child can enter into literacy.

53. It is possible that the *A* and the *S* are also someone's initials, perhaps relating to the granting of the book's privilege, since the initials follow the phrase *Cum gratia et Privilegio.*

54. See Goldberg's discussion in *Writing Matter* of the violence of preparing the quill, 80–84.

55. Goltzius quotes Proverbs in Latin and Dutch. This and subsequent translations are taken from *The Holy Bible, Conteyning the Old Testament, and the New* (London: Robert Barker, 1611).

56. De Certeau, *The Practice of Everyday Life,* 140–41.

57. In the broadest theoretical sense, however—that is, in terms of Derrida's "arche-writing" and de Certeau's "scriptural economy"—writing is indeed always violent. There is no possibility of standing at a critical distance from this scriptural violence that is the very condition of the social.

58. Indeed, as Roy Harvey Pearce points out, the English attitude toward the Indians of Virginia was a relatively peaceful one at first. After the massacre of the English in 1622, however, things changed dramatically. For the remainder of the seventeenth century there was little interest in understanding or even "civilizing" the Indians. See Pearce, *Savagism and Civilization.* However, at the very end of the first section of the *Report,* Harriot does suggest that violence did accompany the effort to establish a colony in Roanoke: "And although some of our companie towards the ende of the yeare, shewed themselves too fierce, in slaying some of the people, in some towns, upo causes that on our part, might easily enough have been borne withall: yet notwithstanding because it was on their part justly deserved, the alteration of their opinions generally & for the most part concerning us is the lesse to bee doubted" (30). Ralph Lane, the governor of the 1585 colony, offers a much more detailed account of English-Algonquian conflict in his "Discourse on the First Colony," written in 1586 and first printed in Hakluyt's *Principall Navigations* (1589). Lane's report is reprinted in David Beers Quinn, ed., *The Roanoke Voyages 1584–1590: Documents to Illustrate the English Voyages to North America under the Patent Granted to Sir Walter Raleigh in 1584,* vol. 1 (New York: Dover Publications, 1991), 255–94.

59. John Evelyn, *Sculptura: Or the History, and Art of Chalcography and Engraving in Copper* (London: G. Beedle and T. Collins, 1662), 8.

60. Gabriel Sagard, *Histoire du Canada, et voyages que les frères mineurs recollects y ont faicts pour la conversion des infidèles depuis l'an 1615,* vol. 2 (Paris: Librairie Tross, 1866), 346–47. My translation is a modification of the passage quoted in Gilbert, *Tattoo History,* 89. In 1789, over one hundred and fifty years after Sagard, Philadelphia naturalist William Bartram was still referencing the chief Western technique of image reproduction in order to explain the tattooing practices of the Creek Indians: "they are performed by exceedingly fine punctures, and seem like *mezzo-tinto,* or very ingenious impressions from the best executed engravings" ("Observations on the Creek and Cherokee Indians," in *Travels and Other Writings* [New York: Library of America, 1996], 534). It is worth noting that Sagard compares tattooing with the actual carving of metal with the burin, while Bartram compares the tattoo with the impression left by the plate. Both these aspects of engraving—cutting and impressing—were used to describe Native American tattoos.

61. For an excellent discussion of the development of the monogram within the context of engraving during the late fifteenth and early sixteenth centuries, see Joseph Leo Koerner, *The Moment of Self-Portraiture in German Renaissance Art* (Chicago: University of Chicago Press, 1993), 203–23. In the chapter titled "The Law of Authorship," Koerner argues that with the emergence of the printed image as a major form of artistic production, the artist—Dürer, in this case—had to confront the problem of his absence both

from his community of viewers and, potentially, from the actual mechanical reproduction of his plates. "The monogram emerges within this absence, as part of a strategy for making mechanical reproduction pay" (204). Koerner's book, particularly the first half, which is devoted to Dürer, has been critical in my understanding of de Bry's authorship.

62. De Bry, quoted in Harriot, *Briefe and True Report,* 41.

63. Albrecht Dürer, quoted in Koerner, *Moment of Self-Portraiture,* 213. The quote is from a Latin colophon printed on the final leaf of a 1511 edition of Dürer's *Life of the Virgin, Large Passion,* and *Small Passion.*

64. On the meaning of *ingenium* in art theory from antiquity to the Renaissance, see David Summers, *The Judgment of Sense: Renaissance Naturalism and the Rise of Aesthetics* (Cambridge: Cambridge University Press, 1987), 99–101.

65. De Bry, quoted in Harriot, *Briefe and True Report,* 41.

66. Perhaps it was an awareness of just this difficulty that led de Bry to stop including his initials in engravings from later books in his *America* series.

67. Revelation 22:18.

68. A copy of Harriot's *Report* at the British Library (G.6837) also includes de Bry's self-portrait tipped in on the opening page, facing the frontispiece.

69. For an iconographical analysis of de Bry's self-portrait that relates his description of an "outer world" (de Bry's *America*) to the depiction of an "inner world" in his self-portrait, see Henry Keazor, "'Charting the Autobiographical, Selfregarding Subject'?: Theodor De Brys Selbstbildnis," *Zeitsprünge: Forschungen zur Frühen Neuzeit* 7, no. 2–3 (2003): 395–428.

70. "Dum Podagræ nodis tophisque innexus inultæ / Tot monumenta parat magnum celebranda per orbem, / Iamque senex plane, sibi tot vernantibus ausis / Immortale facit nomen, seque abdicat umbris" (Jean Jacques Boissard, *Romane urbis topographia & antiquitatum* [Frankfurt am Main: Theodor de Bry, 1597], 3).

71. On early modern prosthesis and the transcendence/devaluation of the body, see Harry Berger Jr., "Second-World Prosthetics: Supplying Deficiencies of Nature in Renaissance Italy," in Erickson and Hulse, *Early Modern Visual Culture,* 98–147.

72. On the symbolism of the compasses, see Anthony Blunt, "Blake's 'Ancient of Days': The Symbolism of the Compasses," *Journal of the Warburg Institute* 2 (1938–39): 53–63.

73. The quotations are from the first English translation of the *Iconologia:* Caesar Ripa, *Iconologia: Or, Moral Emblems* (London: P. Tempest, 1709), 61, 74.

74. Giorgio Vasari, *Lives of the Painters, Sculptors, and Architects,* trans. Gaston du C. de Vere, vol. 2 (London: Everyman's Library, 1996), 736. Michelangelo's trope of the compasses in the eye was picked up in the art theory of the seventeenth century. In *De Arte Graphica,* for example, Charles-Alphonse Dufresnoy writes: "By this means the Painter shall be enabled to conceal the pains, and study which his Art and work have cost him, under a pleasing sort of deceipt: For the greatest secret which belongs to Art, is to hide it from the discovery of Spectatours. . . . Let the Eye be satisfy'd in the first place, even against and above all other reasons, which beget difficulties in your Art, which of it self suffers none; and let the compass be rather in your Eyes than in your Hands" (*De Arte Graphica / The Art of Painting,* trans. John Dryden [London: J. Heptinstall for W. Rogers, 1695], 65–66).

75. For a well-known iconographical interpretation of this engraving, see Raymond Klibansky, Erwin Panofsky, and Fritz Saxl, *Saturn and Melancholy* (New York: Basic Books, 1964). The authors argue that "the compasses in Melencolia's hand symbolise, as it were, the unifying intellectual purpose which governs the great diversity of tools and objects by which she is surrounded" (328). They associate the compasses in particular with

geometry, "the science par excellence for Dürer, as for his age" (339). The compasses would therefore seem to be the instruments which, through their overarching rationality, are able to "encompass" within their circle of reference all the other instruments that are more narrowly directed toward specific tasks. The authors also note that "it is significant that now the artist, too, likes to portray himself with compasses in hand."

76. Pamela Smith has recently stressed the importance of this artisanal background in Dürer's art (*Body of the Artisan,* 67–74). Smith claims that an "artisanal epistemology" undergirds the work of Dürer and other northern artists of the fifteenth and sixteenth centuries, and although she does not address *Melencolia I* specifically, her arguments suggest that the putto could also be understood as a figure for a bodily artisanal knowledge that Dürer never abandoned, in spite of his fascination with mathematics and ideal proportions.

77. Ivins, *Prints and Visual Communication,* 70.

78. On the priority that de Bry placed on financial profit in his book-publishing ventures, see Michiel van Groesen, "Boissard, Clusius, de Bry, and the Making of *Antiquitates Romanae,* 1597–1602," *Lias* 29, no. 2 (2002): 195–213.

79. The following two paragraphs are indebted to a series of articles Walter Melion has published on Goltzius, artisanship, and the authority of the artist's "hand" (in the various senses of that word). See Walter Melion, "Hendrick Goltzius's Project of Reproductive Engraving," *Art History* 13 (December 1990): 458–87; "Memory and the Kinship of Writing and Picturing in the Early Seventeenth-century Netherlands," *Word & Image* 8 (January–March 1992): 48–70; "Love and Artisanship in Hendrick Goltzius's *Venus, Bacchus, and Ceres* of 1606," *Art History* 16 (March 1993): 60–94; and "Self-Imaging and the Engraver's *Virtù:* Hendrick Goltzius's *Pietà* of 1598," *Nederlands Kunsthistorisch Jaarboek* 46 (1995): 105–43.

80. For a reproduction of the full canvas, see Huigen Leeflang and Ger Luitjen, *Hendrick Goltzius (1558–1617): Drawings, Prints, and Paintings* (Amsterdam: Rijksmuseum, 2003), 278.

81. De Bry, quoted in Harriot, *Briefe and True Report,* 41. In the dedication to Raleigh, de Bry notes that he has taken "the paines to cott in copper (the most diligentye and well that wear in my possible to doe)" (4).

82. De Bry was obviously not the only engraver with the problem of claiming authority over images by unknown artists. Most reproductive engravers confronted this problem (although as far as I am aware none produced self-portraits that so boldly aligned themselves with Dürer as does de Bry's self-portrait). For an excellent discussion of many of the issues involved in publishing anonymous images during the sixteenth century and of the problems of authority that accompanied their publication, see Parshall, "Imago Contrafacta."

83. The reproductive engraver's "net of rationality" may be likened to the early modern cartographic techniques of rationalizing the body examined by Valerie Traub and by Tom Conley. See Traub, "Mapping the Global Body"; and Conley, *Self-Made Map.*

84. See Joanna Woods-Marsden, *Renaissance Self-Portraiture: The Visual Construction of Identity and the Social Status of the Artist* (New Haven, Conn.: Yale University Press, 1998), 100–101. On the identification of the sitter, see Cecil Gould, "An Identification for the Sitter of a Bellinesque Portrait," *Burlington Magazine* 110 (November 1968): 626.

85. In Cornelis Cort's 1578 engraving "The Practice of the Visual Arts" (based on a drawing by Jan van der Straet), the compasses are shown to be analogous to the various other arts of incising, including the anatomist's art of incising flesh. Cort's visual inventory of the sixteenth-century scriptural economy includes the architect's compasses, the

anatomist's knife, the draftsman's quill and knife, the sculptor's chisel and rasp, the painter's brush, and, most prominently, the engraver's burin. On Cort's engraving, see Martin Kemp, "Coming into Line: Graphic Demonstrations of Skill in Renaissance and Baroque Engravings," in *Sight and Insight: Essays on Art and Culture in Honour of E. H. Gombrich at 85,* ed. John Onians (London: Phaidon, 1994), 230–32; Michel Bury, *The Print in Italy, 1550–1620* (London: British Museum Press, 2001), 18–21; and Manfred Sellink, *Cornelis Cort: Accomplished Plate-Cutter from Hoorn in Holland* (Rotterdam: Museum Boymans-van Beuningen, 1994), 200–201.

2. Making Sense of Smoke

1. Harriot, *Briefe and True Report,* 62.

2. Ivins, *Prints and Visual Communication,* 70.

3. Caroline Karpinski, "Preamble to a New Print Typology," in *Coming About . . . : A Festschrift for John Shearman,* ed. Lars R. Jones and Louisa C. Matthew (Cambridge, Mass.: Harvard University Art Museums, 2001), 377.

4. See Kemp, "Coming into Line." For other recent reassessments of early modern reproductive printmaking and its techniques, see Walter Melion, "Hendrick Goltzius's Project of Reproductive Engraving"; Karpinski, "Preamble to a New Print Typology"; and Lisa Pon, *Raphael, Dürer, and Marcantonio Raimondi: Copying and the Italian Renaissance Print* (New Haven, Conn.: Yale University Press, 2004).

5. De Bry, moreover, associated closely with some of the most remarkable virtuoso engravers of the late sixteenth century, most notably the Sadeler family of engravers. On de Bry's relationship to the Sadelers, see van Groesen, "De Bry and Antwerp," 36.

6. Paul Hulton, "John White and His Drawings of Raleigh's Virginia," in *Raleigh in Exeter, 1985: Privateering and Colonisation in the Reign of Elizabeth I,* ed. Joyce Youings (Exeter: University of Exeter, 1985), 115.

7. See, for example, Paul Hulton, *America 1585,* 18; and Eric Cheyfitz, *The Poetics of Imperialism,* 188–98.

8. Charles Sanders Peirce, *Peirce on Signs: Writings on Semiotic,* ed. James Hoopes (Chapel Hill: University of North Carolina Press, 1991), 239–40, 251–52.

9. Peirce, *Peirce on Signs,* 251.

10. Saint Augustine, *On Christian Doctrine,* trans. D. W. Robertson Jr. (New York: Liberal Arts Press, 1958), 34.

11. Properly speaking, each line of the engraving is a double index: an index (1) of the engraver's labor and (2) of the line cut into the copper plate, of which the printed line is the impression.

12. James H. Marrow and Alan Shestack, eds., *Hans Baldung Grien: Prints and Drawings* (Washington, D.C.: National Gallery of Art, 1981), 114.

13. "With instances available from Genesis onwards," writes Stuart Clark, "it was straightforward (at least until the onset of corpuscularian philosophy) to argue that the devil could present himself tangibly either by means of what Rémy called 'some concretion and condensation of vapours' or other manipulations of the elements, or by animating corpses" (Stuart Clark, *Thinking with Demons: The Idea of Witchcraft in Early Modern Europe* [Oxford: Clarendon Press, 1997], 185).

14. Notable examples include prints by Dürer, Agostino Veneziano, and Jacques Callot, and drawings by Albrecht Altdorfer and Jacques de Gheyn.

15. See Charles Zika, *Exorcising Our Demons: Magic, Witchcraft, and Visual Culture in Early Modern Europe* (Leiden, Netherlands: Brill, 2003), 411–79.

16. See Léry, *History of a Voyage,* 142–44. The ritual Léry witnessed is engraved by de Bry for part 3 of his *America.*

17. Harriot, *Briefe and True Report,* 54.

18. See Julie Robin Solomon, "'To Know, to Fly, to Conjure': Situating Baconian Science at the Juncture of Early Modern Modes of Reading," *Renaissance Quarterly* 44 (1991): 513–58.

19. For an analysis of the print's iconography, see Zika, *Exorcising Our Demons,* 411–44.

20. That Native American rattles were perceived as conjuring instruments by early modern European collectors of American artifacts is suggested by an item in the Tradescant collection in Lambeth. The 1656 catalog of the *Musæum Tradescantianum* mentions an "Indian Conjurors rattle, wherewith he calls up Spirits." See Peter Mason, "From Presentation to Representation: Americana in Europe," *Journal of the History of Collections* 6, no. 1 (1994): 8.

21. Henry Cornelius Agrippa von Nettesheim, *Three Books of Occult Philosophy or Magic* (Chicago: Hahn & Whitehead, 1898), 47–48. The text I have quoted is from the first English translation of Agrippa's *De occulta philosophia,* translated by James Freake and published in 1651. For a discussion of Agrippa's beliefs about air and dreams and a comparison with other early modern writers on witchcraft, see Michael Cole, "The Demonic Arts and the Origin of Medium," *Art Bulletin* 84 (December 2002): 626–28. On Agrippa's place in Renaissance magic and occult philosophy, see Frances A. Yates, *The Occult Philosophy in the Elizabethan Age* (London: Routledge & Kegan Paul, 1979), 37–47.

22. Agrippa, *Three Books of Occult Philosophy,* 132.

23. That Harriot and Marlowe conversed with some regularity is supported by the testimony of Marlowe's roommate, dramatist Thomas Kyd. See Shirley, *Thomas Harriot,* 186. On the importance of Agrippa in Marlowe's conception of Faustus, see Yates, *Occult Philosophy in the Elizabethan Age,* 115–21.

24. Christopher Marlowe, *Dr. Faustus and Other Plays,* ed. David Bevington and Eric Rasmussen (Oxford: Oxford University Press, 1995), 181.

25. None of the later books of de Bry's *America* displays the same preoccupation with smoke as the first book, but it is worth noting that the de Bry workshop did return in the early seventeenth century to similar techniques of representing smoke, as they developed a more explicitly magical iconography for alchemical and occult works by Michael Maier and Robert Fludd. In the emblems for Maier's *Atalanta fugiens* (1618), for example, this smoke becomes an effective means of suggesting the sublimation of matter through the alchemical process. It is not inconceivable that the engraver of Maier's plates, Johann Theodor de Bry, who helped his father work on the engravings for the *Report,* looked back to those smoke-filled plates of Virginia as he searched for a visual vocabulary for representing the alchemical process. For illustrations, summaries, and English translations of the emblems and epigrams in Maier's book, see H. M. E. de Jong, *Michael Maier's Atalanta Fugiens: Sources of an Alchemical Book of Emblems* (Leiden, Netherlands: E. J. Brill, 1969). On the de Bry workshop and the work of Maier and Fludd, see Frances Yates, *The Rosicrucian Enlightenment* (Boulder: Shambhala, 1978), 70–90.

26. This is the central argument made in Cole, "The Demonic Arts." There have been numerous studies in recent years that treat the subject of witchcraft, magic, and artistic production. In addition to Cole's illuminating article, see also Zika, *Exorcising Our Demons;* Patricia Emison, "Truth and *Bizzarria* in an Engraving of *Lo stregozzo,*" *Art Bulletin* 81 (December 1999): 623–36; Rebecca Zorach, "Despoiled at the Source," *Art History* 22 (June 1999): 244–69; Koerner, *Moment of Self-Portaiture,* 317–62; Claudia Swan, *Art,*

Science, and Witchcraft in Early Modern Holland: Jacques de Gheyn II (1565–1629) (Cambridge: Cambridge University Press, 2005); and Linda C. Hults, *The Witch as Muse: Art, Gender, and Power in Early Modern Europe* (Philadelphia: University of Pennsylvania Press, 2005).

27. Cole, "The Demonic Arts," 630. On the notion that the artist's role is to instill a certain air, or *aria,* into the work of art, see David Summers, "Aria II: The Union of Image and Artist as an Aesthetic Ideal in Renaissance Art," *Artibus et Historiae* 20 (1989): 15–31.

28. For a discussion of the various charges made against Harriot, see David B. Quinn and John W. Shirley, "A Contemporary List of Hariot References," *Renaissance Quarterly* 22 (Spring 1969): 18–23.

29. See Koerner, *Moment of Self-Portraiture,* 326–27.

30. The connection between *Their manner of prainge* and Catholic ceremony is strengthened by the plate that immediately follows it in the *Report,* which is titled *Their danses vvhich they vse at their hyghe feastes* (see Figure 53). As Harriot explains in the caption to this plate, the figures dance around "certayne posts carued with heads like to the faces of Nonnes couered with theyr vayles." Following this ceremony, he explains, they then proceed to "make merrie as is expressed in" the previous figure (Harriot, *Briefe and True Report,* 64).

31. Gaston Bachelard, *Air and Dreams: An Essay on the Imagination of Movement,* trans. Edith R. Farrell and C. Frederick Farrell (Dallas: Dallas Institute Publications, 1988). See especially Bachelard's introduction, "Imagination and Mobility."

32. Harriot, *Briefe and True Report,* 5.

33. These declarations occur on the title page ("sumtibus vero Theodori de Bry"), on the introductory page to the Virginia plates ("now cutt in copper and first published by Theodore de Bry att his owne chardges"), and in the colophon ("At Franckfort, Inprinted by Jhon Wechel, at Theodore de Bry, owne coast and chardges. MDXC"). Harriot, *Briefe and True Report,* 1, 35, 91.

34. Harriot, *Briefe and True Report,* 10.

35. Cummins contrasts de Bry's *America* with the *Historia general* of de Bry's contemporary, Antonio de Herrera. The *Historia general* is an eight-volume narrative history of the New World committed to the glorification of the Spanish crown. See Tom Cummins, "De Bry and Herrera: 'Aguas Negras' or the Hundred Years War over an Image of America," *Arte, Historia e Identidad en América: Visiones Comparativas, XVII Coloquio Internacional de Historia del Arte,* ed. Gustavo Curiel, Renato González Mello, and Juana Gutiérrez Haces, vol. 1 (México, D.F.: Universidad Nacional Autónoma de Mexico, 1994), 17–31.

36. Cummins, "De Bry and Herrera," 30.

37. As Cummins points out, "the 16th century iconoclasm of Protestants which sought to do away with the sacral aura of the image allows here [i.e., with de Bry] for the return of the image detached from belief and ready for the politics of debasement and persuasion" (Cummins, "De Bry and Herrera," 30).

38. In White's models for *Their seetheynge of their meate* and for another engraving (titled *The brovvyllinge of their fishe ouer the flame*) that shows cooking over a smoking fire, there are no human figures. De Bry's decision to add human figures is therefore a significant one, since it makes human labor rather than an isolated, inanimate object into the real subject of the image. There is no surviving original watercolor for *The manner of makinge their boates.*

39. Harriot, *Briefe and True Report,* 55. In his "To the Gentle Reader," de Bry makes the same point: "Yet they passe vs in many thinges, as in Sober feedinge and Dexteritye of witte, in makinge without any instrument of mettall thinges so neate and so fine, as a man

would scarsclye beleue the same, Vnless the Englishemen Had made proofe Therof by their trauailes into the contrye" (41).

40. The foundational text for arguing that perspective is an artificial system is Erwin Panofsky, *Perspective as Symbolic Form,* trans. Christopher S. Wood (New York: Zone Books, 1991).

41. René Descartes, *Discourse on Method, Optics, Geometry, and Meteorology,* trans. Paul J. Olscamp, rev. ed. (Indianapolis: Hackett, 2001), 89–90.

42. See Ernst Kris and Otto Kurz, *Legend, Myth, and Magic in the Image of the Artist: A Historical Experiment* (New Haven, Conn.: Yale University Press, 1979), 71–84.

43. Descartes, *Discourse on Method, Optics, Geometry, and Meteorology,* 90.

44. I don't presume to engage in such theoretical debates here except to say that perspective will be understood as a system whose rules, much like those of language, establish the basic conditions of possibility for producing certain kinds of knowledge. In this regard, my understanding of perspective is indebted to Panofsky's notion of perspective as a "symbolic form" and to Hubert Damisch's structuralist treatments of perspective. See Panofsky, *Perspective as Symbolic Form;* Hubert Damisch, *A Theory of /Cloud/: Toward a History of Painting,* trans. Janet Lloyd (Stanford: Stanford University Press, 2002); and Hubert Damisch, *The Origin of Perspective,* trans. John Goodman (Cambridge, Mass.: MIT Press, 1994).

45. Giovanni Paolo Lomazzo, *A Tracte Containing the Artes of Curious Paintinge,* trans. Richard Haydocke (Amsterdam: Da Capo Press, 1969), 188.

46. See Robert Rosenblum, "The Origin of Painting: A Problem in the Iconography of Romantic Classicism," *Art Bulletin* 39 (December 1957): 279–90.

47. Alberti, for one, discussed the importance of circumscription at length, as the first of painting's three essential parts: "Painting is composed of circumscription, composition and reception of light" (Leon Battista Alberti, *On Painting,* trans. John R. Spencer [New Haven: Yale University Press, 1966], 68). For Alberti's discussion of circumscription, see ibid., 68–72.

48. The earliest known illustrated version of the story is an engraving by François Chauveau, after Charles Le Brun, that served as the tailpiece of the first edition of Charles Perrault's *La peinture* of 1668. On both Gribelin's version and on Chauveau's, see Frances Muecke, "'Taught by Love': The Origin of Painting Again," *Art Bulletin* 81 (June 1999): 297–302.

49. The text was Robert Beverley's *History and Present State of Virginia* (1705). See the discussion on Gribelin in chapter 3.

50. See chapter 4 for a discussion of Ruskin's views on the primitive qualities of engraving.

51. Interestingly, in at least one later version of Pliny's story, engraved by Henriquel Dupont after an 1820 illustration by Anne-Louis Girodet-Trioson, the Corinthian maid also uses an arrow (Cupid's arrow, in this case) to trace her lover's shadow. See Rosenblum, "The Origin of Painting," 286–87, and Figure 12 in this book.

52. Damisch, *A Theory of /Cloud/,* 124. For a discussion of Damisch's *Theory of /Cloud/* and a thoughtful application of Damisch's theory to the work of Agnes Martin, see Rosalind E. Krauss, "Agnes Martin: The /Cloud/," in *Bachelors* (Cambridge, Mass.: October Books, 1999), 75–89.

53. See Damisch, *A Theory of /Cloud/,* 281, n. 115.

54. Erwin Panofsky, *The Life and Art of Albrecht Dürer* (Princeton: Princeton University Press, 1955), 56–57.

55. Damisch, *A Theory of /Cloud/,* 147.

56. The key study on the discovery and early diffusion of grotesques in the Renaissance is Nicole Dacos, *La découverte de la Domus Aurea et la formation des grotesques a la Renaissance* (London: Warburg Institute, 1969).

57. On grotesque wall and ceiling decoration in sixteenth-century Italy, see Philippe Morel, *Les grotesques: Les figures de l'imaginaire dans la peinture italienne de la fin de la Renaissance* (Paris: Flammarion, 1997). No detailed historical interpretation has yet been devoted to the circulation of grotesques in prints, although many examples are collected and discussed in Janet S. Byrne, *Renaissance Ornament Prints and Drawings* (New York: Metropolitan Museum of Art, 1981).

58. De Bry's own background as a goldsmith supports the notion that his ornamental prints were made with goldsmiths in mind; another series of grotesques by this engraver is titled *Grotis for die goldtsmit und andern khunstiger* (1589). On the use of this latter series as the basis for plasterwork decoration, see Anthony Wells-Cole, *Art and Decoration in Elizabethan and Jacobean England: The Influence of Continental Prints, 1558–1625* (New Haven, Conn.: Yale University Press, 1997), 168.

59. De Bry most likely did not design the printer's ornaments, and it can be said with certainty that he did not design the gargoyle tailpiece (see Figure 41), which appears in earlier texts from the press of Johann Wechel, the printer of the *Report*. It is likely that all the printer's ornaments used for the *Report* were part of Wechel's ornament stock.

60. Randle Cotgrave, *A Dictionarie of the French and English Tongves* (Amsterdam: Da Capo Press, 1971), Vv ii v.

61. Some Renaissance writers, to be sure, believed grotesques to contain profound symbolic meanings and related them to other symbolic languages such as hieroglyphs and emblems (although, as Philippe Morel has recently shown, it is on a semiological rather than an iconological level that we should understand these relationships [see Morel, *Les grotesques,* 49–51]). Nevertheless, it appears to be the case that the wide circulation of grotesques in printed form had the effect of emphasizing the purely decorative quality of grotesques over their symbolic power. As Alain Gruber writes, with specific reference to de Bry and other northern printmakers specializing in grotesques in the late sixteenth and early seventeenth centuries: "All these artists collaborated in the miniaturization of a kind of ornament originally intended for large-scale decoration. Simultaneously, grotesques were stripped of allegorical trappings, assuming a purely formal decorative identity" (Alain Gruber, "Grotesques," in *The History of Decorative Arts: The Renaissance and Mannerism in Europe,* ed. Alain Gruber, trans. John Goodman [New York: Abbeville Press, 1994], 214).

62. The watercolors were probably executed in 1577, either during or shortly after the return of Martin Frobisher's second expedition to southern Baffin Island. See Hulton, *America 1585,* 28–30. Gheeraerts may have seen the watercolors while in London, where he lived from 1568 to 1577 and from 1586 to circa 1590, at which time he may have died. See Wells-Cole, *Art and Decoration in Elizabethan and Jacobean England,* 89. It is also possible that Gheeraerts learned of White's watercolors through de Bry himself. Not only was de Bry in London in 1588 while Gheeraerts was there, but he and Gheeraerts were both members of the Guild of Saint Luke in Antwerp while de Bry lived in that city. In addition, de Bry knew and possibly even worked under Philips Galle, the engraver and publisher of Gheeraerts's design (see introduction, note 21). On Gheeraerts's Antwerp period, see Edward Hodnett, *Marcus Gheeraerts the Elder of Bruges, London, and Antwerp* (Utrecht, Netherlands: Haentjens, Dekker & Gumbert, 1971), 15–20.

63. On grotesques as a means preserving an experience of the exotic, see Peter Mason, "From America to Oxfordshire?" in *The Lives of Images* (London: Reaktion Books, 2001), 80–100.

64. Geoffrey Galt Harpham, *On the Grotesque: Strategies of Contradiction in Art and Literature* (Princeton: Princeton University Press, 1982), 3–4. The resistance of grotesques to linguistic classification has led another writer on this topic, André Chastel, to refer to grotesques as "the ornament without name." See André Chastel, *La grottesque* (Paris: Le Promeneur, 1988).

65. On wonder, the New World, and the failure of language, see Stephen Greenblatt, *Marvelous Possessions: The Wonder of the New World* (Chicago: University of Chicago Press, 1991). On Renaissance collecting as a strategy of preserving strangeness, see Steven Mullaney, "Strange Things, Gross Terms, Curious Customs: The Rehearsal of Cultures in the Late Renaissance," in *Representing the English Renaissance,* ed. Stephen Greenblatt (Berkeley: University of California Press, 1988), 65–92. On the relationship of grotesques to wonder cabinets in sixteenth-century Italy, see Morel, *Les grotesques,* 67–78.

66. The Vitruvian critique of grotesques is treated most thoroughly in Chastel, *La grottesque;* and in Morel, *Les grotesques.*

67. On the dialogue between center and margins in medieval art, see Michael Camille, *Image on the Edge: The Margins of Medieval Art* (Cambridge, Mass.: Harvard University Press, 1992). On the continuity between medieval drolleries and Renaissance grotesques, see Chastel, *La grottesque,* 39–43, and Morel, *Les grotesques,* 15–20.

68. Chastel, *La grottesque,* 25. See also Morel, *Les grotesques,* 87–88.

69. Vitruvius, quoted in Harpham, *On the grotesque,* 26.

70. See Chastel, *La grottesque,* 48; and Morel, *Les grotesques,* 38.

71. Motolinía, from the *Memoriales,* as quoted in Gruzinski, *The Mestizo Mind,* 112. A member of the first group of Franciscans sent to Mexico, Motolinía wrote the *Memoriales* between 1527 and 1541. As Gruzinski has shown, there are significant points of commonality between European grotesques and native imagery, so much so that indigenous painters turned directly to this mode to create a mestizo art. The Lafitau quote is from *Customs of the American Indians,* vol. 2, 24.

72. Adolph Loos, "The Luxury Vehicle," in *Spoken into the Void: Collected Essays, 1897–1900,* trans. Jane O. Newman and John H. Smith (Cambridge, Mass.: MIT Press, 1982), 40. The quotation represents Loos's first clear articulation of a position developed at greater length in his famous 1908 essay, "Ornament and Crime." For a recent consideration of the role of ornament in theories of primitive art, see Matthew Rampley, "The Ethnographic Sublime," *RES* 47 (Spring 2005): 255–56. On the relationship between the grotesque and the primitive, see Harpham, *On the Grotesque,* 48–76; and Frances S. Connelly, *The Sleep of Reason: Primitivism in Modern European Art and Aesthetics, 1725–1907* (University Park: Pennsylvania State University Press, 1995), 79–110.

73. Harriot, *Briefe and True Report,* 76. De Bry's next figure, *The trvve picture of a vvomen Picte,* is described similarly by Harriot, and displays a variety of animal and abstract imagery on her body.

74. On the symbolism of the owl in medieval England, see Francis Klingender, *Animals in Art and Thought to the End of the Middle Ages,* ed. Evelyn Antal and John Harthan (Cambridge, Mass.: MIT Press, 1971), 303–6, 402–6.

75. Paul Hulton notes that the decoration on the Pict's body is "inspired by late Renaissance ideas such as the lorica" (Hulton, *America 1585,* 185). The suggestion that Crivelli's *St. George* may have been inspired by theatrical armor is made in Stuart W. Pyhrr and José-A. Godoy, *Heroic Armor of the Italian Renaissance: Filippo Negroli and His Contemporaries* (New York: Metropolitan Museum of Art, 1998), 14.

76. Harriot, *Briefe and True Report,* 46.

77. E. H. Gombrich, *The Sense of Order: A Study in the Psychology of Decorative Art* (Ithaca, N.Y.: Cornell University Press, 1984), 272–81.

78. While some scholars have argued that ornamental headdresses such as that seen in de Bry's tailpiece were inspired by headdresses of Brazilians, Nicole Dacos shows that this motif should in fact be traced to antiquity, and specifically to Etruscan antefixes. See Nicole Dacos, "Présents Américains a la Renaissance: l'Assimilation de l'Exotisme," *Gazette des Beaux-Arts* 73 (January 1969): 59.

79. De Bry, quoted in Harriot, *Briefe and True Report,* 41.

80. As signs of ownership, the printer's ornaments for the *Report* would be more immediately associated with the printer, Johann Wechel, than with the publisher, de Bry. But it is also true that de Bry's interests in protecting his investment directly coincided with those of Wechel; as marks of identity and ownership, the printer's ornaments therefore protect both their interests.

81. John Ruskin, "Grotesque Renaissance," in *The Works of John Ruskin,* vol. XI, ed. E. T. Cook and Alexander Wedderburn (London: George Allen, 1904), 187.

82. Gell, "The Technology of Enchantment and the Enchantment of Technology."

83. Ibid., 166.

84. It is significant that Gell's understanding of the art object is based on Peirce's notion of the index (always leading us back to the causal agent), and not on the icon or symbol. Gell develops his ideas on the index in *Art and Agency: An Anthropological Theory* (Oxford: Clarendon Press, 1998). On Gell's use of the index and on his art theory more generally, see Matthew Rampley, "Art History and Cultural Difference: Alfred Gell's Anthropology of Art," *Art History* 28 (September 2005): 524–51.

85. See W. L. Hildburgh, "Indeterminability and Confusion as Apotropaic Elements in Italy and in Spain," *Folklore* 55 (December 1944): 133–49. See also Gombrich, *The Sense of Order,* 263; and Gell, *Art and Agency,* 83–95.

3. Flatness and Protuberance

1. Gerhart B. Ladner, "Ad Imaginem Dei: The Image of Man in Mediaeval Art," in *Modern Perspectives in Western Art History,* ed. W. Eugene Kleinbauer (New York: Holt, Rinehart & Winston, 1971), 433.

2. See Michael Camille, *The Gothic Idol: Ideology and Image-making in Medieval Art* (Cambridge: Cambridge University Press, 1989); and Herbert L. Kessler, *Spiritual Seeing: Picturing God's Invisibility in Medieval Art* (Philadelphia: University of Pennsylvania Press, 2000).

3. As Patrick Collinson writes, "Nothing demonstrates more forcefully the absolute refusal of so many late Elizabethan and Jacobean religious communicators to appeal to the sense and to popular taste than the pictures which are missing from their books, where you might expect to find them" (Patrick Collinson, *From Iconoclasm to Iconophobia: The Cultural Impact of the Second English Reformation* [Reading, U.K.: University of Reading, 1986], 22). Collinson argues that the most severe iconophobia in England occurs after the initial period of iconoclasm, during the second phase of the Reformation (after 1580).

4. For two insightful accounts of the ways in which a new, early modern regime of representation attempted to come to terms with the religious images of the past, see Bruno Latour, "Opening One Eye while Closing the Other . . . A Note on Some Religious Paintings," in *Picturing Power: Visual Depiction and Social Relations,* ed. Gordon Fyfe and John Law (London: Routledge, 1988), 15–38; and Joseph Koerner, *The Reformation of the Image* (Chicago: University of Chicago Press, 2004), 38–51.

5. Harriot, *Briefe and True Report*, 72.

6. Ibid., 72.

7. Harriot, *Briefe and True Report;* William Strachey, *The Historie of Travell into Virginia Britania,* 1612 (MS); John Smith, *The Generall Historie of Virginia, New-England, and the Summer Isles* (London: Michael Sparkes, 1624); Gerard Mercator, *Historia Mvndi, or, Mercators Atlas,* trans. W. S. Generosus (London: Michael Sparkes, 1635); Robert Beverley, *The History and Present State of Virginia* (London: R. Parker, 1705); Henri Abraham Châtelain and Nicolas Gueudeville, *Atlas historique, ou nouvelle introduction a l'histoire, à la chronologie & à la geographie ancienne & moderne* (Amsterdam: l'Honoré & Châtelain Libraires, 1719); *Cérémonies et coutumes religieuses de tous les peuples du monde* (Amsterdam: J. F. Bernard, 1723–1743); Joseph-François Lafitau, *Mœurs des sauvages ameriquains, comparées aux mœurs des premiers temps* (Paris: Saugrain and Hochereau, 1724). John Lawson offers a verbal description only in his *New Voyage to Carolina* (London, 1709), but it is a description that is undoubtedly indebted to his familiarity with the *Report.* Indeed the influence of the engraving and caption in the *Report* may be felt down to the present. Twentieth-century ethnologists of Native America—largely due to the evidence offered by de Bry's engraving and Harriot's verbal description, along with White's original watercolor—have identified the placement of preserved bodies in a raised temple or ossuary as a common practice among Algonquian and neighboring Siouan tribes of the southeastern coastal region during the early colonial period. See Swanton, *Indians of the Southeastern United States,* 718–29; and Christian F. Feest, "North Carolina Algonquians," *Handbook of North American Indians,* vol. 15, ed. William C. Sturtevant (Washington, D.C.: Smithsonian Institution, 1978), 279. For a more general discussion of the importance of shrines dedicated to ancestor preservation and veneration in the Southeast at the time of the encounter, see James A. Brown, "The Falcon and the Serpent: Life in the Southeastern United States at the Time of Columbus," in *Circa 1492: Art in the Age of Exploration,* ed. Jay A. Levenson (Washington, D.C.: National Gallery of Art, 1991), 531–32.

8. The episode was first related by Smith in his *Generall Historie* (1624): "Before a fire upon a seat like a bedsted, [Powhatan] sat covered with a great robe, made of Rarowcun skinnes, and all the tayles hanging by. On either hand did sit a young wench of 16 or 18 yeares, and along on each side the house, two rowes of men, and behind them as many women" (Karen Ordahl Kupperman, ed., *Captain John Smith: A Select Edition of His Writings* [Chapel Hill: University of North Carolina Press, 1988], 64).

9. See Hans Belting, *Likeness and Presence: A History of the Image before the Era of Art,* trans. Edmund Jephcott (Chicago: University of Chicago Press, 1994), 299.

10. The prophets of the Old Testament describe such idols, as in Isaiah 40:19: "The workeman melteth a grauen image, and the goldsmith spreadeth it ouer with golde"; and Jeremiah 10:3–5: "For the customes of the people are vaine: for one cutteth a tree out of the forest (the worke of the handes of the workeman) with the axe. They decke it with siluer and with golde . . . . They are upright as the palme tree, but speake not."

11. On this reintroduction, see Belting, *Likeness and Presence,* 297–310; Camille, *Gothic Idol,* esp. 27–57; and Ellert Dahl, "Heavenly Images: The Statue of St. Foy of Conques and the Signification of the Medieval 'Cult-Image' in the West," *Acta ad archaeologiam et artium historiam pertinentia* 8 (1978): 175–91.

12. Aby Warburg, "The Art of Portraiture and the Florentine Bourgeoisie: Domenico Ghirlandaio in Santa Trinita: The Portraits of Lorenzo de' Medici and His Household," in *The Renewal of Pagan Antiquity: Contributions to the Cultural History of the European Renaissance,* trans. David Britt (Los Angeles: Getty Research Institute for the History of Art and the Humanities, 1999), 189–90.

13. "An Homily Against Peril of Idolatry, and Superfluous Decking of Churches," in *Certain sermons or homilies appointed to be read in churches in the time of Queen Elizabeth; and reprinted by authority from King James I, A.D. 1623* (Philadelphia: Herman Hooker, 1855), 178.

14. On these distinctions between two- and three-dimensional images, see Margaret Aston, *England's Iconoclasts* (Oxford: Clarendon Press, 1988), 401–8. The special "lifelike-ness" of the sculpted image, as Michael Camille points out, was not tied to the attempt to produce verisimilitude, in the sense of an optical illusion, but to the artist's attempt (always a failure, of course) to "create the ineffable—moving, breathing, speaking 'life' itself" (Camille, *Gothic Idol,* 36).

15. Warburg, "The Art of Portraiture and the Florentine Bourgeoisie," 190.

16. The essential study of this shift is Belting, *Likeness and Presence.*

17. See Charles Talbot, "Prints and the Definitive Image," in *Print and Culture in the Renaissance: Essays on the Advent of Printing in Europe,* ed. Gerald B. Tyson and Sylvia S. Wagonheim (Newark: University of Delaware Press, 1986), 189–205.

18. On the relationship between engraving and sculpture, see Dorothy Limouze, "Engraving as Imitation: Goltzius and His Contemporaries," *Nederlands Kunsthistorisch Jaarboek* 42–43 (1991–92): 448–50.

19. Talbot, "Prints and the Definitive Image," 201. Talbot also points out that some fifteenth-century artists expanded on the relationship between prints and seals by "print-ing images in paste or paper pulp from a seallike matrix. . . . In addition to bearing the authenticity of the original mold, these seal or paste prints also indicate a short-lived effort to make prints defy their usual insubstantiality by taking on the substance of a sculptural form" (200).

20. Ibid., 201.

21. Bruno Latour similarly insists on the presence of Christ in a Sudarium painted by Hans Memling. See Latour, "Opening One Eye while Closing the Other," 20–21.

22. William B. MacGregor, "The Authority of Prints: An Early Modern Perspective," *Art History* 22 (September 1999): 404–16.

23. Evelyn, *Sculptura,* 140.

24. Ibid., 6–7. The best discussion of Evelyn's text is Parshall, "Art and the Theater of Knowledge," 27–31.

25. As Dorothy Limouze points out, Jan Muller's 1597 engraving after Bartholomäus Sprangher, *Painting, Sculpture, and Architecture, Banned by the Turks, Withdraw to Olym-pus,* shows the allegorical figure of Sculpture holding a small statue of Minerva as well as two burins. Muller thus embodies in a single figure an art that includes both religious stat-uary and the practice of engraving. See Limouze, "Engraving as Imitation," 448.

26. See Alois Riegl, *Late Roman Art Industry,* trans. Rolf Winkes (Rome: Giorgio Bretschneider Editore, 1985), 19–27. As Margaret Iverson notes, in Riegl's later work, *The Group Portraiture of Holland,* the opposition between the tactile and optical is "subsumed under a more general opposition between objective and subjective tendencies" (Iverson, *Alois Riegl: Art History and Theory* [Cambridge, Mass.: MIT Press, 1993], 94).

27. Riegl, *Late Roman Art Industry,* 21. On Riegl's treatment of the tactile and optical and their place within his art history, see Margaret Olin, *Forms of Representation in Alois Riegl's Theory of Art* (University Park: Pennsylvania State University Press, 1992), 132–47. Also see Iverson, *Alois Riegl.* In the hands of Wilhelm Worringer, Riegl's opposing cate-gories of the tactile and the optical were subsumed into a developmental scheme for the history of art in which a primitive urge to abstraction and tactile form is always in ten-sion with an urge to empathy and the naturalistic representation of space. See Wilhelm

Worringer, *Abstraction and Empathy,* trans. Michael Bullock (Chicago: Elephant Paperbacks, 1997).

28. While the perspectival structure of *The Tombe of their Werowans* is indeed exaggerated, it is not mathematically correct. That is to say, while the orthogonals do converge toward each other, they do not meet at a single vanishing point, or what Alberti called the "centric point." What is important for our purposes (and, I would argue, for de Bry's) is the *appearance* or *suggestion* of a perspectival space. While there may be no precise central point of convergence for the orthogonals in this engraving, its central point nevertheless seems to be that its orthogonals do converge.

29. Defert, "Collections et nations," 47.

30. Michèle Duchet, "Le texte grave de Theodore de Bry," in *L'Amérique de Théodore de Bry: Une collection de voyages protestante du XVIe siècle,* ed. Michèle Duchet (Paris: Editions du centre national de la recherche scientifique, 1987), 10. On the Protestant politics of de Bry's *America,* see also Bucher, *Icon and Conquest,* 6–10.

31. White's scene appears both on its own sheet and also in miniature in the watercolor drawing of the Indian village of Secoton. The descriptive text I have quoted actually appears on the drawing of Secoton.

32. It has been speculated that a lost drawing by White provided the model for the latter image: see Hulton, *America 1585,* 191. I disagree, since de Bry's enlarged version of the idol—as the text below the image informs the viewer—wears a headdress very similar to that worn in Florida. I take this as a sign of de Bry's own improvisation on the fairly indistinct, cone-shaped hat worn by the idol in White's watercolor. This is typical of de Bry's bricolage method of inventing his own figures out of materials he had available, which in this case would be the Florida images of Le Moyne that de Bry and his sons were simultaneously working on for part 2. On de Bry and bricolage, see Bucher, *Icon and Conquest;* see also Henry Keazor, "Theodore de Bry's Images for America," *Print Quarterly* 15 (June 1998): 131–49.

33. Harriot, *Briefe and True Report,* 72.

34. Aston, *England's Iconoclasts,* 2.

35. For Catholics, too, idolatry provided a critical lens for coming to terms with the Indians of the New World. For a recent discussion of discourses of idolatry in Catholic New Spain, see Thomas B. F. Cummins, "To Serve Man: Pre-Columbian Art, Western Discourses of Idolatry, and Cannibalism," *RES* 42 (Autumn 2002): 109–30.

36. Panofsky, *Perspective as Symbolic Form,* 67–68.

37. See Christopher Wood, "Introduction," in Panofsky, *Perspective as Symbolic Form,* 22–24.

38. Damisch, *Origin of Perspective,* 45.

39. There are strong echoes here of Lacan's mirror stage, in which the subject is captured within a menacing gaze where objects seem to stare back. Damisch argues that the subject of perspective is a Lacanian subject. See Damisch, *Origin of Perspective,* 114–40. For a response to Damisch's interpretation of Lacan and perspective, see Whitney Davis, "Virtually Straight," *Art History* 19 (September 1996): 434–44.

40. Harriot, *Briefe and True Report,* 71.

41. Robert Beverley, *The History and Present State of Virginia,* ed. Louis B. Wright (Chapel Hill: University of North Carolina Press, 1947), 9. Kupperman argues that Beverley's "plain, direct style, so unadorned as to appear naked, was appropriated as the essence of Euramerican identity" (Kupperman, *Indians and English,* 52).

42. Beverley, *History and Present State of Virginia,* 9. On Beverley's interest in savage life for its own sake and in the possibly harmful effects that civilization can have on that

life, see Pearce, *Savagism and Civilization,* 42–43. Five years after the publication of Beverley's book, the noble-savage theme received a boost in England with the visit to London of four Iroquois sachems, whose likenesses were painted, engraved, and widely circulated. See Alden T. Vaughan, "People of Wonder: England Encounters the New World's Natives," *New World of Wonders: European Images of the Americas 1492–1700,* ed. Rachel Doggett (Washington, D.C.: Folger Shakespeare Library, 1992), 22.

43. Beverley, *History and Present State of Virginia,* 63. On Beverley's relationship to Enlightenment thought and especially to sensational psychology with its emphasis on the importance of visual evidence in acquiring knowledge of the world, see Leo Marx, *The Machine in the Garden: Technology and the Pastoral Ideal in America* (London: Oxford University Press, 1964), 82–83.

44. On Gribelin's career, see Sheila O'Connell, "Simon Gribelin (1661–1733): Printmaker and Metal-Engraver," *Print Quarterly* 2 (March 1985): 27–38.

45. The second, revised edition was published in English in 1722. In 1707, *History and Present State of Virginia* was published twice in a French translation by Thomas Lombrail, once in Amsterdam, and once in a pirated version in Orléans. The Lombrail translation was reprinted in Amsterdam in 1712, and again by Bernard in 1718. As Louis B. Wright notes, one of Beverley's motives in writing *History and Present State of Virginia* was likely a desire to attract Huguenot colonists to Virginia. See Wright's introduction in Beverley, *History and Present State of Virginia,* xix–xx.

46. Editions of the *Ceremonies* using Picart's original plates from the 1723 edition, or close copies thereafter, were published in French 1723–37, 1733–39, 1741, 1783, 1789, 1807–10, and 1816–19; in Dutch 1727–38; in German 1727–38; and in English 1733–39. In the first French edition of the *Ceremonies,* the customs of the "Indes occidentales" constitute the very first volume, published in 1723, while in later French editions this material is incorporated, as in the English edition, into the volume treating the "Idolâtres." For an account of the making of the *Ceremonies* and its publication history, see Odile Faliu, "Bernard Picart: dessinateur et graveur (1673–1733)," in *Cérémonies et coutumes religieuses de tous les peuples du monde: dessinées par Bernard Picart,* ed. Faliu (Paris: Herscher, 1988), 9–32.

47. On the Radical Enlightenment and Picart and Bernard's roles within it, see Margaret C. Jacob, *The Radical Enlightenment: Pantheists, Freemasons and Republicans,* rev. 2nd ed. (Morristown, N.J.: Temple Publishers, 2003).

48. *The Ceremonies and Religious Customs of the Various Nations of the Known World,* vol. 1 (London: William Jackson for Claude Du Bosc, 1733), 252.

49. Beverley, *History and Present State of Virginia,* 195–98. For Beverley, the Indians' temple is an obscure place of superstition, and it is the purpose of science to throw light on that obscurity, to clear away superstition. Later in the century, however, the emergence of the sublime as an aesthetic category makes obscurity into an object of interest in its own right. For Edmund Burke, temples such as the one pictured in Gribelin's engraving are to be *appreciated* for their obscurity. "Almost all the heathen temples were dark," writes Burke in his discussion of the obscurity of the sublime: "Even in the barbarous temples of the Americans at this day, they keep their idol in a dark part of the hut, which is consecrated to his worship" (Edmund Burke, *A Philosophical Enquiry into the Origin of Our Ideas of the Sublime and Beautiful,* ed. Adam Phillips [Oxford: Oxford University Press, 1990], 55).

50. See Peter Harrison, *"Religion" and the Religions in the English Enlightenment* (Cambridge: Cambridge University Press, 1990).

51. Henry More, *The Theological Works* (London: Joseph Downing, 1708), 776.

52. For recent new-historicist discussions of Protestant antimaterialism, see Jeffrey Knapp, *An Empire Nowhere: England, America, and Literature from "Utopia" to "The Tempest"*

(Berkeley: University of California Press, 1992); and Gallagher and Greenblatt, *Practicing New Historicism,* 136–62.

53. Charles Blount, "Great Is Diana of the Ephesians: Or, the Original of Idolatry," in *The Miscellaneous Works* (London, 1695), 6, 8. On imposture theory and euhemerism in Blount's thought, see Harrison, *"Religion" and the Religions in the English Enlightenment.* Lord Herbert of Cherbury, who was one of Blount's chief influences, was the first to fully develop the imposture theory in its modern form. See especially the second chapter of Edward Herbert, *Pagan Religion: A Translation of "De religione gentilium,"* ed. John Anthony Butler (Ottawa: Dovehouse Editions, 1996). On anticlericalism in seventeenth- and eighteenth-century thought, also see S. J. Barnett, *Idol Temples and Crafty Priests: The Origins of Enlightenment Anticlericalism* (New York: St. Martin's, 1999).

54. *The Ceremonies and Religious Customs of the Various Nations of the Known World,* vol. 3 (London: William Jackson for Claude Du Bosc, 1733), 123–24.

55. Beverley, *History and Present State of Virginia,* 200–201.

56. David Hume, *Principal Writings on Religion including Dialogues concerning Natural Religion and The Natural History of Religion,* ed. J. C. A. Gaskin (Oxford: Oxford University Press, 1993), 152.

57. David Hartley, *Observations on Man, 1791,* vol. 1 (Poole: Woodstock Books, 1998), 214. On the eighteenth-century's association of the concrete and visual with the primitive stage of human consciousness, see Frank E. Manuel, *The Eighteenth Century Confronts the Gods* (Cambridge, Mass.: Harvard University Press, 1959), 174–75.

58. On perspective as a metaphor, see James Elkins, *The Poetics of Perspective* (Ithaca: Cornell University Press, 1994), 1–44.

59. Lyle Massey, "Anamorphosis through Descartes or Perspective Gone Awry," *Renaissance Quarterly* 50 (Winter 1997): 1148–89. See also Karsten Harries's analysis of the opposition within Descartes's work between a perspectival subject who is "the embodied, concrete 'I'" and an aperspectival subject who is an "angelically pure or transcendental 'I'" (Harries, "Descartes, Perspective, and the Angelic Eye," *Yale French Studies* 49 [1973]: 28–42).

60. One of the chief examples of how the line between the comparative study of religions and Protestant polemic is often blurred during the eighteenth century is Conjers Middleton's *A letter from Rome, shewing an exact conformity between popery and paganism: or, the religion of the present Romans to be derived entirely from that of their heathen ancestors* (London: W. Innys, 1729).

61. Beverley, *History and Present State of Virginia,* 211.

62. Exodus 20:4. The ten commandments appear in two places in the Pentateuch: Exodus 20:1–17 and Deuteronomy 5:6–21.

63. On the teaching and interpretation of the second commandment in the English Reformation, see Aston, *England's Iconoclasts,* 343–479.

64. William Perkins, *A Reformed Catholike* (Cambridge: Printed by John Legat, 1598), 170. Over the course of the Reformation, one witnesses a gradual internalization of this problem of location. One's own mental world rather than the real space of the church increasingly becomes the site from which one must banish false images. See Aston, *England's Iconoclasts,* 453–65.

65. Perkins, *A Reformed Catholike,* 172. Calvin writes: "The permissible images include histories and events *[res gestae],* as well as images and forms of bodies, without historical significance. The former serve to instruct and admonish *[docendo vel admonendo],* while the latter can offer nothing beyond enjoyment *[oblectationem].* Yet it is precisely images of this last kind that have always been displayed in churches. We may say that they did not

serve judgment or enjoyment, but foolish . . . covetousness" (John Calvin, *Institutes of the Christian Religion,* 1.12, as quoted in Belting, *Likeness and Presence,* 551).

66. Thomas Tenison, *Of Idolatry: A Discourse, in which is endeavoured a Declaration of, its Distinction from Superstition; Its Notion, Cause, Commencement, and Progress* (London: Francis Tyton, 1678), 267.

67. By the beginning of the sixteenth century, as Margaret Aston argues, Protestant aesthetics generally assumed a relationship of identity between idol and image (Aston, *England's Iconoclasts,* 450). While this is true in general, there was still much energy spent during the seventeenth century, especially in more moderate camps, on classifying the various types of images in order to determine, in Tenison's words, "how much or how little of the Idol is in each of them" (Tenison, *Of Idolatry,* 269).

68. Henry Hammond, *Of Idolatry* (Oxford: Henry Hall, 1646), 17–19.

69. Tenison, *Of Idolatry,* 269–73.

70. *De idololatria* was bound together with an immense treatise on idolatry by Gerardus Vossius, Dionysius's father, titled *De theologia gentile.* On the Dutch revival of Maimonides's works, see Aaron L. Katchen, *Christian Hebraists and Dutch Rabbis: Seventeenth-century Apologetics and the Study of Maimonides' "Mishneh Torah"* (Cambridge, Mass.: Harvard University Press, 1984).

71. In Hammond's case, however, Maimonides's distinctions did have immediate relevance, since *Of Idolatry* was published in 1646, only five years after the publication of *De idololatria* and at the height of Puritan iconoclasm in England. Hammond, who was chaplain to Charles I and of the moderate camp of Archbishop Laud, would presumably have found some justification in Maimonides's distinctions for defending certain "flat" or "depressed" religious art forms from destruction. On Puritan iconoclasm in the 1640s, see Aston, *England's Iconoclasts,* 62–95. On Laud's use of religious engravings, see George Henderson, "Bible Illustration in the Age of Laud," *Transactions of the Cambridge Bibliographical Society* 8, no. 2 (1982): 173–204.

72. Hammond, *Of Idolatry,* 20. On distinctions in Jewish tradition and in Eastern Christianity between protuberant and flat/depressed images, see also Edwyn Bevan, *Holy Images: An Inquiry into Idolatry and Image-Worship in Ancient Paganism and in Christianity* (London: George Allen & Unwin, 1940), 53–54, 148–49. In the general practice of the Eastern Orthodox, as Bevan points out, the test as to which images should be condemned "came to be whether you could or could not lay hold of the sacred figure's nose" (148).

73. On incarnational thinking and its relation to art during the late Middle Ages and the Italian Renaissance, see Ladner, "Ad Imaginem Dei"; and Leo Steinberg, *The Sexuality of Christ in Renaissance Art and in Modern Oblivion,* 2nd ed. (Chicago: University of Chicago Press, 1996).

74. Tenison, *Of Idolatry,* 271.

75. "An excellent Piece of *Painting,* is to my judgement the more admirable *Object,* because it comes neere an *Artificall Miracle;* to make diverse distinct *Eminences* appear upon a *Flat,* by force of *Shadowes,* and yet the *Shadowes* themselves not to appeare" (Sir Henry Wotton, *The Elements of Architecture* [London, 1624], 83). The source of Tenison's reference to a Virgin and child by Titian is unclear, as I have found no mention of such a work in Wotton's writings.

76. Hullmut Wohl, *The Aesthetics of Italian Renaissance Art: A Reconsideration of Style* (Cambridge: Cambridge University Press, 1999), 3–5, 76–114.

77. Alberti, *On Painting,* 89.

78. The notion of an infinite continuum in which bodies and space are coextensive was not formulated theoretically until 1639 in the work of French mathematician Girard

Desargues, whose new perspective methods were illustrated by Abraham Bosse (see Figure 46). See Wohl, *Aesthetics of Italian Renaissance Art*, 89.

79. Quoted in Erwin Panofsky, *The "Codex Huygens" and Leonardo da Vinci's Art Theory* (London: Warburg Institute, 1940), 72. The author of the *Codex Huygens*, an anonymous Milanese artist who composed the work sometime between 1560 and 1580, devotes a special chapter to the foreshortening of the human figure. On the significance of the dramatically foreshortened figure in sixteenth-century Italian art, see Avigdor W. G. Posèq, "The 'Terribilissima Arte' of Foreshortening in the Mannerist Theory of Art," in *Norms and Variations in Art: Essays in Honour of Moshe Barasch* (Jerusalem: Magnes Press, 1983), 81–103.

80. Robert Smith, "Natural versus Scientific Vision: The Foreshortened Figure in the Renaissance," *Gazette des Beaux-Arts* 82 (October 1974): 230–48.

81. On the relationship between incarnational theology and Italian Renaissance art, see Steinberg, *Sexuality of Christ*. Steinberg's treatment of incarnational theology relies on the work of John W. O'Malley. See John W. O'Malley, *Praise and Blame in Renaissance Rome: Rhetoric, Doctrine, and Reform in the Sacred Orators of the Papal Court, c. 1450–1521* (Durham, N.C.: Duke University Press, 1979), esp. 138–52.

82. I do not mean to equate the kind of foreshortening practiced by Mantegna with the kind of foreshortening that Titian would have employed in painting the *Virgin and Child Jesus* mentioned by Tenison. However, insofar as both Mantegna and Titian represent a general Italian concern for what Wotton and Tenison both call the "roundness" of the human figure, and what Italians called *rilievo*, I think it safe to assume that Tenison would have found Mantegna's *Dead Christ* no less troubling than Titian's painting (which I suspect he never saw).

83. Beverley, *History and Present State of Virginia*, 214.

84. Steinberg, *Sexuality of Christ*, 6.

4. The Art of Scratch

1. For Stevens's own account of his sale of White's collection to the British Museum, see Henry Stevens, *Recollections of Mr. James Lenox of New York and the Formation of His Library* (London: Henry Stevens & Son, 1886), 143–44.

2. I am aware of two other instances between the time of Eggleston's articles in the early 1880s and Binyon's article in 1907 in which selected images from White's collection were reproduced; in neither instance was the reproduction in a widely circulated periodical. Two of White's watercolors were reproduced in color in W. H. Holmes, "Aboriginal Pottery of the Eastern United States," in *Twentieth Annual Report of the Bureau of American Ethnology, 1898–99*, ed. J. W. Powell (Washington, D.C.: Government Printing Office, 1903). Five of White's images, including two maps, were reproduced in Richard Hakluyt, *The Principal Navigations, Voyages, Traffiques, and Discoveries of the English Nation*, vol. VIII (Glasgow: James MacLehose and Sons, 1904).

3. Edward Eggleston, "The Beginning of a Nation," *Century Magazine* 25 (November 1882): 68. Eggleston's view was a typical nineteenth-century response to de Bry, whose *America* was becoming highly desirable as an object of antiquarian interest but less and less trustworthy as an objective report of peoples and events. Thomas Jefferson's 1812 letter to John Adams shows a similar attitude toward de Bry. While Jefferson was proud to own the first "three folio volumes of Latin of De Bry," he also warned Adams that these were books in which "facts and fable are mingled together" (Jefferson to Adams, *The Adams-Jefferson Letters*, 306).

4. Rough copies of Bernard Picart's copies of de Bry's engravings after John White's watercolors are included in Charles A. Goodrich, *Religious Ceremonies and Customs, or the Forms of Worship Practised by the Several Nations of the Known World* (Hartford: Hutchinson and Dwier, 1835). Outline engravings based on de Bry's engravings after John White are included in *Graphic Sketches from Old and Authentic Works, Illustrating the Costume, Habits, and Character, of the Aborigines of America* (New York: J. & H. G. Langley, 1841).

5. Laurence Binyon, "Governor John White: Painter and Virginian Pioneer," *Putnam's Monthly* 2 (July 1907): 400–11.

6. Ivins, *Prints and Visual Communication*, 143.

7. Ibid., 128–29.

8. Estelle Jussim further develops Ivins's ideas, and also offers a thoughtful critique of Ivins's views on the halftone in Estelle Jussim, *Visual Communication and the Graphic Arts: Photographic Technologies in the Nineteenth Century* (New York: R. R. Bowker, 1974). For a critique of Ivins's ideas about the relationship between reproductions and originals, see Gordon Fyfe, "Fugitive Authorship: William Ivins and the Reproduction of Art," in *Art, Power, and Modernity: English Art Institutions, 1750–1959* (London: Leicester University Press, 2000), 31–52. For a rethinking of the objectivity of the photomechanical image as a largely social and cultural rather than technical phenomenon, see Lorraine Daston and Peter Galison, "The Image of Objectivity," *Representations* 40 (Fall 1992): 81–128.

9. As Ivins observes, "the photograph and photographic processes have brought us knowledge of art that could never have been achieved so long as western European society was dependent upon the old graphic processes and techniques for its reports about art" (Ivins, *Prints and Visual Communication*, 156–57). It is important to note, however, that despite the rhetoric of transparency that surrounds photography (especially in Ivins's account), the various types of photomechanical reproduction are affected by a variety of factors dependent on human agents, including exposure to light and exposure to chemical agents. See Fyfe, *Art, Power, and Modernity*, 45. For an analysis of the various codes of photographic reproduction, see Jussim, *Visual Communication and the Graphic Arts*, 45–76.

10. André Malraux, *Museum without Walls*, trans. Stuart Gilbert and Francis Price (Garden City, N.Y.: Doubleday & Company, 1967), 111.

11. For an interesting cultural history of the halftone focusing on publicly expressed concerns about magazine illustration that surrounded the emergence of the new process, see Neil Harris, "Iconography and Intellectual History: The Halftone Effect," in *Cultural Excursions: Marketing Appetites and Cultural Tastes in Modern America* (Chicago: University of Chicago Press, 1990), 304–17.

12. The three articles are Edward Eggleston, "The Beginning of a Nation"; "The Aborigines and the Colonists," *Century Magazine* 26 (May 1883): 96–114; and "Indian War in the Colonies," *Century Magazine* 26 (September 1883): 697–718. All but one of the watercolors reproduced by Eggleston (White's drawing of a Timucua man of Florida, based on a drawing by Jacques Le Moyne) are watercolors that de Bry and his workshop had engraved for Harriot's *Report*.

13. Art history has tended to neglect the significance of reproductive engraving in nineteenth-century visual culture. For a recent treatment of reproductive engraving in nineteenth-century France, see Stephen Bann, *Parallel Lines: Printmakers, Painters, and Photographers in Nineteenth-century France* (New Haven, Conn.: Yale University Press, 2001).

14. Eggleston, "Beginnings of a Nation," 61.

15. On Eggleston's debt to Thierry, see Arthur M. Schlesinger, "Evolution of a Historian," in Edward Eggleston, *The Transit of Civilization from England to America in the*

Seventeenth Century (Boston: Beacon Press, 1959), xi; see also "Edward Eggleston: An Interview," *Outlook* 55 (February 6, 1897): 434, 436. On Eggleston's work as a historian more generally, see William Randel, *Edward Eggleston* (New York: Twayne Publishers, 1963), 124–44.

16. James Gairdner, "On the Sources of History, and How They Can Best Be Utilized," *Living Age* 147 (October 30, 1880): 312.

17. "Dr Edward Eggleston's Historical Papers," *Century* 30 (July 1885): 488. For a relevant discussion of the search for authentic illustrations by nineteenth-century historians, see Francis Haskell, "Museums, Illustrations, and the Search for Authenticity," in Haskell, *History and Its Images* (New Haven, Conn.: Yale University Press, 1993), 279–303.

18. De Bry, quoted in Harriot, *Briefe and True Report*, 41.

19. British Museum, Department of Prints and Drawings, 199.a.3.

20. On the contents of Sloane's albums, see A. E. Popham, "Sir Hans Sloane's Collections in the Print Room," *British Museum Quarterly* 18, no. 1 (1953): 10–14.

21. See Hulton, *America 1585*, 22.

22. Edward Eggleston, "John White's Drawings," *Nation* 52 (April 23, 1891): 340–41.

23. Giovanni Morelli, *Italian Painters: Critical Studies of Their Works: The Borghese and Doria-Pamfili Galleries in Rome*, trans. Constance Jocelyn Ffoulkes (London: John Murray, 1892–93), 76–77. This same passage is quoted in a review of Ffoulkes's translation of Morelli's *Italian Painters* that was published in *Living Age* 196 (February 4, 1893), 325. On Morelli's methods, see Carlo Ginzburg, "Morelli, Freud, and Sherlock Holmes: Clues and Scientific Method," *History Workshop* 9 (Spring 1980): 5–36. Morelli's study of Italian Painters in the galleries of Munich and Dresden was published in German in 1880 and first translated into English in 1883; the study of Italian painters in the Roman galleries, published in German in 1890, was first translated into English in 1892–93. Admittedly, Morelli's work was better known in Europe than in America during the 1880s, and his methods were by no means universally accepted, although in the 1890s he was very influential on American connoisseur Bernard Berenson. I am not interested, however, in establishing a definitive correspondence between Morelli's methods and Eggleston's treatment of White. Indeed, it is hard to draw any conclusions at all about Eggleston's interpretation of White's images, since he offers no commentary on them. But it is precisely this desire to allow the images to speak for themselves that reveals a general affinity between Eggleston's pursuit of authenticity and Morelli's.

24. For an interpretation of White's watercolor of *The Flyer* that reads the medicine man as a figure for the artist, see Solomon, "'To Know, to Fly, to Conjure,'" 547–48.

25. "Dr Edward Eggleston's Historical Papers," 488.

26. See Jussim, *Visual Communication and the Graphic Arts*.

27. Arthur John, *The Best Years of the Century: Richard Watson Gilder, "Scribner's Monthly," and the "Century Magazine," 1870–1909* (Urbana: University of Illinois Press, 1981), 190.

28. "The Outlook for Wood-Engraving," *Century Magazine* 40 (June 1890): 312.

29. Daston and Galison, "The Image of Objectivity," 81–128.

30. That the hand of the wood engraver was particularly suspicious among producers of turn-of-the-century scientific texts is demonstrated in a quote from Johannes Sabotta's *Atlas and Text-Book of Human Anatomy* (Philadelphia, 1909): "No woodcuts have been employed, since the failure of the latter method to produce illustrations true to life has been distinctly shown by several of the newer anatomical atlases. It leaves entirely too much to the discretion of the wood-engraver, whereas the photomechanical method of reproduction depends entirely upon the impression made upon the

photographic plate by the original drawing" (quoted in Daston and Galison, "The Image of Objectivity," 101).

31. John P. Davis, quoted in "A Symposium of Wood-Engravers," *Harper's New Monthly Magazine* 60 (February 1880): 447.

32. John P. Davis, "The New School of Engraving," *Century* 38 (August 1889): 589.

33. W. J. Linton, "Art in Engraving on Wood," *Atlantic Monthly* 43 (June 1879): 713. Linton also authored a history of wood engraving: W. J. Linton, *The History of Wood-Engraving in America* (Boston: Estes and Lauriat, 1882).

34. Linton, "Art in Engraving on Wood," 708.

35. Ibid. Philip Gilbert Hamerton, in a history of the graphic arts published in 1882, clearly distinguished between Linton and the New School engravers by placing Linton among those wood engravers who practice the art "for its own qualities as an independent kind of engraving," whereas the New School engravers stood as the exemplary practitioners "of wood engraving which imitates other arts" (Philip Gilbert Hamerton, *The Graphic Arts: A Treatise on the Varieties of Drawing, Painting, and Engraving* [London: Seeley, Jackson, and Halliday, 1882], 302–27).

36. Timothy Cole, quoted in "A Symposium of Wood-Engravers," 446; Frederick Juengling, quoted in ibid., 447; Henry Wolf, quoted in ibid., 453. For an overview of the New School of wood engravers and of Linton's attitude toward their work, see Edward A. Gokey, "The New School of Wood Engraving," *Courier* 25 (Spring 1990): 53–83. See also Frank Luther Mott, *A History of American Magazines*, vol. 3, *1865–1885* (Cambridge, Mass.: Harvard University Press, 1957), 187–90.

37. John Ruskin, *Ariadne Florentina: Six Lectures on Wood and Metal Engraving*, in *The Works of John Ruskin*, vol. 22, ed. E. T. Cook and Alexander Wedderburn (London: George Allen, 1906), 348, 322. The first edition of *Ariadne Florentina* appeared in 1876.

38. Ibid., 323.

39. George E. Woodberry, "The History of Wood-Engraving, Part II," *Harper's New Monthly Magazine* 65 (July 1882): 261. By the "older manner," Woodberry means the method of wood*cut* rather than white line wood *engraving*. The latter method, first developed by Thomas Bewick at the end of the eighteenth century, involves the use of the tools of the metal engraver (i.e., burins) that cut furrows into the block and then print as white lines; woodcut involves the use of knives that cut away all the wood except for the desired lines, which then print black. The history of wood engraving after Bewick in the nineteenth century is essentially a history of variations on Bewick's white-line method.

40. For a discussion of Ruskin's *Ariadne Florentina* and *The Last Furrow* that ties Ruskin's views on wood engraving to a broader discussion of illustration and the relationships between word and image that that entails, see J. Hillis Miller, *Illustration* (Cambridge, Mass.: Harvard University Press, 1992), 75–96. On Ruskin's attitudes toward mass-produced prints and his deep concern for the gravity of the engraver's work, see also Jonah Siegel, "Black Arts, Ruined Cathedrals, and the Grave in Engraving: Ruskin and the Fatal Excess of Art," *Victorian Literature and Culture* 27, no. 2 (1999): 395–417.

41. Ruskin, *Ariadne Florentina*, 320.

42. Ibid., 347.

43. Linda M. Austin, *The Practical Ruskin: Economics and Audience in the Late Work* (Baltimore: Johns Hopkins University Press, 1991), 8. Austin situates Ruskin's valuing of production over consumption in the context of "the two competing economic theories that governed thinking in the 1870s. These were the labor theory of value and the new utilitarian school centered on demand" (6).

44. Review of John Ruskin, *Ariadne Florentina: Six Lectures on Wood and Metal Engraving* (New York: John Wiley and Sons, 1878), *Atlantic Monthly* 42 (November 1878): 652.

45. Ruskin, *Ariadne Florentina,* 320.

46. The two men actually were acquainted, Linton having sold his cottage at Brantwood to Ruskin in 1871. Although the surviving fragments speaking to their relationship never touch on the subject of engraving, both seem to have had a general sense of shared enterprise in their work. See George P. Landow, "John Ruskin and W. J. Linton: A New Letter," *English Language Notes* 10 (September 1972): 38–41.

47. John P. Davis, quoted in "A Symposium of Wood-Engravers," 446.

48. Walter Benjamin, "The Work of Art in the Age of Its Technological Reproducibility," in *Walter Benjamin: Selected Writings,* vol. 3, *1935–1938,* ed. Howard Eiland and Michael W. Jennings, trans. Edmund Jephcott, Howard Eiland, et al. (Cambridge, Mass.: Belknap Press, 2002), 105. For Benjamin (as for Ivins) photography is considered to be the teleological endpoint of nineteenth-century reproductive practices, and it is above all through photographic reproduction that the masses attempt to overcome their distance from the work of art. What Benjamin's account does not acknowledge is the significance of nineteenth-century printmaking techniques such as wood and metal engraving and the ways in which such practices might support or complicate his narrative. For a critique of Benjamin's lack of interest in nineteenth-century reproductive methods other than lithography and photography, see Bann, *Parallel Lines,* 7–11, 15–18.

49. On Ruskin's desire to preserve the aura of the engraved reproduction in the face of this demand for reproductions, see Siegel, "Black Arts, Ruined Cathedrals, and the Grave in Engraving."

50. Elbridge Kingsley, "Originality in Wood-Engraving," *Century* 38 (August 1889): 578.

51. For a discussion of the importance for nineteenth-century art of Bewick's engraved thumbprint, see Charles Rosen and Henri Zerner, *Romanticism and Realism: The Mythology of Nineteenth-century Art* (New York: W. W. Norton, 1984), 3–5.

52. Even though American authors pushed for an international copyright law that would ensure copyright protection for foreign authors, the idea was to make American authors more attractive to American publishers. Prior to the international copyright law (passed in 1891), it was far cheaper to publish an uncopyrighted foreign work than a copyrighted American work.

53. "Maskwell's Compendium," *Century* 23 (February 1882): 638.

54. Ruskin, *Ariadne Florentina,* 319–20.

55. George de Forest Brush, "An Artist among the Indians," *Century* 30 (May 1885): 57.

56. See George Catlin, *Letters and Notes on the Manners, Customs, and Conditions of the North American Indians,* vol. 1 (New York: Dover Publications, 1973), 145–54.

57. Brush, "An Artist among the Indians," 57.

58. Charles Waldstein, "The Lesson of Greek Art," *Century* 31 (January 1886): 974.

59. On *Century* and the fine arts, see John, *Best Years of the Century,* esp. 181–97.

60. Garrick Mallery, "Picture-Writing of the American Indians," in *Tenth Annual Report of the Bureau of Ethnology, 1888–89,* ed. J. W. Powell (Washington, D.C.: Government Printing Office, 1893), 26. A shorter version of Mallery's study, titled "Pictographs of North American Indians: A Preliminary Paper," appeared in the *Fourth Annual Report of the Bureau of Ethnology, 1882–83,* ed. J. W. Powell (Washington, D.C.: Government Printing Office, 1886), 3–256.

61. Edward B. Tylor, *Primitive Culture: Researches into the Development of Mythology, Philosophy, Religion, Language, Art, and Custom,* 2 vols. (London: John Murray, 1920), 1.

62. Elias shows that the concept of *civilité* first gained currency through Erasmus's popular *De civilitate morum puerilium* (1530), in which civility is tied to "outward bodily propriety." See Elias, *The Civilizing Process,* 47–52.

63. Tylor, *Primitive Culture,* 1. On the culture thesis in the nineteenth century, see Christopher Herbert, *Culture and Anomie: Ethnographic Imagination in the Nineteenth Century* (Chicago: University of Chicago Press, 1991). On the development of evolutionary thought among nineteenth-century anthropologists, including Tylor, see George W. Stocking Jr., *Victorian Anthropology* (New York: Free Press, 1987), especially 144–237. For a discussion of the evolutionary thought of a prominent American anthropologist of the late nineteenth century, Lewis Henry Morgan, see Robert E. Bieder, *Science Encounters the Indian, 1820–1880: The Early Years of American Ethnology* (Norman: University of Oklahoma Press, 1986), 233–46. For an overview of evolutionary thought in late nineteenth-century America, see Richard Hofstadter, *Social Darwinism in American Thought* (Boston: Beacon Press, 1992); and Kathleen Pyne, *Art and the Higher Life: Painting and Evolutionary Thought in Late Nineteenth-century America* (Austin: University of Texas Press, 1996), 11–47. Like other periodicals of the late nineteenth century, *Century* was drenched in the Darwinian rhetoric of cultural evolution.

64. Michel de Montaigne, "On Coaches," in *The Essays: A Selection,* trans. M. A. Screech (London: Penguin Books, 1993), 342.

65. Acosta, *Natural and Moral History of the Indies,* 397.

66. Brush, "An Artist among the Indians," 57.

67. Sylvester Baxter, "An Aboriginal Pilgrimage," *Century* 24 (August 1882): 526–36.

68. For a recent analysis of this confrontation of cultures, see Curtis M. Hinsley, "Zunis and Brahmins: Cultural Ambivalence in the Gilded Age," *Romantic Motives: Essays on Anthropological Sensibility,* ed. George W. Stocking (Madison: University of Wisconsin Press, 1989), 169–207.

69. Frank H. Cushing, "My Adventures in Zuñi," *Century* 25 (December 1882): 191–207; Cushing, "My Adventures in Zuñi II," *Century* 25 (February 1883): 500–511; Cushing, "My Adventures in Zuñi III," *Century* 26 (May 1883): 28–47.

70. John K. Hillers, "A Moqui Weaver at Work" (1879), Western History/Genealogy Department, Denver Public Library.

71. Claude Lévi-Strauss, *Tristes Tropiques* (New York: Penguin Books, 1973), 296.

72. For recent treatments of the materiality of writing in late nineteenth-century American art and literature, see Michael Fried, *Realism, Writing, Disfiguration: On Thomas Eakins and Stephen Crane* (Chicago: University of Chicago Press, 1987); and Michael Fried, "Almayer's Face: On 'Impressionism' in Conrad, Crane, and Norris," *Critical Inquiry* 17 (Autumn 1990): 193–236.

73. Edward B. Tylor, "Picture-Writing and Word-Writing," in *Researches into the Early History of Mankind and the Development of Civilization,* ed. Paul Bohannan (Chicago: University of Chicago Press, 1964), 90.

74. William Hayes Ward, "Our Debt to Cadmus," *Harper's New Monthly Magazine* 46 (March 1873): 521; A. H. Sayce, "The Origin of the Alphabet," *Living Age* 168 (January 9, 1886): 82–83 (originally published in *Contemporary Review*). See also A. H. Sayce, "The History of Writing," *Living Age* 144 (March 27, 1880): 810–17 (originally published in *Nature*). *Living Age* published one other relevant article around this time, originally published in the *Edinburgh Review* and without a cited author: "The Origin of Alphabets," *Living Age* 186 (August 23, 1890): 451–65. The Ward article from *Harper's* contains

numerous illustrations of picture-writing and alphabetic writing. It begins with an example of Native American picture-writing.

75. Alex Nemerov argues that the sense of enervation that pervades *The Picture-Writer*—particularly the limp figure based on *The Creation of Adam*—is due to Brush's inability to transcend his model (Michelangelo) and to offer unmediated access to eternal values. Thus it is a "resentment of the priority of other images, that informs the torpor of Brush's picture." I would add to this that Brush's picture also resents the impossibility of transcending the primitive origins of art in picture-writing. Evolution, *The Picture-Writer* suggests, is enervating work. See Alex Nemerov, "'Doing the Old America': The Image of the American West, 1880–1920," in *The West as America: Reinterpreting Images of the Frontier, 1820–1920,* ed. William H. Truettner (Washington, D.C.: Smithsonian Institution Press, 1991), 323–26.

76. Benson J. Lossing, "The Graphic Art," *Scribner's Monthly* 4 (August 1872): 398.

77. Richard Watson Gilder, "The Recording Tendency and What It Is Coming To," *Century* 53 (February 1897): 634–35.

78. See Harris, *Cultural Excursions,* 304–17, 337–48.

79. Charles T. Congdon, "Over-Illustration," *North American Review* 139 (November 1884): 480, 489.

80. "Knowledge on Sight," *Nation* 57 (July 20, 1893): 42.

81. Theodore L. De Vinne, "The Printing of *The Century*," *Century* 41 (November 1890): 87.

82. Ruskin in fact continued to champion the simple, honest engraved line in an article first published in the *Magazine of Art* in 1888. Ruskin, strolling up and down the Strand in London, encounters "wonderful displays of etchings and engravings and photographs, all done to perfection such as I had never thought possible in my younger days." Because of their highly worked surfaces, he refers to these works as the "black arts" and is concerned that "all this labour and realistic finishing makes us lose sight of the charm of easily-suggestive lines—nay, of the power of lines, properly so called, altogether." John Ruskin, "The Black Arts: A Reverie in the Strand," in *The Works of John Ruskin,* vol. 14, ed. E. T. Cook and Alexander Wedderburn (London: George Allen, 1906), 358–59. On Ruskin's critique of the black arts, see Siegel, "Black Arts."

83. Ruskin, *Ariadne Florentina,* 469.

84. Theodore L. De Vinne, "The Growth of Wood-Cut Printing I," *Scribner's Monthly* 19 (April 1880): 860–74; and De Vinne, "The Growth of Wood-Cut Printing II," *Scribner's Monthly* 20 (May 1880): 34–45.

85. De Vinne, "The Growth of Wood-Cut Printing II," 43.

86. See my discussion of language and the Renaissance collection in chapter 2.

87. See Latour, *We Have Never Been Modern.*

88. Andrew Lang, "The Art of Savages," *Custom and Myth* (London: Longmans, Green, 1910), 276.

89. Ruskin, *Ariadne Florentina,* 360.

90. Ivins, *Prints and Visual Communication,* 108.

Index

Michael Gaudio is assistant professor of art history at the University of Minnesota.

www.ingramcontent.com/pod-product-compliance
Lightning Source LLC
Chambersburg PA
CBHW052032280526
45791CB00010B/2947